Administrative Strategy and Decision Making

SECOND EDITION

C. T. HARDWICK, Ph.D.
Professor of Business Administration
Dean, Center for Continuing Education
University of Detroit

and

B. F. LANDUYT, Ph.D.
Professor of Business Administration
Dean, College of Commerce and Finance
University of Detroit

Published by

SOUTH-WESTERN PUBLISHING COMPANY

Cincinnati / Chicago / Dallas
Burlingame, Calif. / New Rochelle, N. Y.

G75

Preface

IN WRITING the present volume the authors have been motivated by a conviction that much of the literature of administration tends to concentrate on the more mechanical
and stereotyped aspects of management. It is their feeling
that efficient administration demands dynamic action and
that, therefore, the administrative process is not to be described predominantly in terms of steps. They have no
quarrel with the somewhat traditional approach which
wends its way from the settling of objectives through the
preparing of plans, the assembling of resources, the process
of organizing, communicating and the giving of directions,
and which ends with the exercise of the control function.
But they neither see these classical steps as sequential in
any set order, nor do they conceive administration as fully
described by these generic categories.

The orientation of this book may be described as the
strategic approach. It holds that the essence of administration
is the decision or step taken by the administrator in view of
what he knows or believes those with whom he deals are
planning or doing. Good administration is seen as proper
action taken in the light of realism—the realism imposed
through the course taken, anticipated or possible by the
administrator's colleagues in the organization, by his friendly

iii

associates outside, or particularly by his opposition anywhere. There is even a more subtle implication in the strategic approach—that strategy is the aspect of administration which elicits from the administrator the greatest synthesis of leadership knowledge and ability and that, therefore, it is administration at its highest.

The authors believe that their treatment may prove useful to the practitioner, the teacher, and the student. It is their hope that the businessman will find in it a certain substantiation of many of the views and steps he must take in the practical managing of his department or company, suggestions as to effective courses of administrative action, and a frank over-view of the actual process of administration. They believe too that the teacher will find a vital challenge in reading the book and may, as a result, come to a somewhat more realistic view of what business leadership demands, and that the student will take from its pages a greater cognizance of the breadth and depth of dynamic administration and a keener appreciation of the multiple dimensions of the leadership necessary to successful business.

The reader legitimately may raise the question as to the sources of the authors' information and judgment. Their documentation to selected authority suggests a certain perusal of and reliance upon the classics in administration. They have drawn also upon a general background in the social sciences but have gone much further. They have used years of personal experience as administrators, the observations of other administrators in action, and many professional management surveys and audits in which they have participated.

C. T. H.
B. F. L.

Contents

Contents

CHAPTER 1

The Factor of Strategy

> "Strategy permeates the entire process of business management. In every aspect, circumstances arise that bring from the administrators particular action or reaction to meet specific stimuli. Their efforts at appropriate moves—good, bad or indifferent—are seen in all the classical stages: determining objectives, planning, assembling, organizing, communicating, directing, and controlling."

EVERY SUCCESSFUL ADMINISTRATOR is a strategist. Whenever people are assembled into an organization, they will as a group and in the passage of time face different situations. Their leader, if he is to perform his function of bringing them to a goal or goals, must recognize the dynamics of each situation. His position casts him, therefore, in the role of a strategist. Nowhere is this more evident than in the business organization. Top business executives make many decisions which are basically strategic. Middle managers take some decisions which demand the strategic approach. Lower level supervisors may at first appear to make only routine decisions, but, upon further investigation, they will be seen to use politic action when the ordinary procedure is inadequate. Strategy is an all pervasive thread in business administration.

1

A Universal Feature of Business Administration

Strategy permeates the entire process of business management. In every aspect, there arise circumstances that bring from the administrators *particular* action or reaction to meet specific stimuli. Their efforts at appropriate moves—good, bad or indifferent—are seen in all the classical stages: determining objectives, planning, assembling, organizing, communicating, directing, and controlling. Business leadership apparently views strategic action as a practical modus operandi.

Yet, many authorities treat business administration in a rather over-simplified and unrealistic fashion. They view it as a more or less mechanistic process, comprised of a series of stereotyped steps which, if followed, automatically lead to success. Their treatment of the subject tends to fit into a mold of "standardized exposition." For example, in discussing the subject of planning the usual presentations emphasize the prosaic aspects such as the types of plans and their relative merits. Too little is said about the extreme importance of tailoring the plan to fit the peculiar need. Such matters as preselling, timing and surprise, adaptation, multiple offense, full public relations possibilities, and the exploitation of new or unexpected opportunities are given relatively little attention. In a practical sense, however, it is such features as these in planning which give a company its greatest competitive advantage. The strategic considerations in planning begin where the usual mechanistic steps end. It is precisely in the sense of this illustration that strategy is the very lifeblood of the successful administration of a company. The competitive pressures are so great in the modern business world that the usual and the unimaginative are simply not sufficient. Therefore, strategy can be viewed as the very essence of successful business administration.

Definition of Strategy

To be certain, *strategy* has its own peculiar meaning. Originally a term confined to the military frame of reference, it meant, "The art of a commander-in-chief; the act of projecting and directing larger military movements and operations of a campaign."[1] In the beginning, it was carefully distinguished from *tactics* which is defined as ". . . the art of handling forces in battle or in the immediate presence of the enemy."[2] It is obvious that the primitive difference between the meanings of the two terms lay in scope. Strategy expressed the more general and the larger concept; whereas tactics conveyed the idea of the more specific and the smaller.

As years went by, the military term of strategy took on other connotations. It gradually developed a generic application. Today, it is correctly employed to designate skill in planning or managing.[3] Moreover, social scientists have taken the term strategy into their lexicon and given it a bit more specific definition as ". . . the general outline of the ways of achieving certain goals."[4]

In fact, strategy has come to such popular use that its meaning is rarely distinguished from that of tactics. Perhaps this is due to the need of society for a word to express the idea of gamesmanship as movement and counter-movement in the pursuit of object or purpose. It may even be the reflection of the fact that the borderline between strategy and tactics is very dim. The suggestion has been made that the disinction between strategy and tactics exists in the mind of the planner concerned with the issue.[5]

In the light of all this, the word strategy is used to signify throughout this book the general concept and salient aspects of gamesmanship as an administrative course designed to bring success.[6]

Concept of Administration

An explanation of the title *Administrative Strategy and Decision Making* demands analytical attention also to a definition of *administrative.* Immediately, echoes of the battle between the concepts of administration and management are heard. Which is the broader is an issue that seems not to have been settled. Perhaps there is no real distinction in meaning between the two, for high lexicon authority [7] indicates that the words are synonymous and American interchangeable usage in business and literature supports dictionary definition, although with a leaning toward administration as the inclusive term.[8] At any rate, the authors have selected *administration* and the consequent adjective *administrative* to express their point of view for two practical reasons. First, these terms appear to bear no such emotional connotation as *management* or *managerial*—words which can too readily conjure up the unfortunate image of the so-called labor-management dichotomy. Second, they are not as likely as management to generate confusion. Management is too closely associated with the noun manager, which has a narrow meaning in that it designates the executive of a particular organization or part thereof and which, therefore, could cast back a restrictive reflection on management. And so the strategy treated in this book is described as *administrative* which in the words of the dictionary means, "Pertaining to, or dealing with, the conduct or management of affairs."[9]

Background of Modern Administration

Business Practices

In order to provide a common basis for an understanding of the ensuing presentation of the numerous facets of administrative strategy, an effort will be made to trace briefly the major contributions to the modern study of business administration.[10] Of course, the first and oldest contributors are businessmen themselves. These practitioners of the administrative art in business have contributed many ideas and practices. Since the first artisan produced a commodity and the first trader handled a sale, manufacturers and merchants have faced with some success the managing of the men, money, materials, and machines believed necessary to their profit goal. From such experience, many valuable lessons have been handed down with respect to conducting a business. In this category, much information is found regarding the art of buying, selling, and other operational techniques. The serious student of administration may be tempted to minimize this contribution because of a suspected unscientific origin. To do so would be a serious error. Experience is a good teacher, and the literature of the businessman's life and work can be explored to advantage.

Economics

The growing complexity of civilization eventually produced a group of scholars concerned with the general economy and economic behavior. Economists, beginning prominently with Adam Smith in his *Wealth of Nations* (1776), arose to describe and analyze the broad topics of production, distribution, and consumption.[11] Down through the next hundred years or more, the formidable pens of such men as Malthus, Ricardo, Mills, Marx, Menger, Jevons, and Marshall turned out volumes on these subjects. The present century has added its economic theorists; in their ranks are many illustrious scholars—Wicksell, Fisher, Knight, Chamberlin, Joan Robinson, and Keynes. These scholars have broadened measurably the field of vision on matters economic. The student of administration may be tempted to disregard their contribution as being too academic. This disregard would be as serious as overlooking the businessman's part. The economists have helped set the broad limits within which business, and hence its administrators, can operate with efficiency and profit. However, the economists are not to be considered, as common tendency seems to do, the overshadowing source of information on principles of business administration. The truth is that they do not yet have even a universal system of economic theory.[12]

Industrial Engineering

As businessmen continued with their trial and error methods and as economists attempted to describe the workings of the economy and various of its components, another group—yet unnamed—was bestirring itself. Its members were imbued with the growing emphasis on the scientific method. They turned first to the study and improvement of methods of production, and then progressed rather logically into an analysis of business management in general. The pattern of the emergence of these industrial engineers is seen in the work of Taylor, Gantt, Gilbreth, and Cooke.[13] In the early part of the Twentieth Century, Taylor, who is often referred to as the "Father of Scientific Management," brought to bear in the area of management the mind of the scientist. The scientific method—such steps as experimentation, observation, the collection of data, its classification and its analysis, and the formulation of laws and principles—became the order of the day. Proposals for improvement in administration were now to be made on the basis of actual facts regarding methodology and mechanization. From the industrial engineer has come much that administrators presently accept, for example, time and motion study, standardization of methods and procedures, and incentive systems. The contributions of Taylor and his disciples are not to be treated lightly; but obviously administration, which is above all else the handling of individuals, requires much more recognition of the human element than the early industrial engineers were willing to give. Since Taylor's time there has been a broadening in the perspective of industrial engineering and, consequently, a sounder contribution from this source to administration.

Public Administration

In the late nineteenth and first half of the twentieth centuries there was a serious interest shown by certain American scholars in the problem of efficiency in government. With an appreciation of both political science and the scientific method, various of these individuals made real contributions to the field of business administration via the vehicle of public administration. In particular, they added substantially to such facets of business administration as organization, planning, personnel administration, and budgetary control. In the roster of their names there appears prominently Woodrow Wilson and a large number of other scholars including White, Gaus, Frederick, Stene, Bromage, Dimock, Simon, and Merriam.[14]

Psychology

Society was growing more complex. The problem of the individual in the jungle of urbanization and industrialization eventually came to challenge the attention of the psychologist. One of the first psychologists to make a major contribution in this direction was Münsterberg. The nature of his orientation is suggested by the title of his book (published in 1913) *Psychology and Industrial Efficiency*.[15] He pointed out the relation to industrial efficiency of an understanding of the attitudes, interests, and capacities of individuals. Since his time psychologists have concerned themselves more and more with the individual in the business organization. They have given considerable knowledge and numerous devices to business administration. Few modern executives make any major decision without using some data or technique furnished by the industrial psychologist or giving due attention to some principles enunciated by him. Testing and the interpretation of test scores, for example, is a common aid in personnel decisions.

Sociology

Man does not live alone. This has brought the sociologist into the picture.[16] He may not so often be given the connotation of "industrial" as is the psychologist. However, the concern of sociologists with the composition, behavior and problems of groups is the essence of their profession. They have always had an interest in the units of society, even the business unit called the company. Management's attention was sharply drawn to the possibilities of aid from the sociologist by the work of Elton Mayo and his associates, including F. J. Roethlisberger and T. N. Whitehead, in the decade following World War I. In 1927, they opened a series of studies in the plant of the Western Electric Company located at Hawthorne, Illinois. With the cooperation of the management, these scientists conducted controlled experiments with workers performing under changing conditions. The findings, which contained some startling discoveries, concerned among other things, group attitudes and feelings, group behavior, and social grouping. In effect, management was alerted to the need of developing "social skills" in the handling of working groups. Certainly, here we see an early practical emphasis on the human relations aspect of management, a phase greatly emphasized since World War II. Indeed, the contention may be ventured that the contributions of both the industrial sociologist and the industrial psychologist lie largely in the field of human relations.

Related Fields

Undoubtedly there are many other sources of building blocks in the art and science of administration. Mention may be made of the fields of ethics, philosophy, history, political science, and mathematics. However, their contributions are either more abstract or more difficult to isolate than those that have been touched. It is to be hoped that these complicated areas will be brought into focus, for they have given much and still have a great amount to give. The possibilities of ethics alone challenges the imagination.

Administration Itself

Students of administration as such have made definite and significant contributions to their own field. Indeed they are not newcomers, for they can claim predecessors in ancient and medieval times. Sections of the Old Testament are treatises on the handling of people. Classical Greek and Roman as well as early and medieval Church writers found many occasions to write on the subject. Interestingly enough, these early pronouncements not infrequently touched upon the organization and management of people in matters economic. In recent centuries, the tempo of formal concern with administration has increased. However, a veritable mushrooming of students and writers in management has appeared during the last one hundred years. The dimensions of the list can only be suggested. It includes prominently Babbage, Metcalfe, Fayol, Emerson, Follett, Sheldon, Hopf, Schell, Tead, Urwick, Barnard, Mooney, Reiley, Drucker, Simon, and many of their peers or contemporaries.[17]

Institutional Sources

It would be wrong to overlook the contributions that two ancient, if rather antithetic, organizations have made to business administration. The Church and the Military are sources of important administrative knowledge and principles. From the Church, for example, comes much that business administration knows of hierarchy of authority with scaler territorial organization, specialization of activities on a functional basis, and the staff device. The Military has given refinements to the scaler principle, to the usage of staff, to communication, and to the reconciliation of objectives.[18]

As thus briefly traced, business administration can be labelled a multi-dimensional study. It involves the trial and error experience of business itself as well as the fields of economics, engineering, psychology, sociology, mathematics, and other disciplines.[19] *The key question is how can the contributions of these sources which give management its many facets be brought into a unified treatment that may be truly termed the science and art of administration.*

The study of strategy in the action of the administrator is proposed as the answer. It is the point of synthesis at which administration can be studied as a totality. In order to take a correct step, it is necessary to consider all elements of the situation and to act accordingly. This is strategy—the means by which all the executive's knowledge and skills, from whatever source, are brought to bear. In other words, strategy unifies administrative know-how and concentrates it upon a managerial problem. The company economist and market analyst may develop a projection of sales and the personnel office may make an estimate of salesmen needed. But the general manager, to solve the problem of the sales offensive for the next year, must bring together these several dimensions. It is in this process of synthesis that he is seen as the true administrator. To view administration completely one must study administrative strategy.

The Characteristics of Administrative Strategy

Administrative strategy is susceptible to description in many terms, popular and objective. The purposes of perspective are perhaps best served by setting forth first many of the popular concepts of its nature. In this manner, one can rid himself of certain misleading connotations which they carry. In the vernacular, strategy means being clever, shrewd and even tricky, "out-foxing" others, deceptive, winning at all costs, and, in general, Machiavellian conduct. Nothing could be further from the truth than the misleading implications here suggested. To be certain, strategy does connote keenness and gamesmanship, but these in themselves are legitimate and are certainly inherent in the American way of life. One must realize that competition is not always gentle, and he must not mistake its harshness at times for dishonorable conduct. Strategy, like all forms of human behavior, can be perverted and misdirected. It is not in itself immoral.

Right Combination of Factors

The objective features of administrative strategy can here be expressed as generalities, although in one sense this whole book is devoted to them. Strategy, as strongly implied in recent paragraphs, is to be seen as the *right combination of factors*. The first real characteristic means that it requires not only the isolation of the components of the situation but also an evaluation of their relative importance. This may be illustrated in a simple case. The manager of a plant expects a very thorough inspection from personnel representing the president's office. To insure receiving a good report he must think of all the things that may influence them, including their entertainment. Yet, he would probably be unwise to concentrate on the luncheon for the inspection group and overlook the presentation of succinct reports on new profits. In this day and age of overspecialization, it is impossible to place too much emphasis on the necessity for seeing all the parts of the picture, and these in their proper perspective. If there is one thing about which experienced business administrators now complain, it is the superficial and unbalanced answers which so many of their younger assistants propose to company problems. They commonly find that such answers suggest only a partial solution when it is the whole which is demanded.

Relativity

Strategy is *relative,* and relativity is its second essential characteristic. It is action taken in an effort to meet a particular condition, to solve a certain problem, or to attain a desired objective. It has full meaning only with respect to the situation at hand. Strategy may, and generally does, assume many forms, for almost every situation varies in some specific and therefore requires a somewhat different approach. The problem of absenteeism in a Detroit factory may be taken as an example. In the autumn, much of it is occasioned by the deer hunting season, which has a very general attraction for men. The works manager might decide to declare a holiday over the Veterans Day weekend to absorb the anticipated absenteeism. In the spring, however, large numbers of employees may miss an occasional day because of the influence of weather and full purses due to winter overtime, but there is no holiday to cover this type of employment delinquency. The manager, therefore, must take a different tack, perhaps adopt a firm attitude, and use disciplinarian measures such as the lay-off without pay at his discretion. Nothing in the example is intended to overlook the fact that, although it is relative, the strategy applied in different situations may contain some of the same elements. This in itself does not alter the fact that strategy has many forms; it must reflect the circumstances it faces.

Contradiction

Out of this quality of relativity arises a corollary feature which can be somewhat confusing to the consistent mind. Strategic action is frequently *contradictory.* The administrator may take one position or course of action today and reverse his attitude or steps tomorrow; he may do this *here* and that *there*. Yet this is the "logical" pattern for the strategist. Each situation must be seen in all its specifics as well as in its totality. Having appraised it in this comprehensive manner, he then combines his estimate of the situation with his prejudices and resources. Since these three components can differ radically from situation to situation, the administrator may not often take the same action. Many opposites appear in nature such as night and day, love and hate, high and low. This is also true in administration. For example, the administrator is faced with expanding or contracting product lines, increasing or decreasing costs, and adding or dropping personnel. He analyzes and does what he thinks best with the resources available. There is no set of simple, rigid principles to follow except those of basic morality. Of course, one does not wish to paint strategy as the rule of disorder. On the contrary, it is a calculated plan to obtain optimum results by a synthesis of the available components. In this sense strategy means order but a different order, if necessary, in each situation. This basic truth should not be obscured by the essentially "zig-zagging" appearance of the strategist in operation. The administrator gives or withholds information; he attacks or retreats; he is aggressive or passive. The state of contradiction is inherent in strategy.

A further note of explanation regarding the relative nature of strategy is necessary before proceeding to the final feature. The word "action" has been used and will appear many times in this book. The inference may be drawn that strategy generally signifies the vigorous attack. A decidedly different meaning, however, is intended. By the concept of strategic action is meant that "something appropriate must be done." Strategy abhors neglect. The action pattern it may take is most diverse. At times, as pointed out, the frontal onslaught is dictated; upon occasion, circumvention is clearly necessary; sometimes retreat is manifestly the best course; and under other circumstances the maintenance of the status quo is to be preferred. The point to be emphasized is that strategy demands the making and implementation of a particular decision, even though the decision may be to do nothing.

Forward Looking

The fourth objective feature of strategy has to do with orientation toward the future. Strategy is *forward looking*. It is concerned with "doing something about something." The administrator who is hypnotized with his past accomplishments or the historical dignity of his department or company cannot be much of a strategist. He will not be fully able to anticipate the situations that will invariably arise to demand his attention, to evaluate them properly, or to effect that combination of factors which must be focused on these problems to assure their best solution. He will tend to dissipate his time and energy in defending and protecting, whereas he should be conceiving and formulating the unique courses of action required by the evolving situations. Strategic action is impossible unless the administrator focuses his attention toward the frontiers upon which problems and opportunities appear. Nothing new requiring solution can exist in the past, and so strategy is relevant only to the future.

The experienced businessman, or perhaps even the historically minded observer, may disagree with the thought just expressed. He may even arise to the defense of the past with the charge that all new action is possible only because of previous human experience. There is a degree of truth in his stand, even for the strategist. The past does have value to the strategic administrator. He can draw lessons from it; he can use its records to defend his present course of action; and he can when necessary—for even a strategist suffers frustration—mollify his feelings by the rationalization possibilities which history offers. But this concession of the strategist to the past is only in terms of what it can give him to utilize in making the future. It cannot be his center of preoccupation, for above all else he must dream, imagine, and create.

Limitations of Strategic Action

Bounds of Morality and Law

An analytical treatment of strategy is a delicate project. The subject to some may bear a certain Machiavellian connotation. Then too, the twentieth century is peculiarly the era of the "operator." Some observers may view discussion of strategy to be dangerous. They may point out that it suggests the underhanded or improper manipulative handling of people. The possibility that the wrong interpretation or use may be made of an analysis of any aspect of human behavior is always existent. This danger is not denied, but merely avoiding the discussion of administration in its highest form will not deter the immoral from being ruthless.

Strategic action is legitimate only when it is taken within the limitations of morality and law. It is not the contention of this exposition to make the end appear as the justification of the means. As one prominent authority on business ethics writes, "Immoral conduct strikes at the very roots of human nature and works against the final purpose of man's existence."[20] Nothing in this book is intended to tempt leaders into immoral actions in the performance of their administrative tasks. In fact, it is believed that men of true moral fiber who take pains to understand the "internal and external guides of conduct"[21] in business will not be led into a pattern of administrative dishonesty.

Practical Limitations

In order to prevent misunderstanding as to the possibilities of strategy, one should recognize the fact that it simply cannot accomplish the ideal result in all situations. Practical limitations may be inherent in a given administrator's side of the equation. To begin with the organization with which the administrator is associated may be so bound by prejudice, tradition and custom, and formalized structure that he does not have the degree of freedom basic to the "twisting and turning" which is strategy. It should also be recognized that the use of strategy is limited by the capacity of the administrator to take the course which will yield the optimum results; he may be lacking in the knowledge, intelligence, skill and/or courage essential to the proper judgments and required steps. A further possible limitation arises from the fact that the necessary economic resources may not be available, e.g., the budget allowance for hiring the research staff to prove that a new company policy is unwise may be inadequate. The factor of time may impose still another limit to strategy. Time may be so brief that reliance will have to be placed upon the old way, minimum change, or just plain fortune. It may be so long that whatever action is taken in the present or foreseeable future can have little effect on the eventual outcome. Although their restrictions have already been implied, legal controls may exert a negative influence. The administrator, who perhaps could assure the retention by his company of the retailing services of a very large chain through giving preferential discounts, may find that Fair Trade legislation makes this impossible.

Counter-Strategy

The perspective in which this exposition views administrative strategy can be further clarified by a recognition of the influence of counter-strategy. The action or reaction taken by those with whom the administrator must work or cope can be determinative of both the form and extent of his strategic moves as well as of his success in them. This point seems to need illustration. The case of the ambitious and dynamic personnel manager may be examined. He has many ideas and great schemes. At a particular time, he wants to conduct an opinion and attitude survey of all the company employees toward employment terms and working conditions. But union leadership in the plant has other ideas, since it contemplates further demands on management and fears a possible revelation of contentment on the part of the workers. Here is the gist of the matter: shall the personnel manager drop his proposed survey, shall he modify it, shall he attempt to win the union over to the project, shall he proceed with it and try to block union counter-strategy, or shall he simply lower his head and charge? Whatever alternative he chooses, except perhaps the last one, will manifestly have been taken partially at least in response to union moves or anticipated moves. Even if he completely ignores the union he may find that the success of his plan is definitely limited by union opposition immobilizing its members against cooperation in the survey. In each instance the administrator will have been influenced in his strategic action or its result by another entity which threatens to take or has taken its own strategic course. And so it is with strategy in general—one move, inviting another, must adjust to it or take the consequences if any are forthcoming.

Dignity of Man

Today's administrator allies himself with those who believe in the dignity of man. Critics may see in an identification of strategy with administration at its highest a certain negation of religious, democratic and human relations trends that have done so much to elevate man in Western civilization. No plea is presented here for autocracy over democracy in business administration. There is rather an effort to pinpoint the leader in his highest act of leadership and to analyze what really can happen and does happen there. The truth of administration in action is sought, and it is believed that this objective lies within the field of both justifiable scientific inquiry and the limit of practical need. It is not unintentional that this presentation seeks to restore leadership to the individual. It is hoped that the approach will help to protect and restore the role of the individual administrator in the trend toward the anarchy of groupism.

ROLE-PLAYING

A case for role-playing has been included at the end of each chapter. The following explanation of this vitalizing device is given as an introduction to its use.

A. General Explanation.

Successful administration normally not only requires a knowledge of scientific methods and practical procedures but also demands the possession of certain behavioral skills. Strategic leadership, which in part is such a skill, can be developed through psychodramatic demonstrations called "role-playing."

B. Meaning of Role-Playing.

The essence of this method of "learning by doing" is to act out the drama of a business situation. Usually two individuals are assigned specific business counterpart roles such as supervisor of personnel and new employee. The classroom group participates as critical observers and evaluators of performance. Success in role-playing will depend upon effective coaching and realistic acting by the participants and upon objective suggestions of the observers.

C. Suggested Procedure.

The steps enumerated below are offered as a pattern which has been found successful in conducting role-playing for the instructor or business administrator who plans to use it as a training device.

1. Present the business situation in general terms only so that the players will feel free to create and contribute their own strategic ideas to the handling of the problem.

2. Outline the principles of management and strategy involved in the situation.

3. Describe briefly the "setting of the play" with respect to type of business, kind of office, and other simple frame of reference facts to help make the situation real and serious.

4. Select individuals to play the roles involved.

5. Explain to the group audience their part as observers and critical evaluators, and suggest some pertinent questions to be kept in mind or at least urge that they be alert to the *weak* and *strong* aspects of each performer and his performance.

6. Conduct a critical group evaluation of performance.

BUSINESS SITUATIONS FOR ROLE-PLAYING

SITUATION I

The Factor of Strategy

THE SETIF CHEMICAL COMPANY

A. Scene.   An industrial chemical manufacturer. A meeting in the Sales Manager's office on Monday morning for a general discussion of a revitalized sales program.

B. Players.

1. Sales Manager: Mr. Samuel E. Edwards, a young but mature, intelligent, aggressive, college-trained man recently hired away from a competitor.

2. Assistant Sales Manager: Mr. Joseph P. Morgan, an old-timer and a quiet, retiring man of fifty-five who is good at papers, records and office details and who is well respected in the office and by the field force personnel.

C. Situation.

1. Although the meeting ostensibly is called for a general discussion of the sales program, the new Sales Manager also has planned to feel out the Assistant Manager's reaction to strategic leadership approaches to company sales problems. The Sales Manager has heard several disturbing rumors that Mr. Morgan almost fanatically lives by the book and that he has the support of the "old gang" in doing so.

2. Furthermore, Mr. Edwards plans to use this meeting as his first step in a long-run program of persuading and motivating his assistants to go along with the revolutionary new sales program he has in mind.

D. Assignment.

1. In this first case, ask for volunteers to play the roles, and strongly encourage them to be original and realistic in their demonstration of the meeting between the Sales Manager and Assistant Sales Manager.

2. Instruct the group to pay special attention to certain features of the performance which reflect or fail to reflect an understanding of the general nature of strategy.

NOTE: The company titles of all the role-playing cases in this book are fictitious, although each case is a synthesis of common situations reported to the authors.

NOTES

1. *A New English Dictionary of Historical Principles* (Oxford: Clarendon Press, 1919), IX, Part I, p. 1087.
2. *Ibid.*
3. *Webster's New World Dictionary* (College ed.; Cleveland: The World Publishing Co., 1957), p. 1441.
4. JOHN T. ZADROZNY, *Dictionary of Social Sciences* (Washington, D.C.: Public Affairs Press, 1959), p. 333.
5. EDWARD L. BERNAYS (ed.), *The Engineering of Consent* (Norman, Oklahoma: University of Oklahoma Press, 1955), pp. 100-101.
6. The subject of strategy is very broad, and in the field of business administration alone it can be divided into several categories which, as defined by Moore, are external economic strategies, external social strategies, and internal organizational strategies. This book is concerned primarily, but not exclusively, with the latter. A concise distinction among these three types of strategy is given by David G. Moore, "Managerial Strategies" in W. Lloyd Warner and Norman H. Martin (eds.), *Industrial Man: Businessmen and Business Organizations* (New York: Harper & Brothers Publishers, 1959), p. 224.
7. *A New English Dictionary of Historical Principles* (Oxford: Clarendon Press, 1888), I, p. 117.
8. ALBERT LEPAWSKY, *Administration: The Art and Science of Organization and Management* (New York: Alfred A. Knopf, 1952), pp. 34-39.
9. *A New English Dictionary of Historical Principles, loc. cit.*
10. Contributions of the basic and applied social sciences to business administration are suggested by an elaborate chart showing sources of industrial relation knowledge and contained in DELBERT C. MILLER and WILLIAM H. FORM, *Industrial Sociology* (New York: Harper & Brothers, Publishers, 1951), pp. 10-11.
11. A concise analysis of the development of economic doctrine can be found in ROBERT LEKACHMAN, *A History of Economic Ideas* (Harper & Brothers, Publishers, 1959).
12. JOHN VON NEUMANN and OSKAR MORGENSTERN, *Theory of Games and Economic Behavior* (3rd ed.; Princeton: Princeton University Press, 1953), p. 7.
13. For a more extensive treatment of the contributions of the pioneering engineers, see GEORGE FILIPETTI, *Industrial*

Management in Transition (Homewood, Illinois: Richard D. Irwin, Inc., 1953), pp. 1-116.

14. HAROLD KOONTZ and CYRIL O'DONNELL, *Principles of Management* (New York: McGraw-Hill Book Company, Inc., 1955), pp. 28-29.

15. HUGO MUNSTERBERG, *Psychology and Industrial Efficiency* (Boston: Houghton Mifflin Company, 1913).

16. A standard and readable work in industrial sociology is that of DELBERT C. MILLER and WILLIAM H. FORM, *Industrial Sociology* (New York: Harper & Brothers, Publishers, 1951).

17. A collection of excerpts from pioneers in the field of management is contained in HARWOOD F. MERRILL (ed.), *Classics in Management* (New York: American Management Association, 1960).

18. KOONTZ and O'DONNELL, *op. cit.*, pp. 17-18; and JAMES D. MOONEY, *The Principles of Organization* (Rev. ed.; New York: Harper & Brothers, Publishers, 1939), pp. 102-156.

19. The multi-dimensional nature of business administration is recognized by Crawford H. Greenwalt, President, E. I. duPont de Nemours & Company. He writes in discussing the executive function, "The best that I can offer is to say that the basic requirement of executive capacity is the ability to create a harmonious whole out of what the academic world calls dissimilar disciplines." *The Uncommon Man* (New York: McGraw-Hill Book Company, Inc., 1959), p. 64.

   An analysis of the multi-dimensional character of business administration is made more difficult by the fact that complete agreement as to the theory of the firm does not yet exist among economists themselevs. JOSEPH W. McGUIRE, *Theories of Business Behavior.* (Englewood Cliffs, N.J.: Prentice-Hall, Inc., 1964), p. 47.

20. HENRY J. WIRTENBERGER, S.J., *Moral Principles and Problems of Business* (Preliminary printing; Detroit: University of Detroit, 1953), pp. 1-2.

21. *Ibid.*, Chap. III, pp. 17-27.

   Attention is invited to a later publication by Wirtenberger in which he has revised and amplified his earlier work. See HENRY J. WIRTENBERGER, S.J., *Morality and Business* (Chicago: Loyola University Press, 1962).

CHAPTER **2**

Leadership: Strategy in Action

> "Leadership is a dynamic phenomenon. It is the cohesive force which holds the group intact, the accommodating factor which makes it possible for the members to live together, and the disciplinary power that keeps the unit as a whole moving toward a goal. Above all else, it is the directing of followership toward an objective by meeting in a complementary, exploitative, or counteractive move the observable or anticipated actions and reactions of others."

A SOCIAL UNIT cannot function effectively without leadership. It must act as a group to succeed as a group. However, group behavior is neither an automatic outcome of mere association nor can it be attained in most circumstances by completely uncoordinated assembly of individuals.[1] There must be a cohesive and disciplinary force which helps maintain membership, facilitates group interaction, and directs the members of the unit in the pursuit of some goal.[2] The absence of this force, which can be termed leadership, generally means an anarchical situation, except for those rare instances of extreme motivation over a very short period in which the members of the group all run in the same direction, as soldiers caught in sudden gunfire or a crowd in a theater rushing for a single exit upon the discovery of a fire.

23

A Realistic View of Leadership

This is without a doubt a great over-simplification of the meaning of leadership. The concept is one of breadth and depth.[3] It is peculiarly difficult of definition in terms of absolutes. The forms that it takes because of its generative forces, the subtleties it must assume to be acceptable, and the functions it must discharge are so diverse that it cannot be described adequately in a few suggestive sentences. The anatomy of leadership has been the subject of concern, in more or less articulate terms, for millennia. It has bedeviled many ages and many cultures. The writings of Mencius, St. Thomas Aquinas, and Machiavelli testify to this fact.

Strategy, the Essence of Leadership

Leadership is a dynamic phenomenon.[4] The purpose of definition, therefore, will be served by the isolation of its action component, which is properly termed strategy. It is the essence of the leader's highest performance. It is the personal skill by which he meets, in a complementary, exploitative, or counteractive move, the observable or anticipated actions and reactions of those with whom he must deal. In brutal terms, it may be said that the leader is the instrument of the strategy necessary to protect and activate the group. Considered in the light of the strategy which it must exercise, leadership becomes, then, a matter of more than the possession of a list of attributes. It becomes gamesmanship in which the right means, techniques, and devices are understood and used at the right time and place. This thought is not to imply a shallow mechanistic view of the leader. It is intended rather as a basic recognition of the fact that social skills should be great in those who assume the leadership role with its three specific goals of membership maintenance, objective attainment, and group interaction facilitation.

Some Traditional Approaches

There are various traditional approaches to a broad understanding of leadership. It would probably be an unwarranted diversion, though interesting, to attempt an exhaustive review of them.[5] A brief mention of three will help point up this realistic view of leadership.

One common explanation presents a leader in terms of individual attributes, either real or attributed to him by others. These characteristics may include physical features, mental capacities, and moral qualities; or they may simply be that wonderful complex known as personality, the impression the leader gives. Out of this approach may come the popular idea that "leaders are born, not made." It seems to generate the belief that those who have "it" will lead and that those without "it" will follow. Here, is the *great man* fantasy. Such intrinsically insignificant traits as birth to the purple, commanding appearance, persuasive voice, education at a famous school, success in athletics, military position, or the authorship of a publication are equated with ability to lead.

In contrast, a second and more pragmatic approach attempts to explain leadership by starting from the practical situation demanding it.[6] For example, it becomes necessary for top management to put someone in charge of welfare functions in the company. The post goes to a staff person who can be spared. Ipso facto, he is now a leader. Unless by happenstance he has the ability to be a leader, his appointment may be nothing more than the institutionalization of mediocrity in a position of power. But since he has been given the title, it is assumed that the organization now has another leader. This positional theory of leadership probably explains why many unfit individuals are in administrative posts. The tragedy lies in the fact that such misfits frequently are allowed by circumstance to continue in office long after the immediate set of circumstances which led to their choice disappears. The organizational hierarchy eventually will suffer qualitative deterioration in administration, unless it works out informal organizational machinery to help carry his load for which his leadership is not adequate.

A third approach to leadership centers around the degree of involvement of the members of the group in the leadership function. The autocratic school holds that only the person or persons with decision making and enforcing power can be a leader and, therefore, should be a leader. All others can be nothing more than followers. This is best illustrated perhaps by what may be called *der fuehrer* concept—that the leader is all and all is the leader. It prevailed in nineteenth and early twentieth century American industry. The entrepreneur was the dictator. The democratic inroads, which as a rule did not begin seriously in American industry until at least the second generation of the company's life, held that the participation of followers strengthens leadership. As developed since World War I, the democratic trends in administration have gone so far as to achieve significant fragmentation of the leadership function. Today, we see manifestations in the form of extensive use of committees, consultative devices, and rotating leadership. Not a little of this democratic picture is due to the overwhelming influence of the doctrine of equality sweeping the Western World. Quite obviously, the defense that two heads are better than one can be advanced, if one does not forget that the multiplication of ignorance and inability in itself contributes nothing to leadership.

Each of the foregoing approaches explains a fractional, but important, interpretation of leadership. The attribute and personality viewpoint focuses attention on the nature or apparent nature of the leader himself. The positional analysis points up a common practice of equating position and leadership. The group involvement consideration places emphasis on followership. The challenge is to find a synthesis of these and other approaches to leadership in terms of the action core. The theory of strategy as the heart of leadership is proposed as a solution to this problem.

Qualities Basic to Successful Leadership[7]

The qualities necessary for successful leadership are, therefore, those that contribute most to strategic action. Quite obviously, this implies positive degrees of intelligence, industry, character, and personality; but simply to leave the matter here is insufficient. These attributes, inherited or acquired, are generic concepts. They have various aspects and are of many types. The kind of intelligence required to meet the action or reaction of others is not altogether that essential to the analysis of an engineering or accounting problem. This thought can be extended to the other attributes of leadership. Any discussion of the qualities basic to real leadership must attempt to be specific. It must aim to isolate and identify the particular traits of the individual which make him the person who can bring the group to a goal.

Possession of Requisite Mental Ability

Attention logically may be turned first to intelligence.[8] Of the many components which comprise it, five seem of most significance to leadership. They are alertness, imagination, creativeness, judgment and adaptability. The group, whether it be business concern or other, may be conceived of as having two fronts—defensive and offensive. In other words, it must assume certain postures and do certain things to continue to exist, and it must likewise take the necessary stance and steps to forge ahead. For example, a firm manufacturing industrial gases and related equipment will find it necessary to continue the production of standard items as a means of staying in business, and it will also virtually be compelled to spend large sums on research and development to move forward with new products. This two-front war, as it were, that must be fought by a group demands a leader who can look simultaneously in all directions and see where the enemy is weak and where he is strong, where he is vulnerable to attack and where he is most likely to attack. Only the alert leader can do this. This is the leader who is quick, sensitive, and comprehensive in his overview of the entire situation surrounding the group.

Of course, even the most alert leader cannot see what is either not yet present or observable. The general manager of the industrial gas company at an early stage of scientific development in the field could not have foreseen the invention of a certain solid rocket fuel. But the welfare of his company, nevertheless, would have required that it take steps against the possibility of competitive inroads by such a fuel, that perhaps it improve its gas fuels, lower its prices, or go into the development of solid fuels. Obviously, mere alertness would not have been either a sufficient defensive or offensive weapon in this case. Something more would have been needed—the capacity to "conjure up," to dream, to anticipate or, in more psychological terms, to imagine that new fuels of the solid type might be brought out by competitors. Imagination seems to be even a rarer human quality than alertness, for it has more of the abstract in it.[9] Many an alert person is not a leader because he cannot see what is not there to see. He cannot go beyond the bounds of empiricism.

Of close kinship with, but not inherent in, imagination is creativeness.[10] No mental trait, if it is completely a matter of the intellect, is as difficult to define as creative ability. For want of a better practical definition, it may be described as

that human capacity which makes it possible for the possessor to conceive and/or bring into being that which is new,
whether it be of a material or non-material nature. Obviously,
neither the production of successive units of product or
service nor the reproduction of something already made or
done marks an individual as creative, for the element of innovation is not present. The business administrator must be
an innovator, since there are no set formulas for solving all
the business problems he must face. It is impossible to
delimit the amount of creative ability necessary for effective
administrative leadership, but certainly it must be sufficient
for the conception of new ideas, plans, and projects. Perhaps
much of the development of each innovation can be left to
the leader's assistants, providing that he at least take the initiative to insure their proper assignment to it and providing that he make the necessary subsequent control effort to
assure its proper completion.

Yet, this is not the entire story of the intelligence components of leadership. The most alert and imaginative and
creative person might, if he lacked the balancing aspect of
intelligence, be nothing but a source of worry to himself and
his associates. He would notice opportunities, "dream up"
possibilities; and conceive and perhaps move in new directions but he would act in an unwise manner. Judgment is
essential to the evaluation of what is observed or imagined,
as it is to the conception and to the embarkation on or rejection of courses of action. Had the general manager, under
the excitement of discovering or imagining that a rival company might come forth with a solid propellant, decided to
double his research expenditures to the serious detriment of
customer service, he might have lost much of the company's
ability to stay in business. It is what the leader does with
his information, dreams, and creations that is most critical.

Finally the trait of adaptability must be included among
the mental requirements for leadership. By definition, suc-

cessful leadership as action is said to be strategy. Since strategy requires flexibility to meet different situations, the leader should be able to adjust himself and his organization to new conditions and problems. If he cannot, he may, remain not much more than a student of opportunity, despite his possession of all the other of these components of intelligence.

Exertion of Effort

Analysis may next be directed to the basic quality of industry. Success in most lines of endeavor depends upon hard work, and effectiveness in a position of leadership is no exception. In general, industry implies the exertion of continuous and rigorous effort. The industrious man may be thought of as one who applies himself with regularity and intensity to the task before him. But certain elements in the behavior pattern of the leader can make him appear to be something less than a hard worker. To illustrate this point, one may picture the corporation president who always seems to have time for government assignments, community projects, the local golf course, or Florida. It may be that he is simply taking advantage of his position or enjoying the rewards of success. However, it must be emphasized that the leader acts on all fronts, and that methods of defense and offense do not fit necessarily into the simple workbench concept. The whistle does not blow at regular intervals for the leader. While apparently dashing hither and thither, while socializing and posturing, he may be as fruitfully or more profitably engaged in the administration of his position of trust as when sitting at the desk reading or writing directions and reports and performing other routines. His universe of operation is everywhere that people are to be influenced and conditions molded to the wellbeing of his organization. His apparent cavalier attitude toward his office may be the reflection of deep wisdom on his part in delegating routine matters to lesser men, so that he may be free to undertake the real work of leadership, that is, strategic action.

Respect for Moral Values

All really thinking people know that good moral character is essential to the *proper* exercise of power over others. In fact, Western society seems to have come to the historical conclusion that the leader should be a moral man. In this sense, it has taken a much sounder stand than Machiavelli, who seems to have believed that at times it is more important to seem to have virtues than actually to possess them. But the issue at stake in this discussion of the attributes basic to leadership is whether or not morality is *necessary* to the effective use of such power. It can easily be pointed out that many completely bad or even extremely vicious individuals have been truly effective leaders. One needs but cite such characters as Hitler and Mussolini. In the short run, immoral leadership seems possible. His immorality unfortunately may even contribute to the leader's temporary success.

The positive relationship between good character and leadership is certain in the long run, and morality is clearly seen to be a quality essential to lasting, effective leadership. Practical proofs are evident. Many followers see their own high ideals personified in the leader and will not give their fullest support to one who represents anything else. Moreover, in recognition of the fact that their collective security is greatest under the good man, they will be prone to give him their greatest loyalty. Downright fear also is a reason. The immoral leader is sooner or later recognized as a personal danger by many individuals because of his fickleness. He may at any time find it desirable to "turn on" any of his followers. These are evident elements. In addition, there are at least two other more subtle facts to support the contention that morality is a prerequisite for sustained successful leadership. The leader whose conduct is generally above moral approach will be trusted by many followers in his administrative judgments. People tend to trust the honest and honorable man all the way. Moreover, since man has a conscience and since he must live with himself, it is probable that the greatest degree of peace of mind is possible only to the good man. His best work as a leader cannot be done under the pressure of unnecessary conflicts with himself.

There is one phase of character not always associated in the popular mind with morality. The leader must have as a part of his character a large measure of courage. He must make frequent, bold, and often serious decisions, but this is fraught with danger to him and his group. Many decisions and their implementation elicit opposition, and at times this opposition may take the form of reaction so violent as to bring real trouble. The danger inherent frequently prevents timid administrators from discharging their leadership function to the fullest. Only those with courage to face consequences will act, and action is the basis of leadership. The sources of courage are many and deep, and cannot be treated here. However, it is significant to emphasize that the moral man has a special source of courage, namely, his own righteousness. He can always take refuge in the fact that he feels himself to be right, and he can lead into the decision from this position of strength.

Appearance of Superiority

The final attribute basic to efficient leadership is a nebulous concept entitled personality. Whatever this may be as defined by the psychologist, it is in a practical sense the total impression that others draw from an individual as they see him.[11] Certainly intelligence and industry and character contribute to personality because their manifestations are to a degree observable by others. However, it frequently happens that the members of a group will follow one who possesses these qualities in only slight degree, and will not follow another who has the happiest combination of all three. Why is this? The answer would seem to be that they do not recognize the latter as one who can lead them. In this sense, they may be said to be superficial, but even so certain qualities of attraction are missing in him. The absent qualities necessary to make him accepted as a leader are often intrinsically insignificant, but because they are necessary they cannot be overlooked. There come to mind such things as physical appearance, dress, personal dash, voice, standard of living, and social status. If these often superficial characteristics are not significant, how can one explain the popularity and influence which shallow individuals at times exert over or in an organization? It must be concluded that the confidence which is basic to followership, at least in a free society, is the result of many things—some simply strange and others strangely simple. All this suggests that the real strategist in administration is the leader who recognizes his own strong points and makes the most of them.

Leadership Behavior Patterns

There are two distinct patterns of leadership behavior: the non-strategic and the strategic.[12] The former is unchanging and usually implies preoccupation with the routine and the habitual. In other words, non-strategic leadership lives by and for the book. This does not necessarily suggest inefficiency in the routine administration of an organization, for emphasis on the status quo requires and may bring careful procedural order. But strategic leadership is restless. It goes beyond the assurance that the day to day tasks of organizational life are well performed. It seeks to improve much or all that concerns the organization, including the routine procedures as well as the strengthening and advancing of both defensive and offensive frontiers. The essence of strategic leadership is adaptability and creativity. In other words, it is able to draw upon its own experiences and knowledge and that of others, and to synthesize these into a new plan of action; it is productive of new ideas and innovations; it is unsatisfied and curious, constantly seeking out further opportunities to exploit.

The Non-Strategic Leader: One Who Lives by Rules

The non-strategic leader runs with the pack, even perhaps very well; the strategic leader wants to be out in front. This fundamental difference can be seen in an illustration. One may take the case of two district sales managers. The first, perhaps by nature more conservative, concentrates on old customers, minimum service, low expense accounts, and prompt reporting to the home office. When the general sales manager visits the district, he finds a smooth functioning office and staff, but the picture he obtains appears very much the same each visit. The year-end review shows few new customers and little change in sales volume and profit. In contrast, the other district sales manager (an energetic, imaginative and ambitious person) is not satisfied to stand still. He is a strategist. He is constantly on the move about his territory seeking to find further uses for his line of products, larger sales to old customers, and new accounts. He is not hypnotized by the routine. The inference might be drawn that he is, therefore, simply a restless type. However, the truly strategic leader does not neglect the routine, for he realizes that its smooth discharge is essential to the freedom of action he requires. He somehow relegates routine to the background of his life, usually by the development of short cuts to handle it or by delegation. When the general sales manager inspects the more vital administrator and his territory, he senses a vigor and he feels change. He may never be quite certain as to what he will see. Yet in the long run, everything being equal, the yearly reports will show new customers and higher sales and profits for the lively district.

The Strategic Leader: One Who Meets the Situation

The strategic leader needs further description. His actions and their results are easily seen. But how does he really differ from his counterpart? There are two main distinctions. First, he thinks and acts much more dynamically. Second, he possesses those intangible qualities which make it possible for him to "spark" an organization into extraordinary effort. He must have this latter quality in order to obtain the *unusual* performance necessary to strategic action. If the district sales manager sees a chance to land a sizable new account by having three of his salesmen attend a convention of production engineers extending into the weekend, he must be able to influence these employees to the necessary sacrifice of time and home comfort. If he is not able to do so, he is in effect in the same position as the non-strategic, or static, leader who does not even see the opportunity for more business.

A discussion of the strategic leader often raises the specter of a vital, fiery character charging in all directions at the same time. The question of the rate of organizational change and growth, as well as of the diversity of its direction, is involved. Good administration demands both stability and flexibility. There are circumstances when the interests of the organization are best served by the leader's seeming to do or doing nothing. This may be the epitome of strategy, since it may be the logical course for the time. However, conditions usually change sooner or later, and the welfare of the organization accordingly requires ability to shift to meet new circumstances. The point to be emphasized is that the strategic leader follows no one path. He stands still, retreats, or advances as necessary for optimum results.

Situs of Administrative Strategy

Just where can strategy be used by the administrator to advantage in the organization? Part of the answer must lie in the field of functional considerations.[13] In what duties of the leader (who generally is an administrator in a business concern) can strategic action offer the best course? The business leader has two basic administrative responsibilities: (1) the usual administrative processes of setting goals, planning, assembling means, organizing, communicating, directing, and controlling; and (2) constant vigilance to protect and further company interests. Each of these requires some combination of such factors as personnel, time, funds, facilities and methods, as well as a consideration of action and reaction by those with whom the administrator must work or compete. In short, he faces in the discharge of both of his fundamental responsibilities, and their coordinate functions, the necessity for choosing that course of action which will be most advantageous. This, by definition, is strategy, that strategy can be used to good purpose in all organizational functions thus becomes obvious.

Part of the answer concerns the hierarchical structure.[14] Since every leader in the company regardless of his grade has the foregoing two functions in some degree, strategic action can be used profitably by all management personnel from the head janitor to the chairman of the board. The head janitor will have to choose a proper course of action in order to assure his building's being spotless. He may find it necessary to treat his charwomen gallantly, to have them clean after working hours, and to maintain cleaning equipment in top shape. The chairman of the board is also faced with the problem of selecting a course of action. He, too, must be strategic, even though his power is infinitely greater than that of the janitorial supervisor. He may get the best cooperation from his board members by recognizing their advice and judgment, by having board meetings at times convenient to all members, and by providing a status location such as a beautiful board room for the meetings.

The Funnel Theory

In both frequency and scope the opportunities for the use of strategy vary directly with the hierarchical levels of organization. Since strategic action is response to the whole environment, chances for its use occur more often and in greater dimension the nearer the leader is to the top, because he is concerned with a much larger and more important portion of environment. The janitor is expected only to see that segment of the organizational environment having to do with the cleanliness of the buildings. The board chairman has the overview of the total company situation. Between the bottom and top segments of administration, the purview of the environment will increase with each step upward. The chief engineer will have more chances to act strategically than the head draftsman, but not as many as the general manager. This theory as to situs of opportunities for strategy may be described as the *funnel theory*. The many and big chances for strategic action pour into the organization hierarchy from the top.

The funnel theory may explain in part why top administration is sometimes considered less consistent than intermediate or low level management. Its opportunities for the use of various courses of action are multitudinous and often of much more import. Of course, this theory is not a complete explanation of apparent inconsistency by high leadership. The mere fact that such leadership in many cases has more power to act and less fear of consequences is also a determining factor. Moreover, the many and heavy responsibilities that top management must carry no doubt tend to make it eager to exploit situations and to change direction of movement.

In discussing the situs of strategy within an organization, it must be borne in mind that it is also available to and used by the informal leader. This natural leader without position probably makes himself recognized and leads by the use of strategy even more than does the legitimate leader. He has no extra authority in the sense of power granted officially to perform duties beyond those of his company position. Any exercise of his leadership capacity beyond the confines of his status must come essentially from his own ability to act and react. The fact that he must depend upon himself does not necessarily mean that his influence is insignificant. His own peculiar abilities may be very great, and his moves may be far-reaching. Furthermore, his associates, immediate superior, or even most of his superiors may be mediocre or weak individuals; they may simply not care about his informal empire-building; or they may even welcome his "extra-legal" assistance. Finally, his very lack of official status may give him greater freedom of action. Legitimate position usually brings restrictions as well as power.

Conclusion

The real leader is strategic. He is full of contradictions, since he acts and reacts in the light of all the circumstances. He may display a social numbness and either sit still or move ahead without apparent regard for collateral consequences. At other times he may be sensitive to any and all, even solicitous of what others think and want. He may be quite consistent and inflexible, taking the stand that rules must be followed, standards maintained, and all treated alike. Subsequently he may adopt a most inconsistent and fluid course, showing great flexibility of decision and action as circumstances change. It is probably not too maudlin to state that he must be capable of being many things to many people in many situations. If he remembers the values of moral and legal conduct, this requirement will not make him simply an "operator."

BUSINESS SITUATIONS FOR ROLE-PLAYING

SITUATION II

Leadership: Strategy in Action

THE SPAVA GEAR COMPANY

A. Scene.

An automobile parts manufacturing company. Plant Manager's office during a meeting of the Plant Manager and a new shop superintendent who has been on the job for two months.

B. Players.

1. Plant Manager: Mr. William Phelps, who over eighteen years has worked his way up to Plant Manager and who is both extremely industrious and highly respected.

2. Shop Superintendent: Mr. James Rogers, a hard working and ambitious recent graduate of the company's executive training program with little practical background in supervision or administration previous to his present position.

C. Situation.

1. When Mr. Rogers took over his department, production rose steadily for several weeks. It appeared that he was a good leader. Since then production has begun to decrease and rejects to rise rapidly. Moreover, the union has presented management with several grievances from the department.

2. Upon checking into the situation and talking to a few of the older workers, Mr. Phelps has found that Mr. Rogers is "cracking the whip" on the men. He expects an increase of twenty per cent in output and hounds the men consistently. He threatens to discharge them if they do not cooperate.

3. Mr. Phelps believes that Mr. Rogers can be a good leader and has decided to talk to him about the problem. The Plant Manager must apply strategy in his talk so as not to disillusion the ambitious and aggressive young superintendent.

D. Assignment. 1. Select individuals for the roles of Plant Manager and Shop Superintendent, choosing one of the more imaginative for the senior role.

2. Ask them to stress the points of strategic leadership.

3. Instruct the group to describe the probable reactions of Mr. Rogers and to suggest ways by which Mr. Phelps could have handled him better.

NOTES

1. Professor Marshall Dimock eloquently supports this view. See Chapter 12, "Integrative Leadership" in *Administrative Vitality* (New York: Harper & Brothers, Publishers, 1959), pp. 175-198.
2. Statistical analysis incident to the Ohio State Leadership Studies showed that leadership has these three functions or dimensions. CARROLL L. SHARTLE, *Executive Performance and Leadership* (Englewood Cliffs, N.J.: Prentice-Hall, © 1956), pp. 117-118.
3. The complexity of the concept of leadership is recognized in the Ohio State Leadership Studies in that they were conducted as an interdisciplinary project and in that they hypothesized at least three sets of variables—interactions, performances and expectations—as being necessary to account for the leadership role. RALPH M. STOGDILL, *Leadership and Structures of Personnel Interaction*. Research Monograph Number 84 (Columbus, Ohio: Bureau of Business Research, The Ohio State University, 1957), p. vii.
4. "In the broadest sense, leadership refers to that process whereby an individual directs, guides, influences, or controls the thoughts, feelings or behavior of other human beings." FRANKLYN S. HAIMAN, *Group Leadership and Democratic Action* (Boston: Houghton-Mifflin Company, 1951), p. 4.

5. An extensive review of types of leaders has been made in terms of "princes, heroes and supermen" by EUGENE E. JENNINGS, *An Anatomy of Leadership* (New York: Harper & Brothers, Publishers, 1960).

6. Mary Parker Follett in her concept of leadership as obedience to the "law of the situation" takes this approach. MARY PARKER FOLLETT, "Some Discrepancies in Leadership Theory and Practice" in HENRY C. METCALF and L. URWICK (eds.), *Dynamic Administration: The Collected Papers of Mary Parker Follett* (New York: Harper & Brothers, Publishers, 1940), pp. 270-294.

7. For a more comprehensive treatment of qualities necessary in leadership, see ORDWAY TEAD, *The Art of Leadership* (New York: McGraw-Hill Book Company, Inc., 1935), pp. 82-266.

   A detailed analysis of the factors in effective administration is presented in the study by CHARLES E. SUMMER, JR., *Factors in Effective Administration* (New York: Graduate School of Business, Columbia University, 1956).

8. This is not to imply that the possession of high intellect assures good leadership performance. Barnard writes succinctly to this point when he declares, "We all know persons in and out of practical affairs of superior intellects and intellectual accomplishments who do not work well as leaders." CHESTER I. BARNARD, *Organization and Management* (Cambridge, Mass.: Harvard University Press, 1949), p. 98.

9. Imagination is sometimes seen as the basic quality of the intellect. Osborn writes to this effect when he states, "The fact that imagination is the pristine power of the human mind has long been recognized by the greatest thinkers. They have concurred in Shakespeare's conclusion that this divine spark is what makes man 'the paragon of animals.'" ALEX F. OSBORN, *Applied Imagination: Principles and Procedures of Creative Thinking* (New York: Charles Scribner's Sons, 1953), p. 1.

10. Professor Glover defines creative thinking in practical terms. "Creative thinking is that mental process which brings into existence new concepts, methods and products which are of value and can be used for the betterment of the work or project under consideration." JOHN G. GLOVER, *Fundamentals of Professional Management* (Rev. ed.; New York: Simmons-Boardman Publishing Corp., 1958), p. 152.

11. The broader view of personality as "self" in relation to the organization is developed in CHRIS ARGYRIS, *Personality*

and Organization (New York: Harper & Brothers, Publishers, 1957), pp. 20-53.

12. "The word leadership has a wide variety of interpretations. Some may use it to include almost any supervisory or administrative performance." SHARTLE, *op. cit.*, p. 4.

   The authors of this book tend to take the broader view, and so they identify it very closely with supervision and administration. In fact, they go still further in that they often do not distinguish between supervision and administration. They commonly use interchangeably the terms *leadership* and *administration*, and *leader* and *administrator*.

13. Attention is invited to the Ohio State Leadership Studies which were initiated in 1945 and which have been responsible for various publications. Carroll L. Shartle, who was the Director of these studies, points out that in them ". . . the approach to the topic of leadership has been that of examining and measuring performance or behavior rather than human traits." Carroll L. Shartle in the Introduction to RALPH M. STODGILL and ALVIN E. COONS, *Leadership Behavior: Its Description and Measurement.* Research Monograph Number 88 (Columbus, Ohio: Bureau of Business Research, The Ohio State University, 1957), p. 1.

   These studies have been described as providing the best information as to leadership functions. JOHN M. PFIFFNER and FRANK P. SHERWOOD, *Administrative Organization* (Englewood Cliffs, N.J.: Prentice-Hall, Inc., 1960), p. 353.

   Whatever may be the functions of leadership, it is difficult to disagree with the thought that "The successful manager makes things happen." Quotation from GEORGE S. ODIORNE, *Personnel Policy: Issues and Practices* (Columbus: Charles E. Merrill Books, Inc., 1963), p. 221.

14. Leadership structure is discussed by PFIFFNER and SHERWOOD, *op. cit.*, p. 355. They take it to mean that no individual holds all the leadership functions.

   Regardless of their distribution, leadership functions, in terms of behavior patterns, are classifiable into direction, response and representation. See LEONARD R. SAYLES, *Managerial Behavior* (New York: McGraw-Hill Book Company, 1964), p. 53.

CHAPTER **3**

Mobilizing Followers

> "Followership is the reciprocal of leadership. However, in its best form it does not automatically accrue to the leader. He must work to assure it; he must mobilize his followers."

FOLLOWERSHIP is implicit in leadership and along with the leader and the situation it is a basic factor in any leadership problem.[1] There can be no leader without at least one follower,[2] otherwise the individual would have no function as a leader. The leader can exist only as a part of a group of two or more. These laconic statements, which appear almost as truisms, raise an interesting introductory question: What is followership? The reply to this query is more difficult than the definition of leadership.

What Is Followership?

Attachment and Its Sources

The essence of followership is adherence to something or somebody. In an exposition of administrative strategy it means attachment to an individual or individuals. Obviously, there must be reasons for attachment. In the business world, as elsewhere, these are legion in number and variety. Affection, whatever its source, must be cited first. It may not be the most powerful of reasons, but it certainly is the most often mentioned. How many times does one hear on the factory floor or in the office the repetitious statements: "I certainly like the boss!" or "I just can't stand that guy!" The probability that affection is more important in explaining female than male followership should not be overlooked.

Admiration also should appear early in an explanation of followership, for its relation to affection may be close. Admiration may be the result of affection or vice versa, but it is even more. It connotes esteem, i.e. respect or placing high value on a person, and may proceed from a variety of sources. Followers may admire the leader for his appearance, personality, character, ideals, prejudices, personal habits, title, position of power, ability, accomplishments, wealth, social status, or manner of life. Another reason for "enrolling under the banner of a particular leader" is plain selfishness. The follower sees certain practical advantages in the relationship, and so he establishes and/or retains it. Among these considerations, especially in the business concern, are security, economic reward, easier assignments, freedom of action and time, and chance for advancement in the organization. A still further factor which contributes to followership is something now becoming known as "belongingness." It may be described as a type of general compulsion to be a member of a group, but it can also take the more specific form of intra-group affection, without particular reference to the leader. For example, a secretary likes certain of the other secretaries and for this reason alone remains in the organization and retains a vicarious attachment to the "boss." A final reason for followership is simple inertia. This is apparent in the case of the employee who is too lazy or content to be disloyal or to seek change in assignment or employment. In summary, people follow other people because they like them, they admire them, they see practical advantages, they have strong social instincts, or they are too lazy or happy to do otherwise.

The Factor of Compulsion

There may appear to be a major omission in this analysis of followership. No reference has been made to compulsion. People are often forced to follow. This is true in business enterprises as well as in other more obviously disciplined organizations. They are assigned to a certain unit; obedience, cooperation and loyalty to the supervisor or executive in charge are expected. Theirs is not to choose a leader, unless they wish to change jobs. Is this followership? The question may be rather academic, but it does raise the issue of democracy in leadership. It may be contended, with sound argument, that compulsory followership is true followership, whether or not the employees have anything to say in decision-making. The essence of followership is attachment, whatever its origin.

Followership as Something More Than Adherence

Followership, whether voluntary or involuntary, means in a practical sense something more than the mere phenomenon of adherence. It signifies staying with the leader in the pursuance of an organizational goal.[3] The thought here may be rather elusive, but it is highly significant. It leads to the common sense business view that a collection of people within a company has an ultimate economic purpose. Followership in the company as a whole or in one of its units cannot be viewed by the strategic administrator as simply friendly association. It must be effective, and to be so it must mean loyalty until the objective is won. The president of the corporation may have everyone on his team when he speaks of across-the-board salary and wage increases; yet he may, when he wants to institute a new sales program to help obtain the income for the over-all increment, find that almost no one is with him or will lend him assistance. Clearly, he does not have followership in the business sense. The pursuit of a goal as real as profit cannot permit such an "off-and-on" relationship. This is not to imply that the leader's followership is with him to the same degree or is the same in all projects.[4] But it does mean that followership, to be real, must remain with the leader until the goal of the particular situation is assured.

This brief excursion into the nature of followership has been undertaken with a purpose. Followership is an unstable and variable factor in strategy. It must be obtained and retained, conditioned and motivated, coordinated, directed and controlled. The administrator who would perform his duties as a strategic leader must marshal his followers into an effective striking force. It is especially important to this function that he realize why people adhere to him. Such knowledge will not only help him to estimate the limits of his followers' endurance, but also suggest to him their particular susceptibility to his maneuver. This is well illustrated in the case of the vice president who is charged with the establishment of a new branch plant. The work will be intensive for a short period. The obstacles which he will be required to handle on the spot will be numerous. The fact that he knows his core group to be ambitious and loyal people who have hitched their cart to his star in the company with the hope of rising with him may enable him to operate much more efficiently. On the one hand, he will feel considerable safety in pushing his confidants to the limit without overtime pay. On the other hand, he will be able to shift their titles without causing a serious wave of resignations.

The Choice of Followers

The erroneous impression that the largest possible followership is always to be desired tends to prevail in the popular mind. In fact, it is an illusion held by too many administrators themselves. There is here reflected the often spurious American philosophy that bigness is to be desired. The public tends to pay much more honor to the head of a large and nation-wide corporation than to the owner of a local establishment. Similiar adulation is seen in the frequent case of the company administration which gives greatest recognition to the supervisor of the largest number of employees.

Bases for Selection

Objective criteria for judging the proper number of followers are to be found in the use to which they are put. Two quite different uses will demonstrate this fact. Should the leader be interested solely or primarily in the operational efficiency of his group, a salient criterion becomes the span of control. This means essentially how many can he supervise and direct with surety to the desired goal. In a simple, routine, and concentrated job such as the work in a typing pool the number that can be overseen is likely to be much larger than if the job were a complex, unique, and widely diffused task such as selling highly technical electrical equipment. However, should the administrator want to use his followers for the political purpose of impressing top management with the significance of his department and leadership, he may need numbers for numbers' sake.

Perhaps the qualitative consideration in the choice of followers is in general much more important than the quantitative aspect. The leader needs an irreducible minimum of effective performance in his organization. Then too, each leader is known to a large degree by the quality of those with whom he surrounds himself. There is at least one major implication to this latter observation. It suggests that the administrator should select, everything else being equal, the best performer for each job under him. A qualification appears at once, however. The particular job must be seen as a part of the administrative whole which the leader wishes to attain. Without this reservation, the administrator might surround himself with a group of competent specialists incapable or unwilling to fit themselves into his machine. The result could well be as discordant as an orchestra in which each member is playing his own key.

The selection of followers sometimes is based on less noble grounds. The very politically minded administrator may choose his followers, or at least some of them, with the view to make him look better. As a result, some steps that would otherwise be irrational are taken. Mediocre personnel purposefully are employed, since they melt into such a good background against which his relative superiority can shine. Really unneeded specialists are added to his staff in concession to fact or trend as, for example, a cultural anthropologist to a moderate size personnel department. Sometimes people are sought to "complete the leader" in some respect in which he is weak. A case in point is the public relations officer retained to write the speeches of the general manager. The influence of appearances is not to be discounted in a discussion of the assembling of followership.

Unchosen Followership

The foregoing comments on the choice of followership may imply that the administrator has full choice in the selection of his people. This is often not the case. Frequently, he is appointed to handle an organizational unit which is already formed. Such an inherited situation leaves the leader with greatly restricted powers over either the number or kind of his followers. He faces the problem of just using them as he finds them or of endeavoring in some way to change them. There are two ways by which he can attempt to do the latter. He can try to change their attitude, motivation and performance, or he can institute steps to replace them. In electing either or both of these reformative courses he will find himself confronted with an acute necessity for genuine strategy. Many of the "oldtimers" may have intense loyalties to the replaced administrator, they may like the status quo in all its aspects, and they may be in a position to cause the newcomer real trouble. There is, however, one basic principle which the new administrator can follow with advantage to himself. He can resort to the frequently scorned *principle of expediency*, that is, he can do what seems best in the short run, and in this temporizing manner give himself time and opportunity to gain a position of strength from which to take the needed basic corrective action. A new office manager may get along with the office termagant for a few weeks in order to prevent any noticeable break in the stream of office output; and then, when he has established the fact, especially to his superiors, that he is running the office, he can move to have her restrained, reassigned, retired, demoted, promoted, or even fired.

Conditioning, Converting, and Eliminating

The leader may not with safety assume that all his followers are as one with him. Mere membership in his unit does not insure the business administrator that his employees are friendly to him or his organization, that they understand or believe in the established goals, or that they ever can be brought to the desired state of willingness to contribute effort to the organization. Unless the administrator is singularly successful in recruiting people who all are completely "on the team" to begin with or who all are ready to join it,[5] there is, in the over-all function of mobilizing manpower a very real job of conditioning the conditionable and of getting rid of the remainder. Many administrators who lack insight or courage, or who are infected too severely with the germ of tolerance, do not face up to the tiring missionary job necessary in their domain and even less often to the brutal task of ridding themselves of undesirable employees.

If strategic action, in the sense of using the right combination of resources with an eye to the actual or anticipated action or reaction of associates, is ever essential, it is vitally necessary in this conditioning and liquidating process by which the good team is formed and energized. The mere fact of attempting to sell a new point of view or to "clean house" is in itself frequently frightening, for change is often feared. Ill-advised action may raise considerable opposition to the new leader. Early opposition is always especially serious to him, since he needs a relatively frictionless starting period to learn and get control of the new job and to establish a measure of stature in the eyes of his employees, associates, and superiors. Such inappropriate action may also lead him to an irrevocable stand or to a position from which it is difficult or embarrassing to retreat. Finally, the danger always exists that the administrator does not know the real attitude and motivation of his employees. He may take improper action and either miss his target or stir up more antagonism. An administrator may believe that the discontent among his people is due to low wages, and he may, therefore, attempt to get them into a more satisfied mood by giving them a general increment. If he is mistaken and the source of discontent is the inadequate retirement program, their reaction may be quite different from the positive result he sought. His employees in general may feel that they have simply been bribed into the continued acceptance of insecurity with respect to their old age.

Methods of Conditioning Followers

Conditioning, as here conceived, is the process by which the administrator brings his employees to and/or retains them in the frame of mind which makes them willing to accept his leadership.[6] It can be accomplished in three ways.

Resort can be had to enlightenment. He can use one of a number of instructional devices, ranging from personal explanation to the use of the formal training program, to give them the knowledge and understanding with which to analyze their relation to him and the company. He may have as his immediate purpose nothing more significant than making them acquainted with general company policies, rules and practices, or something as involved as a radically new personnel rating plan. But, regardless of the method and immediate aim of the enlightening procedure, it is simply teaching with the belief that the subject matter imparted will do much to lead the members of a group to the desired viewpoint.

As a second method of conditioning followers, appeal can be made to one or more of their urges, drives, ambitions, or desires (the psychologist may be able to suggest more related terms) for such satisfactions as security, personal dignity, affection, pride, social approval, or ostentatious living. This is the old technique of using bait. It is a familiar device, and under proper circumstances is quite legitimate.

The third method to assure the proper attitude on the part of followers is to frighten them. At first hand, this may seem a shocking proposal, but actually fear is one of the most effective and commonly used of all avenues to conversion, and its use is accepted in the highest Judeo-Christian cultures. All human beings are susceptible to fright, and they are constantly changing their thoughts, words, and deeds because of the stimulus of changing fears. It remains, then, for the administrator who would use fear as a conditioner to apply one or more to which he knows his people are susceptible at the time. He must bear in mind certain precautionary thoughts, however. There is probably a limit to every follower's fear; after a point, he may refuse to respond or he may even rebel. It is also possible to frighten him so much that, although he may not dare do anything but support the boss, he will be so worried about doing his job as the boss wants it done that his actual performance will suffer. Finally, the leader should be watchful of the possibility of inducing immorality, which is a real danger inherent in the use of fear, for it is one of the strongest motives to improper conduct. Many people can be led or forced to evil in an effort to protect themselves.

The analysis of these three ways to condition followers does not imply necessarily a definitive and frontal attack on the ignorance, indifference, or prejudice of followers. There is always the possibility of their being converted to the proper attitude by association with other already conditioned employees. The administrator may, for many reasons, eschew the use of the direct approach and rely upon this social osmosis. He may even resort to the more indirect tack of permitting all or certain of his employees to learn the hard way by trial and error. Through their experiences, they may come to see the merit of their leader's viewpoint. This approach can prove time-consuming and otherwise expensive, but the lessons learned can be lasting.

Organizational Overtone as a Conditioning Agent

Strategy in the conditioning process should take into consideration the organizational overtone. The atmosphere of the organization may be aggressive or passive, liberal or conservative, happy or unpleasant, competitive or non-competitive. The incumbent administrator may be totally or partially responsible for this environmental atmosphere; or the new administrator may inherit a particular overtone. Whichever may be the case, the leader should realize that everything he says, decides or does, and much of what he thinks and how he appears, may and frequently does have a definite influence on this overtone. In fact, he simply cannot escape affecting the aura that surrounds his group, because he is a symbol of that which the organization believes, stands for, and desires. It is clear, then, that the administrator is involuntarily engaged in the conditioning process whether he likes it or not. The wise administrator will see to it that the impression he gives is such as to make the greatest possible contribution to the environmental atmosphere. This is extremely important because followers of all types are likely to be deeply influenced in their thinking and acting by the company overtone. The passive and uncommitted person who joins an aggresive house-to-house selling organization may be stimulated by the extremely aggressive spirit of the company and accept the demonstration techniques prescribed by the sales manager. The dynamic and enthusiastic college graduate who joins a static personnel department may be measurably subdued by the deadening effect of the institutional drowsiness and give up his suggestions regarding executive appraisal and development.

There is no one behavior or personality pattern of the administrator best suited to building up or modifying the environmental overtone as desired. In one company, he may be obliged to appear as a good fellow; in another, as a crank; and still elsewhere, as a slavedriver. It is unrealistic to endow the leader, as a conditioner of the group, with uniform characteristics. Here again one sees a reflection of the chameleon-like nature of the leader in action.

But the exploitation of overtone as a strategic device in conditioning means much more than proper example and role adaptation by the leader. There are a host of other sources from which environmental radiation takes place. Among these one may mention prominently the terms of employment, working conditions, union-management relations, manuals and operational patterns, house organs, periodical company reports, training meetings, morale, recreational and health programs, and public relations practices. The list could be extended so long as to lead one to the conclusion that everything the company is or does contributes to its general tone. The strategist in administration realizes the omnipresent possibilities of all his company's policies and practices. Although he will undertake each primarily to accomplish its major objectives, he will always be sensitive to the fact that each can be handled honestly in a manner conducive to even more friendly followership from his employees. An example is to be seen in the annual report of a company which has depended historically upon one product. Times have been hard; the employees know that the company has not been making money. It is necessary for an annual report to be made. Stockholders, internal controls, and government regulation require it. Top management, well cognizant of the pessimism prevailing in the ranks, inserts a glowing but true picture of new product development. An ordinary organizational tool, the annual report, has not only been made to do its financial job but it has also been used honorably to influence company atmosphere.

The Strategy of Conditioning Individuals

Strategy in the conditioning process is not limited to contributions to overtone. Followership is made up of individuals. They are of many types. There are Caucasian and non-Caucasian, male and female, oldtimer and newcomer, the friendly and the unfriendly, the ambitious and the lazy, the bright and the dull, the contented and the malcontented, the imaginative and the unimaginative, *ad infinitum*. What does this mean to the administrator in his conditioning function? It signifies that the conditioning process may become a series of individual problems and, hence, one of great diversity of solution.

Fortunately, there are certain guide lines to the conditioning of individuals which, if followed by the administrator, can make his work much easier. First of all, he must introduce the greatest amount of personal contact into his missonary work. Nothing succeeds in communication like the face to face meeting. A large measure of conditioning is nothing but communication with clarity. The sympathetic approach has a value almost equal to that of direct contact. This approach involves the use of strong lures, understanding and affection. It implies giving the uncertain or unfriendlv individual the feeling that he is not alone. Sometimes the leader will be able to do this by merely listening to complaints or views; in some instances, he will have to agree with his follower; upon other occasions, he will find it necessary to promise and/or render assistance; and, at still other times, the leader will be able best to reach the individual by identification—the device by which he shows the follower that he has or has had the same attitude, belief, or problem. A third guide line has to do with the leader selling himself. It is generally easier to sell oneself than an abstraction called the company. The employee can see and evaluate the leader, whereas the company presents a complex and confusing symbol to him. Moreover, when followers are conditioned to accept primarily the leader, rather than a vague entity, they are much more mobile and will swing more easily with his decisions and movements.

The Strategy of Conditioning Sub-Groups

In the conditioning process, leaders have to be on guard for certain danger areas between the general overtone and individual feelings. Reference is made to the phenomenon of sub-groups either as constituted or as informal units of the company. They range all the way from departments to the morning "coffee break gang." Sub-groups have the power which comes from the fact of association and from the functions entrusted to them or which they may usurp. They are dangerous in that they may oppose the leader with a degree of effectiveness. For both reasons, their peculiar prejudices, feelings, attitudes, and goals must be considered in conditioning followers.

The principles and techniques for influencing sub-groups positively could well be the subject for a specialized research project. Only a few hints can be given in this general treatment of strategy. Their conditioning can be furthered by steps such as the following:

1. Identify and "work on" the leaders of the sub-groups.
2. Isolate the sub-groups for special indoctrination.
3. Play one sub-group off against another.
4. Change sub-group leaders by transfer, promotion, demotion, or discharge.
5. Give the informal sub-groups organizational status and responsibility.
6. Recognize and publicize the good performance of the sub-groups and, in extreme cases, their bad performance.

The Hard Cases

It seems reasonable to admit that the suggested conditioning process may not achieve the necessary conversion in certain cases. Therefore, especial steps will be in order to convert the most perversely motivated, the completely indifferent, or the outwardly opposed—whether they be individuals or groups. The initial step is to identify the real recalcitrants through such means as complaints from others, poor performance, and outright opposition to the leader and/or organization. The next step is to isolate them from as much support as possible within and without the company, so that they must stand alone. Weakened in this manner, they will be easier subjects for conversion. The final step is to bring to bear on their case whatever "persuaders," hidden or open, are necessary and legitimate. These may be as diverse as efforts to make them into personal friends or attempts to frighten them by front-carpet treatment, group pressure, personal disgrace, and/or punitive measures.

If the employees cannot be converted, there remains only one course for the administrator who will not tolerate them as they are. This is to eliminate them from his group. He may do so by indirection, that is, by making it too uncomfortable or impossible for them to stay. One needs but mention encouragement to seek a better job elsewhere, isolation, attrition of powers, demotion, repeated passing over in promotion, no compensation increment, and very strict supervision and discipline as forms of indirection. He may, on the other hand, choose direct action. This does not always mean discharge, for there are other opportunities, especially in a large organization, to attack the problem frontally. The nonconvertibles may be transferred to another unit of the organization or reassigned within the department to positions which their attitudes fit or in which they can do little or no harm. Direct elimination does not always entail harm to the "victim's" standing or pocket book. He may be pushed upstairs to an even better appearing and rewarding job in order to remove him from the position where he is an obstacle. How many executives have been placed in higher positions for this very reason?

Elimination is not to be disdained as an instrument of administrative strategy in mobilizing followers. There are situations in which certain individuals or groups cannot be retrained to insure reasonably coordinated action. Nothing in this dictum is intended, however, to advance elimination as an easier way out for the peace-oriented administrator who simply wants calm at any price. It should always be realized that among non-convertible personnel may be the real innovators, the original thinkers who simply cannot be brought to conform because they do see better ways of doing things and greater opportunities. Obviously, these can be valuable people. It is up to the strategist to sort out and keep somehow the "good" bad people and get rid of the other undesirables.

Coordination

All the conditioning and converting of followers possible will not in itself give that degree of mobilization of employees which will assure their working together effectively. Something more is needed: coordination. It is not a definite stage in administration but rather a basic need in all steps. Coordination, reduced to its most simplified terms, is the fitting together of the separate efforts of the individuals and groups that make up an organization.[7] Its purpose is smoother operation and the better achievement of organizational goals. The widespread contemporary application of the *principle of specialization* makes coordination unusually important to modern business administration because it involves great division of labor.

Proportions of the Coordination Function

The task of coordination is much more involved than the complexities of the organization may suggest. Specialists are often assigned to do or supervise the various parts into which the job is broken. These specialists are human beings, and each brings with him his own prejudices, loyalties, beliefs, and other individual characteristics. These differences may, therefore, add to the administrator's expected burden of coordinating the work of the various organizational units. They may be reflected in the peculiar ways in which the job is done or supervised. The task of coordination is also made more difficult by the mere fact of group individuality, which may or may not develop as a reflection of a specialist's views. The various departments and other divisions of a company do evolve their own objectives, philosophies, and ways of doing things. These group idiosyncrasies obviously can cause great difficulty for the administrator.

When a situation arises in which individualistic specialists are running several divisions of the company and in which a number of divisions have taken on their own definite characteristics, the administrator as a coordinator has a major challenge. The strategist who now seeks to weld his organizational domain into a good team for harmonious work faces his perennial problem of evaluation in an extreme form. He must pick and choose the individual and department he wishes to emphasize, as well as those he wants to subordinate, under the circumstances of the time and place. The point to be understood here is that he will not be able to coordinate effectively by treating all people and parts of his organization with the same emphasis and even terms. Coordination frequently demands favoritism; it is not always the nice process of elevating all to the same high place or reducing all to the same lower level in order to get them to work together. The coordinating problem of a vice president in charge of purchasing may be taken as an illustration. Under his control are the old established divisions of buying, traffic, inventory control, standardization and specifications, and salvage headed by real specialists. In certain market conditions he must stress minimum inventory investment and pay relatively little attention to economical buying. This may mean that for the time he will find it necessary to favor the inventory control group and especially its manager. The phase of mobilizing followers which is here termed "coordination" has little to do in practice with the democratic ideal of equalitarianism. The vice president who administers purchasing may be accused of having his favorites, but he will find it necessary to treat the components of his organization differently from time to time simply to keep them working together properly.

Thus far it has been made to appear that coordination is concerned only with people, alone or in groups. The issue that it means more probably can be argued with merit. Whatever the truth, it must be conceded that there is a necessity for obtaining a degree of compatibility in objectives, philosophy, organizational parts, methods and procedures, since without it the administrator cannot successfully mobilize his followers into coordinated action. The difficulties which can arise if it is missing are illustrated in a few rhetorical questions. How can a president be expected to coordinate the people in his company if its objectives are as diverse as cleaning sewers profitably and producing exquisite cosmetics? How can he hope to attain a unified effort on the part of his employees if the company wants items of gold-plated quality to be sold at dime store prices? How can a top executive successfully weld the employees of his company into a harmonious whole when the organizational scheme demands a separate accounting office responsible to him for all accounting and also an accounting division in each department independent and responsible to another top executive? How can a department head coordinate his team members when the general manager at times gives direct orders to this administrator's subordinates and upon other occasions is most meticulous about respecting channels? Whether or not all this suggested necessity for compatibility in things other than people connotes a component of coordination, it is nevertheless essential to mobilizing the human factor into a successfully functioning force.

This line of reasoning leads to the inevitable conclusion that the administrator immediately responsible for coordinated effort in output may at times find himself stymied by company factors beyond his personal control. The plant manager may not be able to induce his men employees to work for the same wage as women, and yet company philosophy and policy demands it. What can he do? In such an apparent impasse the plant manager may evade the issue by not letting the dilemma arise. He may do this through avoiding the employment of women or assigning them to job classifications not in competition with men. He may ignore the whole question and let the consequences educate his superiors. Or finally, he may attempt more directly to effect a change in the attitude of some component of the situation; for example, he may attempt to educate his men to the merit of women as fellow workers or he may resort to suggestions to his superior. The point illustrated here is that the strategic administrator is not helpless even when he is faced with the apparently binding rules of the top echelon.

Sometimes the administrator in his ambition to increase output, to use more specialists as a concession to managerial fads or trends, or to resort to further decentralization as an attack on control problems, may splinter his operation into so many parts that coordination becomes increasingly difficult. He should beware of this mousetrap of overspecialization. The difficulty of getting people to work together will be enhanced for various reasons, among which are: the physical fact that it is "harder to fit more pieces together"; the lengthening communication links with officials, associates and subordinates; multiplication of power centers and vested interests; and the loss by his workers of the pride which comes from doing a more meaningful segment of the job.

Personal specialization, real or imagined, is today at a premium. Few people see themselves as general yeomen. This in itself poses a coordinating problem for the administrator interested in efficiency, as suggested earlier in this chapter. He will be tempted to obtain for a particular job the individual who knows the most about it and who can be presumed, therefore, to be the best performer. But this action may not be without its peculiar cost. Highly specialized personnel are, because of their specialization, likely to be less versatile than others. The administrator will find himself in the unpleasant situation of having obtained a good performer in a narrow field but a poor general organizational team member. This dilemma may be made even more sharp by the specialist who, in addition to a lack of general capacity, is hypnotized by his own importance or the significance of his profession or line of work. The expert accountant may never have had training or experience in handling personnel. This alone can give his executive in the company real trouble when, for example, it becomes necessary to give him a battery of clerks. And, if this narrow specialist suffers from the personality disease of blind pride, the supervisor will really need all his strategy to induce other more balanced people in the organization to work with him.

The Leader as Coordinator

The huge dimension and the complexity of the problem of coordination, as well as the fact that it is found in all phases of management, may frighten the ordinary administrator.[8] He can and is increasingly taking refuge in a number of protective devices, including committees to effect greater unity of action, liaison personnel, specialists called expediters or coordinators, and a host of other entities bearing strange and wonderful titles. However, the old axiom that responsibility cannot be delegated certainly applies to coordination as one of the most important features of administration. If the administrator seeks to shirk the responsibility by attempting to place it on the shoulders of lieutenants he will not only lose a degree of stature as a leader, but he may also find that he has a new problem of mobilizing followers, namely, to coordinate the efforts of his coordinators.

Conclusion

The expression "mobilizing followers" may seem quaint or awkward. It has been used to describe a group of related functions of the leader, who is also called the administrator in this business administration oriented treatment. These functions are the understanding of followership; the choice of followers; their conditioning, conversion, and elimination; and their coordination. Since the literature of administration has no generally used terminology to cover this family of duties, the somewhat bizarre phrase which is the title of the chapter was adopted. Moreover, the concept of leadership that is essentially the subject of this book is most clearly defined in the military vocabulary, which frequently uses the related idea of mobilizing. And even more, there is an action connotation in the phrase "mobilizing followers"—and action is the essence of this thesis on strategy.

As a subject for analysis, the problem of mobilizing followers possesses almost unlimited possibilities. An effort has been made to keep its treatment in this chapter manageable by delimitation and exclusion. Yet, it is felt that one special aspect of the subject is of such overwhelming importance and has been given so little mention that it deserves the dignity of special treatment. The chapter which follows immediately, therefore, is devoted to the *reconciliation of the objectives of the administrators themselves.* It may appear to contain some repetition, but the issue is unique and the approach quite different. Such similarity of thought as may be present is either unavoidable or intentional and designed for specific focus and emphasis.

BUSINESS SITUATIONS FOR ROLE-PLAYING

SITUATION III

Mobilizing Followers

THE GARAPAN NATURAL GAS COMPANY

A. Scene.   A public utility company. The office of the Director of Personnel who is discussing the attitudes of a senior buyer with the Director of Purchasing.

B. Players.   1. Director of Personnel: Mr. Max Hightower, who is a middle-aged, well-bred and sophisticated executive.

2. Director of Purchasing: Mr. Joseph E. Ternes, a tough and rough negotiator, who has held his office for twenty-two years.

C. Situation.   The problem at hand concerns an employee of the Purchasing Department.

1. Mr. Edward Jordan, a senior buyer, has long been a constant critic of the company. He is known everywhere as a malcontent who enjoys attacking the company policies and practices he considers weak. But he is an efficient buyer.

2. Many times in the past few years he has been the spokesman for office employees engaged in some grievance presentation.

3. Yesterday, the grapevine reported to the personnel office that Mr. Jordan is circulating a petition for the revamping of the retirement program for office workers.

4. Mr. Hightower is urging Mr. Ternes to take action aimed at keeping Mr. Jordan working at his desk instead of roaming around stirring up trouble and in general acting as a poor follower.

D. Assignment. 1. Select two individuals to act out the roles of Mr. Hightower and Mr. Ternes.

2. After the demonstration by these first two players is finished, choose a new player to act out the role of Mr. Jordan and use one of the previous actors as Mr. Ternes.

3. Suggest all players emphasize the "mobilization" approach.

4. Have group contrast the two performances.

NOTES

1. RALPH CURRIER DAVIS, *The Fundamentals of Top Management* (New York: Harper & Brothers, Publishers, 1951), p. 51.
2. FRANKLYN S. HAIMAN, *Group Leadership and Democratic Action* (Boston: Houghton Mifflin Company, 1951), p. 5.

3. For an attempt at leadership to be an act of leadership, the follower must be motivated to move, to some degree, in the direction desired by the leader. Haiman, *op. cit.*, p. 5.
4. "The follower's persistent motivations, points of view, frames of reference or attiudes will have a hand in what he perceives and how he reacts to it." Fillmore H. Sanford, "Leadership Identification and Acceptance" in Harold Guetzkow (ed.), *Groups, Leadership and Men* (Pittsburgh: Carnegie Press, 1951), p. 51.
5. In regard to willingness to contribute to a given specific formal organization, Barnard states, "The preponderance of persons in a modern society always lies on the negative side with reference to any particular existing or potential organization." Chester I. Barnard, *The Functions of the Executive* (Cambridge, Mass.: Harvard University Press, 1956), p. 84.
6. Acceptance of the administrator's leadership means also identification with the group already responsive to him or to organizational goals if the group is just being formed.

    Professor Simon writes that "a person identifies himself with a group when, in making a decision, he evaluates the several alternatives of choice in terms of their consequences for the specified group." Herbert A. Simon, *Administrative Behavior* (New York: The Macmillan Company, 1958), p. 205. Quoted with the permission of the Macmillan Company.
7. "Coordination . . . is the orderly arrangement of group effort, to provide unity of action in the pursuit of a common purpose." James D. Mooney, *The Principles of Organization* (New York: Harper & Brothers, Publishers, 1947), p. 5.
8. Elmore Petersen and E. Grosvenor Plowman, *Business Organization and Management* (4th ed.; Chicago: Richard D. Irwin, Inc., 1958), p. 218.

    Mary Parker Follett suggests the enormity of the task of coordination by devoting four principles of organization exclusively to coordination. Mary Parker Follett, "Individualism in a Planned Society" in Henry C. Metcalf and L. Urwick (eds.), *Dynamic Administration: The Collected Papers of Mary Parker Follett* (New York: Harper & Brothers, Publishers, 1940), p. 297.

    "Unfortunately, no plan is perfect for resolving the conflict between freedom and coordination." William H. Newman and Charles E. Summer, Jr., *The Process of Management* (Englewood Cliffs, N.J.: Prentice-Hall, Inc., 1961), p. 407.

CHAPTER 4

The Reconciliation of
Administrative Objectives

> "Efficient administration demands recognition of the unpleasant fact that not all administrators of the company *naturally* have the same personal objectives in working with it or even know or agree upon organizational objectives."

IT IS DOUBTFUL that man in his conscious hours is ever without some objective or objectives. On the one hand, he is a creature of infinite wants; on the other, he rarely, if ever, finds it possible to suspend his thought processes when awake. These two factors suggest that he always has "something in mind."

Of course, the nature of his aims will vary greatly with the individual and with time. They may be the dominating forces of his life or the ephemeral desires of the moment. They may be practical goals or idealistic dreams. They may be the essence of morality or the way to evil. In fact, few human phenomena possess as many contrasting natures.

Consciousness of objectives is most significant to the organization and the administrators who are responsible for its functioning.[1] It supplies justification for the organization,[2] and it provides motivation and direction for thought, plan, and action. Since these steps may either be oriented to the utility or disutility of the organization, the importance of the goals which help generate and chart them is obvious.

Provincialism

A Real and Not Uncommon Phenomenon

This somewhat philosophical approach is not as academic as perhaps it may appear to the problem-harassed president of a corporation or to his line and staff officers who, in their respective departments, are confronted with their own peculiar, if rather less general, questions. It is incorrect to assume that all the members of management have the same purposes in the company, or unit thereof, or that they even know or always care deeply about its principal objectives. Owners and employees alike are simply a cross-section of the race, having all the peculiarities, positive and perverse, to which it is heir. Moreover, they are creatures of many different loyalties: those acquired before they enter the company or department; those which they must give, at least superficially, to it; and those developed within the organization to a symbol, individual, clique, or some other attraction. Common sense demands, then, that all management officials, whether of top, intermediate or low level, should frequently take stock of their personal objectives and those of their fellow administrators with reference to the over-all purpose of the company. Failure to do this can be most prejudicial not only to the more immediate cause of good human relations but also to the ultimate efficiency of operation as reflected in the annual profit and loss statement, in future competitive ability, and even in company survival.

Whatever they may be termed—objectives, aims, purposes or goals—ignorance, misunderstanding, or disregard of the ends which motivate and direct one's self, associates or organization will result, except under the most fortuitous circumstances, in what an earlier generation wisely described as "working at cross purposes." But there is no room for this in the business concern. It exists, at least under the free enterprise system, to make as high net return on unit of cost as competition, government regulation, ethical conduct, and social obligation will permit.[3] Lack of coordination and friction resulting from provincialism of administrators is likely to boost cost without giving the company any greater ability to raise its selling price or increase its market.

Provincialism is probably a common phenomenon in the administration of all types of organizations. It is generated to a large degree by the intense desire to succeed. The term "provincialism" connotes narrowness. It, therefore, seems logical to apply it in business to mean a degree of narrowness on the part of the administrator with respect to his own objectives, with respect to those of his associates, and most importantly with respect to the relation of both categories to the goals of the company as an entity.

Factors Contributing to Provincialism in Objectives

Various factors contribute to this provincialism in a business organization. Although technical and professional ability is of prime importance to the heads of small concerns and the lower management grades of large concerns,[4] one such factor is that many business administrators, especially in the United States, are recruited or "evolve" from the ranks of able technicians and professionals, e.g., engineers, salesmen, and accountants. From specialization, they are moved to positions demanding more generalized views. Some require time to acquire this new orientation; others never attain it. It is erroneous to assume, as is commonly done, that a man who is a good engineer automatically will make a satisfactory plant manager; that an accurate accountant will naturally turn into a successful controller over night; or that a dynamic salesman will become an efficient sales manager by mere appointment.

Another factor which lends itself to administrative provincialism in business is the size of the managerial job. Modern companies are generally large enough or give promise of sufficient size in the foreseeable future to demand considerable departmentalization. Necessary as it is to efficient management in all except small concerns, this is not an unmixed blessing. It frequently throws blocks on the roadway to an understanding and reconciliation of the diverse objectives within the company. Among these obstacles may be noted the substitution of department aims for over-all company goals, the rise of new and unbalancing centers of power, the switch away from organizational to departmental loyalty, and the appearance of further difficulty in intra-company communications.

The final factor giving rise to administrative blindness as to conflicting objectives, and one which is often found in American companies, is the traditional Western characteristic of individualism. Few people seem to be as independent as Americans both in outlook and action. It is traditional that each shall hoe his own row, and to a large degree this tradition prevails in all lines of endeavor. Business administration is no exception. Here, as elsewhere in American life, the premium is on getting a job done without help or with comparatively little assistance. Although this is undoubtedly a great national virtue in that it means wonderfully productive self-initiative, it also gives rise to a certain reluctance to analyze the fabric of motivation existing in the company. The great drive in American business administration is to act and to keep acting.

Approaches to Reconciliation

It is now more than ever necessary that those in charge of the management of a business get together on their objectives and those of the company. This is an era of seriously diminishing "profit margins" and many social pressures on business. It is a time of great economic growth in which many companies are risking the dangers of unprecedented expansion to meet an anticipated deluge of demand. Both present financial health and future company welfare require extremely smooth teamwork among all the members of management. This is obviously possible only when there is a reconciliation of the objectives of the various administrators, be they shop foremen or president, with the over-all goals of the company.

Attention is invited to the concept of reconciliation. It implies something less than complete surrender of individual objectives. Its essence is the understanding and acceptance of the fact by the individual administrator that his best interests, and his ethical conduct as a member of the management of the particular company or department which employs him now, can be served by so submerging and/or adapting his own personal aims as to contribute most to the success of the organization. It further suggests that he may find it necessary to reappraise his position with the company in terms of its potentials to fulfill his ambitions and in terms of his desire and capacity to serve it properly.

Certain it is that anything more would carry with it definite dangers to good administration. The case of a hypothetical medium-size manufacturing concern may be used as an illustration. This company has a proud production manager who has risen from the ranks on the basis of sheer merit. He glories in his ability to keep the shop running, his men busy, and the maximum product coming off the line. But this concern has a very cautious purchasing agent who does not wish to add to the inventory of raw materials more than is absolutely necessary to maintain minimum output. He is constantly watching for price declines which will yield him bargains. Were the higher administration of the company to clamp down hard on the production manager's frequent over-enthusiasm to maintain the highest possible output, he might become disgruntled, lose his drive, and in these days of essentially great demand for experienced production people even move to another job. On the other hand, if the higher echelon of administration urged the purchasing agent to be a bit more liberal in stocking material, he might react in similar fashion. Yet both of these need some curbing of their present courses of action. Each is also most valuable to the company, and is, in an isolated sense, doing his job well. The problem is clearly one of getting them together on organization objectives, rather than destroying their initiative or favoring one over the other. Their goals need a measure of reconciliation.

Let Someone Else Do It

There are many approaches to the matter of reconciling the objectives of administrators. The simplest, though most negative, is for each administrator to take the attitude that the task of getting people together belongs to someone above. The person who assumes this "do-nothing" view is a poor administrator, for administration is the job of the whole administrative group, even though it is ultimately the responsibility of the president. Furthermore, this passive individual is failing to exercise the degree of leadership inherent in his position. If it is true that one generally rises in the business world in relation to his exercise of leadership, he obviously is also missing an opportunity to further his own interests.

Seek Department Agreement

A somewhat more constructive approach is the effort by the administrator to see that his particular office, division, or department is in practical agreement on its own aims. Quite obviously, this approach has a measure of good in it. A company consisting of a number of such parts would undoubtedly have a better chance of successful operation than one with a lack of agreement on objectives even within its component parts. Partial teamwork is better than none.

However, there are dangers inherent in what may be called "compartmentalized unity." One is the possibility of too much loyalty to a function or segment of the organization. For example, the sales department may see its job clearly and do it extremely well but in this very departmental devotion develop an overzealousness, an orientation detrimental to the best financial interests of the concern. Its drive and success in selling may result in the granting of credit to an unwise degree. More is clearly demanded in the way of company-wide teamwork. Another danger is the temptation to "empire building." This can be seen in the case of the personnel department created as a staff or service unit that reaches out to the production area and assumes complete cognizance over discipline. Such assumption of power and consequent proliferation of personnel people will hardly encourage cooperation and coordination.

Relate Individual Aims to Company Goals

The approach which promises most in ultimate unified company action is for the individual administrator constantly to relate his aims to the broader company objectives. In this connection, he will find it necessary to keep three questions in the forefront of his administrative decisions: (1) What am I really planning to do? (2) To what extent, if any, will it interfere with the intentions of any of the other administrative units? (3) In the last analysis, to what extent will the pursuit of this aim contribute to the over-all goals of the company? It is clear that this truly constructive approach to the problem of reconciliation of objectives presupposes a large degree of company loyalty not always found in administrators. Yet the most successful administrators do seem to possess it. There is little reason to believe that playing the lone wolf or selfish gang game of a unit can generally insure a person continued success in business administration, even though it may help the administrator get ahead by establishing a quick reputation upon which to transfer to a position with a different organization. Neither of these extremes is likely to result in that total company effort necessary to maximize profits, which, at the risk of being considered "old fashioned," one can continue to suggest as still a basic long run purpose of a business in a free society.

Strategic Devices

The issue now arises as to the devices which can be used to attain the high degree of reconciliation in aims necessary to most effective administration. There are undoubtedly a large number. The possibilities of political action, improved communications, and downright manipulation are almost unlimited. Six devices seem to be of prime importance and may be treated briefly at this point.

Formulation of Objectives

The first is the formulation of general organizational objectives. What are they: survival, growth, economic contributions, social obligations, and/or profits?[5] Unbelievable as it may seem, there is much evidence to indicate that many concerns do not have other than perhaps the general idea that they want to "make money." If a business does not have clear goals, certainly it cannot expect the greatest degree of unified action from its administrators. Each may have his own ideas as to the direction in which the company ought to be headed and at what rate of speed. The results can be, and have been, fantastic in many cases.

General, over-all company objectives are basically the responsibility of top management, including the board of directors, the president, the chairman of the board, and the members of the executive committee.[6] This raises the danger in the twentieth century era of rampant democracy that certain lower level administrators may feel themselves ignored. The complete avoidance of this repercussion is obviously impossible. There are decisions in all organizations which are of such major and pervasive import that they must be made topside without complete regard for the views of subordinate echelons.

The use of the policy committee may mitigate against a negative reaction to such authoritarianism. If this committee is constituted in a company, care should be taken to see either that its membership is only of the very top figures or that it has quite full representation based on a coordinate level of responsibility. Otherwise, a peculiar and unpleasant situation may arise in which some significant departments may be neglected and in which a major department has no more to say than a minor administrative division. This can lead to even more discontent than a pure and simple unilateral decision from topside. It raises the implication that rank means little in the company. Of course, it should mean much, since the possibility of its attainment is one of the better rewards for administrative cooperation and leadership and since it certainly ought to reflect ability.

It is true that the degree to which top management wishes to be explicit on its over-all goals depends upon the emphasis it wishes to place on one or more of them.[7] The measure, then, to which it spells out its commitment to each of them is in itself a strategy friendly to general agreement among company administrators on the matter of goals, if for no other reason than that it lets them know what the top echelon most desires and mayhap indicates the hierarchy of goals it has in mind.

The question inevitably arises at this point as to whether something more specific than agreement on general goals is not needed as a basis for effective reconciliation of the aims held by various administrators. The answer would seem to be in the affirmative. Much of the disharmony among executives comes because they do not know, understand or appreciate the specific aims which they and their colleagues should have, or do have, within the framework of what may be called general objectives generally stated.[8] These specific objectives can range from matters of small import to issues absolutely vital to over-all purpose; for example, they may involve a proposed reduction in number of carbon copies of correspondence or the intent to make a major department operate at twice its present speed. Whatever the relative significance, specific aims, too, must be set; else executives, who should be laboring mightily in the peaceful light of set company goals, may come to blows over the intermediate aims necessary to reach these ultimate ends. The specific aims may be decided by a superior or by a particular executive, but decided they must be.

No doubt the introduction of an element of democracy into the formulation of objectives may contribute to their saleability. People tend to accept and agree with their colleagues upon decisions which they have helped make. This is, of course, a reason for the recommendation just made that the policy committee be used to arrive at general, over-all company objectives. While it is quite possible that similar, if lower level, committees can be created to help fix specific aims, it is much more likely that specific goal formulation by department managers and other subordinate administrators may have to rely on less pretentious means to use the democratic device. The executive can in numerous informal ways make an effort to ascertain the feelings, views, and recommendations of the other executives with whom he must work. He has at his command the powers of observation, communication, and common interest.[9]

Publicizing of Objectives

A second means which can be used to insure that all administrators are leading in the same general direction has to do with publicity. It is to make goals known as far as publicity is compatible with the dictates of other significant management problems and of good competitive practice.[10] This can best be done by definitive intra-company announcements through such means as memoranda for general distribution, administrative staff meetings, and house publications. It is generally not wise to rely upon administrators finding out major decisions as to company aims by reading of them first in the public press. This may not only lead to confusion because of the lack of reportorial accuracy but it may negate much of the good influence on administrative personnel which may come from being "in on the know."

In announcement or elaboration, definite reconciliation possibilities are to be found in the manner and tone with which publicity is given organizational goals. If it is timed when the executives are receptive, the goals may be accepted by all or most of them. Certainly then, higher management officials should gauge administrative feeling toward the company or department before announcing new objectives or explaining older aims. Moreover, objectives can be stated in inviting terms so as not to arouse more than necessary opposition.[11] In fact, it may be possible in given situations so to present an objective that it appears to administrators as an inspiring ideal to be pursued vigorously.

Procurement of Friendly Personnel

A third device to assist in attaining agreement on objectives lies in the selection of sympathetic personnel. There seems to be no single English word adequate to express the meaning here intended. The idea can be approximately expressed in the statement that a company should obtain and place in key positions personnel who believe, think, and act in a manner complementary to the organizational goals. For example, a company which has decided to change from a centralized to decentralized structure may wisely seek, and place its reliance upon, personnel predisposed to more independent action. American companies have not always made use of the recruitment of proper team members to fit their particular philosophy of management. They have often overlooked this device and have, in dismay, found it impossible to pursue the goals upon which they have decided. Perhaps inertia, lack of courage, and institutionalized resistance are largely responsible for the neglect of this device.

The Management Conference

A fourth way to eliminate diversity in the aims of administrators is to go a step beyond definition and statement of company objectives and selection of willing personnel, and to use a relatively new technique in great current favor. Reference is had to what is generally termed *management conference*.[12] This type of conference is a special event planned as to subject matter and techniques. Generally, it is best to place its organization to a considerable degree in the hands of a representative committee of company administrators not too high in the echelons of staff and command. This will help to mobilize the younger and often more eager and critical personnel behind the effort, as well as to assure a certain freshness of view commonly most existent in those who still have their spurs to win.

The advantages of the management conference as a means of attaining greater agreement regarding aims are many. The management conference appears above all else to be a democratic device, and it reflects interest on the part of the organization in its higher members and their ideas. It supplies an opportunity for members of administration to become better acquainted socially and professionally. It furnishes a means by which the young and/or new members of administration can be further indoctrinated and assimilated. Obviously, as a meeting the management conference provides an additional two-way channel through which higher echelons looking downward can clarify and emphasize organizational aims, plans, and problems and through which individual administrators and groups looking upward can voice criticisms and suggestions. It can focus special attention on the management problem as a whole, or at least on significant segments of it, and it can divorce the problem from the many routine functions confronting the usual business administrator from day to day. The management conference can constitute a controlled situation as far as subject matter is concerned, for it can be devoted to about any phase of conflict or uncertainty which it is desired to treat. It is a means by which many administrators can be recognized through being invited to attend and/or participate. The flattery involved is one of the better ways of bringing them together in aims. The human race is still surprisingly caste conscious.

To these numerous positive possibilities of the management conference as a means of reconciling the aims of executives, there must be added the fact that it can be made to serve a certain evangelical purpose in that departments are expected either in preparation for the conference or during the sessions to reveal their ambitions and plans, and after the conference to digest, evaluate and perhaps even apply what they have learned. This introspective and analytical aspect not only helps hold up the good for praise but also exposes the weak or trivial or frankly provincial to criticism. Here is powerful motivation to become truly oriented toward the whole team. Closely akin to the evangelical possibilities of the management conference is its potential as a safety-valve through which the critical can give vent to their feelings.

There should be one other important reconciliation advantage common to all well planned management conferences, and it well may be the most significant value of the device. The inspiration and guidance of good lectures and demonstrations and the give and take of seminar type and problem-solving meetings can provide the kind of education and cross-fertilization necessary for sound administrative agreement on aims to be pursued. There is still truth in the oft-repeated statement that many heads are better than one. The management conference is a practical means for mobilizing and pooling views.

A treatment of the management conference must mention the more serious cautions with respect to its use. It is a delicate device and needs careful attention. A basic caution concerns its capture by one or more "power centers" or by natural leaders in the company. If the conference is thought by the rank and file of administrators to be the creature of some vested interests with their inevitable axes to grind, more harm than good can be done. Resentment will be certain, suspicion of its real purpose probable, and even more divergence of views as to aims possible. Another caution relates to what may be termed "commitment paralysis." It seems almost inherent in the democratic processes of the management conference. An issue may be so raised, discussed, and terminated by a consensus agreement that management cannot afford to accept the group decision. An effective strategy for avoiding commitment entrapment is to have and use a carefully prepared agenda and to entrust the chairmanship of conference meetings to skilled chairmen sympathetic to top management ideas. A still further cautionary suggestion, although not as significant, is well worth mentioning. If feasible, the conference should be held on company time and attendance arranged at company expense. Like most human beings, business administrators look forward to such special perquisites as release from regular duties, free registration, and company entertainment. If such psychic lures are not extended, proper attendance and participation may not ensue. Furthermore, these features will tend to accent the special and important nature of the event. As a concluding caution, the thought that a management conference generally should have a worthwhile program must be underlined, for lacking such it loses much of its potential to instruct. Most particularly, it should have an element of challenge and inspiration so that it may exert the desired pull toward teamwork.

Formal Instruction

Formal instruction is a fifth device for bringing about the realization that the company is the team and that the basic goals for all lie in the same direction. It may assume many forms as diverse as departmental staff meetings, company sponsored courses, or attendance at colleges and universities. Regardless of which form is used, the important thing is motivation to learn. This can be encouraged by the forward looking attitude of top administration and an organizational atmosphere which encourages learning. Example is strong tonic. Administrators, and even non-administrative personnel with ambitions toward management, can be powerfully influenced to improve themselves by the attitude and action of their superiors in keeping the company and its management up to date. They can also be encouraged by company recognition of efforts toward improvement through study. Without doubt, a strong recognition is the salary increment and promotion in rank, but even lesser steps, such as formal recognition by letter or house organ of enrollment in or completion of a course, can be most stimulating.

Rewards

There is a sixth reconciliation device—the whole matter of rewards. Those who identify themselves and their interests with the over-all purposes of the company should be given, everything being equal, the higher rewards in salary, promotion, and company honors. It would seem that this would always be the case. However, the fact is quite different. In a considerable percentage of cases, company rewards are granted on the basis of one or more of a number of rather questionable criteria. Among these are nepotism, friendship, erroneous evaluation of worth, fear of reaction at failure to reward, and custom.

Command as a Reconciliation Technique

Of some relationship to these devices for obtaining reconciliation of aims is executive command to work toward a goal. The ordering of cooperation can be a ticklish proposition. It is a management truism that an order which cannot or will not be obeyed must not be issued, for it will destroy authority, discipline, and morale;[13] but at times it is difficult for the issuing executive to ascertain beforehand and with surety that it can or cannot be carried out. Moreover, the very fact that it is considered necessary to order may indicate a tense situation in which cooperation is not forthcoming. Finally, the decision to compel carries with it the necessity to enforce obedience, and pressure (punitive or otherwise) can always cause reaction. This reaction can be especially serious in a large organization because of the great number of subordinate administrators, the necessity for heavy reliance by the "commanding official" on these many people, and the complex structure into which they are organized. In other words, the stern administrator in the large company is likely to be subject to much more reaction, and of a type most subtle to isolate and liquidate, because the possibility of unfriendly subordinates and centers of power hiding in the labyrinth. Nevertheless, there are times in all companies, large and small, when the command function must be exercised with determination. For example, one has the instance of the general manager who is implementing an organizational decision to buy more from the company's customers in the interest of public relations and sales promotion. In exploring this matter with the director of purchasing, he encounters violent opposition to his proposal, which is labelled reciprocal buying. The director of purchasing seems quite hypnotized by the fact that the purchasing clan in general considers this action very unprofessional. After due discussion and complete blocking by the orthodox director of purchasing, the general manager orders that it be done. An impasse in voluntary cooperation has occurred; the organizational objective can be pursued only by command.

New Management

A Strategic Pattern of Conduct

An especially difficult situation may arise, either within the department or the company as a whole, when new and aggressive management takes over. Fear may be generated among the personnel by the feeling that past faithfulness will be overlooked. Even despair can appear if the new president, general manager, or department head is believed to possess radically different prejudices, goals, and criteria of efficiency than the former incumbent. It commonly behooves all newly appointed administrators, especially those from outside the company, to tread lightly down any new paths. The vigorous leader will find this hard to do. He may be inclined to interpret his new employment as a mandate from the company "to straighten things out." But he should bear in mind that precipitous action can create a situation even worse than the existent problems and confusion. Certainty of the facts, consideration of the human element, and calmness of action should be his guiding principles.

Within due time after assuming office, the new management should make a definitive estimate of the situation and decide as to whether or not a satisfactory degree of agreement on objectives exists. It must be borne in mind that it is possible for new management to move into a situation demanding little in the way of reconciliation of goals. However, if his estimate of the situation is sufficiently negative to demand remedial action, he has at his disposal, and will be required to use, one or more of the same devices as are available to management in general. It is true that new leadership can impart a new appearance to an old device by the mere fact of using it a bit differently or with a different degree of vigor and emphasis. For example one may take the management conference. The former president used the training department to organize and conduct management meetings, and saved even more money by requiring them to be held at the plant after dinner in the evenings. The new management, more acquainted with professional services and human psychology, engages a famous professional consulting service to put on the conferences in the form of a dinner meeting at the local country club. Strategy is here apparent in a job of face lifting done on a tried and true mechanism.

In addition to the usual devices for reconciliation, face lifted or not, new management will find another promising technique in a form of "administrative courting." Reference is had to the "winning over" of selected oldsters in the existing organization. In all situations involving a shift in power, there is likely to be found a number of retained administrators who particularly desire to gain acceptance from the new superior. He should not ignore this opportunity of winning support. Although in the long run confidence perhaps can be won only by deserving it,[14] their support is often to be had quickly and almost gratuitously, demanding nothing more than recognition. Oldsters are often most valuable to the newcomer, not only in performing the duties of their positions but also as sounding boards, avenues of communication, advisors, and propagandists.

When all efforts at reconciliation have been made, there may still be situations which clearly demand more revolutionary action than the use of patience and the continuing application of reconciling devices. Commonly these situations can be handled, or at least an approach to their solution made, by the removal through discharge, transfer, demotion, or promotion of key old-timers in administration or of the whole old management group and by their replacement with other personnel. The use of this extreme remedy in a situation of basic conflict as to objective is not uncommon in American business and industry. Its most effective use, however, demands a good deal of subtlety. On the one hand, it rarely happens that the entire old management is beyond utilization. In fact, some of the old group usually possess knowledge, connections, and ability which no new appointee could bring or obtain quickly. Selectivity, therefore, must be the guiding rule in replacement. On the other hand, there is always the possibility that members of the former management left in power can prove harmful to the incoming administration. They may not perform efficiently; they may defend old positions; and they may effectively work toward the sabotage of operations and the blocking of new goals. At times, then, a certain aggressiveness seems dictated in clearing out the old and installing the new. Here is the dilemma of the incoming president, general manager, new department head or foreman faced with the necessity of cleaning house. How far can he go in replacement without doing more harm than good?

The Management Team

During the last generation, there has been a large number of cases in which the new business administrator has ignored the implications of this question. He has simply brought with him his *own management team* composed either of tried and true subordinates from the company or department he is leaving or of other trusted personnel variously selected. In certain instances, the accompanying team has been large enough to assume all major administrative posts in the concern or organizational sub-unit to which he is moving. In other instances, it has consisted only of a few individuals either as executive or staff assistants or as appointees to key subordinate administrative positions. Whatever the size of the incoming team, its introduction, although it may make the transition easier for the top man involved, is not an unmixed blessing. The fact that he has chosen certain individuals to bring with him indicates a type of favoritism, even though it is thoroughly deserved, to both them and those with whom they must work in the recipient company or department. It is as if the administrator says, "Come with me, you whom I know and trust, for I can't and don't wish to place my confidence in the lieutenants already on board." A degree of flattery is undoubtedly felt by his people and a converse measure of insult by the established personnel. Of course, if this were the only result of team transfer, mention of the subject would scarcely be justified; but the dangers go further. The flattery involved may lead the members of the team to assume airs and to presume upon the good graces of their patron administrator in not doing their new jobs to the best of their ability. This and the inherent insult in being overlooked may produce a measure of unfriendliness, opposition, lack of cooperation, and even poor performance in the "old" employees.

An even greater danger of team transfer, however, is inherent in the ties that such action demonstrates to the organization and its community. The leader, whatever his rank, must maintain and show a degree of loyalty to his team members often in excess of their merit. Not to do so might alienate these favored sons upon whom he especially depends and also might prove to his other associates and the general public that he made an error in bringing them along. Moreover, the demerit of unwise or improper personal conduct or administrative action by any of his people reflects inevitably upon him. Having chosen them above all others, he is burdened with them to an extent not present in his relations with the other subordinate administrators under his supervision. In a very real sense, the incoming administrator must stand or fall with his team.

Conclusion

Nothing in the case just presented for reconciliation of the personal aims held by the various administrative personnel with those of each other and more importantly with the broader purposes of the company should be interpreted to mean support of conformity for its own sake. Only that reconciliation of aims is deemed wise which is necessary for the attainment of these broader purposes. In fact, it is held desirable for administrative personnel to have great diversity in what they expect to obtain from life. It is the pursuit of these different aims that helps to produce the desirable variations in rate and depth of diligence with which men perform their appointed or chosen tasks.

Yet reconciliation of the particular objectives, and the concepts of objectives, held by the administrators of an organization does mean a degree of submergence of self for the legitimate purpose of clearing the way for command and control. No one seems to have set forth the real meaning of the reconciliation of objectives better than Urwick who states, "Organization—the design on the drawing board—takes life and fire, becomes an organism, only through personality, a commander who can lead helped by subordinates whose spirit is fused with his."[15]

BUSINESS SITUATIONS FOR ROLE-PLAYING

SITUATION IV

The Reconciliation of Administrative Objectives

THE PAFICO DISTRIBUTING CORPORATION

A. Scene. A food processing, canning and distributing firm. The Executive Vice President is conversing with the Controller about public relations.

B. Players. 1. Executive Vice-President: Mr. John S. Upright, a polished and aggressive public relations expert, who has recently assumed responsibility for executive direction of this old-line firm.

2. Controller: Mr. Edward E. Elson, an old-time, tight-fisted accountant, who has been the chief financial officer for many years and who was recently named to his present position.

C. Situation. The meeting is to treat a serious conflict in company objectives.

1. The Controller, as spokesman for the conservative element of the company, has been very outspoken in favor of an economy program.

2. The new Executive Vice President has been working out a program for growth, expansion and invasion of new markets. He has been receiving excellent cooperation from the Manufacturing, Research, Purchasing and Sales Departments, but the rumor has been circulating that the Controller is getting ready to "put an end to this nonsensical daydreaming."

D. Assignment. 1. Explain the situation in preceding group meeting and ask the group to prepare a list of strategies to be used by each party.

2. Select two individuals to act out the above roles, and have them do so with vigor.

3. Call for group critique of stratagems.

NOTES

1. The fallacy of the single objective is exposed in PETER F. DRUCKER, *The Practice of Management* (New York: Harper & Brothers, Publishers, 1954), pp. 62-94.
2. JAMES D. MOONEY and ALAN C. REILEY, *Onward Industry!* (New York: Harper & Brothers, Publishers, 1931), p. 77.
3. "The business organization is primarily an economic institution. Its primary objectives, therefore, must be certain economic values that it is expected or required to create, acquire, preserve, or distribute." RALPH CURRIER DAVIS, *The Fundamentals of Top Management* (New York: Harper & Brothers, Publishers, 1951), p. 96.
4. HENRI FAYOL, *General and Industrial Management*, trans. CONSTANCE STORRS (London: Sir Isaac Pitman & Sons, Ltd., 1949), p. 11.
5. Professor McFarland cites these as the long range, general objectives common to all business enterprises. DALTON E. MCFARLAND, *Management Principles and Practices* (New York: The Macmillan Company, 1958), p. 97.
6. *Ibid.*, p. 97.
7. *Ibid.*, p. 103.
8. *Ibid.*, p. 102.
9. *Ibid.*, p. 106.
10. "Definite objectives whose requirements are known, understood, and accepted by the organization are a requisite for effective cooperation. . . . The quantification and written statement of those values that constitute business objectives tend to increase the economy and effectiveness of business organization and operation." DAVIS, *op. cit.*, pp. 114-115.
11. Suggested by MCFARLAND, *op. cit.*, p. 106.
12. For a brief treatment of the conference method, see ROGER BELLOWS, *Creative Leadership* (Englewood Cliffs, N.J.: Prentice-Hall, Inc., 1959), pp. 211-223; for a full discussion, see NORMAN MAIER, *Problem-Solving Discussions and Conferences* (New York: McGraw-Hill Book Company, 1963).
13. CHESTER I. BARNARD, *The Functions of the Executive* (Cambridge, Mass.: Harvard University Press, 1956), p. 167.
14. CHESTER I. BARNARD, *Organization and Management* (Cambridge, Mass.: Harvard University Press, 1952), p. 11.
15. L. URWICK, *The Elements of Administration* (New York: Harper & Brothers, Publishers, n.d.), p. 82.

CHAPTER **5**

The Power Complex

"All effective administration demands the possession and utilization of power to some degree. This is as true in the twentieth century as in the days of rampant autocracy."

FEW COMPONENTS of our social structure are viewed as superficially by the majority of Americans as the business enterprise. It is commonly seen as various things other than a pulsating organic unit of society. To many, it means a place at which of necessity they must spend eight more or less unpleasant hours five days each week. To large numbers it is the source of subsistence, the pay envelope which is forthcoming with a sort of rhythm and to which, therefore, employees are somehow entitled. To still greater numbers, it is a brand, a symbol or a TV show. To all, it is a place where upon occasion things and services are bought.

This superficial attitude seems to stem from two rather divergent factors. One is the human tendency to find work irksome and reward pleasant. Therefore, people tend to feel both dislike and affection for the business that employs and pays them, and to suffer a degree of hypnosis in the emotions aroused. The company becomes a stimulus for reaction, and not a subject for analysis. The other factor probably responsible for the superficial attitude is the almost childlike faith

89

which Americans in general have in American business. The nation is prosperous; its businessmen have contributed immeasurably to its prosperity and, in doing so, have themselves emerged as the wealthier class. In general, Americans are not inclined to look much below the surface. The magic in the success of any segment of the nation tends to deaden desire to study its operation. As the popular mind reasons, "American business knows what it is doing. Why worry about it?"

Were this uncritical view confined to the consuming public and the working classes, it might not be so alarming. However, the fact remains that all too frequently management itself seems to entertain a most unanalytical feeling toward the general nature of a business organization. Often there is little managerial introspection within the particular company itself. Nothing else could account for many of the serious and costly errors that are hidden by an apparently favorable profit and loss statement or by one for which there is no standard of comparison.

Management's unconcern with the organic nature of the company may stem from a number of influences, among which are the condition that most management personnel are themselves employees; the hypnotism of success in terms of profits expected or made; and the contagion of mass apathy toward the subject. Whatever the forces responsible, it is now a most serious condition. Competition grows apace; costs increase and profit margins narrow; foreign producers are less and less to be ignored; and socialistic pressures are becoming increasingly threatening.

The Company as a Social Unit

Perhaps the most important aspect of the basic nature of the business organization, which is commonly overlooked by Americans in general and business management in particular, is the fact that the business enterprise is actually a type of social group. In a sense it is a society in itself. It consists of a group of persons more or less voluntarily banded together for the accomplishment of some common ends or special goals which an individual or a segment of the group finds most convenient to pursue in this particular union, fears to pursue without association, or cannot attain alone.[1]

Why is the recognition of the company as a social unit of such prime significance? The answer is simple. It points the way to a critical understanding of the requirements, in terms of proper administration, for the success of the enterprise. The successful functioning of any society demands a certain relationship which may be described in brutal terms as domination and submission.[2] This may be hidden or softened by the human relations approach, but it will exist underneath as the essential moral and survival force of the contractual relationship between employer and employee. *Successful business administration demands power on the part of management just as the effective functioning of any other society—political, military, or religious—requires it.* No organization can long function in the anarchy of "discontrol" or the idyllic condition of equal decisive influence. Domination by all and submission by none, or vice versa, would mean chaos and death to any social unit.

The people who make up the social unit called the company, from the janitor to the chairman of the board, are individuals. They are blessed with varying abilities and levels of education and culture, many different personal objectives which they hope to gratify by being associated with the company, ancient prejudices and ties, and partisan loyalties within the company. Even though they do have some common goals in being together, it is obvious that they cannot operate with any measure of success unless there is in the hands of some one or more people the force to dominate, that is, to lead through influence, persuasion, or decree.[3] There are many people who may be troubled by such reference to power.[4] If so, it may be that they mistake the "smooth" handling of human beings for their efficient administration, that they believe the company to be a place in which people socialize for pay, and they do not realize that human relation techniques often can provide only the lubricant which makes administration easier and more effective.

The Nature and Origin of Power

Power and Obedience

Power in the group is the ability to effect obedience.[5] It can be defined in less harsh terms as the capacity to win compliance, to obtain followership, or to impose the will. Regardless of the niceties of definition, power is absolutely essential to achieve coordinated results. Unless power is lodged in the hands of some, and not all, within the enterprise, only disaster can follow. Individual differences are so great that spontaneous and comprehensive cooperation toward a common goal will rarely, if ever, take place. This is a truism.

Sources of Power

Power may stem from various sources.[6] It may adhere to the individual or individuals who have a large proprietary interest in the company such as stock ownership, capital lent, or patents owned. It may be granted by the charter or articles of partnership. It may be inherent in organizational position. It may come from some particular technical knowledge which others in the company do not have. It may proceed from force of personality. It may result from personal status within the group such as seniority. It may come from ties of blood, marriage, or friendship. It may even be seized by manipulation and chicanery.

The power obtained by belonging to the correct gang, clique, or team is of special import to larger companies and of some significance even to smaller enterprises. There are cliques (one may use this word generically here, since it does not necessarily imply either the ruthlessness of "gang" nor the desirability of "team") in all organizations of more than a few people.[7] Although their origin may be diverse, the members can have real power under one or both of two conditions. They may control certain very strategic operations in the company, for example, the personnel department, which frequently must be courted to obtain even an efficient secretary; or they may have a leader with considerable power, granted or assumed, who sheds power upon his henchmen by protecting them, for example, the sales manager who fights the controller over the general issue of expense accounts for his salesmen. Regardless of the situation which generates their power, members of a clique can be troublesome in administration because the organizational structure makes no formal allowance for their existence and because they, therefore, can become the source of constant friction. The antidote is very concise procedure from which deviation is rarely allowed, or the wise utilization of the clique, or its integration within the formal organization.

A caution is here dictated. A vacuum as regards power will not long be allowed to exist within the company. If no administrator has power over a particular area someone will attempt to obtain it. It may be an established official of the concern, an ambitious youngster, an outsider such as a person seeking a position, or even a professional agency in search of a client. The old axiom that power abhors a vacuum is quite applicable to the business enterprise because of the possibility of political, economic, and psychic gain to be had by filling it. It should be remembered that administrative vacuums can exist in mature as well as in new companies. The difference may simply be one of type and/or frequency.

The erroneous impression that power always flows down-ward is not intended. Subordinates possess power which may be exerted on their superiors, although it is generally exercised over lower echelons. An example in point is the case of the good secretary who, even though she "bosses" many of her supervisor's underlings, also exercises real in-fluence over him. This line of reasoning suggests the exist-ence of an interplay of forces in the exercise of power, and a necessary qualifying thought to this discussion which is oriented primarily in the downward perspective.

Significance of the Source of Power

The issue of the source from which an administrator gets power is not merely an academic exercise. Very practical implications are inherent in it.[8] The matter of permanence of power is prominent. This point is evident in the contrast of two very different ways of getting power. If the adminis-trator is the chief stockholder, his power position is likely to be secure and, at his will, quite long. However, should it be that he has simply assumed power from having been the only experienced engineer on duty during an influenza epidemic, his tenure as a kingpin, large or small, may be unsafe and shortlived.

Among these practical considerations, the effect of the source of power upon the administrator's morale, personality, and character is also important. For example, an experienced individual appointed to head up sales may have pride in his recognition, whereas a young man made sales manager of a corporation because his uncle is president may feel and exhibit certain negative tendencies such as insufficient pride in accomplishment, lack of self-reliance, or real arrogance.

Then too, the reaction of others within the company to the manner in which power was obtained may be of practical significance. A chief purchasing agent who is appointed be-cause of his known ability may get considerably more respect from his associates in the organization than one who obtains this power position because he married the daughter of the vice president in charge of production. One should always bear in mind that the higher the regard in which one's associates hold him, the greater will be his chances of success in the administration of the group.

Finally, it must be mentioned that the source of an administrator's power is of significance to his associates and competitors in dealing with him. The source of power may well indicate its degree. A department head who is the son of the leading stockholder may actually have more power because of this connection than another department head who succeeded to his job because of seniority, and he may, therefore, be either harder or easier to handle in business relations. The source of power may also determine how the administrator will use his power. If it is from an impregnable source he may be more inclined to act in larger, more precipitate, and even more decisive terms. These lines of thought imply strongly that knowledge of the source of an administrator's power can be of value to those who deal with him, since it may tell them something of what to expect from him.

The Degree of Power Necessary

There is no more elusive or delicate subject in the field of business administration than the degree of power necessary to its success. The individuals with greater power in the organization will believe at times that they have insufficient ability to make others do as they wish. Those with lesser power occasionally will feel imposed upon. Unfortunately, there are no objective criteria for concisely determining how much or how little power individuals within the company should have. About the only thing which can be done is to equate power with authority (a not altogether proper thing to do, since authority connotes institutionalized, or built-in, power[9] to discharge certain responsibility), and to seek refuge in the well established principle that each member of administration should have sufficient power to discharge his responsibilities.

The Factor of Responsibility

The determination of the correct amount of power demands, above all else, a clear delineation of responsibilities. This suggests such usual devices as organizational charts, job analyses, and operating manuals. It would seem a problem which reasonable men of good will could solve without too much trouble. However, the real difficulties do not appear on paper, even when administrative wisdom succeeds in establishing the clearest statement of responsibilities in the most concise hierarchical and procedural arrangement. One of the more significant practical difficulties comes in actual operation when circumstance necessitates an actual shift in the relative importance assigned to particular responsibilities or groupings of responsibilities.

An example is to be found in the situation when competition makes it imperative for the research and development department to obtain a larger share of the budget at the expense of sales promotion for an older product. For a longer or shorter period, the research and development staff are the "fair-haired gang." They have the green light; and they may run into friction with other departments because they now have more power.

Shift in Responsibility

It would appear that a certain strategy is here indicated. When a new balance of power is to be created or is permitted to develop, by the upgrading or downgrading of the responsibility held, top administration should be forehanded in attempting to win the support or acquiescence of the administrative personnel most likely to feel endangered. Whatever devices are used to attempt this sometimes very difficult task, three principles should be followed. First, there should be apparent frankness as to the nature of the shift in what can be called "company emphasis or organizational structure," because frankness has a tremendous human appeal and because it is an effective disarming technique. However, complete frankness, despite its high popular evaluation, may weaken the competitive position of the company, endanger plans for further administrative changes, or bring a serious internal upset. Second, the aggrieved individual should be informed by a top administrator of major shifts. Generally, reaction to change in degrees of power held comes from fear, and the greatest worry is usually of the intentions of the "headman." Since he, be he president, executive vice-president or general manager, is in the position to inflict the heaviest injury by change, he also has the greatest power to allay anxiety. Third, the personnel likely to be hurt or feel injury generally should be told as early as possible. Secrecy is well nigh a fiction even in the best run companies. The news or suspicion of impending change will out. Irreparable damage to morale can be caused by others learning of the change before the parties most likely to feel the negative impact come to know it, and by a long period of concern before the real truth is known.

There is at least one condition when quite the opposite of frankness, directness, and promptness are dictated with respect to a change. At times, the administrator desiring the shift may not feel certain of the attitude in other parts of the company whose acceptance or support is needed for the anticipated power shift. In this case, it may be wise to let the news leak out so that any sudden antagonism may be avoided and a gradual conversion process take place by the possible opposition becoming accustomed to the idea.

Perspective demands return for the moment to the original

thesis that the business concern is a society. Much of what has been written in the above paragraphs suggests that this discussion of power is confined to the company as a whole. It should be pointed out, with proper deference to sociological considerations, that there are sub-societies within the company. The best examples are the so-called departments. Therefore, the considerations here most often advanced in the company frame of reference apply also, if on a smaller dimensional base, to the intra-department scene. In this line of thinking, one may properly substitute *department head* for *company president* and *chief file clerk* for *department head*.

The Dynamics of Power

Appraisal of Power Held

The use of power is a function of strategy. Its wise employment depends upon many circumstances. The degree to which the leader realizes that he possesses power is undoubtedly foremost. It is not an uncommon phenomenon for the administrator to fall short of the most effective use of power simply because he does not know how much power is in his hands. Either he underestimates the degree to which he can impose his will or he oversteps his capacity to back up his decision. The reasons are many and include ignorance, lack of imagination, indolence, and fear.

Whatever the cause of the leader's failure to make a correct appraisal of his power position, it should be emphasized that each power position has two components: the core, which is the authority given or permitted by the organization as a right, and a periphery or aura of power surrounding the core and shading out into the pervading darkness of opposition. The administrator who fails to realize the dimensions of this elasticity will not be able to exercise his total power most effectively. If he overjudges the limits of what he can do and asserts himself too far, he will run into the fiercely defended power areas of others and encounter possible failure. If he underestimates them, he will leave unexploited opportunities for leadership.

Unity of Command

The proper use of power depends secondly on what has been aptly termed the "unity of command." This principle holds that for any action the subordinate should receive orders from but one superior.[10] The practical manifestation of unity of command is to be found in the carefully established and correctly functioning chain of command, in which each domination and submission relationship illustrates or constitutes a unity of command. Without unity of command, the possessor of power will run the danger of his orders not being obeyed, since the subordinate may be getting orders from other superiors and either heeding them or simply surrendering to the confusion of multiple orders either by executing each to only a degree or by simply following none of them. The management situation in a company or department which suffers from a serious lack of unity of command can well be imagined. Subordinate administrators and employees will not know whom to obey or will obey those whom they like, respect, fear or desire to please for various reasons. The higher officials, who may enjoy the freedom to command as an expression of their status, will discover that they do not seem to be able to use fully the power which is supposed, as authority, to reside in them. There is in all this the serious implication that the best use of power depends in part upon how well the organizational structure has been conceived and instituted.

The Handling of Opposition

The concept of opposition has been mentioned. Except in the rarest and most sanguine circumstances, there is generally some opposition to every act of leadership as an exercise of power. This brings the discussion, then, to the third circumstance upon which the effective use of power depends. It may be stated as the ability of the administrator to forestall or overcome opposition to his will.

There is no doubt but that ingenuity is always necessary to the successful handling of opposition. The forms and places and times at which opposition to the leader's decisions may arise are infinite in number and often totally unexpected. No general pattern can be laid down for the meeting of opposition. However it may be suggested that, as a rule, the leader should anticipate trouble and lay his plans as if it were inevitable, but to his associates appear calm. Adherence to this principle will enhance his readiness for difficulty, his ability to lead from strength, and his capacity to inspire confidence.

It should be emphasized that there is a general quality which may adhere to leadership and prove of almost as much importance to the evading or liquidation of opposition as ingenuity itself. Reference is had to trust, i.e., faith in the motives and judgment of the administrator making the decisions. Trust is built upon many things: general character, prior success, personality, acquaintance, identity of interest, and cultural ties. But one element stands out and seems of salient import, and that is morality. If an administrator is unfailingly honest and honorable in his dealings with his fellowmen, he will develop eventually among many a reputation for moral trustworthiness. This can be of the greatest and most direct assistance in mitigating suspicion of wrong motives. It must be remembered that the human mind has the trait of slipping from good thought to good thought and from bad to bad. If the leader's motives are not held suspect by associates, there is a greater chance that his judgments also will not be questioned. In other words, the trust of one's associates in his moral conduct can become a built-in shield to other types of opposition.

Power as a Changing Possession

Much of what has just been said may imply that power is a static attribute of position, that once given or acquired the problem simply becomes one of using it. Quite the contrary is true. Although power structures within an organization may tend to be stable,[11] the power and concomitant leadership of the individual administrator are dynamic phenomena. They either grow or diminish in response to the influence of a complex of power accrual or attrition forces always present with respect to any leader.

It should be a major function of the top administration of a company to see that the growth in a particular administrator's power is the reward for the proven effective use of a lesser entrustment of power. Unfortunately, the interplay of circumstances, both internal and/or external to the company, may thrust power upon an administrator who does not deserve it, cannot exercise it properly, or is an unknown quantity. Seniority of service is high among these circumstances. In many instances, seniority is simply a biological gift of comparatively better health or greater longevity.

The issue of seniority in the power complex of a business concern is likely to be the source of considerable trouble. If it is ignored in promoting to positions of higher responsibility, the company may be said to be ungrateful. Motivation for good and long service may be injured. On the other hand, if seniority is the principal ladder to higher position, incompetents may rise to levels well above their ability.

What can a sincere administrator do? It would seem that a number of steps can be taken. Above all he should maintain the highest standards feasible for appointment to each administrative level, so that the possibility of an individual's reaching consideration for a position at each higher level cannot be based simply on seniority. Moreover, he should see that there are non-promotional rewards for seniority so that it may have its due recognition without requiring the elevation of mediocrity. Among these, one can mention salary increases, retirement benefits, new titles of dignity, and public recognition of long years of service. It should not be forgotten that many administrators use a slightly Machiavellian procedure to handle the old employee who is neither qualified for particular promotion nor amenable to seduction by non-promotional rewards. Reference is had to promotion in another direction—either in an area in which he is better qualified or to a job in which he can do less harm.

The skeptic may raise the question as to the significance of all this concern with seniority as a part of a discussion of power. He may consider the individual with the long record as just another employee who can and should be ignored in the promotional process if he does not well fit into it. Unfortunately, this may be a questionable ethical stand. Also, if seniority is actually ignored, the results may be costly. The employee who has been with the company for a long period of time has acquired by many processes, notably by intimate knowledge of the organization or portions of it and by loyalties won within it, a certain degree of power. If he is a natural leader, this measure may be considerable. The implication is clear. Should he be passed over in the promotional process but retained in the company, he may exercise his influence to obstruct and defy subsequent company policies and actions. It may even, therefore, be necessary eventually to demote, transfer, or discharge him, and thus occasion a net loss to the organization, if he is efficient in some respect.

The Loss of Power

Now what about the loss of power held in the company? Power may be lost in many ways. It may simply wither away with the passage of time due to a gradual shift in the nature of the company's business, inexorable changes in its organizational structure, or the slow theft, consciously or unconsciously, of power by other, frequently new and more dynamic administrators within the company. It may be lost through disuse. Either others may assume it when it is not used frequently enough; or it may be found wanting when, on the rare occasion the administrator decides to apply his will, he discovers that his associates now have other ideas and will not submit. It may be thrown away by abuse. If a given administrator uses his power for improper purposes or to an excessive extent, his superiors may decide to curb him in one way or another. Then too, it may be lost in what is termed the "power struggle," the fight for dominance so common in organizational life.[12] Finally, power may be taken away by higher power for a large number of reasons peculiar to the judgment of the superior. Such reasons might be dissatisfaction with the subordinate's character, personality or work, desire to embark upon a new company policy into which the old subordinate does not fit, recognition of pressure from within or without, or desire to appoint a friend or relative.

This may be rather frightening to the sincere, hardworking executive who has thought that his efforts will eventually prove him capable for and be rewarded by a boost up the administrative ladder. He may, however, take consolation in various facts. First, he should recognize that his company, in a practical sense, is a society; that it cannot prosper without the services of efficient administrators; and that his superiors in general want efficient subordinates, since it is the productivity of these lower orders who, in large measure, make it possible for the higher echelons to maintain their greater power and grow into even more power. Second, he may take heart in the fact that he is not helpless to protect himself in the company. His best weapon is, of course, hard intelligent work. This, more than anything else, will give him that degree of indispensability which not only does much to preclude replacement by someone else but also contributes greatly to the possibility of promotion.

There are many who will brand this as so much sentimental rationalization. They will say that virtue does not always triumph, that top administration is not always concerned first with efficiency, and that efficiency is not generally enough protection. To a degree, such critics are correct in this more cynical stand. Even if this is granted, however, there are still things which the subordinate can do and that all administrators can undertake to see that their virtue is rewarded.

A few of these steps may be mentioned. No matter how friendly and just the company environment in which he is employed, the administrator should always keep himself alert—in popular parlance, "in the know." This implies that he must spend much time in company circles, e.g., be on the job early and late; read all its literature he can get; attend as many group meetings as he can; and become acquainted with the thinking of his superiors, equals, and subordinates by analytical study of them and by politic association with them. It is only through a keen knowledge of what is taking place or probable in his company that he can chart the best protective or upward course for himself. This is so obvious as to seem trite. Yet, many frustrated administrators, who find their positions in jeopardy or do not advance, simply sit and complain. They are never fully aware of what is happening about them and are therefore unable to do much about it.

Another step which the administrator may take to protect and further himself is to seize every opportunity, within the bounds of ethics, to call himself and his merit to the attention of his superiors. Higher administrators are not always in a position to learn of the relative virtue of all their subordinates. One way to sell oneself is by doing a bit more or a little better job than is expected. Such action may not be immediately noted, but chances are good that it eventually will be. When it is noticed it becomes the very best self-selling device. The employee who "puts out more or better" than the job demands is rare indeed, and most superiors are eager for his services.

Anxiety to be safe in a position or to be certain of advancement should not be permitted to overshadow good moral conduct in dealing with others in the company. If it does, it may well defeat its purpose. Any group of people working together will for its own protection demand, as far as it can, proper internal relations. Quite apart from the origin of this demand in moral concept, which may be its source more often than one supposes, is the simple sociological need of the group for a substantial degree of peace, harmony and mutual respect, without which it can neither function most efficiently nor give its members a sufficient feeling of security to retain all of them. The practical meaning of all this is not obscure. He who would retain or enhance his position of power within the company should not be so eager to pry into its secrets or sell himself that he forgets the welfare of his associates, ignores their rights, and rides rough-shod over them. Unfortunately, many ambitious power seekers get whatever information they can wherever and however they can, and use every device to sell themselves at the expense of others within the company.

Living with Power

Perhaps the most difficult aspect of the power position is to learn to live with power. Many an administrator has failed in his work, grown unpleasant, become an evil character, or even died of ulcers because of his inability to "philosophize" his position.

Power Breeds Loneliness

The nearer the administrator is to the top, the more he will be alone. He who has power in considerable quantity will find it necessary, in order best to discharge his probably heavy responsibilities, to hold himself aloof from his associates.[13] If he does otherwise, he may become enmeshed in the woof and warp of entangling loyalties and enmities which will make objective decision and decisive action difficult, if not impossible. Furthermore, in the last analysis the leader must stand alone; he and he alone cannot escape ultimate responsibility, for responsibility is obligation. This in itself sets him off from his fellows and creates within many administrators a sense of being alone.

Power Tends to Corrupt

Power has been compared to Medusa's head, with the thought that whoever has looked upon her countenance remains forever under her spell. The possession of power has dangers to the possessor. The administrator, finding himself able to impose his will in one direction, may use it for other purposes less legitimate. In the passage of time, such usage may not only make him a tyrant but also give him the reputation of being one. The temptation to use power capriciously and to extend its application beyond proper limits is very great to many leaders. It promises so much of self-flattery and, in many cases, social and material reward. However, the administrator who succumbs is not only essentially disloyal to his associates since he is perverting the mutual objectives of their association as a company, but he is also laying the basis for attack by those who see themselves endangered by his exploitation of his power position.

The Possession of Power May Frighten the Possessor

Probably more administrators than might be thought are actually afraid of the power in their hands, and even more likely fear additional power. How else can one explain the reluctance of able and industrious officials of the company to decide and act? This fear may proceed from so many inherited and environmental influences that it would be folly to try to isolate them in this short treatment. The basic issue in the situation which finds an administrator afraid of his job is the age-old problem often facetiously expressed, "Do I wish to live as a mouse or a man?" No one can give the right answer to an executive faced with this deep internal conflict. If he feels that he cannot find adequate courage to wield the power necessary to discharge his responsibilities, he should not seek higher power, and in many cases should try to find satisfaction and livelihood in a position, perhaps technical or professional, in which the phenomenon of power and its use are not so essential.

Conclusion

Power in the social group has been of universal interest to man since he first saw woman and formed the basic social unit, the family. Recent trends have tended to obscure the fact that it is the very energizing force within organization. Without it, there can be no real leadership. This is as true of the business concern as of any other type of society. The business administrator must learn to live with power, even though it makes him a lonely man, may tend to corrupt him, and can even frighten him.

BUSINESS SITUATIONS FOR ROLE-PLAYING

SITUATION V

The Power Complex

EROM WHITMAN AND SONS, INC.

A. Scene. A tool and die manufacturing concern. The office of the Executive Vice President who has called in the newly appointed Director of Public Relations.

B. Players.   1. Executive Vice President: Mr. Wendell Hall, a shrewd official of many years' experience with the company, who understands the necessity for politic action in power shifts.

2. Director of Public Relations: Mr. Fred Goodyear, a new executive of the concern who has been employed away from a lucrative position as a public relations director with another company but who has always worked in a rather easygoing and stable environment.

C. Situation.   1. Erom Whitman and Sons, Inc. has recently been receiving poor publicity concerning its products and labor relations in the local press. In an effort to correct the situation, the Executive Vice President has created the Office of Public Relations Director. The incumbent is to work closely with the Director of Industrial Relations and the Vice President in charge of Manufacturing.

2. The new Director of Public Relations has been on the job sixty days but so far has been receiving very poor cooperation from other executives.

3. The meeting being held is concerned with ways and means by which the new Director of Public Relations can get and exercise adequate power over the old line departments.

D. Assignment. 1. Select two persons to act out the above roles. Try to obtain unusually imaginative individuals.

2. Assign one-half of the group to criticize the performance of each.

NOTES

1. For another viewpoint, see Knickerbocker who declares, "The group of people comprising an industrial organization is not a group which has arisen to achieve an objective common to all its members. The owners, or the managers, have recruited a number of isolated individuals—created a group—

because the combined efforts of many people are required to achieve the owner's objective." IRVING KNICKERBOCKER, "Leadership: A Conception and Some Implications" in SCHUYLER DEAN HOSLETT (ed.), *Human Factors in Management* (Rev. ed.; New York: Harper & Brothers, Publishers, 1951), p. 15.

2. Unfortunately, the term "domination" bears a rather brutal connotation, and appears at times in the literature of administration to mean a primitive method of administration quite in contrast to integration and obedience to the Law of the Situation. See the compilation under the "principle of centralization" in L. URWICK, *The Elements of Administration* (New York: Harper & Brothers, Publishers, n.d.), p. 127.

3. Mary Parker Follett suggests a certain qualification of this conclusion. She declares, "So far as my observation has gone, it seems to me that whereas power usually means power-over, the power of some person or group over some other person or group, it is possible to develop the conception of power-with, a jointly developed power, a co-active, not a coercive power." MARY PARKER FOLLETT, "Power" in HENRY C. METCALF and L. URWICK (eds.), *Dynamic Administration: The Collected Papers of Mary Parker Follett* (New York: Harper & Brothers, Publishers, 1940), p. 101.

4. DELBERT C. MILLER and WILLIAM H. FORM, *Industrial Sociology* (New York: Harper & Brothers, Publishers, 1951), p. 310.

5. *Ibid.*, p. 310; and H. H. GERTH and C. W. MILLS, *From Max Weber: Essays in Sociology* (New York: Oxford University Press, 1946), p. 180.

6. JOHN M. PFIFFNER and FRANK P. SHERWOOD, *Administrative Organization* (Englewood Cliffs, N.J.: Prentice-Hall, Inc., 1960), pp. 332-338.

7. A discussion of the types of cliques is to be found in MELVILLE DALTON, *Men Who Manage* (New York: John Wiley & Sons, Inc., 1959), pp. 57-67.

8. PFIFFNER AND SHERWOOD, *op. cit.*, p. 332.

9. For an interesting comment on the forms in which power appears, see ROBERT BIERSTADT, "Power and Social Organization" in ROBERT DUBIN, *Human Relations in Administration* (New York: Prentice-Hall, Inc., 1951), p. 180.

10. HENRI FAYOL, *General and Industrial Management*, trans. CONSTANCE STORRS (London: Sir Isaac Putnam & Sons, Ltd., 1949), p. 24.

11. ROBERT DUBIN, *The World of Work* (Englewood Cliffs, N.J.: Prentice-Hall, Inc., 1958), p. 29.

No doubt, the fact that the power held by the individual in the organization tends to be a changing factor is due in part to his ambition and the ambitions of others. Odiorne states flatly, "Deep inside nearly every successful man is an intense desire to be the best." GEORGE S. ODIORNE, *How Managers Make Things Happen* (Englewood Cliffs, N.J.: Prentice-Hall, Inc., 1961), p. 158.

12. DALTON, *op. cit.*, Chaps. III–VI, pp. 18-191.

In his compilation under the "principle of the general interest," Urwick takes note of the lust and struggle for power which is a danger in growing organizations. URWICK, *op. cit.*, p. 127.

13. It is true that successful executives have a unique type of association in that they seek each other out. This is probably based on what Mills calls "a kind of reciprocal attraction among the fraternity of the successful." C. WRIGHT MILLS, *The Power Elite* (New York: Oxford University Press, 1956), p. 281.

Managers as such may tend toward a sort of attitudinal association, since they share common beliefs and, in fact, prejudices. For example, Morris concluded, from his conversation with a number of managers, that they appeared to hold some common doubts about the scientists and engineers serving as their advisers. WILLIAM T. MORRIS, *Management Science in Action* (Homewood, Ill.: Richard D. Irwin, Inc., 1963), p. 4.

CHAPTER **6**

The Exploitation of Opportunity

"Opportunities are situations which can be used to advantage. They may be fortuitous or man-made. Much of the competitive advantage enjoyed by the administrator, his department, or company flows from his attitude toward and utilization of opportunities."

OPPORTUNITY is a key concept in the defense of capitalism. The free enterprise system is claimed to afford man the greatest possible chance to use his initiative and individual ability in his own interest. It is further contended that this freedom is essential to the highest degree of economic progress. Each individual basically free to develop his peculiar capacity largely for his own reward is seen as the production and consumption unit par excellence. The driving effort of free individuals, wisely curbed only to prevent license and educated to accept necessary social responsibility, is held to mean the greatest prosperity for the nation. Although the forces of the Left apparently do not concede this point, common sense indicates that there is no general rebuttal.

Opportunity and the Leader

Obviously, however, this argument in support of the free economy is meaningless in a practical sense, unless the

111

lauded factor of freedom is reflected in business leadership sufficiently farsighted, analytical, and courageous to see and seize opportunity.[1] Most Americans are convinced that it is so reflected. In fact, the belief that American business executives are dynamic is certainly a prominent element in the American *credo*. There is excellent evidence in the history of such businessmen and industrialists as Rockefeller, Carnegie, Firestone, the Fords, the Fishers, Chrysler. And general proof positive lies in the unprecedented high scale of living enjoyed by Americans, which certainly cannot have been attained without effective business leadership.

This is not, of course, either a eulogy or an essay in complacency. There is nothing in the free enterprise system which automatically assures dynamic leadership to every specific company. The economy may be most prosperous and give the appearance of over-all good leadership, but various individual companies—and the operation of specific companies is the orientation of this study of administrative strategy—may be directed by mediocre or really incompetent executives. This is a distinct probability in the United States. Our great prosperity enables our society to carry poorly run businesses. Although their costs are high, Americans can afford to buy their products, for such is the national wealth. Yet there may be an even more common danger than this social cover-up of an occasional badly run company. It is the probability that many allegedly successful businesses are not managed as efficiently as they could be. To ignore this issue is really to indulge in pride or self-satisfaction.

Certainly one element which prevents many business administrators from measuring up to the highest standards of efficiency is their failure to use their freedom. In other words, they do not see or use fully their opportunities. Opportunities are situations which can be used to advantage. They do, of course, suggest departure from the normal course; they frequently smack of outright innovation. Since this is the case, many an ordinary executive, desiring primarily peace and calm, views them as something less than desirable. To him they represent unpleasantness; they appear as potential disturbances to his smooth routine and even as threats to the security of the familiar. Opportunities, therefore, are to be overlooked, avoided, and minimized. If the situation is clearly recognized by his superiors or associates as one which should be exploited, he may be driven to action. Yet this, in all to frequent instances, may be only half-hearted and assume one of the familiar frustrating techniques such as further and long study or reference to past abortive efforts in the beckoning direction.

The administrator who neglects opportunity for improvement in the operation of his department or company may feel himself perfectly justified. After all, he may remind himself that he and his people are doing their job well. To seize an opportunity for change might, quite apart from disturbing him, redound to the disadvantage of the company. For example, an office manager might "lie low" on the subject of central files or a typing pool when the installation of a new president would give him the opening to recommend their introduction. He might feel that the so-called forward steps would bring more confusion than exists under the status quo, and he might be correct. The implication here seems to be that it is not always desirable to seize opportunity just for the sake of appearing progressive. The rational exploitation of opportunity demands selectivity.

Despite this preliminary caution, the truth remains that much of the competitive advantage enjoyed by an administrator, his department, or company flows from his attitude toward and utiliziation of opportunities. The strategic leader is well aware of this fact. He knows that the "extra something" which may be gained by the judicious investigation and use of situations may make him or his a winner. He tends to seek out and to view opportunities in a positive light; he may even be so sensitive to their possibilities as to attempt to create them. Since this book holds the strategic leader to be the truly efficient executive, it now proposes to turn to an analysis of opportunity and its role in the strategy of administration.

Classification of Opportunities

Opportunities are of no one mold. Composed of different circumstances interwoven variously, they are of many types. This is not to suggest that they are so different as to preclude any study of their anatomy. It is rather to suggest the necessity for some type of categorization, for classification does place them in an artificially static condition in which they can be the more easily observed and analyzed. There are many ways of grouping situations which promise advantage. Those that appear to be of most significance to the strategist will be described.

Large and Small

At the risk of appearing facetious, one may cite as the first grouping of opportunities the prosaic classification into large and small. Some situations promise great things; others hold out hope of only small gain. The contrast is seen in two illustrations. The rapidly rising cost of operating the family car at mid-century presents to the administrators of various automobile manufacturing concerns high hope of a good market for economy vehicles. On the other hand, the contemporary American demand for ever-increasing physical comfort and the development of air-conditioning for automobiles adds only a little extra sales appeal to the low and medium priced cars.

A pertinent question arises here. Should the administrator concentrate on the "big chance" and ignore the more numerous little opportunities which present themselves? The *principle of selectivity* in the choice of opportunities to be seized has been laid down, and the application of this principle certainly means paying more attention to situations whose exploitation offers the most. Yet, it is possible to concentrate too much upon the hope of the big at the expense of the small opportunity. The situation which promises large gains to the administrator may never come. Companies and their departments do reach a plateau of operational smoothness at which few greatly challenging situations are met or can be engineered. The administrator who looks only for the big break may never "get off the plateau" of routine accomplishment. It should be remembered that the positive effects of exploiting small opportunities can be accumulative. Many small gains for the department or the company may add up to something of real significance. Thus the constant taking of opportunities to please customers who complain about service can mean much better public relations in general. Attention to small opportunities can have even further accumulative results. It can provide self-training in dynamic action for the executive who follows this alert course. It can also contribute to his reputation as an alert and progressive administrator. His subordinates will tend to see him as a real leader who can take them somewhere; his associates will be influenced to recognize him as their peer and even as a tough competitor; his superiors may notice him more often or with greater favor and come to identify him as a go-getter they want for higher assignment.

A warning is in order. This somewhat enthusiastic presentation might make it appear that the exploitation of opportunity is the sure way to self-elevation in the organization.[2] To be certain, it is an essential step in the competitive battle for internal advancement, but the pitfalls must be recognized. The administrator who seizes opportunity may, by this act, disturb his colleagues who are content to sit and protect the status quo or who are interested in different opportunities. A case in point is the sales manager who wants to take on a new product made by a small independent manufacturer but whose own research, engineering, and production people do not wish to see the company's activities expanded or who plan to develop certain other products. The aggressive sales manager may, if his offense to them is sufficient, expect their animosity and opposition. Perhaps, and in a more justifiable sense, they may be aroused because they consider his step precipitate or otherwise inimical to company interests. In short, he who seizes opportunity can by his very action disrupt the atmosphere of contentment and, therefore, may find his upward progress slowed or blocked by those he has disturbed.

An even deeper pitfall awaits the aggressive executive in the form of possible failure. There is always the possibility that the pursuit of an opportunity will prove fruitless or too costly. This is a particularly serious outcome when his embarkation upon the course was opposed by important personages in the organization. They can declare, "We told him so;" they can hold his failure against him; and, if they feel strongly enough and have the power to do so, they can take punitive action. Failure is also an especially serious result when the department or company commitments to the new course of action have been substantial. The executive who takes the opportunity to write a letter of recommendation in support of a subordinate's application for transfer to another department but whose subordinate does not get the job may hide his failure or find it ignored by all save the candidate. But the administrator who sells his superior on a scheme for a multi-million dollar plant expansion which is undertaken just before the beginning of a market recession may fare much worse. Risks to the adventurous leader are often in direct relation to the possible cost of failure to his superiors or group.

Fortuitous or Created

Opportunities, regardless of size, can be classified as fortuitous or created. The former are due to conditions beyond the control of the executive or in which he has no significant determinative influence; in the main, fortuitous opportunities just happen. The latter are in some major sense brought into being by the individual himself. It is impossible to say which is more frequent in business administration. A purely deductive view would suggest that both are more often seen in new or expanding companies. This conclusion is based on the facts that such organizations are operating with less precedent and routine, that their managerial philosophy is still fluid and friendly to innovation, and that their management probably must seize opportunity or fail in its objective to start a new enterprise or to expand. Although either type of opportunity may not be as common in older or more static companies, maturity does not render such concerns completely barren. An aggressive administrator can make his own opportunities. The life of any business may be described as a series of situations, and it is reasonable to expect that in any series of situations there will be some that can be used to advantage. Situations are different conjunctures of the same circumstances or conjunctures of different circumstances and cannot always be met by the routine attack. At least to the extent that they demand unique attention they offer opportunity to do something different, even in the staid company.

How to Recognize an Opportunity

Failure to See Opportunities

Without doubt, most ordinary administrators whose continuing mediocrity stems from their failure to see chances to improve and expand their operation really have some desire to be more successful. Much of their weakness lies in the fact that they do not know an opportunity when they see it. This deficiency may be due to one or more of a number of circumstances. First, the individual's inclination to favor personal safety and peace and/or his natural laziness work a type of hypnosis on him so that he cannot see beyond the routine. Whatever ambition to progress he may have is overwhelmed by the stronger negative force. Second, he may lack the intellectual attributes of the type necessary to analyze a situation or problem in terms of its potentiality. One mental element here missing is imagination.[3] A third circumstance which prevents the administrator from seeing opportunities is his indoctrination. Many an administrator in his formative years as a business executive, if not in all his prior education and experience, has been steeped in the philosophy of conservatism and conformity. He has been trained away from risk taking and so dare not look for opportunity, at least not for situations that are quite uncertain. (In fairness, it should be admitted that this administrator may be retrained, if his blindness is only an acquired trait.) Finally, the administrator may not detect situations which can be turned to advantage because of the confining effect of the organizational environment. Tradition or the direct will of the top administration may dictate that each executive stay on his assigned track. He is quickly checked or diverted if he starts off on a new scent.

Where to Look for Opportunities

Opportunities are where they are found. This truism is significant. It means that the administrator should look for advantageous situations in those places and at those times where they are most likely to occur. However, he should give especial heed to the *principle of problem situations:* in searching for the solution to a specific problem, opportunities are frequently uncovered and occasions to make opportunities are met. A large percentage of opportunities are a by-product of attempted problem-solving. The administrator who remembers this fact will often find a wealth of promising situations at hand.

Changes in Scope of Operation

The specific sources of opportunities are legion. Prominent in any list would be a change in the scope of the operation of the organization. Either expansion or retrenchment create temporary total or partial vacuums. Things are in a state of flux; policies are not yet completely defined; the ultimate assignment of functions is still uncertain; controls are likely to be inappropriate; and power centers in general are upset and shifting. The strategically minded executive can here find a rich lode. Problems with all their possibilities of exploitation are generally more numerous at this time. Possible opposition to his aims of long standing may be off-balance or removed in the changes taking place. The administrator may find himself peculiarly free to pursue new opportunities, since old commitments and loyalties are liquidated or weakened and since innovation is the order of the day.

Opportunities arising from a change in the magnitude of operation can be illustrated by the case of the well established small manufacturer of lawnmowers who is expanding into the toy and sports goods fields and who is, therefore, building two new plants. The controller has been restricted in his activities by a close family ownership clique dedicated to old fashioned personal management. He has been able to do nothing truly important, except to maintain routine accounting service. Well aware of the real functions of a true controller and cognizant of what he could contribute to improve administration and his own status, he is squarely confronted by a major enlargement involving complexities which the family is not able to shrug off or meet with their old procedures. Specifically, he realizes the need for standardized records, uniform reports, budgetary control, and profit planning in a multi-plant management. Expansion now affords him the chance to move forward by impressing upon ownership the necessity for these steps.

Internal Organizational Changes

Internal organizational change is also high in the enumeration of sources of opportunity. This may take various forms, e.g., centralization, decentralization, or redepartmentalization. Every change in organizational structure disturbs some established relationships. The upset situation may offer opportunities to the smart administrator. Old bonds are severed; new people are to be sold and new loyalties to be won; positions are created and need to be filled; personnel is to be reassigned and reallocated; and goals, especially those of departments and other divisions, may be modified or enlarged.

Situations which can be exploited with gain are particularly common in a program of decentralization. Each decentralized unit is likely to be somewhat of an imitation of its parent, paralleling to a goodly degree the home office. It therefore provides a multiplication of jobs, titles and power centers, and a certain proliferation of administrative problems, both of which may present opportunities. In fact, decentralization fairly reeks with opportunity. The mere creation and staffing of more (even if smaller) administrative units creates an empire situation with some controlling mechanism. Many chances for contributions to administrative improvement as well as to personal advancement lie in its tentacles.

Difficult Situations

There is one school of thought which holds that opportunities to help group and self are to be found in facing difficulties. Problems are said to be the source of real opportunity. Are there grounds for the belief? There are substantial reasons to believe the affirmative. On the one hand, problems are inherently motivational forces to all except those who ignore them. They induce thought and action simply because they are obstacles to the courses already charted. The more thinking and doing man undertakes, the more avenues are likely to open up to him for his excursions. On the other hand, problem solving demands both analysis and synthesis—one a process essentially of exploration and the other basically of experimentation. In all aspects of human behavior, these are the steps by which frontiers of opportunity are revealed. Certainly, the traffic manager faced with a carrier strike and the resultant pile-up of goods and stringent complaints of his vendors is forced to consider alternate means of transportation. His problem virtually thrusts upon him the opportunity to revise his mode of shipment.

Administrative Crises

The administrative crisis is related to the problem as a source of opportunity. Something totally unexpected, or of such import that it overwhelmingly attracts attention away from routine functioning and ordinary difficulties, suddenly appears. The crisis may be internal or external. The former is illustrated by the death of a hard-driving young executive, a serious clash between two or more officials of the company, the discovery of a major neglect or sell-out by a trusted employee, or even a strike or lock-out. The latter is seen in many forms also: the beginning of a war or the declaration of an armistice, the passage of legislation by Congress which did not seem to have a chance, a surprising decision by a court or public regulatory body, an important invention or discovery by a competitor, a tactical shift in a competitor's pattern of competition, or an unanticipated negative response by consumers to an expansive advertising campaign. Whatever its form, a crisis calls attention away from the every-day pattern of administration and tends to relegate former aims, at least for a time, to less significant status. New ideas and seemingly fantastic schemes, as well as bold action, become acceptable. Here is opportunity laid bare.

Again a note of warning seems in order. There are superiors who administer intentionally by crisis, and who even stimulate or invent artificial crises as stepping stones. Their motivation may be most noble; they may have in mind nothing but the welfare, honor, and progress of their organizations. Contrariwise, they may be drawn by the most selfish desires to become recognized and rewarded for their successful meeting of near catastrophe. The administrator working under a superior addicted to the crisis technique will do well to watch himself. Apparent opportunities will abound. There are two worrisome questions. Does the superior want his subordinate administrators to chase each chance they see in his milieu? Perhaps he does not, for he knows his organization cannot be run by a group of people chasing butterflies. Then too, if he is a truly venial chief, he may want all the glory from crisis liquidation for himself. Can the subordinate afford not to seize the big opportunities revealed? It may be that the top echelon will hold him negligent for not grasping them and that he may lose face, position, or chance for advancement by not doing so. This is not to belittle administration by crisis. It can be a most effective pattern of management, as the history of certain large American industrial concerns proves. There is no doubt some substance to the belief that a great degree of progress can be made by a business organization through the constant jolting effect of successive crisis situations and the efforts to meet them.

Personal Alliances

Nothing has been said of personal alliances as a source of opportunity. Yet, it is probably one of the most fertile. These alliances arise out of blood kinship, marital relationship, ties of youth, obligations of friendship, indebtedness for past favors, affiliations of a religious, political, fraternal or social nature, recognition of mutual views or interests, and chance contact. All personal alliances have one element in common which can yield opportunities. It is the link between the parties that transcends hard and cold criteria of business values. Therefore, the alert administrator who enjoys a personal alliance has a bond with another or others beyond the basic financial nexus of profitable operation. This may introduce him to situations which he can use to his advantage. The administrator who would avail himself of the openings made possible by a personal alliance should be constantly aware of the danger of taking unfair advantage of personal connections. Such connections, in the possession of unscrupulous persons, may be used by the latter to the detriment of the party with whom they have the alliance or as an unfair weapon against third parties.

Social Drift

Social drift will be cited as a final origin of opportunity in this selective presentation of sources. It is a phenomenon hard to describe. It may be either merely a fad or fashion, or a real secular trend. It signifies an acceptance by the public of something, for instance, a commodity, a service, a system, a method, a procedure, a title, or even a symbol. The strategic administrator should have no trouble in understanding the two major openings offered by this group acceptance. First, there is the greater possibility of his successfully proceeding toward a goal which is currently in favor. A wide-awake office manager now has a much better chance to get an electronic computer setup simply because automation has become the symbol of progress. Second, there is the possibility of using public acceptance, whether it is national or confined merely to the industry or company, figuratively to beat opposition into submission. An old-fashioned treasurer who believes in manual computation and simple machine usage can be persuaded to "go modern" by the argument that everybody wants and many are using high speed data processing equipment.

Here is a chance for some administrative self-hypnosis. The ascertainment and measurement of public approval is very difficult. An administrator may be convinced that the tide is running his way and take the opportunity to swim in the direction he thinks it is moving. In reality, what he sees may be simply a fad. Fads at their peak can be very convincing. He may also lead himself into believing that his pet belief or project has the necessary "public" acceptance just because it has been endorsed by some top business executive, academic authority, research agency, professional society, or trade organization. Such an error is easy to make in a free society where all are at liberty to express their views and where endorsement is a popular form of social behavior. So the ambitious administrator, misguided by partial approval, erroneously thinks he has the opportunity to sell his expensive foreign market development plan. To his chagrin and disadvantage he discovers that his superiors, who know that their particular industry as a whole is still very doubtful of the profit to be made abroad, turn down his proposal decisively. Perhaps he is more to be pitied than blamed, for he is in a measure a victim of the times. He has overestimated the pertinent support of his proposal.

How to Make an Opportunity

Determinants of Action Necessary

Any situation is composed of a number of elements. If the leader can provide one or more of these elements or if he can somehow direct or control them, he can determine to this extent the nature of the situation. In such sense, business administrators can make their own opportunities, or at least contribute to the development of situations which they can use to advantage. The action necessary thus to make the future may be heavy and involved, or it may be nothing more than a minor and simple step. Its dimensions and directions are set by the type of opportunity the leader desires and by the obstacles in his way.

It is impossible to discuss the type of opportunity sought in any definite sense because it will vary greatly with administrator, time, and other circumstances. Suffice it to state that the ambitious executive who wishes to push himself, his department, or his company ahead by tailor-making openings for forward action must define clearly in his own mind and for his own guidance the kind of opportunity he seeks. The executive who does not do this may be disappointed in one of two ways. If he does not have in mind a clear goal in terms of the opportunity sought, he may either find that the opening he has made is far too little for the plan he wishes to effectuate or, quite differently, that he has caused unnecessary disturbance in the organization by over-manipulation.

Contrasting illustrations may serve to place these dangers in sharper perspective. A superintendent of buildings and grounds thinks that all the buildings should be sanded; in fact, he desires this so strongly he constantly reminds the top echelon of administration through direct report and innuendo that it is housed in a disreputable looking structure. But he is disappointed when he is informed that the general manager has approved the sand-blasting of only the administration building. The superintendent has underestimated the proportions of the situation it was necessary for him to create. He apparently has not understood the type of opportunity he should have attempted to make—further agitation of the general manager. At another time, disgusted with the cigarette butts and other debris almost constantly present in the main corridor of the administration building, he "makes so much noise" that the general manager forbids all office personnel to smoke outside of their offices. The white-collar workers are indignant at this curbing of their freedom, and the result is a certain lowering of their morale. The problem could have been solved with much less repercussion if the superintendent had not overplayed the seriousness of the condition. It probably could have been handled with a proper remonstrance to the employees by the general manager and with the provision of necessary receptacles. The superintendent in this case, overestimating the opportunity necessary for him to create, worked too hard and did more harm than good.

As just mentioned, the other determinant of the nature of the action necessary in opportunity making is the obstacles to its creation. These obstacles include unfriendly company policies, opposition by superiors or other influential personnel in the organization, moral and legal principles and sanctions, time, money and facilities, and a host of imponderables. It is a truism that the more formidable the obstacles, the greater or more clever will be the action required. The important point to be emphasized here is the necessity for a proper appraisal of these obstacles. They may be so insignificant as to require only slight nudging or they may be so large as to make the effort to create the opportunity inadvisable. Many an administrator has suffered serious setback to his aspirations for self and organizational advancement by attempting to surmount barriers in a certain way or to attack them at all. Obstacles, especially unknown human ones, have a way of effectively fighting back. Had he correctly gauged their strength, he would have proceeded differently. Furthermore, a realistic view of obstacles may even reveal other opportunities not planned or anticipated.

But the question posed still remains. *How* can an opportunity be created? Different techniques are required under specific circumstances, for there are many variables. Nevertheless, a general formula can be suggested and expressed symbolically in a pseudo-mathematical form. Let O equal the opportunity sought, that is, the immediate goal of the administrator's action; E stand for the elements of the desired situation already positive or under his control; E_1 for the elements to be added; N the known obstacles to the attainment or the bringing under the administrator's control of E_1; and N_1 the unknown obstacles.

$$O = \left(\frac{E}{N}\right) + \left(\frac{E_1}{N_1}\right)$$

This equation, while unworkable mathematically, highlights the real job of the opportunity maker. There are always present some favorable elements about which he will need to do nothing. His real job is cancelling out N by E as far as possible; identifying E_1 and N_1; balancing E_1 and N_1 as far as possible; and then adding the residues, the sum being the measure of the work to be done. He has now reduced the opportunity-making task to its essence. His attack, therefore, well can be that of the strategist. He will proceed to take appropriate steps, as dictated by the circumstances, to liquidate opposition and to introduce necessary missing elements.[4]

The Five Elements of an Opportunity

This line of reasoning raises the necessity for recapitulating the elements that make up a situation which can be turned to advantage—in other words, the components of an opportunity. There are five. One is *critical moment,* the exact time in the development of a situation at which the other necessary elements can best be synthesized. Assume that a director of research wishes to create the opportunity to launch a research project and has obtained his superior's general approval, the requisite authorization for funds, the necessary facilities, and the project director and his staff. One element is missing in this simplified example. It is the answer to the question: When should he launch it? In this case, the propitious moment occurs when the company needs the stimulation of new product development, and so he seizes upon it and announces the project.

Possession of power by someone in the sense that he has the capacity to take or to induce exploitative action is a second element of opportunity. Obviously, no situation can be used to advantage unless someone has the power to seize it and use it. If our administrator with the research project in mind had not been an official, he probably could not either have sought or obtained the authority from the vice president in charge of product development to launch it. In short, he had to have power. In this case it came largely from his position. Opportunities, in the vernacular of the hunter, are birds flying within range.

Next there is *availability of means of exploitation.* While it might be considered so closely related to the possession of power as to be a part of the second element, it is of such import as to demand separate mention. In a practical sense, no opening for action exists unless the means necessary to act exist or are attainable. Had the research director lacked the necessary funds, facilities and personnel, the opportunity for him to start his project could not have been said to exist in reality. He would simply have had an ambition and perhaps seen a need.

A fourth component of opportunity is *absence of effective resistance and interference.* Freedom to decide and to act on the part of the opportunity seeker or maker is essential. If someone or group within or without his organization is sufficiently influential as to block his use of the situation, it loses its promise for him and is not, therefore, an opportunity. The degree of freedom essential is found in a condition of vacuum, an area in which no one has as yet moved;

in a condition of neutrality, a state in which possible inter-
ferers are still open-minded; and in a condition of conversion, an accomplishment of having sold the idea to its
potential enemies. The director of research, having no real
opposition within the company, had the necessary opening
for his desired course of action.

The last element of an opportunity, which might logically
have been treated first, is *possibility of gain* of some type.
This element is so obvious, however, that it scarcely needs
discussion. By definition, an opportunity is a situation which
can be used to advantage. It should be understood that the
gain may be small or large, immediate or ultimate. The important thing, very clearly seen in the created opportunity,
is that there be some expectation—that rewards be recognized
as possible. Certainly, the research director saw or sensed
some promise of gain to himself or his group or he would not
have worked to create the opportunity.

Can administrators at all levels make or help to make their
own opportunities? The answer would seem to be in the
affirmative. Any administrator has some influence over pertinent circumstances. "Opportunities to make opportunity"
exist in most organizations. The hypothesis, however, that
the ability to create favorable situations is greater in the
echelon of middle management seems reasonable. It at once
has a measure of irresponsibility and freedom not enjoyed
by top administration and a degree of power to explore and
act not possessed by the lower level supervisors. Perhaps
belief in this proposition is the reason that so many corporation presidents look to their department heads for dynamic
action and complain when it is not forthcoming.

Hints for Exploitative Action[5]

Opportunity exploitation is one of the many aspects of human
behavior. It can be done wisely or unwisely; it can be under-

taken honorably or dishonorably. There are no set rules which, if followed, will assure the wisest and most honorable action; rather the best use of opportunities demands that the administrator be truly dynamic. However, common sense suggests certain guidelines. The following list of hints may be useful.

1. Remember that the exploitation of an opportunity will involve moral values, and that the truly strategic leader will take the ethical course.
2. Be the first to seize good opportunities.
3. Examine dubious opportunities and, if they look too uncertain, let someone else take the first steps in their cultivation.
4. Remember that others may be attempting to use the same situation; there may be advantage in "taking them over" or joining them at some point, as far as fair play will permit.
5. Live dangerously with good sense; take risks in proportion to expected gains.
6. Remain flexible; compromise and redirect when feasible and ethical.
7. Manipulate fairly before you fight, but fight if the stakes are high enough.
8. Be willing to progress by steps and build sub-opportunities into a whole.
9. Leave an avenue of retreat; it may make possible an effective and interim tactic or provide a way of saving something if things go wrong.
10. While pursuing the main chance, be alert for new openings; the foment may reveal by-products in the form of other opportunities.
11. Get as much publicity for your intentions and efforts as will further them.

The foregoing list of hints may suggest the advocation of what is commonly and distastefully known as opportunism,[6] but nothing could be further from the intention of this work. The legitimate seeking, making and seizing of opportunity, which is the subject of the chapter, is something very different. Opportunism implies a certain unprincipled operation. An opportunist is popularly seen as one who takes the course of expediency dictated by the moment and primarily for his advantage alone. The proper administrative exploitation of opportunity means the pursuit of possibilities without the abandonment of moral principle. It is directed at gain for the organization and administrator, not just for the latter. This distinction places no stigma on personal ambition, but it frowns upon the butterfly and totally selfish gambles of the self-centered executive.

The real strategist will realize that, despite all the good maxims, he may possess or develop a pattern of operation peculiar to himself because of his own ability, character, and personality. For example, if he is a brilliant, hard-driving but pleasant individual, he can perhaps use a bold, domineering approach. His methods may be unique also for a reason quite outside himself. He may be well aware of the fact that he is one of a group and that he is always under the compulsion to maintain certain relations with it or various of its numbers. The nature of these relations can be an important influence in shaping his actual modus operandi. For instance, if he wants his associates, or any level of them, to be kept in the dark, he will be constrained from revealing plans and actions.

Conclusion

Two courses beckon the administrator, the routine and the dynamic. Should he choose the former, he may be able to live by the book peacefully and uninterruptedly. If he chooses the latter (and the true strategic leader will do so), he will try to find in promising situations that which is profitably new or expansive for his organization. His life may be troubled but eventful. The dynamic course is marked by milestones of opportunities exploited.

The purpose of this chapter has been to emphasize the necessity of, as well as to suggest avenues and means for, departing from the placidity of routine administration. Underlying the whole presentation has been the belief that progress in management, and even in career, is largely dependent upon the use of situations which promise gain. The viewpoint has even been emphasized that, if fortune does not lay favorable circumstances in the lap of the administrator, he will do well to bestir himself and make or help create his own opportunities. Frequent reference to ethical conduct has been made to set the moral limits to the exploitation of opportunity.

BUSINESS SITUATIONS FOR ROLE-PLAYING

SITUATION VI
Exploitation of Opportunity
ABLE ZARCO AND BROTHERS, INC.

A. Scene.   A paint manufacturing company. The office of the President in which a meeting is taking place between the President and the Vice President in charge of Sales.

B. Players.   1. President: Mr. Everett Goodsmart, dynamic executive, long with the company, self-made, and somewhat impatient of conservative subordinates who cannot see opportunity or who are afraid of it.

2. Vice President in charge of Sales: Mr. Philip P. Provost, also a long time official of the company who has been in his present position for eighteen years and who is to retire in two years; a slow-moving individual motivated primarily by consideration of safety and surety for self and company.

C. Situation.   1. Upon the recommendation of the Board of Directors, the stockholders have recently approved a merger with a national toy manufacturer. The President, in his usual enthusiasm, is anxious to move ahead with an aggressive market program. The Vice President in charge of Sales has been opposed to this type of new venture, which he believes will merely create more problems.

2. The President is trying to point out the opportunities offered by this current expansion into new lines.

D. Assignment. 1. Select two individuals to act out the above roles. Try to match them with personality types of the two officials.

2. Have the players step out of the room before they begin; then instruct the group to pay especial attention to how well the job of persuasion is done by the President. Tell the members of the group that they will be called upon to comment when the performance is finished.

NOTES

1. The literature of business administration is quite silent on the exploitation of opportunity. The authors have, however, drawn considerable inspiration for their treatment of the subject from a work written by Mr. RALPH J. CORDINER, President, General Electric Company: *New Frontiers for Professional Managers* (New York: McGraw-Hill Book Company, Inc., 1956).
2. Some interesting comments on the new administrator's use of opportunity are contained in EDWIN HASKELL SCHELL, *Administrative Proficiency in Business* (New York: McGraw-Hill Book Company, Inc., 1936), pp. 51-58.
3. Imagination as an attribute important to the perceiving of an opportunity is recognized by DAVID G. MOORE, "Managerial Strategies" in W. LLOYD WARNER and NORMAN H. MARTIN (eds.), *Industrial Man: Businessmen and Business Organizations* (New York: Harper & Brothers, Publishers, 1959), p. 219.

4. It is interesting to note that Barnard in discussing the "Theory of Opportunism," which sees opportunity in different dimensions than the authors, does identify, however, the strategic factor as ". . . the one whose control, in the right form, at the right place and time, will establish a new system or set of conditions which meets the purpose." CHESTER I. BARNARD, *The Functions of the Executive* (Cambridge, Mass.: Harvard University Press, 1956), p. 203.

5. This exploitation is consistent with the general behavior pattern of the strategic administrator. As Dimock puts it, "He [the executive] must live by his wits, his competitive instincts, his understanding of social forces, and his ability as a leader. He does not operate in a fixed environment." MARSHALL EDWARD DIMOCK, *The Executive in Action* (New York: Harper & Brothers, Publishers, 1945), pp. 65-66.

The great breadth of possibility in opportunity exploitation may be indicated in PETER F. DRUCKER, *Managing for Results* (New York: Harper & Row, Publishers, 1964), pp. 203-217. His analysis therein of the kinds of opportunities is particularly suggestive to the authors of this book.

6. The concept of opportunism used here is not to be confused with the meaning of opportunism advanced by Barnard in his "Theory of Opportunism." He applies the term much more broadly. BARNARD, *op. cit.*, p. 201.

CHAPTER 7

Maintaining Organizational Peace

> "There is no such phenomenon as a completely peaceful company. The company has goals, policies, plans and procedures, and their fullest possible attainment or utilization demands smooth coordination and cooperation among all its members. Since these may be interrupted by trouble between any two or more of the company family, the issue of internal peace is not to be ignored by realistic management."

WHEREVER man is gathered together for any appreciable period of time, he is almost certain to clash, in a greater or lesser degree, with his associates. Such is his nature and culture that disagreement, friction, and conflict are practically inevitable. His instincts, his intellect, and his free will, as well as the less natural features of his character such as acquired values and prejudices, predispose him to trouble.[1]

The Approach

The executive or the worker in the business concern is no exception to this categorization of man as a troublemaker. There is no such phenomenon as a completely peaceful company. War—hidden or open, cold or hot—is virtually always present in some measure, for personnel of the organization are members of the human race, no more or less. This is not to imply that the company is to be viewed as a hornet's nest in which each person is busily engaged in buzzing around to sting the man at the next desk or bench. It is rather to emphasize the fact that man cannot work long together in complete and continuing harmony with those about him.

Peace is a very real issue within the company. The contrary state can interfere with the attainment of its goals and with policies, plans, procedures and methods attuned to these objectives, the fullest possible pursuit or utilization of which demands smooth coordination and cooperation among all its members. Since these may be interrupted by trouble between any two or more of the company family, the issue of internal peace is not to be ignored by alert management.

What really is peace within the company? The concept is difficult to define, for it is a condition which to the practical mind means the absence of conflict. The ordinary businessman, when asked if "things are peaceful" in his company or division of a company, is most likely to answer in terms of the existence or non-existence of trouble. It seems necessary to fall back upon the philosopher for a positive definition of peace within the business organization. As defined by one of the great Christian philosophers, peace is the "tranquility of order."[2] Peace, then, would seem to be tied up with order. Complete peace may be said to exist within a company or a portion thereof when human relations are such as to permit the greatest degree of orderly functioning possible, that is, the highest degree of coordination and cooperation among employees and officials attainable.

There are undoubtedly many ways of getting at the subject of peace within the company. However, the approach which seems to promise most in terms of objectivity is the study of the antithesis of peace, namely, *conflict*.[3] In the first place, it is more easily identifiable than peace, because it is generally a somewhat unique phenomenon. Even in this day of social confusion, few companies suffer from conflict as the usual state of affairs among their personnel. In the second place, the prevention and liquidation of conflict is a real aim of business administrators concerned with peace in their own ranks. In this presentation, conflict is conceived as the advanced state of disagreement wherein the parties which are involved, as groups or individuals, no longer can work together to a reasonable extent.

There are many types of conflict within a company and several ways of classifying them. Conflicts may be distinguished on the basis of breadth of involvement, i.e., clashes between labor and management, disputes between units and between units and individuals within the organization, and trouble between individuals in it.[4] They may be categorized as of major or minor import to smooth operation of the concern. They may be grouped into avoidable and inevitable classes, with the idea that some can be prevented and others not. They may be divided on the basis of their duration as old or new. They may even be grouped as open or hidden, depending upon the extent to which associates, including management, know of them.

Information as to Conflict

The Problem of Detection

The first problem which confronts the business administrator with respect to conflict within his own organization is the detection of it.[5] Obviously, he has no difficulty in learning of conflicts of major import which have erupted into the open. He is generally made all too aware of them, for when a real clash comes it will sooner or later end up on his desk with considerable noise. However, there are two instances in which he may be effectively insulated from what is happening. One is during the period of fomentation when either no serious impasse exists or when associates and friends of the warring parties are still able to effect some kind of reconciliation or truce between them. The other is in the case of covert conflict, the type which for one reason or other just does not come to the executive's attention or at least is long buried.

Both of these blind spots can be of real significance. Knowledge of impending trouble may enable the company official under whose cognizance it falls to take preventive action. For example, if the company president knows that the chief auditor from the central office and a branch accountant are in serious disagreement over accounting procedures, he may be able to forestall it by clarifying instructions, strengthening the hand of one, or even reassigning one or both. Information as to a hidden conflict also may be of great value to the proper official. It can enable him to take the advantageous position or action necessary for its quiet liquidation. Undercover conflicts are frequently of an especially serious type, because they may continue for months or years with a resulting long-term debilitating effect on the efficiency of one or both of the parties involved or on that of the people dependent upon them within the organization.

What can the business administrator do to increase his sensitivity to conflict? Clearly, he can do more than just depend on a formal reporting system, which is too often almost the sole source used by the non-strategic executive. First and foremost, he can be on the job as much as possible. His knowledge of what is transpiring in his company or unit will generally diminish in direct proportion to his geographical distance from his office. It has been remarked facetiously that relatively little bad information of company affairs filters down to Fort Lauderdale. Another helpful action is to circulate through his company; nothing is quite as revealing as personal observation.

A third way to increase sensitivity to conflict is to develop and use feedback devices. There are a multiplicity of these devices, but all are really two-way communication channels.[6] Still a further positive step is to cultivate non-hierarchical sources of information. If this is done without bribery or other unethical influence and discreetly, it can be a perfectly proper device to gain a fuller picture. He who neglects this informal avenue is not making full use of his legitimate learning opportunities. Regardless, however, of his specific actions to obtain information about the conflict within his domain, the administrator should make every effort to develop an alertness to trouble. This will grow with an expanding and deepening knowledge of human nature. He should address himself, as should all leaders of men, to a life-long study of this most interesting phenomenon.

The Use of Informers

Deeply ingrained in the American character is an antipathy toward informers and their use. Rash indeed is the company official who makes wide practice of using them. The stigma attached to them is certain in substantial measure to rub off onto him. Of course, there is a great difference between keeping employee pipelines open and having informers. The former implies "family relations" within the company; the latter, the use of spies, one of whose functions it is to bear tales to the top. In actual practice, the distinction between these two lines of action demands a substantial degree of moral and political sensitivity on the part of the executive. His operation, to remain out of the espionage classification, must be unsolicited in the sense that he does not actively seek information from employees. It must be open in the sense that he is receptive to confidences from all. It must be non-rewarding in the sense that he does not give rewards for reports on others beyond the proper recognition of official communications from competent inferiors.

Above all else, the obtaining of information from subordinates as to conflict within the ranks should not, except in the case of direst necessity, be sought by pressure on possible informers. The executive does have the perfect right, which he can exert without fear of bad human relations and which he should exercise in the interest of smooth administration, to question his subordinates about trouble in their respective jurisdictions. But what he should not do, with any degree of regularity if he is to maintain the highest respect of his group, is to ask for, or, even worse, to attempt to squeeze out information from someone who has no direct responsibility for the conduct of the person or persons in conflict. An example may sharpen this point. A district sales manager habitually sends in a heavy expense account. The assistant treasurer regularly raises objections and openly doubts its validity. The district sales manager counters by telling his associates that the assistant treasurer uses a company car over the weekends for private purposes. A running feud is born. The chief draftsman lives in the house adjacent to the home of the assistant treasurer. The treasurer of the company is well aware of the size of the district sales manager's expense accounts, but he has no direct means of checking on his assistant's misappropriation of company property. The temptation might well arise to ask the chief draftsman, especially since he is a loyal company employee who can be easily pressured into "cooperation," if he has seen the assistant treasurer with a company car on the weekends. To yield to this easy method of ascertaining the facts would, if known to the company personnel, help brand him as an individual who "goes behind your back to find out things about you." Little that an executive can do will make him more unpopular than to learn the facts by this means.

Knowledge of the Anatomy of Conflict

In addition to the necessity for learning the facts of the case in the interests of maintaining leadership stature, there is another reason for the executive to be fully informed. It is even more strategic in import. Conflicts, although they may differ from each other in many aspects, do have a certain common anatomy. Every conflict has an underlying causation; a period of fomentation; an immediate causation which precipitates it from mere friction into deadlock and even embattlement; two or more parties who may be individuals, informal groups, or established entities; a point of crisis; and a coefficient of attraction to people not directly involved in it. Knowledge of the essential parts of a particular case not only can assist the executive in appraising its seriousness and import, but it also can give him valuable data as to where it is most vulnerable to attack.

To explore and appraise fully the opportunities afforded the executive by a knowledge of the components of any given conflict complex would require very considerable space. Suffice it here to say that the executive concerned with handling a conflict should do his best to isolate and explore them. He is almost certain to detect at one or more points a facet or facets which will be useful.

A brief survey of the strategic possibilities for the administrator which arise out of an anatomical knowledge of conflict is revealing. Perhaps the basic causes lie in some company or department weakness such as ignorance on the part of one or both parties, lack of adequate communication, unjust policies and practices, or simply ineffective leadership. These are defects which executive action can decisively move to correct. There is always the possibility that during the evolutionary stage the parties have done something, such as false accusation or indiscreet criticism, which the administrator can use to make them "draw in their horns" and stop fighting. The conflict may not yet have been precipitated and the immediate issue or situation which could do this, such as a promotion of one party when two unfriendly department heads have been bucking for it, may be delayed or avoided by the administrator. If the crisis has been precipitated, the immediate cause may reflect the real reason for the trouble (e.g., a niggardly company policy of recognizing and rewarding dynamic unit executives) and thus it may reveal to the administrator the remedy for prevention of future similar conflicts. The nature of the disputants and their position in the company power complex may dictate the manner in which they can be most effectively handled. A partially Americanized janitorial supervisor may be calmed down by a show of higher authority, whereas the sensitive son of the general manager may require a much more subtle approach as, for example, appeal to his family pride. The point of crisis—be it approaching, present or past—may imply the proper timing for executive interference, whether the problem is dispute over the use of brooms or over the most lucrative sales territory. If the crisis is a long way off the official may have no immediate urgency to act; if it is at hand, he may be required to move promptly; or if it has already occurred, he may find it wise to wait and see whether or not the problem wears itself out. The degree to which the conflict is known in the plant, company or outside world, as well as the nature of public reaction to it, may indicate the severity of action for the executive to take. For example, if a conflict involving an office manager and his female employees over his prejudiced attitude toward them becomes widely known in the plant, the general manager may find it wise to discharge him without further to do; but, if this trouble is known only to the four women in his office and perhaps a few of their associates, it may be sufficient in company interests to transfer him to an all-male operation.

It is well to remember that, although each of the component aspects of conflict has its own peculiar significance to the administrator, the basic causes are of most importance to him. It is against these that his principal effort normally should be directed, for, unless they are removed, circumvented or nullified in influence, similar conflicts may continue to appear. The repetition of conflict, in addition to sapping his time and energy, commonly has the unfortunate effect of crystallizing sides, enhancing issues, deepening personal wounds, and glorifying participation. Certainly then, the executive should make a special effort to ascertain and analyze the fundamental causation of any conflict which he must handle. He will find that the forces deeply underlying advanced disagreement are many. They include real differences or felt differences such as exist between stereotypes (e.g., labor and management who usually think they must disagree) as well as actual or imagined differences over objectives, methods and procedures, time, democratic involvement, quantity and quality of performance, and relative rewards. He will also discover that conflicts proceed from a host of much more subtle forces which may be summarized under the heads of personality clash, personal dislike, and professional jealousy.

The point being emphasized is that the executive can learn much about the proper handling of a conflict by studying its essential parts. If he takes the pains to consider it as having, in the language of the production engineer, "standard parts," he will find it much easier to diagnose the trouble, make the necessary repairs, and re-establish the smooth running of his human engine which, after all, is not an inaccurate description for the company or any combination of people within it who must work together.

What to Do About Conflict

Speed and Decisiveness

Once conflict becomes known to the executive, the question arises as to what he should do about it. The dynamic but inexperienced or rash administrator may often rush into the fray to settle matters, whether by domination, compromise or integration.[7] In this manner he seeks to re-establish order and discharge his sense of personal responsibility. In many cases, prompt action is best. However, there are circumstances when it may be well for him to wait: for example, the information he has may simply be gossip, the conflict of little consequence, or the issue one best not noticed by the executive. And then, of course, waiting may eliminate the necessity for any action, because the conflict may be settled by the warring parties themselves or by other third parties, or because it may simply wear itself down until it no longer exists or is of significance.[8]

But, no matter what the speed and decisiveness of his action, the executive should observe one caution. He should learn as many as possible of the facts of the case before taking steps to settle the matter. No one can look quite as foolish as the administrator who assumes a stand but then discovers that there really is no dispute or that the side he favors is in error. Suppose, for example, that a division head discovers that certain standard operating procedures are being disregarded and the employees responsible for the activities carried on by these procedures are seriously divided in their opinion of the value of the procedures which have in effect been abandoned. If the division administrator acts to reinstate the earlier procedures, will he not be compromised when he learns that these operating procedures have been changed by higher authority so that division personnel have no alternative but to act in accord with the directive changing the procedures?

Maintenance of Objectivity

One of the difficult things for the executive to do in settling a conflict is to maintain objectivity. His purpose should be to see to it that the conflict is settled on the basis of facts, and this is not always easy to do. To begin with, one can note that such action may involve the executive's taking the side held by a person or group against whom he has a decided prejudice or whom he thoroughly dislikes. For example, the senior department head, who has fought his way up without anyone's aid, may find that the union steward, whom he considers an abomination, is right in his dispute with a foreman over the foreman's use of obscenity in supervision. Yet the necessity for assuring settlement on the basis of truth may involve more and be even harder than this agreeing with the enemy. It may require taking a view or decision unfriendly to the supervisor's personal interests, as might be the case when facts show his trusted clerk to be the dishonest party in a dispute with the cafeteria manager over the handling of coffee money. Even this may not be the most difficult position in which to maintain objectivity, which is so necessary to justice. There is the possibility that the delicate situation may arise in which interests of the department or company are contrary to the just course. A case in point is found in the dispute involving a number of supervisors who were promised good promotions in the lush days of defense contracts, providing they would remain on the job and not demand bonuses, but who now are in open rebellion against the company because it is delaying promotions due to uncertain economic conditions. For a particular administrator to support the cautious company would be to protect its interests at this time, although it might be an open disregard of a company agreement with its personnel.

Respect for Justice

The maintenance of administrative honor demands that the executive endeavor to settle disputes according to the dictates of justice. This is easier said than done for reasons other than the difficulty of his maintaining an objective viewpoint.

Concepts of justice unfortunately vary among people. Even though he may correctly believe in absolute standards of right and wrong, not only may the executive in a particular situation be in doubt as to the course proper from the moral viewpoint, but one or both sides, their sympathizers, his colleagues or even top management may disagree with the fairness of his decision. Nevertheless, he must take a definite stand in many such conflicts, and he can do no better than decide them according to "his own lights." This may not please the disputants, and their supporters, his associates, or company officialdom, but it is the honorable course and, therefore, the one which in the long run may be expected to gain him the most respect from his associates. There is great defensive strength in the position of having done what one believes to be right.

Suppose, however, that the apparently just decision by the executive may be one highly detrimental to the interests of the company. Assume even that, as in the case of promised wage and salary raises, it might seriously endanger, if not force, the company to the wall. What strategy is here dictated? Shall "justice" be done at all costs? The decision probably would be taken, in most cases if the company had the power, not to fulfill its immediate obligations and commitments on the theory that its interests transcend those of the individuals working for it. If such a decision were made, the company, as an entity apart from the aggrieved parties, should attempt for ethical and human relations reasons to do at least two things. First it should explain to its personnel, and if essential the public, the necessity for the unpleasant action. Secondly, it should pledge itself to ultimate justice, that is, to take all compensatory steps possible, as, for example, in the case of the promised wage and salary raise, other rewards now or in the future. This pledge should always be most realistic, for successive failures to keep the company's word will prove disastrous to any good morale its employees may retain and even to outside public relations.

When an administrator finds it necessary to reverse company policy or pledges in the solution of an internal conflict, he should pay especial attention to the matter of timing. It is a well recognized phenomenon that reactions are partly the result of the timing of the stimuli. Common sense, then, would suggest that the negative reaction to reneging can be decreased by proper timing. Unfortunately, there is no comprehensive formula to cover the matter. The administrator must play largely by ear. On the one extreme, he will be faced with conflicts which can best be settled by an abrupt reversal of the company stand. This is illustrated in the situation wherein the real root of the trouble is company policy itself, as when two of his department heads are in conflict because the existing rules and regulations regarding the borrowing of office equipment favor one department greatly and unfairly over the other. Here his prompt decisive action will do much to remove the cause of the conflict as well as to add to the stature of the administrator and company in being willing to admit and rectify error. On the opposite extreme, he will be confronted with disputes which he can best handle by a slow change in company stand—a shift at a rate of speed which will permit the idea of innovation to be absorbed gradually and negative reaction perhaps to be "talked to death." For example, the internal dispute over the number of secretaries in various offices might be handled by the creation of a secretarial pool. The loss of private secretaries would undoubtedly cause a clamor among the executives of the company. If the move were started by the establishment of a typing pool, expanded into a central file division, and finally culminated with the creation of a true secretarial pool, the aggrieved executives might become accustomed to the new organization, having gotten most of the venom out of their systems without ever uniting into effective opposition.

Action Not Always Wise

Despite protestations in preceding paragraphs, the line of thought thus far may have implied strongly that the management of a company should always act to settle significant internal conflicts. This implication is not intended. There are numerous situations in which interference may not be wise. A few of the major instances may be illustrated. The executive may simply deem it too dangerous to interfere; perhaps one of the warring parties is an indispensable person who will brook no reconciliation. The executive may in another case decide to use the perfectly valid technique of ignoring the trouble. He may feel that, if unrecognized officially, it will somehow dissipate itself, as may happen when two foremen get into a dispute over an isolated aggression by one of them. In still another set of circumstances, he may decide that the eruption or continuation of the fight will serve his purposes. A conflict between two top engineers over laboratory space if allowed to erupt and/or drag on, may help convince the finance committee that a new building is needed. A final illustration of instances when the executive may decide to remain aloof involves his effort to settle the dispute by indirection. He may want to rely upon the good influence of a third party, perhaps an old and respected colleague of the disputants; or he may wish to use the committee approach and therefore may allow the issue to go to some company grievance settling group.

Irrespective, however, of the reason for remaining aloof from conflict, the administrator who does so should maintain a certain poise. If he does not he may suffer an important loss of face. It is evident that he should be calm, noncommittal, and serious in his demeanor. Should he not be calm, his public may quickly develop the idea that he wants to interfere but is somehow being restrained. This may be interpreted as leadership weakness on his part. Should he express opinions on the trouble, he may automatically destroy the very attitude he is trying to take, that of aloofness. Should he be humorous or disparaging in his attitude toward the issue at stake or the parties involved, he may appear foolish or cold.

Stimulation of Conflict

There are administrators who go even further than simply "staying out" of conflict in their domain. They are of the Machiavellian breed, and attempt to encourage or create conflict in an effort to further certain ends. The more timid or unimaginative of this stripe may employ the device but occasionally. In order, for example, to clear the way for their own advancement, they may manipulate a rival or enemy into a battle with someone else, from which fray he will probably emerge with a stigma sufficient to block his promotion. The bolder and more visionary, if even less ethical, character may seek to make conflict within his company or department a general condition, so that he can operate to his advantage within the attendant confusion. There is strong suspicion that this technique is not unknown to some top administrators who see it as a means of creating artificial opportunities for their leadership as well as a device for keeping potential opposition unorganized or off balance.

Whatever the course taken by the executive in his treatment of a conflict, he must always bear in mind that his chances of remaining untouched by it are slight. He does have the immediate responsibility for it as he does for everything which happens in the company or part thereof under his management. And it may be that the conflict is fundamentally or immediately, partly or fully, the result of his action or omission, or of company policy or practice. It is always good common sense for him to consider and approach any conflict under his aegis with a bit of soul-searching. Much guidance can be gained from the correct answer to the self-addressed question, "Am I or the company involved in this dispute, and, if so, how far?" The executive who realizes, for instance, that his two division chiefs are fighting over an issue because his or the company's instructions on a certain matter are not clear, is at a distinct vantage point from which to settle the fracas.

Constructive Possibilities of Conflict

No essay on the strategy of peace could claim to be realistic without some mention of the fact that conflicts are not necessarily unfriendly to company interests. To the degree that they, or their developmental stages of disagreement and friction, engender greater or more intelligent action within the organization, conflicts may be a constructive force for progress.[9] A case in point is to be seen in the corporation whose sales and credit departments are continuously engaged in the battle over sales volume versus credit integrity. The sales manager has his annual goal set at $10,000,000. The credit manager is equally determined not to grant credit to the 15 or 20 per cent of the existing customers whom he considers poor risks. The situation possesses distinct possibilities of company gain. The sales manager, realizing the credit brake on him but bent upon his over-all sales volume, may seek better customers. His adversary in the credit department, happy at the opportunity of improving his portfolio of short-term paper, may be more willing to extend liberal credit to the safer purchasers. The company should emerge the winner.

Differences in the concepts of conflict and competition must be carefully distinguished. It is a generally accepted belief that rivalry is a powerful motivating force in most forms of human endeavor. Individuals or groups within the company may work harder and more efficiently in an effort to beat their associates. Usually the goal is some reward— a fatter pay envelope, promotion, recognition in company publication, or any of a long list of other material or psychic gains. The point to be emphasized is that such drive to excel does not necessarily involve conflict, at least as defined in this paper. Conflict means that situation wherein the disputants will not work together to the degree to which higher management deems reasonable. It signifies a breakdown in coordination and cooperation to a serious degree. Although a given conflict may possess it in some measure and although striving to outdo each other may lead to conflict, competition in itself can be, and commonly is, a healthy intra-company phenomenon, simply the effort on the part of various of its employees and segments to excel their bench and desk mates. Accordingly, competition so conceived can flourish within coordination and cooperation and by increasing the amount and quality of output contribute to successful operation. In short, conflict, although occasionally productive of some company good, is generally negative in effect; whereas competition, occasionally a source of conflict, is in essence the drive to do more and better.[10]

A Positive Program for Peace

Internal Peace—An Organizational Norm

Peace within the organization may be seen as a norm. It is the condition generally desired. It is a condition which, when disturbed, usually sets in motion forces which attempt to re-establish it, and to borrow phraseology from economics, may even be described as a point of equilibrium around which organizational behavior fluctuates. People join themselves together into a company for some common or individual goal which they believe can be obtained or best reached only in association with others. Although the goal is sometimes completely predatory in that an individual associates himself with an organization solely to exploit his fellow workers, this is certainly not the rule in business. So deep generally is the desire and need for peace in order to make the most profit, obtain the highest salary or wage, enjoy the best promotion, or have the steadiest employment, etc., that the company family will almost always resent conflict and show its feelings in efforts to obtain and assure peace.

Strategic Principles of the Positive Program

Despite the fact that peace is a norm within the organization, it cannot be taken for granted. The leader will find that it is a goal which challenges his strategic abilities. The establishment and maintenance of internal peace is a task which varies in nature with a host of circumstances, such as the kind of the company or department, time, type of employees, and external pressures. It is nowhere the same problem. However, there are certain strategic tenets which, if understood and applied by the leader, will help him achieve peace. The leader is the instrument by which the organization attains order. His conduct of the management function is the real key. As is true in all human behavior, he is confronted with "right and wrong" courses of action which will either bring the order of tranquility or the disorder of conflict to his organization.

Since peace is as much a state of mind within the organization as it is a condition of employee relationships, a first tenet to be suggested is that the *leader should consciously endeavor to create an atmosphere of harmony among his people.* The influence of environment is very great upon the conduct of the members of a group. Imitation is a powerful human urge, and potential trouble-makers can be prevented from becoming real trouble-makers by assuring them a working environment in which their associates generally behave peaceably. Then also, most employees will lack the initiative to break the peace barrier where peace is strongly established. It takes a rather unusually courageous, misguided, or motivated individual to embark upon a pattern of conduct contrary to that prevailing. If he does so, he becomes a belligerent in a peaceful world, and thus he makes himself in a sense a social outcast. To be a focal point of trouble invites disapproval in the peaceful atmosphere, and, as the psychologists of another generation correctly emphasized, one of the great instincts or drives of man is for social approval. The *Law of Contagion* is operative in the peaceful atmosphere; peace does beget peace.[11]

It is much easier to expound upon the necessity for the atmosphere of peace as a means of attaining internal order than it is to identify the steps by which the desired feeling can be generated. Among these steps is the establishment by the leader of the fact that he expects peace and that the premium conduct in his organization is that of harmony and cooperation. He may implant this idea in the minds of his people in various ways—by his own example of calmness, by his reward of peacemakers, and by his decisive action against trouble-makers. Among the steps which the leader may take to assure a peaceful tone is also something much more subtle: the constant surveillance of all aspects of the operation under his cognizance to isolate quickly and remedy promptly any developments which may upset or seriously irritate his employees. An example of this step will help to clarify it. A heavy equipment manufacturing company has received many complaints about certain features of new machines which it has recently sold its customers. As a result, the president commands all of them to be recalled and the faulty features to be corrected. To assure this being done promptly and well, he orders a task force of his best engineers and production people to the job. It means lucrative overtime for them. The president, who desires the maintenance of the greatest degree of peace in his organization, recognizes the possibility of jealousy arising out of this situation in which some of his employees will earn more money than others. He immediately moves to inform his whole organization of the urgency of satisfying the customers, and to make it clear to those unassigned overtime that they will not be forgotten in future demands for overtime.

Even in the most peaceful environment, inter-personal, inter-group, and person to group trouble will occasionally appear. If it is allowed to go unsettled, it may grow into something larger and dangerous to the whole fabric of peace. As peace begets peace, so conflict breeds conflict. This leads to the suggestion of a second tenet for the leader who desires harmony. *He must provide a system of what the engineer might term "blow-off valves."* This system should be considered as a safeguard to peace and prior in use to the utilization of what has long been called a grievance procedure. It involves the provision of opportunity for complaining individuals and groups to rid themselves of their irritations by expressing them. There are many of these so-called valves. Top management should let it be known that every employee can express himself, if he does so in proper manner, to his supervisor without fear of reprisal. A formal suggestion program may be established to invite constructive contributions. Training conferences may be held for the ventilating of feelings. Committees may be utilized for the exchange of views and the compromise of points of difference. Mass involvement in a real or pseudo-social meeting may be used as the occasion for friendly discussion. The assignment of individuals with high intelligence, critical attitude, and strong initiative to positions challenging their abilities may be made to siphon off their energy and use their ability to the fullest. Even the encouragement of personnel to attend formal university courses may prove a safety valve. The gist of the thought here expounded is that much trouble can be dissipated by permitting and facilitating the expression of complaints and criticism and the rechanneling of thoughts and energies. Not all trouble demands judicial decision, and to the extent that it can be handled outside of the grievance machinery it tends to remain less belligerent. Moreover, the power of the leader to adjudicate is not called into use so often, and it is thus better retained for the bigger issue.

Of course, there will always be an irreducible number of conflicts in every organization which cannot be settled except by proper adjudication. *The peace-minded administrator must provide for a "judicial process."* For him this is the third tenet in building a positive program for peace. The process may be kept very direct. Immediate supervisors may be given the power to adjudge, so that, for example, a foreman faced with the question of who has lost some tools can decide the issue himself. It may be involved and complicated, requiring referral to designated special personnel or bodies,[12] so that a dispute between two major departments regarding capital equipment outlay for the current year must be submitted to the finance committee for settlement. Regardless of the simplicity or complexity of the judicial process, it must contain certain elements if it is best to be used in the interest of organizational peace. First, someone must have the responsibility for settling the dispute, otherwise more trouble and ill will may be generated by the frustration of trying to get a decision which no one seems willing to make. Second, all possible complainants and defendants must know who has the final authority for decision making and the general procedure by which the dispute reaches him. This implies the definition within the company of the chain of command and the education of all concerned to it. Third, the organization must have criteria for settling its internal disputes. Just as a court of law has its statutes, the common law and precedent to guide it, so the executive or body before whom company disputes come must have something by which to judge them. These criteria may be many and varied, but they are necessary in the interests of that objectivity which is essential to justice. Among these criteria are moral principles as well as practical considerations necessary to the legitimate welfare of the company such as its public relations, competitive position, and profit. Whether or not the criteria used should be made known to the disputants is a consideration of strategy and must be decided in each case. Probably, however, the disputants will have a greater feeling of having received justice and will retain less motivation for making further trouble if, at least at the time of the settlement, the criteria upon which it is made are revealed to them.

It is suggested as a final tenet for the leader to follow in his positive program for organizational peace that *he utilize sub-leaders in the role of "apostles of peace."* Even though peace is contagious, it is inherently an unstable state of affairs because of personal differences among those who make up an organization and the pressure of a variety of other internal and external factors. It needs constant guarding and stimulating. The leader cannot be everywhere at all times doing all things nor should he be if he wishes to maintain the dignity inherent in his office. He needs sub-leaders at all managerial posts who are eternally on guard against friction and conflict among their workers, who are willing and able to settle as many disputes as possible without fanfare and at as early and low a stage as possible, and who continuously by precept and example promote the cause of working together.

Therefore, it is provident for the top administration to assign, as far as possible, to all levels of management those who, while remaining dynamic, see eye to eye with him on the basic relation between harmony and efficiency. Yet this is not all that is necessary. Like all human beings, subordinate administrators may lose their faith, at least momentarily, because of immediate pressures. The office manager who starts out in his job thoroughly in tune with the viewpoints of his superiors may find that his supervisory problems come to undermine his dedication to the cause of harmony. He may need occasionally or even constantly to be resold the doctrine of peaceful operation. And so the harmonizing efforts of the superior must be more or less continual.

Conclusion

Internal peace is vital to the most efficient administration of a company. If it does not prevail, the optimum degree of coordination and cooperation cannot be attained. The net effect inevitably will be something less than the greatest possible efficiency of operation, with the result that costs will be higher than necessary and net earnings less than could be had and with the result that even outcome other than profit will be less favorable. The subject of peace within the organization cannot be overlooked by the alert administrator or the analytical student of the managerial process, even though industrial sociology has been slow to investigate it.[13]

Emphasis upon a state of internal harmonious relations is not to suggest the desirability of constant and complete agreement among the personnel of the company. This would probably prove most deadly to organizational advance. Common sense and experience have demonstrated time and again that much progress comes from differences in opinion and judgment. The condition of peace here urged precludes neither healthful divergence of views and plans nor the ordinary ephemeral clashes of personalities engendered by the very fact of living and working together. It presupposes both and is something much more. It is the absence of conflict, that advanced degree of disagreement wherein the parties at odds no longer can work together to a reasonable extent. In conflict, forward action is slowed or stopped.

However, organizational peace is not automatically forthcoming.[14] It rarely happens without specifically directed effort toward its building and maintenance.[15] The responsibility for the action is clearly upon the shoulders of all members of administration working within a more or less clearly conceived program for internal harmony. The top echelon leader who fails to recognize this fact can hardly be called a strategic executive.

BUSINESS SITUATIONS FOR ROLE-PLAYING

Situation VII

Maintaining Organizational Peace

MALOLOS INTERIORS, INC.

A. Scene.   A furniture distribution chain. A meeting in the Controller's office to inform the Market Research Supervisor and staff that a new filing system is under consideration.

B. Players.   1. Controller: Mr. Larry Kales, a dynamic administrator who likes modern methods.

2. Market Research Supervisor: Mr. Carl Finch, a methodical individual who has been with the firm for thirty years and who originated the present filing system.

3. Secretary to Mr. Finch: Mrs. Janice Williamson, a graduate of the city's leading secretarial school.

4. Market Research Analyst: Mr. Ralph Currill, a new employee who is a graduate of a leading college of business administration.

5. Market Research Analyst: Mr. James Gerber, who has been with the firm for seven years but who has never gone to college.

6. Stenographer: Miss Mary Jane Neave, an alert young woman with ideas of her own.

C. Situation.

1. The present filing system is similar to that used in most libraries, namely, the Dewey Decimal System.

2. The Systems Engineering Company has been called in by Mr. Kales to review the filing system, and it has recommended a change to an alphabetical subject file which would completely eliminate a numerical system.

3. The staff is divided as to which method they prefer. Mr. Finch considers this a personal affront and Mr. Gerber sympathizes with him. Mrs. Williamson and Miss Neave are more familiar with an alphabetical filing system, and therefore, gladly accept the new proposal. Mr. Currill had added nothing to the argument, but, after the other employees have given their opinions, he states his on the strength of their arguments.

D. Assignment.

1. Select individuals to play the respective roles. If possible, choose those with some office experience.

2. Have the group comment particularly on the manner in which Mr. Larry Kales conducts the conference.

NOTES

1. "Conflicts arise from the facts of living. . . . We are social beings. There is interdependence between one person and another person, between one person and a group, between groups. Conflict arises out of this interdependence." ROGER BELLOWS. *Creative Leadership* (Englewood Cliffs, N.J.: Prentice-Hall, Inc., © 1959), p. 162.
2. ST. AUGUSTINE, *The City of God*, XIX, 13.
3. The concept of conflict as used in this chapter may be described as *social* rather than *individual*, or conflict within self. For a description of the latter, see CHRIS ARGYRIS, *Personality and Organization* (New York: Harper & Brothers, Publishers, 1957), p. 39.

4. It is in this broad sense that Mary Parker Follett sees conflict. She declares in her paper *Constructive Conflict,* "We shall not consider merely the differences between employer and employee, but those between managers, between the directors at the Board meetings, or wherever difference appears." HENRY C. METCALF and L. URWICK (eds.), *Dynamic Administration: The Collected Papers of Mary Parker Follett* (New York: Harper & Brothers, Publishers, 1940), p. 30.

5. Occasionally authorities in the field of administration emphasize detection of conflict even more. For example, Leavitt in speaking of adapting organizations to people declares, "Perhaps it is more fruitful for an organization to locate and correct its difficulties than to try to avoid those difficulties altogether." HAROLD J. LEAVITT, *Managerial Psychology* (Chicago: University of Chicago Press, 1958), p. 281.

6. Suggested to authors by *loc. cit.*

7. Mary Parker Follett sets forth these three courses of action as the main ways of dealing with conflict. She defines domination as victory of one side over the other, compromise as each side's giving up a little, and integration as a solution in which both desires have found a place and neither side sacrifices anything. METCALF and URWICK, *op. cit.,* pp. 30-32.

8. In discussing "Social Groups and Antagonism," Dubin makes an interesting observation which, in itself, is applicable to this line of thought. He states, "Maintaining a long-term position of antagonism is difficult under most circumstances. People find it hard to maintain the emotional indignation that is necessary for long periods of time. Antagonism for its own sake is not easy to sustain." ROBERT DUBIN, *The World of Work: Industrial Society and Human Relations* (Englewood Cliffs, N.J.: Prentice-Hall, Inc., © 1958), p. 309.

9. "It is possible to conceive conflict as not necessarily a wasteful outbreak of incompatibilities, but a *normal* process by which socially valuable differences register themselves for the enrichment of all concerned." MARY PARKER FOLLETT, *Creative Experience* (New York: Longmans, Green and Co., Inc., 1930), p. 300.

It is doubtful, however, that she saw conflict as necessarily advanced disagreement. Although she does suggest that conflict as continued unintegrated difference is pathological, she specifically states that conflict means difference. METCALF and URWICK, *op. cit.,* pp. 30 and 35.

10. Professor Pfiffner expresses an interesting view on this subject. "Competition, rivalry, and opposition produce social health, provided institutions and behavior patterns provide peaceful means for resolving conflict," JOHN M. PFIFFNER, *The Supervision of Personnel* (2nd ed.; New York: Prentice-Hall, Inc., 1958), p. 203.

Conflict is believed by some to stimulate the growth and development of both the individual and the organization. CHRIS ARGYRIS, *Interpersonal Competence and Organizational Growth* (Homewood, Ill.: Richard D. Irwin, Inc., 1962, p. 2.

11. This does not imply any particular pattern of work behavior. Peace generates peace in both the organized (formal) and voluntary (informal) groups, even though the type of group to which the people belong influences their behavior. For comments on this latter relationship, see DUBIN, *op. cit.*, pp. 303-309.

12. A formalized grievance machinery does much to reduce the danger of more violent conflict, since it standardizes conflict. This idea is suggested by Dubin with reference to management-labor conflicts. DUBIN, *op. cit.*, pp. 324-326.

13. See MELVILLE DALTON, "Conflicts between Staff and Line Managerial Officers," *American Sociological Review*, XV, June, 1950, p. 342, as quoted in ROBERT DUBIN, (ed.), *Human Relations in Administration* (New York: Prentice-Hall, Inc., 1951), p. 128.

14. "Effective organizations are characterized by extraordinary capacity to deal effectively with conflict and to resolve it." RENSIS LIKERT, "A Motivational Approach to a Modified Theory of Organization and Management," in MASON HAIRE (ed.), *Modern Organization Theory* (New York: John Wiley & Sons, Inc., 1959), p. 204.

15. Valuable background material for the attack on conflict can be found in JOHN S. ELLSWORTH, *Factory Folkways* (New Haven: Yale University Press, 1952), Chap. 8, which bears the intriguing title of "Antagonistic Cooperation"; and in ROSS STAGNER, *Psychology of Industrial Conflict* (New York: John Wiley & Sons, Inc., 1956), although the emphasis is on the union management conflict.

Haiman devotes two chapters to the resolution of social conflict. FRANKLIN S. HAIMAN, *Group Leadership and Democratic Action* (Boston: Houghton Mifflin Company, 1951), Chap. 9, "Resolving Social Conflict: Integration"; and Chap. 10, "Resolving Social Conflict: Majority Vote."

CHAPTER 8

The Strategic Approach to Morale

> "Morale is a most subtle concept to isolate. In business,
> it can be said to be the worker's over-all attitude to-
> ward the work situation. The strategic administrator
> will generally want what may be considered good or
> high morale in his company or department. He has at
> least four basic objectives which he wishes to ac-
> complish with respect to his subordinates. The accom-
> plishment of each of these four objectives will be made
> much easier if his subordinates have the 'right' atti-
> tude toward their jobs."

FEW SUBJECTS in the field of administration attract more
public attention than morale. The term itself has a familiar
sound to people interested in human relations, and seems
to evoke a certain emotional response from them. For these,
and their number is legion in this day of great economic,
social and political equality, it connotes something good or
bad, and so it arouses their active, if at times uncritical
interest.

Conceptual Framework

Morale is a most subtle concept to isolate. Although the term
and idea are common in the literature of business administration, its real meaning is beclouded by a host of more or less
different definitions. This variation may be attributable to

differences in the philosophical, psychological, anthropological and/or sociological orientation of those writing on the subject.[1] On the other hand, the problem of defining morale may be nothing more than a semantic difficulty, for words do not always mean the same to all people.

In the interest of practicality, a short definition is probably best for a treatment of morale in the business environment, since it will help keep the essential problem of attainment and maintenance of *good* morale in bold perspective. There is always a danger of confusion, if not hypnosis, in too much concern with involved definition of an aspect of human relations.

Since morale is a state of mind and emotions,[2] it seems reasonable to think of it in terms of its manifestation as the *general* attitude toward the job and organization complex. Attention is invited to the word "general," the implication being that morale is the reflection of a group of feelings. Morale in business, therefore, can be said to be the worker's over-all attitude toward the work situation.[3] But, in addition to having the characteristic of generality, morale is a matter of degree. This fact is also implicit in the definition, for any general attitude can be described as good or bad or placed in an intermediate zone.

The strategic business administrator will generally want what may be considered *good* or *high* morale in his company or department. This desire is quite understandable. He has at least four basic objectives which he wishes to accomplish with respect to his subordinates: (1) to motivate them to do their work promptly, well, and economically; (2) to hold them; (3) to draw from among them the best personnel for assignment to positions of greater responsibility; and (4) to assure their being effective missionaries for him and his department or company. The accomplishment of each of these four objectives will be made much easier if his subordinates have the "right" attitude toward their jobs.

Businessmen at times seem to equate right attitude with friendliness. However, the word "friendly" when used to connote good morale may be found somewhat wanting. In actual practice, the administrator who understands the strategy of leadership needs a number of feelings in the hearts and minds of his people, including prominently industry, loyalty, enthusiasm, and pride.[4] Industry is perhaps the most important of these feelings which together contribute to good morale. It leads people to work diligently, and diligence is generally necessary to successful operation of any business. Loyalty induces employees to stay on the job, and it is an effective antidote for personnel turnover, that perennial bane of administration. Enthusiasm is the state of mind which carries subordinates into all types of competition; and it is the competitive process which squeezes out on the top side much of the new and additional leadership so often sorely needed. Pride can contribute mightily to quantity and quality of output. It also can bring men to talk and to react in such manner as to give company or department good public reputation. It is this reputation which does much to attract proper applicants and even profitable customers.

Students of morale, regardless of whether or not they identify morale with like and dislike for the work situation, frequently concern themselves with the question as to whether this general attitude is an individual or group phenomenon. It seems proper to speak of it as either, and to use the phrase *employee's morale* or *employees' morale,* for both individuals and groups may have general attitudes.[5] However, the issue is avoided by adopting a view that morale is a quality attaching itself to neither the individual nor group, but rather a real, pulsating equilibrium relationship between employees and company or department.[6]

But there is still another somewhat troublesome issue occasionally injected into the definition of morale. At times the suspicion is voiced that the relationship between satisfaction with the work situation and productivity is not as positive as generally felt.[7] If there is any substance in this view, it may be a reflection of the fact that some motivation other than what is commonly called good morale is making itself felt. Among these may be specific factors of great influence such as dire economic necessity on the part of the employees, the irresistible momentum of their past, and strong negative stimuli such as fear and hate. The general truth, however, seems to be that output tends to rise with improvement in morale.[8]

The Top Administrator as Chief Morale Officer

The question arises at this point as to who is responsible for the attainment and maintenance of good morale. Without quibbling, it may be asserted that the top administrator of the company has the ultimate responsibility for this important task, just as he has in the last analysis for any other task in the company under his administration. The morale activities of the personnel department and other staff divisions interested directly in the personnel problem are to be seen as simply part of his action in discharging his morale responsibility. Their existence is not a sign that he shirks it. A corporate president or top executive of a non-corporate business who attempts to pass this responsibility downward is not only running counter to the basic principle of organization that an obligation cannot be delegated, but he is also almost certain to encounter serious trouble because there are aspects of the morale problem which only he can solve.

Respect for Unity of Command

The top administrator, first of all, must see to it that the organizational structure of his company is conducive to the right feeling.[9] Specifically, this signifies that he should respect the *principle of unity of command* in setting up or changing organizational relationships. In other words, he should attempt so to organize that the authority of each echelon flows from one higher official, and that, in instances where this is not feasible, a mechanism is available to assure the coordinated application of power. Nothing can be as destructive to good morale as to be required to work for two or more conflicting bosses. An example of this occurs when an operating department head receives uncoordinated orders on a particular matter from both the general manager and a staff or service department chief such as the head of the accounting office.[10]

Strategic Placement of Service Departments

Akin to his direct duty to give substance to the principle of unity of command, is another task of the top executive in the cause of good morale. Reference is had to the grouping and over-all supervision of the activities of the company in such manner as to make service departments truly and smoothly serviceable to the other units of the company. A major source of irritation, especially to subordinate administrators and to supervisors, is the difficulty of dealing with service departments. These now include a goodly number of units in the ordinary medium or large size company and range all the way from the mail room through the printing office and a long list of other entities. It is perhaps not an exaggeration to state that most experienced business administrators and supervisors, as well as many plain employees, have frequently become extremely annoyed, if not seriously frustrated, with the block thrown in their way as a company ball carrier by some often very minor service person or regulation. How many such people have torn their hair and condemned the whole organization to places unmentionable at the mail room's refusal to dispatch an urgent document after a late afternoon hour, the printing office's blurring of a blueprint or a stencilled explanation, the motor pool's failure to send a car for an important prospective customer, the payroll division's tardiness in issuing checks, or the central records office's misplacing of an urgently needed document. The point to be emphasized here is that only the supreme executive authority seems to have the necessary power so to organize and direct service activities as to prevent or reduce this friction endemic to all going organizations. It can be a serious friction, and it can spread widely, especially if continual. The end result can be either constant bickering with service departments or the surrender of the operating departments to their bureaucracy. This is not to imply that the service departments are to blame for all the friction, but rather that, since theirs is the secondary function of service to the staff or operating departments, it is the duty of top management in the cause of morale to see that this role is understood and maintained.

Institution and Enforcement of Proper Over-All Personnel Policies

The chief executive has still another direct morale function. It is for him to make certain that proper over-all personnel policies are promulgated and enforced. To be certain, this is sometimes a difficult task. He may be circumscribed, for example, by an active board of directors, by the strong advice of his staff, or by the consistent pressure of unions. Yet, he should always remember that his influence in any company matter is commonly no greater than he attempts to make it, and that a dynamic and well-informed president, for example, can frequently persuade his board, successfully stand against his advisors, and handle union demands.

Setting Example as a Leader

Finally, the top administrator, as the chief morale officer of his company, must set the best possible example as a leader. He must command when command is required; generally appear courteous; be firm and honorable in all dealings with his personnel; accept advice when sincerely given by his subordinates; reward and punish without partiality; and remain fiercely loyal to all in his company who deserve it. Example is generally a better teacher than precept; and the higher the individual setting the examples, the more influential the example. It is a distinct human tendency to emulate highest superiors.

The Significant Role of the Immediate Supervisor

Reasons for Importance

With the exception of these broad aspects, the problem of getting and keeping proper morale is primarily that of the immediate supervisor.[11] There are a number of reasons. First, the immediate supervisor is the company *in loco* as far as most subordinates are concerned. He represents and enforces company authority;[12] he sympathizes, criticizes, rewards, and punishes for the company. Second, he is in the best position to ascertain the morale of his people as individuals and groups. Finally, if the span of his supervision is proper, he will have more time and opportunity than others to take necessary morale action when and if necessary.

Basic Morale Principles for the Immediate Supervisor

In approaching his job as the morale officer of his particular unit, the immediate supervisor should be guided by the basic principle that human beings have and feel a certain dignity, no matter what their position in society or the company; and that it is not only morally wrong to violate this essential human dignity but also unwise to do so, since even the dullest or weakest person will react when pushed too far. In the pressure of modern business and industry, it is sometimes easier for the supervisor to regard each subordinate as a mere cog, and no more, in the drive for efficiency. This view is also encouraged by the fact that generally supervisors nowadays know their people less well personally and, therefore, tend to feel less sympathy for them. The supervisor who wishes to develop the proper attitude in his people toward their jobs and organization must make each feel that he is essential to the group—that he has real worth. He should look upon them as much more than incidental instruments.[13] This is a high recognition of human dignity, and will generally be rewarded by some or all of those positive feelings the administrator usually wants in his group such as industry, loyalty, enthusiasm, and pride.

There is at least one other guiding principle which the immediate supervisor should observe in facing the morale problem. It involves the consideration of totality. Morale is a most complex human phenomenon[14] and has its roots in numerous and many unknown sources.[15] Roughly speaking, the feeling of the employee toward his job is the result of four categories of factors: heredity, pre-employment conditioning, employment terms and working conditions, and contemporary outside life. The supervisor who believes that he can invariably correct a morale situation by changing some circumstance in the individual's employment situation, such as raising his wages or patting him on the back, is generally deceiving himself. So intricate and interwoven are the factors that determine the nature of morale and so important is their proper evaluation by the supervisor that he must, in all morale matters, give full recognition to their diversity.

The hereditary traits contributing to an individual's feelings toward his job could include qualities as diverse as his natural physique and his innate mental capacity. For example, a strong individual might not resent repeated demands to stay at his desk until the dinner hour, whereas one who tires easily might come to resent the source of his fatigue. A bright person might enjoy analyzing the cost of equipment replacement, but a less critical mind might want to run from the job. Regardless of its manifestation, inheritance is the one source of morale which cannot be changed.

Pre-employment conditioning is sometimes quite difficult to separate from inheritance as a source of good or bad feelings toward the job.[16] Many characteristics acquired through the long years of childhood, adolescence, and previous employment may be for the administrator just about as serious as inherited traits, since they are so strongly embedded in the employee's make-up. The employee who comes from an environment that has demanded little from him may prove as much a weakling or dullard as the one born with less gifts. The man who was always sheltered by his parents and who has known little physical exertion may react to a fatiguing sales assignment in the same manner as a naturally weak individual. The man who majored in "basketweaving" in high school or college may be as frightened by the job of reconciling an accumulation of invoices and customers' checks as a person with lower intellect.

Employment terms and conditions are commonly considered the principal source of employee morale. There can be little doubt that job security, recognition, day-to-day treatment by the supervisor, size of the pay envelope, the hours of work required, vacations, the physical features of the place where he performs his task, and his compatibility with his associates within the company are of great influence. However, they are not the whole story, for, if they were, one would not find an appreciable number of disgruntled individuals in all companies, since some of the more "enlightened" concerns do offer almost ideal employment. Man's attitude is rarely, if ever, determined by just the immediate bait.

The final source of morale, the individual's life outside

the company is of incalculable importance in many cases. It undoubtedly plays a part in the reactions of all people to their employment. Human beings are not automatons who can turn off the influence of the hopes and fears, the beliefs and anxieties, the victories and failures, the happiness and sorrows of outside life when they assume their employment duties. They carry much of it with them to work just as they carry much of their employment influence home. A good example of this contemporary outside force is the approval by their relatives, friends, neighbors, and other associates of their employment. Perhaps the best example of this external force, however, is that which proceeds from domestic relations. Administrators should realize that a happy family life contributes much to happiness on the job, and that an unpleasant one has the contrary result.

Nothing in this underlining of basic principles is intended to cast doubt upon the effectiveness of techniques in obtaining and retaining good morale. It has been presented as an introduction to the steps which the immediate supervisor can take, since the dignity of man and the complex origin of morale generally must be realized and respected as a prerequisite to the effective use of any technique. For instance, even the use of that which is popularly considered best bait of all, higher pay, will not assure a proper frame of mind in a situation in which men are treated as less than men and their feelings are attributed to a particularistic cause or two. From this line of thought, then, one may proceed to an enumeration of certain morale building and defending techniques open to the immediate supervisor.

Morale Techniques for the Immediate Supervisor

The use of his power over the selection and assignment of personnel stands in first place among the techniques available to the supervisor. Although the actual hiring may be done by an employment manager or other official, the supervisor is not helpless. There are a number of things he can do, and of these none is more important than to establish the reputation for being hard to please in personnel assigned. He can insist on certain types of employees for given jobs. If this is not possible formally, he can do it by word of mouth, by frequent request to have an undesirable worker transferred, and by strong demands to have the incompetent or recalcitrant fired. A carefully picked, assigned, and sorted team— each member of which is possessed of good character, personality and ability to do his job—is the very best assurance of high morale in a department. The supervisor should remember in his desire to get such a team that it is the "squeaking wheel which gets the grease."

Regardless of how successful he is in creating a first class team by selection and placement, every supervisor should assume from the very beginning of his contact with his department and each member in it the "posture of leadership." This is a technique almost *sine qua non*. It is a truism that leadership encourages followership; lack of it, or of its appearance, is conducive to confusion, frustration and disdain, all enemies of good morale. The concept of posture of leadership implies that the supervisor consistently conduct himself in the manner of a leader. This demands above everything that he be decisive in all matters. Subordinates generally prefer the supervisor who can make up his mind and stick with his judgment. They are prone to interpret this characteristic as a sign of strength, and human beings generally respond favorably to strength, everything else being equal. How often is seen the disappointment and let-down in the employee who awakens to the fact that his supervisor just cannot decide what to do about the department trouble maker? Conversely, how frequently is seen the look of approval for and pride in the boss who will stand for no bullying and who, with dispatch, effectively chastises or gets rid of the tough character?

All this stress upon decisiveness, however, is not to be interpreted as support of capricious and irresponsible action on the part of the supervisor. There are two qualifying thoughts necessary. Decision should be based on the best knowledge attainable in order to avoid the chance of an embarrassing action. It must be remembered that really intelligent decision making can attract followership. Furthermore, decisiveness, to be most conducive to good attitude in the department, must be accompanied by the willingness to correct a wrong decision with equal dispatch. Otherwise, subordinates will come to see the boss as obstinate or even stupid, rather than of strong character. The effect on morale may be quite negative.

The fact that the posture of leadership requires decisiveness has been stressed. It also demands a strong sense of honor on the part of the supervisor. This is a quality almost impossible to describe briefly in comprehensive terms. Suffice it to say that it does signify high moral character and conduct. The supervisor's character is of great importance to the department member. It means that he as a subordinate can feel surer of getting a square deal from his boss who is to him, for all practical purposes, the company. One may imagine, for example, the good feeling generated by the supervisor's insistence to others that a poor tool really was defective when issued to one of his workers, and the converse in disillusionment and disgust when the supervisor accepts unwarranted criticism from colleagues or superiors that his men are careless with equipment.

But there is still a third component of leadership posture. It is the supervisor's early establishment of and consistent adherence to what may loosely be termed the ground rules of the department. This does not necessarily mean any formal codification of "do's and don'ts" for the members and the rigid enforcement of same. It implies something broader: a clear communication to the department personnel, in one way or the other, as to what the supervisor will and will not tolerate and as to what he expects. All human beings have an innate desire for security, and they tend to feel much safer when they know what the leader's reaction most likely will be. Certainty on the part of the department personnel can contribute much to morale. A common illustration is to be found in quality of work demanded. If the department personnel know that only first class work will be accepted by the supervisor, most of them will eventually come to expect this of themselves and their colleagues in large measure. On the other hand, should they observe that the supervisor vacillates in what he will accept as satisfactory work, some will do slipshod work, others will feel themselves unappreciated, and most will be upset by the ensuing turmoil when he does crack down.

Posture of leadership as a technique for getting and keeping morale means, then, that the supervisor make decisions promptly with honor and consistency. To this as further attributes there could be added with logic and in simple enumeration all the subsequent morale techniques suggested in this treatment. But to do so might obscure their importance, so they will be presented as separate devices.

A third technique, and in many cases as useful as selectivity and leadership stance, is to play to the human instinct for recognition, social approval and status.[17] Few people are so dull or so completely satisfied with their lot, that they do not crave more positive regard by their fellowmen. A number of things are required of the supervisor who would use this trait as a morale building and holding device. He must, obviously, learn all he can about each of his subordinates, particularly their likes, dislikes, and ambitions. He must also be prepared to act quickly in recognizing good work, for prompt recognition is usually more desired and appreciated. He must exercise ingenuity in seeing to it that the best publicity is given the accomplishment, and this suggests

that the publicity be lateral as well as downward and upward. The subordinate desires approval by his fellow workers
as well as by his inferiors, supervisors, and supervisors'
superiors. Where possible and otherwise feasible, the supervisor should crown the whole social regard process by giving
the employee some tangible symbol of earned status, such
as a seniority rank, title, work privilege, or special facilities.
This action makes it possible, as it were, for the employee
to continue "to draw" interest on his good work.

The alert and ingenious supervisor can do a great deal
more than just "pep up" an individual in a particular case
with this social regard device. On the one hand he can use
it with respect to an individual or group at almost any time,
since he can always find something to commend. Hence, it
can be used as a tonic when needed to offset other forces
debilitating to good morale. For example, a salesman has
not been doing well in selling replacement items, but he
succeeds in a long campaign to land a big order for machinery. Recognition of the latter accomplishment can be a
most invigorating tonic to him and perhaps to his fellow
salesmen, who also may be having a slow period. On the
other hand, he can utilize it to gain a larger measure of
affection and loyalty for himself by carrying the ball directly
in the sense that he goes out of his way to assure recognition
for his employees by the proper people. An example may be
necessary to clarify this point. A salesman receives a warm
letter of appreciation from a customer for whom he expeditiously obtained some badly needed equipment. He shows
the letter to his supervisor, a regional sales manager, who
can gain much in response from the salesman by promptly
sending the letter, or carrying it in person if possible, to the
sales manager of the company, and by placing it when returned, or a copy of it, on the office bulletin board or in
the house organ.

There are cautions to be observed in the appeal to the

desire for social regard as a morale builder and holder. Too much recognition is dangerous. This is especially clear in the case of the individual, although the thought is somewhat applicable to the group also. It may go to his head or create resentment on the part of his associates. Even the mere fact of approval of an individual's accomplishment may be undesirable or dangerous to his and his associates' morale. He may have been a symbol of disdain by his fellow workers; he may be personally disliked by them; he may be in need of toning down rather than stimulating; he may even be an undesirable employee who should be encouraged to leave or who is slated for separation or transfer. In addition to these two cautions, it should be remembered that approval must be timed in order best to accomplish its expected morale objective. It may be wise to withhold approval from an individual, or unit, that recently has had too much favorable recognition; or conversely it may be wise to focus it on individuals, or groups, who currently need a stimulant to their feelings. Then also, the supervisor and the organization may grant status to an individual, or group, that may not live up to its continuing demands, and thus management may find itself with a difficult self-created personnel problem.

Closely related to social regard are the devices of disapproval and punishment. Good morale would seem to demand just as much certainty with respect to negative recognition as it does for approval. However, supervisors who have the morale of their department seriously at heart should observe one ironclad rule. Disapproval and punishment generally should be in private. There are a large number of reasons: such action is usually as effective as negative steps can be; it saves face for the "culprit," since it gives him a chance to correct his ways without public shame; it argues for calmness in deliberation; and it eliminates much of the possibility of a public quarrel between the supervisor and the subordinates, an action often very detrimental to the supervisor's standing and even the company's cause. Furthermore, the supervisor should always remember that he may be wrong in part or in toto, and that private conference and action will afford him a better opportunity to change his decision, for it can assure less public disgrace, censure, and influence. Nothing stated here is intended to deny the fact that public disapproval and discipline are always out of order. There are times when the open expression of negative reaction by the supervisor is most therapeutic.

Some supervisors follow the doubtful practice of taking open note only of poor performance, and simply accept efficiency as a matter of course. These supervisors also commonly have the practice known as "needling," and make it almost the only recognition bond with their subordinates. In general, they are probably not making their greatest contribution to morale, and frequently are themselves morale detractors. It can be crushing to a subordinate to work faithfully and effectively without notice by his superior and then to have the superior tartly call a mistake to his attention. The reaction is likely to be very negative to the supervisor and the organization he represents. No such supervisor can hope to attain that team spirit among his people which represents one of the highest types of morale and which is often absolutely essential to the best over-all performance of a department. Good spirit is built to a large extent upon affection for the superior, but affection for a supervisor who notices only mistakes is hard to develop.

Another morale technique available to the immediate supervisor is quite intangible and therefore requires close description. Reference is had to the *adoption* of the department by the supervisor as his family. This signifies many things on his part, but it means above all else the development of a spirit of real affection for his people, deep sympathy for their employment and outside problems, and fierce loyalty to their cause in general. How does a supervisor do this? There is no formula to be prescribed. The problem is a personal one with each supervisor, and it is intimately related to his regard for his fellowman. But no matter how he attains this feeling for his personnel, he and, through him, the company will be repaid in good morale many times. There are always exceptional people who do not respond to affection and protection, but the majority react positively if for no other reason than that they are made to feel more important. Moreover, in the twentieth century, when the personal contacts between superior and subordinate are so much less close than in the days of small companies and communities, employees are likely, after an initial period of suspicion, to grasp with almost pathetic eagerness the hand of friendship and care extended by the supervisor. Cynics may laugh and declare that their experience as supervisors suggests all people to be ungrateful creatures more than likely ready to bite, rather than grasp, the extended hand. It may be that they never really understood or went all the way in developing the *pater familias* nexus, or that they have had unusually unfortunate experiences in their supervision career.

Somewhat connected with the family device is the common venture. The technique involves doing things together with the hope of raising morale through mutual victory or sacrifice. In the practical environment of the office or shop, this means more than just working together on routine jobs. The technique is distinguished from ordinary cooperation by two features: the task or objective is a critical one of high importance and its accomplishment is beset with many or serious obstacles. A feeling of being wanted may be fostered by the fact of invitation and inclusion in the pressing and difficult task, and the feeling of comradeship developed in struggling jointly over the problem. Both these feelings can be very significant to good morale.[18]

This is the age of the democratic spirit in the United

States. Americans are strongly imbued with the spirit of equalitarianism. They are likely to respond warmly to invitations to participate in any decision making process affecting themselves. This suggests a final morale device for the immediate supervisor. He can contribute in many instances to an individual's good feelings toward his job by seeking his opinion on matters affecting him directly or indirectly. In general, it seems true that the closer a free individual is to the source of decision making, the happier he seems. It is probably due to the inflation of ego so characteristic of social freedom.

Participation in decision making is a matter of degree, and the supervisor's good judgment as well as company policy will set the extent. However, no matter how much advice and other participation the supervisor seeks from his personnel, he should remember that there is an advantage in democratic procedure quite apart from catering directly to a strong desire in free men. The mere consultation with subordinates has a diagnostic value. The supervisor will learn much of their various feelings and will be better able, therefore, to take proper steps to improve or maintain their morale in general.

Over-Emphasis on Morale Techniques

The subject of morale devices open to the immediate supervisor is figuratively limitless, though a distinct danger lies in its overemphasis. The erroneous impression may be given that the development and maintenance of good morale is primarily a matter of "techniques and gadgets" used by those immediately responsible for the work and attitude of a given number of employees. The truth is quite contrary. Good morale is certainly in part simply a consequence of good supervision.[19] It is also the result of a complex of factors, many of which are beyond the control of company officials and their devices. Furthermore, as not yet stressed sufficiently, sustained good morale is basically the reflection of fair and intelligent treatment of employees by the company through its policies and practices. All the techniques imaginable cannot whitewash an absence of the desire and effort to treat people properly and to win their desired allegiance.

The Reflection of Low Morale

Multiplicity of Symptoms

To be certain, the harassed administrator is concerned with more than just possible approaches to the problem of morale. In fact, these may be his second consideration, his first being the symptoms of bad or deteriorating feelings which suggest remedial action. Although morale is truly an elusive phenomenon to measure, an enumeration of such symptoms, at least to a reasonably complete degree, is possible. The list includes employee irritability, complaints, friction with associates and supervisor, reduced output, tardiness, absenteeism, joining or organizing resistance or bargaining groups, and outright resignation or plain disappearance from the job. The administrator must understand that the signs of bad morale are not the same in all people and groups or at all times. For example, in a production department which has been under the pressure of overtime for months, the best indication of declining morale might be tardiness or absenteeism; whereas among the various white collar employees the sign might be interest in union affiliation to get higher salaries. Another striking example, but involving the element of time, might be tardiness in this same production department in March after five or six months of overtime during the dark days of winter, but reduced output in July when business is slow and the chance of layoff quite probable.

Pseudo-Indications of Poor Morale

Unluckily for the administrator, the problem of ascertaining the state of morale is even more seriously complicated by the fact that the so-called signs of deteriorating morale can be nothing more than pseudo-indications whipped up by the pressure of forces interested in creating discontent in otherwise contented employees. Among these artificial forces, one may note the efforts of labor recruiters representing other companies and the emblandishments of union organizers. The best mechanical tool[20] for measuring the state of morale, whether it is the interview, the rank order method, the questionnaire, or the listening-in-technique, cannot give complete assurance of being able to distinguish between real and pseudo-deterioration. About the only other recourse open to the administrator is keen personal observation and shrewd analysis, especially of any sudden change for the worse in morale as suggested by a rash of negative signs. Naturally, the good administrator tries to be foresighted and forehanded so he may, with reliance upon only a moderate degree of intuition, see artificial pressures coming. If he can and does take prompt and efficient action to forestall their influence, he can come out a double victor. Not only will he have prevented a raid on his spiritual capital (in this case, the good feelings of his employees), but he may have contributed positively to their morale if his action gives them something which they otherwise would not have gotten.

The Level of Morale—An Unstable Phenomenon

Morale in employment is not to be seen as a stable feeling. It is, in fact, very mercurial.[21] Work is generally irksome, and employment, therefore, tends to create in the minds of most people a certain, if not always admitted, resistance. Any additional unpleasantness, then, in the work situation is likely to bring disproportionately serious reaction. On the other hand, since the prevailing attitude toward work is one of automatic acceptance of a necessity, any mitigation of its rigors or enhancement in material or psychic rewards is likely to be more than welcome as making a bad situation better. The challenge to the administrator, regardless of his echelon, is to avoid enhancing the irksomeness of employment and to take all steps, compatible with the goals of his company, to add to its attractiveness. Both fortunately and unfortunately for him, changes in degree of morale on the part of any employee or employees are *contagious*. This characteristic probably stems from contradictory elements in the character of modern Western man. The normal member of this species entertains a warm sympathy for the victim of adversity, which means that most employees will react negatively when one of their group suffers a setback either from the company or life itself; and, at the same time, he possesses an almost childlike faith in good actions and the doers thereof, so that anything done to elevate the morale of a group is likely to give the majority a boost. A top administrator, for instance, may create undue anxiety by cutting the salary of one department head; and he may also appreciably stimulate the friendliness of all department chiefs by fighting for the retirement rights of the oldest. Truly the business administrator deals, as do all executives, with the "slipperiest" of all clay, man himself.

Conclusion

Morale is a state of mind as reflected in attitude. The concept of friendliness toward the company, department, administrator, supervisor, or work assignment is not quite adequate to embrace the practical meaning of morale. In actual practice, the administrator wants a number of feelings in the hearts and minds of his people; and among these are industry, loyalty, enthusiasm and pride.

The top administrator must be considered the chief morale officer of the company. He cannot escape the general responsibility for the feeling of his employees toward their jobs, and he does have certain morale stimulating and assuring tasks that only he should discharge. However, the problem of getting and keeping proper morale is primarily that of the immediate supervisor. Many devices are available to him for accomplishing this task. Their full description and evaluation have not been attempted in this chapter; they demand extended and careful attention by experts in the field, including psychologists and sociologists. An effort has been made simply to suggest a few of them in a critical sense. More importantly, an attempt has been made to emphasize the fact that good morale is not primarily a function of gimmicks and techniques. It is the authors' view that morale is the result of a complex of factors and that the greatest contribution which administration can make to it is fair and intelligent treatment of employees.

Morale is not a stable quality. There are few aspects of humanity which change more often. The administrator who fully appreciates this fact will understand the extreme importance of strategic action. He will remain alert in his treatment of his employees, and will be quick to take that action or counteraction necessary to "shore it up" or build it higher. To this end, reference is suggested to the elements and devices of strategic action previously described or implied in this book.

BUSINESS SITUATIONS FOR ROLE-PLAYING

Situation VIII

The Strategic Approach to Morale

THE SPRUE & ELLIS COMPANY

A. Scene.   A freight forwarding company in a large city. A meeting between the Personnel Director and a personnel department trainee after his two months of training and observation in various departments of the company.

B. Players.   1. Personnel Director: Mr. Joseph A. McNally, who has been with the company for twenty years and has come to believe that everything is fine so long as the company is making a profit.

2. Personnel Department Trainee: Mr. Philip P. Phillips, a recent graduate with a master's degree in personnel from a leading university, eager to analyze and criticize but intelligent and sincere.

C. Situation.   1. Mr. Phillips believes he has found several sources of possible discontent in the company. The employees are not well acquainted with company policies, there is no generally known grievance procedure, the pay scale is twenty-five cents per hour less than in comparable industries. An over-all personnel problem is developing, and the men are thinking of organizing a union.

2. In his enthusiasm to do the right thing, Mr. Phillips has decided to discuss the situation with Mr. McNally, point out the dangers, and offer possible solutions.

D. Assignment.   1. Select players to act out the roles of the Personnel Director and the Trainee.

2. Have the Trainee stress the importance of definite company policy, and the value and methods of keeping peace in the organization.

3. Use the performance as an opening for an extended group discussion of causes of poor morale.

NOTES

1. JOHN M. PFIFFNER, *The Supervision of Personnel* (New York: Prentice-Hall, Inc., 1951), pp. 208-209.
2. MICHAEL J. JUCIUS, *Personnel Management* (4th ed.; Homewood, Illinois: Richard D. Irwin, Inc., 1959), p. 338.
3. ROGER BELLOWS, *Creative Leadership* (Englewood Cliffs,

N.J.: Prentice-Hall, Inc., 1959), p. 74; and DALTON E. MCFARLAND, *Management Principles and Practices* (New York: The Macmillan Company, 1958), pp. 449-450.

4. Professor Dubin introduces even the element of zeal in performing the activity. ROBERT DUBIN, *The World of Work* (Englewood Cliffs, N.J.: Prentice-Hall, Inc., 1958), p. 217.

5. MCFARLAND, *op. cit.*, p. 449.

6. For this view of the situs of morale, see F. J. ROETHLIS-BERGER, *Management and Morale* (Cambridge, Mass.: Harvard University Press, 1946), pp. 192-193.

7. An interesting finding was made by Katz et al. in a study of railway section gangs. "This study has revealed very few differences between high and low producing employees with respect to their attitudes toward the work situation. The great majority of men in both high and low sections express satisfaction with the work, the company, their fellow workers and their future prospects." DANIEL KATZ et al., *Productivity, Supervision and Morale among Railroad Workers* (Ann Arbor: Survey Research Center, Institute for Social Research, University of Michigan, 1951), p. 24.

8. The authors agree with Pfiffner when he writes that "high morale is a complex combination of many factors that make people do what the organization expects them to do." Adapted from JOHN M. PFIFFNER, *Supervision of Personnel* (2nd ed.; Englewood Cliffs, N.J.: Prentice-Hall, Inc., © 1958), p. 210. This view precludes, in effect, the necessity for discussing at length the issue as to whether or not high morale means high productivity, for by definition morale is consonant with that degree of productivity the organization desires or with any other objective it pursues.

However, the direct relationship between good morale and output was suggested long ago by the Western Electric studies. DUBIN, *op. cit.*, p. 220; and F. J. ROETHLISBERGER and WILLIAM J. DICKSON, *Management and the Worker* (Cambridge, Mass.: Harvard University Press, 1946), *passim*. It was further supported by later studies conducted under the Survey Research Center of the University of Michigan. DUBIN, *op. cit.*, p. 220. And it has received more substantiation in subsequent investigations by various scholars.

9. JAMES C. WORTHY, "Factors Influencing Morale" in SCHUYLER DEAN HOSLETT (ed.), *Human Factors in Management* (Rev. ed.: Harper & Brothers, Publishers, 1951), p. 323.

10. For a succinct analysis of the principle of unity of com-

mand, see HENRI FAYOL, *General and Industrial Management,* trans. CONSTANCE STORRS (London: Sir Isaac Pitman & Sons, Ltd., 1949), p. 24-25.

11. DELBERT C. MILLER and WILLIAM H. FORM, *Industrial Sociology* (New York: Harper & Brothers, Publishers, 1951), p. 469.

12. It is true that the supervisor may find himself somewhat constrained in his morale function since he must see to it that the purposes of efficiency are served. Roethlisberger writes to this point. F. J. ROETHLISBERGER, *Management and Morale* (Cambridge, Mass.: Harvard University Press, 1946), pp. 37-39.

13. This idea is underscored by Selekman and Selekman with a terse admonishment. "When men appear before him as employees and staff members . . . the business administrator must view them not only technically, as does the scientist, but also politically and ethically, psychologically and socially, as does a teacher, minister, or physician." SYLVIA KOPALD SELEKMAN and BENJAMIN M. SELEKMAN, *Power and Morality in a Business Society* (New York: McGraw-Hill Book Company, Inc., 1956), p. 109.

14. Urwick is eloquent on this point. "It is brittle, sensitive stuff—the spirit of any great undertaking. When it is good it is unmistakable: when it is bad it is a choking fog, which undermines the courage and stifles the effort of even the best men and women among the personnel. And yet it is almost impossible to define precisely the elements which go to make or mar this 'atmosphere.'" L. URWICK, *The Elements of Administration* (New York: Harper & Brothers, Publishers, n. d.), p. 89.

15. Pfiffner refers to a recent psychological analysis that drew from a sampling of attitude surveys the factors related to how employees felt about their employment. Five showed up with regularity. Arranged in the order of their consistency of appearance, they seemed to be " '. . . (1) economic and related rewards, (2) adequacy of immediate supervision, (3) effectiveness of the organization as a system, (4) satisfaction with the job itself, and (5) compatibility of fellow employees.'" JOHN M. PFIFFNER, *The Supervision of Personnel* (2nd ed.; Englewood Cliffs, N.J.: Prentice-Hall, Inc., © 1958), p. 238.

16. It has been observed that the "basic attitudes and sentiments which employees themselves bring with them to the workplace" are the common factor underlying high morale. BURLEIGH B. GARDNER and DAVID G. MOORE, *Human Re-*

lations in Industry (Rev. ed.: Chicago: Richard D. Irwin, Inc., 1950), p. 348.

17. There is evidence from employee attitude surveys that "job satisfaction and morale are dependent upon the extent to which supervisors take into consideration employee's needs for recognition and status." Morris S. Viteles, *Motivation and Morale in Industry* (New York: W. W. Norton & Company, Inc., 1953), p. 325.

    This emphasis upon recognizing the employee desire for recognition, social approval and status should not be allowed to becloud the fact that the bad performance of the worker himself may be a major factor in causing his bad morale. This thought is suggested in Charles D. Flory (ed.), *Managers for Tomorrow* (New York: New American Library, 1965), p. 141.

18. Robert H. Roy, *The Administrative Process* (Baltimore: The Johns Hopkins Press, 1958), p. 155.

19. William H. Knowles, *Personnel Management* (New York: American Book Company, 1955), pp. 212-213.

    Some authorities go much further than simply holding that good morale is in part the result of good supervision. The staff of Rohrer, Hibler and Replogle are responsible for the statement that "A well managed firm typically has high morale as an inevitable by-product of executive effectiveness." Flory, *op. cit.*, p. 149.

20. See Davis for a summary of the principal ways of measuring morale. Ralph Currier Davis, *The Fundamentals of Top Management* (New York: Harper & Brothers, Publishers, 1951), pp. 578-581.

21. Jucius, *op. cit.*, p. 354.

CHAPTER **9**

Stratagems in Planning

"In some form, planning occurs prior to most decision
making and action. Its nature, dimensions, and potential cannot be explained adequately by an exposition
of the classical steps commonly identified in its description. Planning is gamesmanship, and proper planning is gamesmanship of a high order."

PLANNING is not necessarily a chronological step in administration. It is rather an aspect of the whole administrative
process and pervades administration from beginning to end.
Therefore, it is especially important that the administrator
not only understand its nature but that he appreciate the
opportunities it affords.

There is no unanimity of thought as to the nature of
planning. Some presentations see planning as all prior
thought on decisions or actions to be taken; others view it
as some sort of formal mental process of preparation for
decision and action.[1] It is the contention of this treatment
that both extremes are correct but that neither leads to an
adequate analysis of the subject.

Planning, to be understood thoroughly, must be considered as gamesmanship, just as administration itself—the
whole of which planning comprises a part—is to be seen as
this form of behavior. When such perspective is assumed, a
whole vista of analytical possibilities opens up. The planner

188

is not seduced by the simplicity of either plain early thinking or the precise niceties of formal procedure. Planning implies in its minimum dimensions (1) knowledge of and strategic reaction to goals; (2) objective estimate of resources needed and, if the plan must be approved by superior authority, wise presentation of this cost factor; and (3) respect for precedent, courage to break it, and imagination to think creatively when necessary. Certainly these are subjects to challenge the administrator.

The Influence of Goals on Planning

The purpose of gamesmanship in administration is to win, i.e., to achieve desired organizational goals. The role of goals in planning is not always the same. Under certain conditions, the goals will have been set by higher authority or circumstances. In other situations, the planner will be confronted with the necessity for selecting goals. Both cases frequently appear in business. The top policy committee of a corporation establishes a sales target of 2,000,000 units, and here the sales manager is caught in a situation in which he must plan toward a fixed goal. An example of the freer situation is to be found when the chief executive simply orders the sales manager to work out the entire sales program for the year at the district level.

Planning under Fixed Goals

In the hierarchy of organization, it is normal for higher authority to establish goals, and it is especially normal for subordinate administrators to accept and, when necessary, to plan for the attainment of these goals. There may, however, be cases in which the administrator upon whom falls the burden of planning toward these goals, will for adequate reason decide that he cannot or should not plan in terms of the stated objectives.

It may appear as if he has no choice, that he *must* plan in terms of these goals. Actually, there are a number of other strategic courses open to him. One of the more obvious is a frontal attack on the goals by arguments against their unsoundness. Obviously, this is risky; it may even endanger his position. If he undertakes to oppose them in this manner, he should take care to demonstrate the specific and cogent reasons why the goals are unsound. The higher administration of his organization generally will not wish to make a mistake, and may, therefore, listen to his arguments.[2] A further bit of strategy in making the frontal attack less objectionable to superiors is to delay presenting arguments against the fixed goals until such time as the first phase of planning demonstrates them to be unsound.

A second course open to the opposing administrator planning under imposed goals is to resist them indirectly. There is a host of indirect actions possible, a few of which approach sabotage. The planner can build into the plans such heavy demands for resources that the goals come to appear too costly. He can arrange the time schedule in the proposed plans so that their effectuation would seriously interfere with other programs of the company. He can purposefully plan to reach the main goal through a number of unwise or ridiculous sub-goals, so that the top administration simply gives up. He can keep the plan on the "drawing board" by the technique of constant change in its features so that time will defeat the accomplishment of the imposed goal. Finally, he can always resort to the time honored technique of misunderstanding so that the plan is never proper for the goal. Some or all of these procedures may, in a particular frame of reference or in general, be downright unethical. If they are, they should be shunned. Unfortunately certain types of administrators, inordinately driven by the desire for success, will resort to them.

Of course, the ordinary administrator presented with a

goal by his superiors will generally seek to plan accordingly and without effective reservation. But even this conforming executive has available certain strategic maneuvers. First and foremost, he can enthusiastically accept the goal by some formal expression. Superiors may occasionally grimace at his courage in approving their stand, but generally they will be flattered that someone agrees with them and may, therefore, give him more support in planning. Next, he may immediately get to work on the plan, and thus by action assure his superiors that he is with them and show his colleagues that he believes the goal proper. This immediate action, then, can elicit both favor from above and support from his environs. Furthermore, he can resort to phase planning. This is such a promising technique that it seems to deserve special comment.

Phase planning refers to the preparation of plans in terms of periods of time, application of degrees of effort, utilization of particular facilities, movement in a given direction, or establishment of sub-goals. Regardless of the terms in which it is done, it implies breaking down the whole projected operation into some arrangement of parts and organizing distinctive plans around these parts. Naturally, there must be a coherency in the whole, and the plan for each phase must fit harmoniously into the picture either as a continuity or conditional step. Phase planning, however, must not be confused with alternative planning which means setting up a second or third plan for use if the first is found sufficiently lacking. Confusion arises between the two concepts because in phase planning the action taken in the implementation of a succeeding phase is often determined by what has occurred in the preceding phase.

Interesting as the anatomy of phase planning may be, the issue here is how the administrator, who accedes to the goal set by superior authority, can use the device to advantage. Certainly, the administrator can use phase planning to demonstrate to higher echelons the dimensions of the task set by the goal, and, by so doing, create a basis for selling the plans to them. Most human beings think in terms of specifics. The board and president of the corporation who set the goals are much more likely to understand, for example, the total personnel needs demanded by the plan if they can get a clearer picture of the time and point at which the utilization of different labor components will be asked. Furthermore, the administrator can use phase planning to allay the fears of top administration. Not infrequently, top management formulates and announces an aim, and then figuratively trembles at what such boldness will demand in terms of innovation, public relations, and cost. But, if the planners or planning group presents their proposal "in bits," they may be able to make it look much less frightening, just because the plan in parts does not look as large as it does *in toto*. Then, too, in this matter of allaying administrative fright over big goals, it must be pointed out that phase planning can be used to present avenues of safe advance, and points for wise retreat, by making movement to each succeeding phase dependent upon a certain degree of accomplishment in the previous phase. Top management can be shown by the planner that, if the goals of each plan are reached, the next phase will be undertaken on this justification or that, if they are not reached, further action in the direction indicated by the advanced phase will be halted.

Planning by phases places in the hands of the planner even greater power than is suggested by the two strategic possibilities just described, because the planner has the opportunity for the creation of sub-goals. Since he creates the phases of the plan, he obviously provides the criteria for movement from phase to phase. In a realistic sense these are, in part at least, sub-goals. Here lies indeed great power. The criteria he sets for advancement may be easily reached, and thereby movement stimulated toward the accomplishment of the over-all objective or toward an accumulating disaster which makes final attainment of organizational success much more difficult or impossible. On the other hand, the criteria selected may be hard to attain or completely out of the realm of possibility, so that progress toward the imposed main goal is retarded or prevented. In fact, if his sub-goals are either too easy or too elusive, the planner may cause the top administration in suspicion, satisfaction, or despair to modify or even abandon the big objective.

The process of phase planning is itself a valuable *modus operandi* for planners. It gives them more flexibility than they would have in unitary planning. Since parts are involved, they can make changes in the proposal with a greater degree of ease. Consider this example. A food processing company has determined to introduce a new line of dog food. The staff planning group is given the general goal of nation-wide sales coverage. It decides to plan by phases, and to do so on a certain geographical basis. When the plan is presented to the company's policy committee, objection develops along the line that the trial sales campaign in the rich New York area appears to be inadequate. Since the plan is presented in phases, the planners can meet the objection by the modification of a part. They can change more quickly than if the whole plan were the target for objection. Incidentally, they thus can maintain their prestige as a responsible entity.

Planning When Goals Are to Be Set by the Planner

The subject of strategy when planning toward an imposed goal presents almost unlimited possibilities. However, there is a parallel question which, for purposes of contrast, may now be raised. How about strategic action in those planning situations in which circumstances require that the planner set his own goals? Two such situations are readily apparent. One is when the top administration, which always has the responsibility to chart the course of the organization, decides not to do so in terms of goal setting. The other exists when the departmental head or another subordinate administrator has a particular mission so complicated that he must set a whole array of specific objectives toward which to plan.[3] This latter situation is clearly indicated in the case of the director of purchasing who must assure the organization of steady suppliers, effective competitive bidding, and scheduled delivery of necessary materials and supplies as a part of his very complicated task of procurement.

Both situations involve the making of what may be called "value judgments." Any planner left on his own to set goals toward which to plan must determine certain standards for their selection if he would be strategic. A myriad of questions thus confronts him. What do I want? What is best for my organization or department? What do my superiors really desire? What do my other "publics" expect? Which goals will be most certain of attainment? What objectives are most dangerous to me? How legal are my aims? Are they professional and ethical? These questions suggest the necessity for a hierarchy of values, a subject which cannot be avoided in organizational planning.

The obvious sequence of a hierarchy of values with respect to goals is the necessity of setting objectives in terms of importance. This involves considerations that are personal, professional, organizational, and social. The planner will not often find it wise to arrange his objectives on the basis of one of these considerations to the exclusion of the others; in almost all cases, more than one of these factors will demand recognition. To be certain, the selfish man may attempt to set his goals in terms of personal advantage alone. He is likely, therefore, to present a plan unacceptable to both his associates and superiors, for his action will in many cases require him to overlook much of the greater necessity and good. The narrowly specialized administrator may determine his goals by professional standards alone, and so he may produce an unrealistic plan in terms of organizational needs and resources. The ideals of the engineering or accounting professions, for example, may be too rich for the company blood. The devoted administrator entrusted to set objectives in planning is commonly impelled to do the "right" thing in terms of the organization by concentrating on the goals of gain for the company. This is good if it does not mean the exclusion of all other values, for such omission may build into a plan the basis for improper conduct and bad human relations. Individuals and groups have inalienable rights which even the greatest economic power cannot ignore. The broad-minded idealist often is inclined to fix his goals in terms of social welfare, e.g., to emphasize the number of laborers that can be hired rather than the efficiency of the labor factor. Planning along this line can lead to serious increase in costs and eventual financial difficulties.

Is there here an impasse beyond which the conscientious and intelligent planner cannot go? The true strategist is sanguine on this point; he sees that there is a way out. And so he recommends action along the lines of synthesizing, which as used here means arranging objectives to reflect all four bases—personal, professional, organizational, and social. His recommendation is based on the cognizance of elements of common interest. For example, he shrewdly recognizes that his or his superior's promotion may depend upon his insistence on professional standards, attention to company profits, and concern for the community standard of living. The strategist also has an answer with respect to the dilemma situation, in which there is no reasonable possibility arising out of common interest, of the reconciliation of two or more of these four bases for goals. He is aware of the great strength to be found in moral conduct and urges that conflict in goals be settled on the basis of ethical principles. He knows that the morally *right* course is likely to attract unusual support when the situation is one of real difficulty.

This does not mean that he should neglect justice in his attempts at compromise when it can be effected, but rather that he should advance it here as the sole grounds for settlement.

While the immediate task of the administrator who must plan without prior goals is to reach a decision on goals, he should realize that his arrangement of objectives into a hierarchy of significance will necessitate a hierarchy of plans. This is in the nature of an obvious fact. Prime objectives will require plans of the first order, and less important objectives, plans of lower order. The activities of a large organization are directed and coordinated by a pretentious arrangement of plans in vertical succession.[4]

There is more to this issue of strategy by the planner who is to set his own goals. Most planning administrators probably have sufficient political and moral sensitivity to set objectives in a reasonably good perspective. However, some of them do not believe firmly in that which they proclaim as their aims. It remains, once he has fixed his goals, for the unbelieving planner to discipline himself into their real acceptance. This may sound too nebulous for the realm of practical administration, but it is actually a fundamental psychological necessity in many cases if the best planning is to be done. Planners—and, in fact, all men—not infrequently determine the direction to take but then, in their weakness or dislike of the indicated path, actually hold back in taking it. It is risky to trust the administrator unconverted to his own goals to produce an effective plan.

Strategic Handling of the Resources Factor

Idealism is a real asset in business administration. It can result in the highest type and statement of ends. It can help free the mind for creative thinking. Yet business to survive and prosper must be practical. One of the more important aspects of practicality has to do with the necessary resources which often are described as money, men, machines, methods, and materials. The planner must consider the availability of these resources, as well as their right combination, if he is to produce a workable plan. Unfortunately few, if any, companies or administrators have real access to free and unlimited resources, and certainly in no company are resources combined automatically. Therefore, the possibility for strategic arrangement enters planning through the resource door as well as through the avenue of goals.

Estimating Resources Needed

The planner who approaches the factor of resources must first of all make an appraisal of those which are necessary for the successful implementation of the plan. This is a very difficult task, especially when it comes to the stage of concretely estimating in the plan specific resource requirements. The temptation undoubtedly exists in the minds of many planners to overestimate in the interests of safety. Although this practice may have some advantages, it can have undesirable repercussions in frightening the top echelons whose approval of plans is necessary, in economic waste, and in the eventual disrepute of the planner. Underestimation is also serious, for it may doom the plan to failure in execution.

It would seem that the wise planner might well use the strategy implied in the *doctrine of sensible leeway*. It signifies provision in the plan for maneuvering up or down the scale of requirements during the execution of the plan. This provision can take one of three forms. A common form is the more subtle one of boldly stating in the plan uncertainty as to requirements beyond those necessary to get started. This provides at once both the greatest flexibility and the most inexactness. It might facetiously be considered planning resources by not planning them. Another is the plus or minus estimate, which has both merit and demerit. On the positive side is its complete simplicity. What is easier for the planner to provide than a margin of error? On the negative is its indefiniteness which may make superiors suspicious of the plan and which may prove most worrisome to the comptroller. The third form may be described as the multiple-level device. Here, the various estimates of requirements are provided contingent upon different degrees of accomplishment. To illustrate, take the case of a toy manufacturer drawing up a plan for the production of small flying saucers. He has several targets: 50,000, 100,000, and 150,000 units. Therefore, he makes several different estimates of his resource requirements. This multiple-level device is the most scientific method of estimating resources needed, since it basically pegs input to output. The one obvious disadvantage is the difficulty of proceeding to procure resources in these different dimensions. Planners can do something about this, however, by a number of concrete steps such as provisions for a line of bank credit, overtime, temporary hiring, additional plant shifts, leasing of extra space and equipment, and sub-contracting.

Reference to the budgetary concept of the resource factor in administrative planning has been omitted. It is felt that modern budgetary procedure is simply a method of putting into effect one of the above forms of maneuvering resources. By omission of the term budget, the real core of action suggested may be made a bit clearer.

Scheduling Procurement of Resources

But estimating the quantity and quality of resources needed may not be the only step in the planning of logistics. The complete plan may also show when to obtain resources. It goes without saying, however, that no sensible plan should so restrict the decision making power of the operating personnel that they cannot in attempting to carry out the plan make the necessary movements to meet unexpected and changing circumstances. Therefore, the planner should beware of too great detail in treating the matter of timing procurement. Few things are as unprofitable or demoralizing to the administration of an organization as to have money borrowed but unspent, machines idle, and employees sitting around. The one unquestionable rule for the timing of resource procurement is to provide a general schedule so that there is a minimum chance of either a major tie-up or significant waste. This involves prominently priority time. Steps are taken early to start procurement of those items, such as long term finance or heavy equipment which commonly requires much more time, for example, than the hiring of a labor force.

There is a common danger in any planning for resource procurement. A factor always disturbing to management is new and additional costs. High company officials, if they deserve the appellation "dynamic," are generally receptive to proposals for new ventures. But they become wary when the plans call for substantial outlay. Top administration is of necessity both leader and watch-dog. The careful statement, in the plan, of resources needed may challenge the "guardian instinct" of the superior authority, and thus invite his negative reaction to the whole proposal. This danger can be really serious when the company is in a period of cost consciousness due to poor business or keen competition.

Disarming Potential Objections from Above

Since a plan of any proportions generally must include the subject of resources needed to implement it, the planner might well address himself to strategies of disarming potential objections from above. Among the possible moves in this direction, one may mention prominently the confinement of resources outlined to idle or partly used facilities and factors. A metal products company loses a defense contract. The new products division conceives and plans the entry into the production of hospital equipment. Aware of the financial worry of the board of directors, who must approve plans for the introduction of any new product, the new products division points out in the plan that little additional in fixed costs will be needed to launch production of the new line, since plant space and equipment are not now fully utilized.

Closely related to the assurance that the plan does not demand more fixed investment is the strategy of assuming in the plan that existing facilities and factors can carry the extra burden which will be imposed by it. This is not uncommon in American business administration. It simply means giving existing divisions of the organization more work. This procedure is not only carried out but is rationalized commonly by the argument that the new assignment is just *one* more task, and any good organizational unit can do one more thing. It is difficult to ignore the illustration of this common strategy of "piling on" to be found in the recent practice of thrusting the administration of retirement plans onto the existing personnel office. That such strategy so often succeeds in execution may be attributed to either pride or fear by the subordinate administrators on whose shoulders the new burden falls. They may wish to appear willing and capable, or they may distrust the consequences of objecting.

Under certain circumstances, the planner, as a positive approach to the matter of resources demanded, can recommend diversion of expenditures from an existing less promising company activity to the new venture. The potential saleability of this approach is to be found in two facts. It helps assure those who will make the decision on the acceptance of the plan that important additional outlays are not really involved. It also suggests to higher administration more efficiency, and may actually show them a way of rationally getting rid of a low yielding or losing operation. A plan of leasing automobiles for company personnel, for example, is made attractive by pointing out that the money now being spent to buy, service, and maintain a company owned fleet probably would more than meet the cost of a leasing program.

A final strategy for selling the new plan, as far as its resource needs are concerned, is to minimize them. There are undoubtedly many ways of doing this, but two appear to offer the most. One is to emphasize the probable big returns on the expenditures indicated. This is best done by the use of ratios. Nothing is as appealing to the executive who must manage profits as the good probability of a high percentage return on outlay. The other way may be described as the use of the pilot device. The plan is written to propose a minimal effort, with the provision that no further expenses are to be incurred unless the pilot experiment proves profitable. The new products division in the metal products company would, by such planning, recommend the manufacture of two hundred hospital cabinets and their sales display at key places throughout the nation. It would emphasize the fact that these cabinets were simply an experiment before further commitment of resources to their full production. This would place the approving authority, if he doubted the wisdom of the plan, in a position for objective judgment.

Precedent, Imagination, and Creative Thinking

Precedent: Pro and Con

Every organization in existence for an appreciable period of time has developed or accepted certain policies and practices of operation. These tried, if not necessarily true, norms constitute a body of precedent which has great significance to the planner or planning group for the organization. The mass of accepted ideas and ways of doing things may, on the one hand, prove of great assistance in planning. It may provide an objective base from which to start thinking, a frame of reference within which planning can politically be done, and certain lessons from past experience. On the other hand, precedent may be a virtual "Old Man of the Sea" to be carried by the planner or planners. It may so influence the planning activity as to delimit seriously the dimensions and nature of its work.

A consideration of precedent in its relation to planning lends support to the contention that many things in life are neither completely white nor completely black, but have both positive and negative implications. An illustration may be useful. Take the case of seasonal delivery planning in a large department store. The company, an old and established concern, obviously had lived through many Christmas rushes and had delivered millions of dollars worth of merchandise during these times. As the Christmas season of last year approached, the issue of planning the delivery service arose. Some in the company were not altogether satisfied with past delivery performance. They succeeded in having a group assigned to recommend action plans. When the committee came to face its job, it discovered that the company traditionally had relied upon contract delivery services to handle overflow and that this reliance seemed justified, since the job had thus generally been done well enough to get all Christmas orders delivered before 6:00 P.M., Christmas Eve. The committee also learned that the President, still powerful and revered although living in Ft. Lauderdale most of the time, himself had instituted contract services many years ago. Obviously, precedent pointed a way which again could be taken with some assurance of success, and it certainly indicated a course of action which probably would not bring down the wrath of top administration. Everything else being equal, the influence of precedent would here be to the good as far as the planners might be concerned. But assume that, even though the use of commercial delivering services had moved orders on time, the cost thereof had been rising so much as to make their continued use questionable. This problem may well have been the reason the store manager and his aides formed the committee. They wanted to learn if a cheaper satisfactory delivery arrangement were possible. But the committee now found itself in a dilemma. If it departed from precedent, it would step into relatively new grounds and tempt disapproval and censure from the top, and so it took the easy way out and decided upon the status quo. Here the force of precedent, which indicated one effective and safe way to proceed, constituted a restraining influence on the thinking and recommendations of the planners.

Stratagems for Overcoming Precedent

A planner or planning committee may decide to disregard precedent, at least to a considerable extent, and to proceed along new lines. How can obstructing precedent be handled by planners? There are undoubtedly many approaches; yet the following actions seem particularly promising:

1. *Show drastic changes to exist in circumstances.* This is an attempt to motivate those bound by tradition into acceptance and support of change. In the delivery example, the planners might have emphasized the longer hauls necessitated by suburbia as well as the marked rise in contract delivery costs occasioned by the increased mileage.
2. *Demonstrate to administration that there is a better way of doing the thing in question.* Of course, this may prove difficult, if not impossible. The new idea can be sold more readily, however, if the planning activity makes a sincere effort to demonstrate to those supporting precedent that the innovation is better in ways peculiarly significant to them. The president of the department store probably was vitally interested in showing his board of directors continued and rising earnings per share. Therefore, if the planners could have advanced prominently the idea of cheaper deliveries as an argument for a new system, their chances of obtaining the president's acquiescence or support might have been enhanced.

3. *Make the new plan appear as similar as truth will permit to the existing plan or other accepted norms of operation.* This implies many steps: for example, the retention of insignificant traditional principles and procedures; the usage as far as feasible of similar titles, positions, and even personnel; and the statement of the nature and extent of the changes with as little publicity as possible. This suggestion is well described in the adage, slightly twisted to express the idea, that it is easier to sell new wine in old bottles. The president might have bought a new delivery plan more easily had it been made to appear similar to the old.

4. *Give as much as honorably possible, if not all, of the credit for the new idea to those who support precedent.* This action frequently succeeds, for there is little salesmanship as effective as discreet praise. The president made to see in the new delivery plan an effort to follow the principle of economy—a tenet to which he has always given public service—might not have been too hard to win over with the idea that the change was really based on this guiding principle which he long since had laid down.

5. *Show, when appropriate, that competitors, particularly the effective ones, are planning for change or actually taking new steps.* Static and dynamic business leaders are both generally influenced by the action of their competition. The former, perhaps either lazy or ignorant, commonly do what one may in juvenile terms describe as "follow the leader" because they are too sluggish or uniformed to proceed on their own. The latter, keenly attuned to the danger of being outstripped, constantly keep their ears to the ground and, when they detect movements on the part of competitors become much more motivated toward change. The department store executive may have been either static or dynamic, but it is doubtful that he could have ignored more efficient delivery services being planned or instituted by other department stores in the city had he been clearly informed of them.

6. *Plan for gradual change.* Many cautious administrators, seeking safety by following old policies and procedures, are nevertheless not greatly alarmed by small changes. Here the planning entity can find an opening for the initiation and development of a large or radically new proposal. The idea

is to move in such small steps that each new proposal is acceptable, and in such numerous steps that the desired total change is eventually pushed through. Leasing delivery trucks to service out-county customers as a first step toward a total leasing plan for Christmas delivery might not have evoked the president's opposition.

7. *Announce the new plan as a completely revolutionary idea when grounds exist for so describing it.* This specific step, the boldest of these suggested ways of handling precedent in planning, demands courage and at times a great measure of it. However, it may have a surprisingly good chance of success. The strategy lies in taking the offensive so that the opposition must go on the defensive to protect the old. It must be remembered that it is easier to attack than defend, since the attacker has the advantage of surprise, mobility, and the public interest inherent in new things. The president of the now much belabored department store might not have found it easy before both his board and public to oppose, at least directly, new plans for cheaper delivery.

These suggested stratagems for overcoming precedence are in reality ways of helping to sell any plan. One additional way, which is of such broad import that it cannot justifiably be listed with a set of more or less specific techniques, has to do with the mobilization of as many of the organizational family as possible and feasible into the planning process. It should not be difficult to enlarge the participation in planning, since so many people like to be heard and since all people within the organization have duties which require some planning.[5] This involvement can be a major and practical method of liquidating precedent, since precedent is the function of firm ideas and habits held by large numbers and since their participation in planning an innovation is a form of self-liquidation of prejudice.

A caution is in order. It must not be thought that precedent is dangerous to planning simply because it may have supporters willing and able to fight the new idea. Precedent is also dangerous because of its hypnotic effect on the planner. The course of least resistance is always tempting, and the acceptance of traditional policies and procedures can be this course. The sincere planner needs to fear himself, for the very existence of precedent may deaden his vision.

Imagination and the Freedom to Imagine

The planner must have something which is called imagination. Even psychologists seem put to it to define this quality concisely. Suffice it to say that imagination is a mental power which enables one to visualize situations and possibilities beyond present reality. In a poetic sense, imagination is the ability to dream; in the most practical business connotation, it is the capacity to think of the future in terms of what might be. Whether this mental power is inherited or acquired, or partly both, is a matter properly of concern to the psychologist and geneticist. It is simply desired here to point out that planning is impossible without a degree of imagination.

One real issue regarding imagination in the planning process may seem rather prosaic. It is the freedom of the planner to imagine sufficiently. This will generally demand time, release from pressure of other duties, and the absence of fear to deal with matters beyond current acceptance. This does not imply that the planner should insist upon being treated as a prima donna or that his organization should as a matter of course treat him as a delicate thinking machine. It suggests rather that the exercise of imagination is a particular task which, like all other specific jobs, requires some special circumstances for its best accomplishment.

Motivation to Imagine

This emphasis upon freedom to imagine is not to imply that the designated planner will use his imagination automatically just because he is free to imagine. He is human, and the assurance that he will do his best projection into the future demands certain motivation. This motivation may proceed from at least three general sources: the recognized desire or actual order of the superior to plan; the challenge to the planner's ability to think creatively which is inherent in that which is to be planned; and the hope of reward whether in material terms, social recognition, or any of a host of other desired ends.

One must go still further with this idea of imagination, or what is here loosely called "creative thinking," by pointing out that the optimum freedom to imagine and the best motivation to do so may be made ineffective in part or whole by a negative organizational overtone. The feeling may be rampant and deep among the company's personnel that in the last analysis nothing new, and especially nothing daring, will be tolerated or supported by the company's controlling hierarchy. Worse still, discouraging statements of a wide variety may take their toll upon the attitude and actions of the planner. He may hear such comments as these: "Why make new suggestions, nobody listens anyway?"; "If you make a suggestion for some new project, you get saddled with it!"; "There isn't any money, why dream?"; "We tried it before and it failed!"; "Can you prove that there is a demand for it or that it will work?"; and "Policy will not permit it." Many an administrator who deplores the lack of new ideas coming up from his staff should cast a critical glance at the organization's overtone as related to dreaming and the forward look. Creative thinking flourishes best in an atmosphere of receptivity.

The Pattern and Process of Planning

The Good Plan

In the discussion of planning, it is customary to devote some attention to the characteristics of the so-called good plan.[6] Such qualities as clarity, flexibility, and workability are often mentioned. These and many other positive features may be qualities of a good plan. However, there is a distinct, if frequently overlooked danger, in any categorical description of a plan as good. That plan is best which, within the bounds of morality and law, best suits the situation demanding it. This view is in keeping with the whole concept of administrative strategy. The line of reasoning can be advanced more concretely by pointing out that there are instances when quite the opposite of qualities commonly set forth in administration literature are necessary to make the plan fit the situation. Some examples will clarify the point. The president of a corporation, desiring that his bold forward step be given much developmental discussion by his staff, may intentionally neglect the cause of clarity and describe his plans in only the vaguest terms. A district sales manager, under orders from the home office to push "bread and butter" replenishment items at the expense of new equipment being developed by the company, may draw up rigid plans for a sales campaign, allowing neither himself nor his staff any real opportunity to modify them. The personnel officer, directed from above to hold the line on executive compensation but also pressured by the executives to do something for them, may draw up a plan calling for such a radical increase in expenditures that it is not acceptable to the top echelon and, hence, unworkable. Such are the dynamic implications of realistic administration that obscurity, rigidity, and impracticality may be necessary attributes of a plan. And so it is plain that no one list of characteristics can be given as descriptive of the good plan.

Good Planning

Although it is not possible to define a plan as *good* in terms of fixed characteristics, it does seem possible to describe good planning as a process.[7] Whatever may be the type of plan most suited to the dynamics of the particular situation, there are a number of basic principles of planning to which the planner or planning entity must adhere if the best results are to be attained.

The first principle is the fact that there is no way of planning best for every administrative need, but rather that there are clear alternative methods to fit different situations. A few alternatives will be suggestive.[8] If time is short and close coordination between fields of activity being touched not absolutely essential, planning by an individual or small group may be most practical. Should time be short but close coordination vital, this individual or group should be one with strong central authority. If acceptability to large numbers is more important than speed or coordination, planning through conferences and committees may promise most.

Normally, the organization should draw upon the best planning ability available.[9] This is the second principle. The reason is quite obvious in terms of end product desired. However, there may be circumstances arguing against the use of the best planners. For instance, such individuals may have a point of view which the organization can not afford to have reflected in the plan; they may not possess the standing and respect necessary for the selling of the plan; or they may represent interests whose power the organization cannot afford to enhance by any further recognition of their ability.

A third principle logically follows. The actual work of planning should be entrusted either to the operational administrator or to some person or entity knowledgeable of the operational pattern and problems of the organization.[10] In most cases, it is only through the tempering effect of their practical and particular knowledge that the organization can be assured of a realistic plan. Unfortunately, it is possible to draw up and even sell to the top administration of a company a plan which is little more than a beautiful staff exercise. The president or other high official wants planned proposals. He is in the front line of company offense and defense. A well-written plan may appear to him to be almost a providential weapon, and plans totally unrealistic can be made, by their comprehensiveness, consistency of parts, conviction of tone, and format of writing, to appear most desirable.

The fourth principle recognizes the internal and external public relations implications of planning and the plan being drawn.[11] It can be stated thus: the planning activity should be such as to cause the minimum disturbance to company overtone, morale, and image or, if the planning activity is designed as a motivational device, to bring the type and degree of disturbance desired. The implementation of this principle quite obviously demands an overview and estimate of attitudes and expected reaction both inside and outside of the organization. There is here a possibility of balancing risk against risk and proceeding as the net balance indicates. Reference is had to situations in which one organizational administrator or administrative clique may be strongly opposed to the direction of planning but others firmly in favor of it. Reference is had also to the situation in which one set of attitudes and reactions is expected from the organization and another from the community, the company's customers, or even the nation as a whole.

The fifth and final principle lies in the flexibility of planning activity. This is not to be confused with flexibility as a characteristic of a plan. It means rather that the planning entity keep itself so free from binding commitments that it can be selective in its direction of thinking, manipulative in handling resources for planning, and strategically poised to use either defensive or offensive planning techniques. Unfortunately, superior authority whose stamp of approval is frequently necessary on "plans for planning before planning can start" sometimes places restrictive policies, rules, and regulations on those who are to do the planning. Therefore, the planner, or the leader of the planning group, may be compelled to take steps to circumvent these restrictions, and so he may find himself assuring the top administrator that he agrees with him and will comply with his desires, interpreting the orders and expressed wishes of the top administrator most fully, and/or deliberately not reporting planning deviations unless and until it becomes feasible to make them known in successful terms. What has just been written is not intended to suggest the wisdom or desirability of deceit. The aim is rather to recognize the fact that in a busy world the administrator whose approval is necessary may not see the planning picture clearly, may need education from below, and may, in fact, be quite agreeable to wise interpretation of his dicta.

Cognate Uses of Planning

Planning is ordinarily done to lay the course of some future action. However, the administrator may occasionally find it to be a device well suited to accomplish one or more of a large category of other objectives. Yet he should be wary of the dishonorable course, for planning can be rather easily perverted to uses and ends which smack of the ethically improper. Among the cognate objectives of planning at least five may be mentioned prominently.

To Delay and Divert

The activity of planning can be used by subordinate administrators as a stalling device. There is a certain action implication in planning. Sometimes the superior in the organization can be satisfied or mollified at least momentarily by being assured, when he presses for action on a problem, that the first step in action, planning, is being taken. Furthermore, many a superior is afraid to demand more and faster action when his subordinates confront him with the report that the necessary planning is not yet finished. The possibility of wrong movement, and of the failure and criticism which may ensue, may loom up alarmingly in his mind when he hears the strongly advanced statement, "but we still are in the planning stage."

Planning also can be used as a delaying and diverting device by the administrative superior. There are many occasions when he may order planning to avoid making a decision or taking action. He may need more time to study and evaluate not only suggestions or requests but also the total background against which action decisions on them must be taken. He may wish to force pressuring individuals or groups into a cooling-off period. He may feel that, if they are given the actual job of planning, they will convert themselves away from their original ideas by studying the difficulties and repercussions inherent therein. He may even want time in which to formulate and weigh alternative plans, get approval for them from his superiors (perhaps the board of directors), and maneuver his employees into a mood or position receptive to these counterproposals.

To Raise a Smoke Screen

Planning may be utilized as a means of confusing associates or competitors regarding the direction of movement. This might, for example, be the step undertaken by the administrator who employs a management consulting service to draw up a new manpower program, when in reality he simply wants facts brought out into the open which will make it possible for him to fire the personnel director. It might, for example, also be the course pursued by the Agrahan Baking Company in ordering its branch bakeries to run a bread preference survey and in openly planning an advertising drive, when actually it is seeking information upon which to base its asking terms in a merger proposed by the Wotje Bread Company. Planning which results in deliberate confusion may raise ethical questions.

To Make Busy Work

A further cognate of planning is to be found in its use as company "busy work." Business concerns at times find themselves overstaffed but for some reasons do not wish to discharge any personnel. In order to assure reasonable morale in the department or company as a whole or to avoid criticism from some financial watch-dog, a responsible administrator will put the temporarily idle personnel to work on writing plans—an activity which seems to have no limit. But overstaffing is not the only occasion to use planning as busy work. Another pertinent situation would be the existence within the organization of an energetic critic or critics whose attention and efforts could be diverted from criticism by assignment to a planning project to ventilate their feelings by such activity. And still another case in which planning might be used simply as something to do is found in the necessity for keeping the formal planning office of the organization busy so that its gears do not get rusty between more regular planning projects.

To Pace Organizational Growth

A further special use of planning may aptly be described as "planning to pace institutional growth and development." No organization, business or otherwise, can with safety always entrust its expansion to chance. There are factors, such as financial resources and an uninformed but promising potential market, which definitely set a measured pace for wise growth. There are also other factors, such as the enthusiasm or capacity of personnel and the immediately profitable market for products, which argue for a more headlong forward movement. The planning device can be used to keep these two opposing forces in balance. For example, the long term capital sources which would have to be tapped to finance the building of a new plant in an outstate location are asking high interest rates, but the general sales manager may be excited over growing family formation and the large market it promises. By ordering a long market study and an extensive sales plan drawn up, the president can delay commitment to high financing costs and at the same time save some of the enthusiasm of the general sales manager. Here is planning truly pacing company expansion.

To Launch a Trial Balloon

The utilization of planning to send up the well-known trial balloon is a distinct cognate technique. The company management may not be certain as to the public receptivity of a new brewing plant in a suburb. The president decides, as a preliminary planning step, upon the employment of a market survey service to study publicly the local beer market and to submit data along with recommendations regarding expansion. Apart from the fact that he actually may want the information and recommendations, he can analyze the reactions of people sampled, of the newspapers, and of civic organizations to the whole idea of a new brewery. Should these gauges of public feeling indicate negative attitude of serious proportions, he can well retreat, having done nothing more than plan; and, of course, he can make the decision to build the new plant more surely if they indicate a positive reaction of the public involved.

To Test Ability

A final twist to the use of planning for other than future action guidance is found when the administrator orders a subordinate to give him a plan on some matter for the real purpose of studying the analytical and constructive ability of the individual. No doubt this use is commonly combined as a corollary with the more usual role of planning. The superior, really wanting the plan for its own sake, gives the job of planning to whom he desires to test.

Conclusion

Planning is a fertile field for administrative strategy. It occurs in some form prior to most decision making and action.[12] Its nature, dimensions, and potential cannot be explained adequately by an exposition of the classical steps commonly identified in its description. Planning is gamesmanship, and proper planning is gamesmanship of a high order, since it involves the selection, use, and maneuvering of ideas, people, money, things, and time to meet the needs of a particular situation. Properly done, it demands respect for precedent as well as the ability and courage to imagine and think creatively.

A definite purpose is commonly assigned planning by the more or less superficial student of the topic. It is the laying of a scheme for future action. But he who concerns himself more analytically with planning comes to see that it can be used for purposes other than future guidance. These purposes constitute an enlargement of its role, but, if left within the framework of morality, a legitimate category of usage.

BUSINESS SITUATIONS FOR ROLE-PLAYING

SITUATION IX
Stratagems in Planning

THE STATE BANK OF COMMERCE

A. Scene.   An insular commercial bank. The Chairman of the Board has called in the President to discuss plans for celebrating the fiftieth anniversary of their business.

B. Players.   1. Chairman of the Board: Mr. Jose Dimenez, son of the founder, aristocrat, lover of pomp and ceremony who, however, always keeps a sharp eye open for business promotion.

2. President: Mr. Archibald Mortimer, a state-side young financial genius and graduate of a College of Business Administration in a great eastern university, who is motivated largely by an intense desire to operate an efficient bank.

C. Situation. 1. The Chairman of the Board is very unhappy about the way the twenty-fifth anniversary was celebrated, so he instructs Mr. Mortimer not to bother with the "old plans" but to start all over with some new and different approaches.

This is the second attempt to review progress on celebration plans. The President has not given the planning much attention, and has not consulted with his subordinates. Up to now, he has suggested little more than coffee hour and souvenirs for the group.

D. Assignment. 1. Select two persons to act out the roles with emphasis on the strategic considerations in planning, especially as they relate to overcoming precedent and unimaginative thinking.

2. After the performance, elicit from the group six practical devices not brought forth by the performers which the President could have used in drawing up a new and interesting program.

NOTES

1. This chapter is not intended to be a comprehensive exposition of planning, but, in conformity with the purpose of the entire book, it confines itself to a discussion of strategic possibilities in planning.

   For a thorough treatment of the general subject of planning in administration, see WILLIAM H. NEWMAN, *Administrative Action*. (Englewood Cliffs, N.J.: Prentice-Hall, Inc., 1950), Part I, pp. 13-120.

2. The thought that sound objectives and principles should not be compromised in business planning is emphasized by RALPH CURRIER DAVIS, *The Fundamentals of Top Management* (New York: Harper & Brothers, Publishers, 1951), pp. 72-74.

3. Professor Drucker comments on the necessity for each subordinate manager to set goals. PETER F. DRUCKER, *The Practice of Management* (New York: Harper & Brothers, Publishers, 1954), p. 129.
4. BILLY E. GOETZ, *Management Planning and Control* (New York: McGraw-Hill Book Company, Inc., 1949), p. 66.
5. MARSHALL EDWARD DIMOCK, *The Executive in Action* (New York: Harper & Brothers, Publishers, 1945), pp. 123-124.
6. Fayol and Urwick enumerate what they believe to be its broad characteristics. See HENRI FAYOL, *General and Industrial Management*, trans. CONSTANCE STORRS (London: Sir Isaac Pitman & Sons, Ltd., 1949), pp. 44-45; and L. URWICK, *The Elements of Administration* (New York: Harper & Brothers, Publishers, n.d.), p. 34.
7. Planning as a process is treated at length by NEWMAN, *op. cit.*, pp. 81-99.
8. Suggested by COMSTOCK GLASER, *Administrative Procedure* (Washington, D.C.: The American Council on Public Affairs, n.d.), p. 72.
9. "One of the striking management developments of the decade of the 'fifties was the appearance of formal organization planning units. It is safe to say that by 1960 organization planning had become one of the most influential staff activities in larger organizations. . . ." JOHN M. PFIFFNER and FRANK P. SHERWOOD, *Administrative Organization* (Englewood Cliffs, N.J.: Prentice-Hall, Inc., 1960), p. 242.
10. WILLIAM J. McLARNEY, *Management Training: Cases and Principles* (Homewood, Illinois: Richard D. Irwin, Inc., 1952), pp. 114-117.
11. NEWMAN, *op. cit.*, pp. 110-119.
12. ". . . even where the future bears a high degree of certainty, some planning is necessary. In the first place, there are many ways to consider accomplishing an objective, and there is the necessity of selecting from among these the best way. . . . In the second place, when the decision as to a course of action is made, it is necessary to lay out plans or blueprints so that each segment of the business will contribute toward the job to be done." HAROLD KOONTZ and CYRIL O'DONNELL, *Principles of Management* (New York: McGraw-Hill Book Company, Inc., 1955), p. 437.

    Competition is responsible for an increasing amount of planning. CHARLES E. ST. THOMAS, *Practical Business Planning* (New York: American Management Association, 1965), p. 14.

CHAPTER **10**

The Reorganization Vehicle

> "Reorganization is a valuable device for the executive who sees administration as strategy. At first thought, it may be concluded that reorganization is simply a means by which company organizational structure is changed. Actually, it can be made to serve a considerable number and variety of purposes, some of which are quite far removed from the fact of structure."

THE TERM "organization" bears two connotations. It may be interpreted to mean structure[1] or to designate the act of arrangement.[2] The former meaning is of importance as of a point of time, for it signifies accomplishment. One correctly speaks of the schematic plan or structure of a company, as its organization. The latter meaning is dynamic, and so is here of greater import. In a treatment of administrative strategy, it is the act, and not the result, which is the prime subject. Attention will be devoted, therefore, to organization as the *process of arranging*.

Orientation

In the sense of arranging, organization is more or less continual for the business concern. This laconic statement needs explanation. The entity known as a company or department

218

thereof has various components which can be arranged into a structure: the intangibles commonly described as goals, responsibilities, power, and functions; and the well known tangibles—resources, facilities, men, and already established policy making or administrative units. But not only *can* they be arranged; they *must* be arranged. It is only by the establishment of certain relations among these components that the entity's goals are to be attained. For example, sufficient power must be given the administrator to discharge his responsibilities; and resources, facilities, and men must be assigned to functions or the latter cannot be carried out. All this is rather academic, but the question remains, "Why describe organization as a continual process?" The answer is found in the fact that the company or department operates in an everchanging environment, which places different demands upon it in the pursuit of its objectives, and in the fact that no one arrangement of components is for long adequate to meet these demands with satisfactory efficiency and results.[3]

Yet, in its strictest meaning, the act of arrangement can take place but once. That is at the time when the company or department is first established. From then on, rearranging to meet new needs and problems becomes the pattern of conduct.[4] A new term obviously is demanded and, consequently, it seems proper to select *reorganization*. A wit has said that the only significance of organization lies in the fact that it is the first step in reorganization. Some may deny the overwhelming role of reorganization, because they do not see major changes being made in the relationships of company or department components. This is not a valid basis for denial. Many, rather than large, changes are the evidence necessary to establish the existence of continual rearrangement. That it is a reality is seen by the analytical administrator who, in meeting or handling better the challenge of such strains and stresses as rising costs, internal conflict, or pressure from competing products or services, must frequently shift (though often only to some small degree) intra-company or intra-department relationships.

Reorganization is a valuable device for the executive who sees administration as strategy.[5] At first thought, it may be concluded that reorganization is simply a means by which company organizational structure is changed. Actually, it can be made to serve a considerable number and variety of purposes, some of which are quite far removed from the fact of structure.[6]

What are the usages to which reorganization may be put? Certainly no exhaustive list can be attempted, for the reason that they vary so much with the circumstances and nature of the rearrangement. However, four require special mention and treatment because of their possibilities. They may be described as correction of the statics of company or department structure, liquidation of particular roadblocks to efficient operation, change of organizational image in the minds of employees and other "publics," and the acquisition, retention, and promotion of personnel.

Correction of the Statics of Structure

The impression that everything is fluid in the arrangement of company or department components may have been encouraged by the preceding paragraphs. This was not the intention. It must always be remembered that, although the administrator should be alert and ready to change various aspects of the structure of his entity when circumstances require such action, there are parts of it that are designed to, and commonly do, remain fixed for long periods of time, even for the life of the business concern. These may be thought of as comprising the hard skeletal core of organization. Some illustrations come to mind with respect to a given company: its line arrangement of board of directors, president, general manager, and subordinate officials with a predominantly downward flow of power; its complex of multiple plants; its decentralization of administration; and its entrustment of immediate supervision to shop foreman and office managers.

Yet, these more or less fixed features of a company's or department's structure can become obsolete and inadequate. It should always be remembered that no aspect of structure is sacred. A particular organizational scheme is to be justified only in terms of its contribution to effective administration, since, in the last analysis, structure is but one device by which management pursues its operational goal or goals. Therefore, even though they may enjoy relatively more immunity from change, these so-called fixed features of the organization may properly be made the subject for attempted improvement.

Circumstances Requiring Change

There are at least three circumstances which, in the interest of more effective administration, require some change in the relatively stable aspects of the organizational structure. Certainly, one is the inability of the existing structure to function with sufficient speed. This condition may be illustrated by a television broadcasting company whose final acceptance of an advertising contract depends upon the action of a standing contract committee having all the slowness inherent in the committee organism. Obviously, the committee, as a final approving agency, must be removed or shorn of its decision making power. Another circumstance calling for reorganization of the firmer building blocks in the structure is difficulty in communication. Although the common problem of arteriosclerosis in communication channels is not necessarily the result of some wrong stable arrangement in structure, it does occur as a result of fixed features. For example, the office of general manager in an old line automobile parts manufacturing company long may have "run the whole show." Directions from the president to plant managers rarely reach them in their original meaning, suffering attrition as they pass through the general manager's bottleneck. Suggestions from the lower echelons and the field likewise rarely get beyond the office of the general manager, where they are entrapped. The solution is reorganization of the general manager's hierarchical position, responsibilities, power, and functions. The third circumstance that demands change in the status of organization is the degree of rigidity which prevents it from having the adaptability necessary to the various challenges of administration. This condition is seen, for instance, in the case of the cosmetic manufacturing company that repeatedly fails to meet the competition of concerns producing more glamorous beauty aids because its staid research department has the final word on the adoption of new products. Here is a case for the relocation or liquidation of a really fixed feature of organization that brings too great a degree of rigidity.

The Direct Approach

Changing the nature or status of the so-called fixed features of the organizational structure is not always to be approached in the same way. For want of better terms, one may state that the task can be handled directly or indirectly. In the direct approach, the company officials with necessary authority recognize the difficulty and move to correct it with action aimed directly at it. The president of the television broadcasting company abolishes the committee and appoints one contracting officer for all advertising. The board of directors of the automotive parts firm proceeds to have the corporate by-laws amended in such manner as to reduce the position of general manager to that of first executive assistant to the president and thus to destroy the effectiveness of the general manager's bottleneck. The president of the cosmetic firm attaches the research department, which formerly acted with great independence, to the office of the director of marketing, who thus receives sole authority to make all new product recommendations to the president.

Oblique Movement

However, some conditions may make it unwise or even impossible to move so logically and expeditiously against the sacred cows of time-honored structure. Among these conditions are the degree of influence in final company decisions enjoyed by the offending organizational unit; the likelihood of this entity reacting in some retaliatory action dangerous to the company, department, or attacking executive; the negative influence on internal morale or public attitude resulting from the disturbance of change; and the possible slow-up of or other disturbance to operational efficiency incidental to the change-over. In the light of these repercussions, it may behoove the "reforming company authority" to move obliquely.

There are a variety of oblique courses open to him. He should note, because of their potential effectiveness, such courses as the employment of a special internal systems group or of an outside consultant to study and recommend changes which are expected to include modification or realignment of structure, abandonment of certain units, or creation of new structural entities. He should also take cognizance of the so-called proliferation procedure by which superior authority in a company or department leaves officially undisturbed the offending structural unit or aspect but moves to circumvent it by the by-passing of it. The reorganizing official may do this either by simply ignoring the stumbling block and dealing with some other official or office of the organization on matters traditionally entrusted to the offender, or by the employment of personal assistants or specialists to undertake many of the functions previously handled by the established official or office. The expression "proliferation procedure" seems quite apt here, for its use really involves the creation of additional or super-administrative machinery. (It is in this context that one finds the so-called informal leader commonly being used by top echelons to "get around" administrative opposition.) In extreme cases, top authority may, in an effort to circumvent effective organizational resistance, go so far as to bring about the creation of whole new departments or even companies without touching the established organizational entity.

A final indirect device for reorganizing the static aspects of company or department structure is more subtle than those just mentioned and, in reality, is probably a step in the direction of more forceful action. Reference is had to a campaign by the administrator of publicizing the weaknesses of an existing feature in his own organization. Higher management not infrequently undertakes to discredit one or more of its own subordinate entities in an effort to set it up for final radical change or destruction. Such an action may pose an ethical issue.

Liquidation of Particular Roadblocks

In rearranging organizational components to modify or remove more or less permanent features of the company or department structure, management is, in effect, practicing self-surgery of a basic corrective nature. However, reorganization is an instrument which can also be used to change or excise organizational roadblocks of a less fixed and general nature. These roadblocks to administration are found in personnel, policies, and practices. They could be, for example, a senior member of intermediate management who opposes the president's program; a policy which prevents the president from taking a necessary inconsistent step; or an administrative practice that places company affairs in a worse than necessary light.

There may be a temptation to view this category of organizational ailments as composed of relatively superficial matters which higher authority can handle by plain executive decree. Many of them are of such nature as to be amenable to this treatment. It is also true that many of them are very difficult problems to solve, problems so stubborn that they cannot be swept away by mere command. The great degree of human interest involved accounts for much of their resistance to solution by order from above. Even more so than in the attack on the so-called fixed organizational features are human loyalties, feelings, and opinions likely to be involved in the effort to modify or liquidate personnel, policy, or practice obstructions in the organization. These obstacles are frequently of closer concern to members of the organizational family (since they participated in their development or employment) than the rigidities built into the organizational structure by a founding father or other company official well removed in time or authority from them. Resort, then, can be had to reorganization to sweep aside these roadblocks by changing the frame of reference in which they arose.

Personnel Obstacles

Inefficient or obstreperous personnel may be considered as a primary roadblock which demands reorganization in one of a number of instances. A common case is that in which the offending individual has great potential value to the company, and higher authority does not wish to lose his services. Therefore, in an effort to get him out of the way of progress but at the same time keep him in the organization, his office may be abolished and another position created. This step will place him where he can be less dangerous and more helpful in the pursuit of organizational aims. It is clearly more than a simple transfer. It is an act of reorganization, for there has been a rearranging of company components.

Another need for the reorganization technique in handling personnel problems may appear if the repercussion of more drastic action (discharge, transfer, demotion or promotion) promises to be great. The undesirable official or employee may have support from sources that are able and willing to cause real trouble if he is the clear target of corrective action by the company head. These sources can range all the way from company employees who like the unfortunate person or persons, to a member of the board of directors who resents the president and is willing to brand any punitive or corrective action by him as improper, and on to customers of the company who have been given special deals by the person in trouble with management and who, therefore, have good reason to try to protect him. Unfortunately for the company president, the types of opposition and other trouble from these sources can be just as diverse as their number. It is necessary but to mention representations widely publicized, let-down in productive efficiency, internal maneuvering "to get" the president, and threatened or actual shift of purchases to other companies. The point in this instance is that the president, or whoever the company executive responsible may be, simply cannot afford to make a martyr or martyrs of the offending individual. Here, of course, resort can be had to reorganization to solve the dilemma. By some juggling, eliminating, or adding of organizational components (responsibilities, power, authority, functions, positions or any other) the president can create a structure which has no need for the person in question or which at least places him in a spot which is sufficiently good to satisfy his supporters but from which he can do less or no harm to smooth operation. Quite clearly, such use of reorganization can involve delicate questions of administrative ethics, and it therefore behooves the official who undertakes its employment to analyze and channel his actions carefully.

A final personnel situation open for the use of reorganization is one of the more delicate problems which an administrator must occasionally face. It is the necessity, in the interests of company efficiency, to rid the organization of a person with whom he is closely tied by bonds other than immediate efficiency, e.g., by blood or marital relationships, by past services from the subordinate or subordinates, by personal association, or by plain affection. Perhaps the purpose usually served by using reorganization to eliminate or downgrade "close connections" within the company is that of face-saving and avoidance of unpleasantness or revenge. Executives, like all human beings, at times do make decisions in response to emotional considerations. A device, such as reorganization, which may be used honorably by the executive to free himself in decision making from the undue influence of sentiment has a place in the administrative toolchest. There is no intention in this statement to deny the nobility of loyalty nor to contend that administrative decision should never be based on it alone. Quite to the contrary, one should remember that honor itself may demand that loyalty be an overwhelming influence in executive decision. Even further, one should bear in mind that decision on the basis of loyalty may be very wise strategy in winning and keeping the support not only of the personnel involved but of the employees in general. This suggests that the executive who is embarrassed about the deed can, through the degree of disassociation which reorganization gives, remove himself further from the fact of having to break a personal tie and so take greater courage to do it. The formula is simple. Rearrange the components of the organization so that the job of the target individual disappears and so that there simply are no other jobs for him. One additional idea may be added by advancing the thought that the executive can further insulate himself against the pain of injuring a friend or other associate by having as little direct connection as possible with the planning and implementation of reorganization. One way for the executive to reduce the repercussions of personal involvement is to use outside consultants for recommending reorganizational changes that will eliminate undesired personnel with whom he has close personal connections. This device is often employed.[7]

Policy and Practice Blockades

Personnel do not constitute the only "particular" organizational obstacle to more efficient administration. As mentioned in preceding paragraphs, there are also policies and practices which may stand in its way. Here again the question arises, "Why bother to change the structure of a company or department simply because it has a policy or practice inimical to better administration?" The answer is partially implied in the preceding paragraphs which attempt to justify the use of reorganization as a means of removing personnel obstacles. Yet there are other distinct and peculiar reasons for its justification.

That policies (settled courses adopted) and practices (repeated or customary actions) can be pervasive and entangling phenomena must be emphasized. A policy or practice well developed and long followed by any company or department can become a type of cancerous growth so inextricably embedded in the organizational structure that the only way it can be changed or eliminated completely is to modify or get rid of the existing arrangement of organizational components, that is, to reorganize. This may be a rather obscure concept, and it probably can best be explained by illustration.

The hypothetical case of the Calumpet Publishing House which, since the turn of the century, has been placing its printing with the small but well run Market Alley Press may be analyzed to make the idea concrete. Practice has become, in fact, more than a usual procedure. Constant satisfactory dealings with the Market Alley Press have gradually crystallized into a Calumpet policy of neither considering nor placing printing with any other press. The years have, however, greatly enhanced the volume of business being done by the Calumpet Publishing House. Its president is becoming increasingly aware that there are other good printers, that there is the possibility of receiving competitive price bids from them, and that the Market Alley Press is at times unable to handle all the increased demands which Calumpet is placing on its productive capacity. The president of Calumpet's decides, therefore, to revise the policy of dealing only with Market Alley Press and to throw open his company's printing work to competitive bids. He discovers, however, that over the many years of exclusive dealing with Market Alley Press the organization of his production department has become closely geared to Market Alley's manner of doing business. He learns to his dismay, upon discussing his ideas with the various administrators in the production department, that any shift away from Market Alley would make it impossible for the present department to operate with anything like reasonable efficiency. He is face to face with a hard cold fact of administration. Performance of organizational functions according to certain principles and in a certain way over an appreciable period of time brings an evolution in the nature and capacity of organizational structure. He is forced to reconsider his approach—and so he comes to the conclusion that the only avenue open is reorganization. Hence, he orders the production department to be overhauled and a contract negotiating office added, so that Calumpet may adopt the new policy of open market placement of printing.

There is an even more complex policy and practice commitment than the one illustrated above, and it, too, can be liquidated through reorganization. This is found in the situation in which a department of a company holds the power to determine some of its own policies and practices, and becomes so possessive of and identified with this "right" that it can resist successfully normal action by higher management to get it to change them. The department may have come into the possession of such power in many ways, for example by long usage of independence allowed it in the organization, through the personality of the chief or some other person in the department, or as a result of leadership cowardice or lack of ingenuity on the part of top management of the company. But, regardless of how it got the power, it does appear impregnable to ordinary executive attack. The president of the company (or some other official with the authority to effect rearrangement in company structure) can bring about changes in the undesirable behavior pattern of the department by reorganizing the department.

Perhaps this reorganization would take the form of splitting the department into two or more mutually independent parts, or it might be carried out by consolidating it with a department friendly to the president's views. Whatever way the structure is changed, the act of reorganization does have certain advantages in handling departments recalcitrant on matters of policy and practice. It has a good chance of success, because it breaks up the combination of factors that constituted the effective resistance. It may well be a long, if not lasting, solution to the particular undesirable behavior commitment inasmuch as time will generally be necessary for a new area of similar rigidity to arise. Finally, reorganization may in part screen the real purpose of higher officialdom, since it can be done apparently for many considerations other than breaking the particular resistance front. This is an especially important advantage of the reorganization technique when the department in question has long been a favorite of management even higher than the reorganizing authority (as it may well have been to acquire the independent power it possesses). A frontal attack under these circumstances might be interpreted as a manifestation of bad faith on the part of the echelon making it. Concealment of real purpose can also propose a question of fairness which must be answered by the administrator in each particular case.

Change of Image

The image of a company or unit thereof is "the way it looks" to the people cognizant of it. There are two basic types of images of anything: a true picture, the image which reflects the subject as it really exists; and the false impression, the image in some manner distorted from its actual subject. This difference does not necessarily connote any element of chicanery on the part of the company or department, since untrue images are frequently the result of factors well beyond the control of the entity itself. Nor does the difference necessarily imply that there are two patterns of public reaction—one to the true and one to the untrue image. The stimulus of an incorrect or a pseudo-image can be exactly the same as that of a correct reflection of a subject. Examples of this fact are rife in all aspects of life.

Regardless of the nature of mental impressions, the image of his company or department is of vital import to the administrator. The reaction of its "publics" to it will be based in large measure upon how it appears to each. This fact has both internal and external implications, because there are publics both within and without the company or the unit of it he administers. In a loose sense, the former consists of his staff and other employees; the latter of all those not directly associated with the company. Strictly speaking, there is a third public—the intermediate zone of people who belong neither to the company nor department but whose associations are closer than plain outsiders. In this intermediate zone are company personnel, if the administrator handles less than the whole company, not in his division of the organization and a host of other close organizational associates such as professionals on contract to the company, relatives of employees, and vendors or customers of long and very intimate standing.

With this superficial analysis of image, there may be raised the real question at issue, "How can reorganization be used to effect a change in the image of a business or industrial entity?" There are various angles from which this question can be answered. One approach, within the framework of a treatment of administrative strategy, is to seek an answer in terms of the different types of publics involved, since the wisest use of the reorganization device to change image seems to demand a different pattern in each case.

Reorganization and the Internal Image

It is a truism that proper public relations begin at home. Therefore, attention must first be devoted to changing the image held by the internal public. This task can be either very simple or most difficult. The administrator under certain circumstances scarcely needs do more than drop a few hints as to new company or unit organization, policies, or practices, and his people will eagerly seize upon a new picture of their employing entity. One such fortuitous circumstance is an intense and general desire on the part of the administrator's subordinate executives and employees for company change. This desire may be generated by their deep dissatisfaction with something in the company. Another of these happy conditions is great attachment for and confidence in their company, division or administrator, which may express itself in a receptivity to company suggestion and action. In neither of these circumstances would it seem necessary to bring out the big guns of reorganization to clear the way for the evolution of a new image.

Yet, there is reason to suspect that the job of changing the internal image is often more difficult. It can involve a re-education of the people most intimately associated with the subject of the image, i.e., those who work for it and see it as their employer. They are in a good position to know the truth, and efforts of real intent and substance may be required to make them change their minds as to what the company or their division in it is really like. It is not always easy to give them a pseudo-image by minor organizational changes, blandishments, plans, and promises. Their "hard-headedness" may even be enhanced by their close emotional tie-up with their employing entity. Many of their ambitions, hopes, fears, and satisfactions spring from the company or unit, or are otherwise associated with it. Strangely enough, this close emotional involvement may cause them either to feel strong ownership for the entity or to wish to disavow it. Either state of mind is a potentially effective barrier to image change by the administrator. The ownership complex generates a protective stance for the existing image; the disavowal attitude, commonly a "don't-care" or suspicious feeling toward anything company representatives may say or do.

The administrator facing the task of changing the internal image may thus be confronted with a really tough problem, the solution of which demands nothing less than the creation of the necessary new subject for the image. The use of reorganization is indicated. By effecting a rearrangement of the organizational structure, he can do a great deal toward influencing his sub-leaders and employees to develop the new and desired mental picture. The boldest feature of company or department personality is its organizational structure, and a shift in it is most likely to impress all who work for it.

An illustration may be helpful. In a meat packing plant the management and employees of the stockyard division, which receives the incoming livestock shipments, have long looked upon themselves as scarcely belonging to the company family. The administration of the company is anxious, in the interests of better performance in the stockyards, to effect a change in this attitude. It has tried higher pay to compensate for unusual working conditions, but to no avail.

It has meticulously provided stockyard workers with all social perquisites, such as nice dressing rooms and refreshment facilities. In spite of these efforts the stockyard division continues to sulk. Realizing finally the difficulty of the problem, the president decides that the only solution is to abolish the stockyard organization as such, so that its employees cannot continue to identify themselves with what is, in their minds, a low-brow or unrecognized division. Therefore, he orders that the stockyard division be made a department of the butchering division, that it be administered by the head of this division, that complete integration of personnel policies and practices take place, and particularly that promotions in the future be made in either direction from those working in the stockyards and from those employed "inside." In short, he has resorted to reorganization.

Changing the External Image by Reorganization

Reorganization would seem to be a particularly useful device to bring about a different image in the mind of the external public. The public without the company generally does not see it or any part of it in as intimate detail as do those who work for it. It is reasonable to assume, therefore, that outsiders think of it in terms of its boldest feature, and organizational structure is certainly one of these. Public image in terms of organizational features is illustrated by two limited surveys recently completed. A cross-section of two hundred mature individuals in Detroit were questioned as to how they saw the General Motors Corporation. Over 75 per cent of the answers described it in some manner as a grouping of car producing divisions. In an effort to verify these findings, an effort was made to ascertain the external image of a company whose image may not be as much affected by popular identification of product as that of General Motors. When two hundred Detroit men and women were solicited for their impression of the E. I. DuPont de

Nemours and Company, more than 67 per cent replied in some manner as to indicate that DuPont has a vast business empire, including a large element of control in the General Motors Corporation. Two limited samplings of this type by themselves may mean nothing, but they are suggestive of the impact which organizational features can have on the outside public. If the assumption is correct then obviously reorganization, especially if of a nature and dimension ample enough to attract public attention, can help change the external image of the company and its parts.

The Reorganization Device and the Intermediate Public

The so-called intermediate public remains to be discussed. The administrator concerned with changing the picture in the minds of these people can be encouraged by two possible conditions. They may be less blinded by a commitment to an old image than are the personnel of the company or department, since they have not been as intimate with the organization. They may also be more knowledgeable of the true picture than are those who make up the external public, because they have been closer to it than the outsiders. The happy significance to our administrator lies in the fact that this group is probably easier to re-educate than either of the other two publics.

As a matter of fact, it seems that few administrators ever concern themselves particularly with reconverting the intermediate public. They usually see only the two more commonly recognized publics. Yet, the strategic administrator, especially the one who has decided to get at the matter of image change through reorganization, may find in this intermediate zone a proper testing ground for his reorganizational proposals. Appropriate individuals can be asked for their opinion on decentralization, for example, with less fear of receiving a prejudiced answer than from company or department personnel and with less fear of receiving an unenlightened reply than from rank outsiders. An occasional administrator sometimes employs the intermediate public still further and in a manner which may be dishonorable. Since it is not a cohesive unit, the executive easily can search in it for those who will support his reorganizational proposals and steps, ignore those who do not or whom he does not contact, and present the opinions of the supporters as the views of "other employees, vendors, customers, etc.," with little worry that any tide of rebuttal will appear.

Cautions

Before leaving the topic of reorganization as an image smasher and builder, certain cautions in its use must be noted. Foremost is the fact that, to be effective, the reorganization required may have to be "larger" than good administration, exclusive of image changing, may demand. To assure better morale on the part of the stockyard employees, the president was forced to merge their division with the key division of his business. Yet is it not likely that few stockyard workers qualify easily in the butchering department and few butchers want to move outside to drive the animals about. Desire to change images via the reorganization route can bring administration to over-do reorganization. Another caution must be stated. Sometimes a company or department may by design proceed to create an unrealistic image of itself by organizational changes which it heralds as far-sweeping and of major significance but which are actually important or existent only on its organizational charts. A clever publicity campaign may delude all the publics. When expected results in improved administration and operation are not forthcoming the danger that a serious reaction will set in against the company or unit is always present. This reaction may be particularly strong from those who expected direct gain from the reorganization and did not see in it merely a public relations move. The stockholders can be expected to become most clamorous when it becomes apparent that the reorganization was largely window-dressing. It scarcely need be stated that stockholders can cause real trouble for company management!

A danger to public relations is inherent in the process of image changing by reorganization. The various publics may draw the wrong image from the rearranged organization. There is no magic accuracy of impression-giving that accompanies reorganization for any purpose. It may be necessary, therefore, to communicate early and accurately any organizational changes. Delay and incomplete education as to change can be costly.[8]

The Acquisition, Retention, and Promotion of Personnel

It is an old and well known practice to try to "purge" a company or department of unwanted people by reorganizing it. This procedure seems common among companies of all sizes and respectability. Perhaps less well known is the use of reorganization to attract, keep, and move up desirable personnel. Yet reorganization is admirably suited to this purpose also.

Reorganization as a Positive Personnel Measure

The use of reorganization as a positive personnel measure to protect and acquire good performers may be a more delicate task than its utilization as a negative weapon to clean out undesirables. The reason lies in the fact that reorganization as a positive measure is likely to involve more innovation in the form of new assignments, positions, organizational units, and/or personalities. This does not deny that the reorganization broom brings a certain amount of newness and strangeness; it does so. However, the removal, shunting, or consolidating processes normally are more matters of simple readjustment.

Innovation to obtain, keep, or elevate personnel in an organization holds certain dangers. There is always the possibility that the new step may accomplish its immediate purpose but prove less "good" in the longer run. The establishing of an office of operations research in order to bring into the organization a first class research man and his team may result in getting them, but it may fail to contribute much to the profit and loss statement because of the enormous cost and of the lack of appreciation and cooperation by the oldtimers in the administration hierarchy. There is occasionally the chance that the innovation will become an organizational monster which management cannot control. The creating of a company department to handle government relations in order to provide a promotional opportunity for a presently employed dynamic executive, who cannot be held without being given advancement, may result, as he functions in his normally aggressive manner, in the acceptance of defense work that comes to overshadow the real corporate purpose and seriously interfere with the normal and proper functioning of the company. Nor can one overlook the possibility, however slight, that the innovation may ultimately undermine the leadership of the administrator who introduced it. The general sales manager, who feels it necessary to give an able assistant an executive job of his own, is successful in urging the company to establish a New York sales office to handle a special product, but this young and vigorous new executive soon, by his effectiveness or "fireworks," comes to overshadow his mentor in company status.

Some Simple Guiding Rules

The dangers inherent in reorganization should not discourage the administrator from considering this means of procuring and retaining proper personnel. That these dangers exist may not be denied. A number of simple rules, if followed by the administrator, will do much to reduce these hazardous possibilities. They are listed without comment.

1. Analyze carefully the basis for self-acclamation or reputation of the outsider who appears to be potentially such a valuable addition to the company. Will his worth justify reorganization?
2. Weigh carefully the claims of a present employee that he is highly marketable outside the company. Offers hinted at or waved about may not be founded in fact. Why in such cases run the perils of reorganization or at least of major structural changes?
3. Evaluate the personal ambitions, objectives, and character of the individual under consideration for employment, retention, or promotion. He may be a very able wolf in sheep's clothing; safety may demand that the reorganization necessary to keep or get him also surround him with checks and balances strong enough to restrain his rapacity.
4. Weigh precisely the power shift or dilution brought about through the reorganization, with special reference to its potential effects on self and team associates. A new office or other organizational unit created in the interest of keeping or getting good people may prove a veritable sword of Damocles over the innovator; it may be wise for him to move slowly in placing appreciable power in the hands of a new department.

It may appear that the immediately preceding line of thought is unfaithful to the tone of the book, which is intended to be positive and dynamic. Certainly, the rules just set forth could be interpreted as arguing for the maintenance of the *status quo*. This is not their purpose. They are simply expressive of the sound basic administrative philosophy that the wise administrator fit his decisions and actions to facts and that he be neither necessarily the first nor last to innovate.

Respect for the Classical in Organization[9]

Without appreciation of the fact that organization in itself has a recognized anatomy and body, an analysis of reorganization as a strategic device would not be respectful of the great body of literature on administration, nor would it be sound, because the classically identified aspects of organization have strategic implications. Insofar as they are real, they truly set the stage and determine limits for strategic action. To a certain extent they do this when they are fictional but firmly accepted by the rank and file of administrators.[10] It is proposed to set down and examine from the viewpoint of strategy some of the real, and unreal but firmly accepted, aspects of organization.

Bases for Organization

Without endeavoring to be humorously alliterative or alliteratively humorous, one may point out that the basic fact of organization is the *bases of organization*. Most expositions of administration at some point treat this subject. The first step in organization is often held to be the grouping of activities, an action sometimes called departmentation. Various bases are identified for this step.[11] These include products, customers, geography, time, process, functions, subpurposes, and some other criteria.

Certainly, there can be no facet of organization as significant to reorganization as basis. There are few skeletal features of an organization that cannot be profoundly changed by a shift in the grounds of departmentation, for this will produce a different grouping of activities. Moreover, most inter-departmental relations can be influenced by such action, since they are determined in no small measure by the nature of the departments. The relations among sales departments based on geography will obviously be different from those among a regrouping on the basis of product. But all this is more or less a truism. A few rhetorical questions can add realism. Wouldn't the possibility of organizational re-arrangement be stupendous if the board of directors of the General Motors Corporation were to abandon product as one of its bases for organization (Chevrolet, Pontiac, Buick, Oldsmobile and Cadillac) and substitute, in its place, a purely geographical basis by which production of all makes would be concentrated in area plants? Can one even imagine the potential for reorganization which would proceed if the top management of the Metropolitan Life Insurance Com-pany were to abandon the geographical district office basis for doing business and adopt a centralized mail order basis? Would not the opportunities for organizational change stag-ger the imagination were the F. W. Woolworth Company to abandon the handling of many price classes of its merchan-dise in one type of store in favor of dividing them among fifteen types of stores on the basis of price? Clearly, the reorganizer has the most powerful device for reorganization in the possibility of changing the categorization foundation of organization. Its use demands that the reorganizer have great power in the company. It is probable that the approach to reorganization here suggested is in practice available only to boards of directors, presidents, and other chief executives of the company.

There is yet another way in which bases of organization are of significance to the reorganizer. Administrative strategy has been defined as gamesmanship. A condition which makes successful gamesmanship easier is the possession by the "player" (the reorganizer here) of the widest and easiest movement possibilities. The administrator in his influence over the bases for grouping company work has this condition in his grasp. Each basis is another position from which to retreat or to which to advance. Of course, it must be added that few organizations are structured on a single base and that, therefore, the strategist may have both more opportunities and more headaches in using them as a reorganizational device than here implied.

Chain of Command

A salient feature of all organizations is a concept or relationship best recognized for its military connotation. A chain of command is a requisite for the existence of an organization. Responsibility for the attainment of organizational goals ultimately rests with the top administrator. He must have a concentration of power adequate for the discharge of this total responsibility. If he does not, the organization (barring the most unusually fortuitous turn of fate) will fail to accomplish its ends, for the simple reason that its chief executive will not be able to make the decisions and enforce the action necessary. But, regardless of the adequacy of his power, he cannot personally do all the things essential to a full discharge of his responsibility. He must delegate duties to subordinates and, in order that they may carry them out, he must also see to it that they have the authority to enforce their will. The first level of subordinates, finding the delegated duties too much, may require that some of them be passed on with the further sharing of authority to the second level, and it to the third, and so on downward.[12] The progressive distribution and diminution of duties and concomitant power should not obscure the fundamental requisite of effective administration that each level of administration must know who its superior is and recognize his superior authority. A succession of these "domination and submission relationships" beginning at the top of the administrative ladder is properly known as chain of command.

At least two significant opportunities are hidden in the formality of the chain of command relationship for the administrator who wishes to effect changes in the organization. One has to do with the degree of power he entrusts to his subordinates on the management ladder, and may offer temptation for really vicious administrative practice. By placing too little authority in the hands of one or more of these officials, he may assure their failure to discharge the duties assigned them. Thereupon he may proclaim this failure as intolerable, and, by laying the blame for it at the door of organizational structure, use the situation as a reason to propose and work toward some desired reorganization. Or he can move in an opposite direction. By giving too much authority to a given subordinate or category of subordinates, the administrator can encourage their over-influence and action. If they are susceptible and make a nuisance of themselves within the organizational family, he officially can also find this situation to require correction and thus use it as a stepping stone for organizational change. Oddly enough the strategic administrator may be aided and abetted, perhaps innocently, by the very individual or individuals whom he places in the "impossible" power situation. In their frustration at failure from too little authority, or stinging from the criticism of their associates because of too much, they may lend the administrator their weight in demanding and bringing about his desired changes in the organization.

Another opening in the chain of command for the would-be strategic reorganizer can be found in the entrustment of authority to a subordinate or subordinates whom he knows to be innovators. These individuals, possessed of good imagination, strong desire, and creative ability can be expected to introduce the new and different. In the vernacular of the sports world, this means giving the ball to those who will run with it. The administrator places his hope for reorganization in the hands of a dynamic and able person or persons, believing that the latter will either proceed to revamp that section of the organizational complex over which he presides as executive or supervisor, or advance reorganizational suggestions and plans so strongly that he, the administrator, may justifiably take them for consideration and eventual implementation.

An interesting feature about potential innovators is that they may be found in the ranks of management officialdom somewhat removed from the administrator wishing to use them as an instrument of reorganization. This fact may serve to make them all the more useful for his purposes, since they may use their authority to direct criticism, blame, suggestions, and outright demand for change at organizational roadblocks between them and the higher echelon of the administrator. The dynamic subordinate with power in the organization may thus become management's hammer for beating it into desired shape.

There is even a more subtle opportunity for using the chain of command concept as a strategic device for reorganization. In general, the chief executive has the choice of maintaining, sharing, or assigning duties and authority. These possible alternative actions mean that his pattern of operation may be left fluid, and so it will be more difficult for his opposition in the organization to prepare for any reorganization moves on his part. The opposition simply may not know in what direction he next moves.

Centralization and Decentralization[13]

A question which seems to arise in all appreciable reorganization efforts is that of the degree of concentration of administration and operation desired. This expresses itself in the issue of centralized versus decentralized organization. It is a classical field of argument admitting of many points pro and con. The strategic administrator who wishes to make some change in organizational structure can often find in the debate substantiation for his desires. By identifying his cause with a larger one, which in the second half of the twentieth century is still unresolved as to relative merits, he will appear to be proceeding on much broader and objective grounds than were he to make his reorganizational proposals on the basis of personal arguments. Thus, he finds in a "traditional hassle" a helpful means of selling his ideas.

Another opportunity for the reorganizer which is found in the dichotomy of centralization and decentralization is associated with the breadth of action which each process permits. Centralization theoretically has only one limit—and that is one person. This would be, of course, a ridiculous condition for almost any but the tiniest organization. The reduction of the process to this unusual limit does, however, serve to suggest the extreme contracting possibilities inherent in centralization. Decentralization likewise, even though it is action in an opposite direction, has an extreme limit, which would be such complete autonomy of office, department or plant that only a common name might bind the entities together. These pseudo-theoretical considerations suggest that in the apparent process of centralizing or decentralizing the strategic reorganizer can find almost any limit to which he wishes to go.

As a matter of fact, he can do even more under the generic umbrella of centralization or decentralization than to proceed toward one pole or the other. He can actually reorganize in both directions, centralizing one operational or administrative function such as accounting, and decentralizing another such as employment. Indeed, the administrator who likes to change things organizational has a rare chance to indulge himself under the aegis of centralization and decentralization. An example is to be found in the case of a gas company which decided to reorganize its stores department in the interest of reducing personnel. A specialist who was called in gave the general manager his analysis of the situation, which was to centralize the twenty-one warehouse locations into three area distribution centers. The general manager, in this case the individual desiring reorganization, followed his advice. Centralization of stores was accomplished. But at the same time the general manager also decided upon the suggestion of the specialist to decentralize purchasing to the same three locations. It is clear that reorganization in opposite directions can be carried out under the mantle of scientific management conferred by the phenomena of centralization and decentralization.

Line and Staff[14]

The most discussed concept in the core of administration is that of line and staff. The "line" is said to be the chain of divisions, departments, sections, personnel, etc. which pursues directly the objective of the company. It is described as the operational part of the organization. The "staff" is considered to be those parts and persons of the organization whose function it is to advise.[15] It is not the purpose of this discussion to argue the issue as to whether or not this is a real distinction in actual practice. True, one must admit that at times the two functions of operation and advice are so intertwined in performance that identification as operating entities or as staff becomes difficult if not impossible. The question to be answered is simply "What implications for reorganization lie in the historical distinction between line and staff?"

One implication to reorganization is negative. In a situation demanding reorganization, the line and staff may appear as permanent features, difficult to touch. Each, having been distinguished on past organizational charts and in past organizational thought as separate administrative worlds, now argues strongly for continued separation. In cases in which the strategist sees the wisdom of general company reorganization, or even the shifting of units or personnel between traditional line and staff assignments, he may be countered with strong general resistance. As if to make the situation more difficult, it may be augmented by a number of circumstances. Among these rigidities, one may note the inaptitude, real or assumed, of professional advisors "to do" and the inability of "professional operators" to study and recommend; the reluctance of braintrusters to lose status by moving out of the category of thinkers into the plant; the fear of line personnel to be thrust into research and paper work; and the feeling of uncertainty in each camp about promotional possibilities if transferred to the other area.

The line and staff complexus, however, is not altogether unfriendly to reorganization. It promises an outlet for the administrator who is reorganizing with the objective of shifting a power center without too much opposition. He can use the staff category as a shelf on which to place a unit or member of the organization whose direct influence he desires to curtail. For example, he can sidetrack an operationally inefficient Vice President in charge of Manufacturing by assigning him to the President's Office as Special Consultant. The strategic reorganizer can also use the line and staff arrangement to move a dynamic and farseeing adviser into a position of much more command influence. He can remove from the company brain-trust the young man in the Staff Office of Market Research who has analyzed clearly the possibilities in the African market but whose influence is slight because of his junior position among a group of firmly entrenched senior analysts, and he can assign him to head up the new African Sub-Division of the International Sales Department.

Another situation in which the line and staff distinction can be used to advantage by the reorganizer is more indirect in nature. It arises when superior authority wishes to guide, strengthen, stimulate, or otherwise change line decision at a particular spot without removing the operational incumbent. The superior can create a staff adjunct directly attached to the line office in question, place proper personnel in it, and depend upon them to effect the change in the line officer's thinking. This is obviously a reorganizational exploitation of the staff vehicle. It is quite common in American business, and it is probably a root cause of the great staff proliferation which has characterized our business administration for the last two decades.

Control[16]

The best laid plans of a company or any other organization do not carry, so to speak, an inherent assurance that the machinery of the organization will carry them out as intended. One of the functions of administration, therefore, is to make up for this lack, i.e., to follow the progress of operation according to the plans adopted. Whatever steps this may involve—observation, analysis, correction, motivation, and follow through action—it is properly termed "control." The classical literature of administration commonly so describes it.

The control function demands machinery for its accomplishment. This may assume complex and technical proportions in large and intricate operations, and so one sees arising, for example in the great automobile factories, such devices as production control, quality control, budgetary control, and operations research. But whatever form the control mechanism may take, it is an integral component of the organizational structure.

Fortunately for the administrator who seeks to bring about some reorganization in his company or other organizational entity, there are aspects of the control mechanism which he can use to advantage. First of all, there is the matter of standards. All control mechanisms must have standards in order to measure accomplishment. The strategic administrator can, to the extent that he has the power to set or change them, so determine such standards that they will require organizational change for their satisfactory attainment.

Next is the possibility inherent in control points. Quite

obviously, rational management in the interest of economy and speed will seek to "check on" operations in as few places as necessary and at those points where the results can be measured reliably. These are the control points. Wise administration will usually select as control points so-called "narrows" in production, those stages or places in the operational process through which all the to-be-observed operations, products, or services pass. These narrows may vary all the way from an inspection station of the production or quality control service to the desk of the officer in charge of budgetary analysis. But, whatever and wherever they may be, the number and location of control points is a matter for administrative decision. The executive who has the power to decide upon them may, by his choice, bring about a situation demanding organizational change. He can decide to increase or decrease the number of control points or so change their situs that the present organizational set-up cannot accommodate them.

Finally, the administrator who is determined to reorganize can use control reports as a weapon with which to push some reorganization dear to his convictions or ambitions. One of the necessary features of the control mechanism is the report made to the administration on observations at the control points. Reports of any kind may be allowed to languish, handled in some routine manner, or seized and exploited for a purpose. The change-oriented administrator can often bring about "reforms" in organizational structure by the adroit use of control reports that come into his possession. He can analyze them carefully and use the results favorable to his aims as support for his reorganizational views. Here again delicate questions of honorable conduct may appear. The temptation can arise to hide unfavorable facts revealed in the report, action which well may be unethical.

There are many other classical concepts in administration

which, when translated into features of organization, can be studied with some hope of profit for possible ways to effect reorganization. One may mention such subjects as informal leadership, democratic processes, lines of communication, and span of supervision. It is believed, however, that enough has been written to suggest the richness of the general field of investigation and that, in a real sense, the five features explored—bases for organization, chain of command, centralization and decentralization, line and staff relations, and control mechanism—contain the greatest opportunities.

Conclusion

In the realm of administrative strategy, reorganization may be viewed as a subject of more significance than organization. This conclusion proceeds from the belief that reorganization is the much more common process, for organization takes place but once. It also proceeds from the feeling that dynamic administration, always alert to the necessity for change in order better to meet its problems and competition, will be interested in the opportunities for and techniques of reorganization.

Reorganization is not to be regarded as a certain sign of trouble or instability within an organization. It is a tried and true tool of the administrator for arranging resources and processes more effectively to accomplish objectives. The significance of its employment tends to be great since, if effective, it changes some feature of the organization, creates a new arrangement of organizational components, and in general sets off a number of actions and reactions in the company or department. If the bonds-of-organization concept is sound,[17] these effects may constitute a veritable chain of events! So great is its potential for results in the organization that reorganization must be used with astuteness and a sense of what is ethically right.

BUSINESS SITUATIONS FOR ROLE-PLAYING

SITUATION X

The Reorganization Vehicle

ULITHUS FOOTWEAR, INC.

A. Scene.   A major shoe manufacturer. The conference room of the Vice President in charge of Marketing who is holding a conference with the Sales Manager and the Director of the Systems and Procedures Section concerning reorganization proposals.

B. Players.   1. Vice President of Marketing: Mr. Donald J. Dickinson, a truly professional administrator who is hard pressed by the fact of successful encroachment of rival firms and by the reaction of the President to this unpleasant development.

2. Sales Manager: Mr. Sterling T. Strong, a typical hard-bitten salesman with an outstanding record of accomplishment in all the positions he has held, who is inclined to believe he can repel competition by harder work.

3. Director of Systems and Procedures Unit: Mr. Yancey R. Youngblood, possessor of an inquiring mind, who is a real disciple of scientific method and who, therefore, always wants the facts of the case before deciding what to do.

C. Situation.   1. The Vice President is determined to reorganize the Sales Department because the competitors have been taking a growing share of the market.

2. The Sales Manager merely wants to shift a few District Sales Managers and inaugurate more contests or some other incentives.

3. The Director of the Systems and Procedures Unit has just completed a field survey, and he is trying to sell a reorganization scheme in which the fifteen district offices are recentralized into three new super "zone" offices.

D. Assignment. 1. Select three players to enact the reorganization discussion, and try to assign the role of the Director of the Systems and Procedures Unit to an imaginative and vocal individual.

2. Assign the group the task of analyzing and summarizing the arguments which could be advanced for reorganization in this case.

NOTES

1. Albert Lepawsky, *Administration* (New York: Alfred A. Knopf, 1949), p. 219.
". . . the structure of organization is almost inevitably a hierarchy of superiors and subordinates in which the higher levels exercise authority over the lower levels." Frederick Harbison and Charles A. Myers, *Management in the Industrial World* (New York: McGraw-Hill Book Company, Inc., 1959), p. 3.
2. Louis A. Allen, *Management and Organization* (New York: McGraw-Hill Book Company, Inc., 1958), p. 57.
3. "The vitality of an enterprise is measured by its power of spontaneous reaction to changes in conditions, and of internal modification and arrangement to meet such changes. . . . This power must be continually fostered and factors unfavourable to its development watched for and eliminated." Quoted from L. Urwick, *The Elements of Administration* (New York: Harper & Brothers, Publishers, n.d.), p. 121.
4. Alvin Brown, *Organization: A Formulation of Principle* (New York: Hibbert Printing Company, 1945), p. 246; and Ralph J. Cordiner, "Efficient Organizational Structure" in Edward C. Bursk, *How to Increase Executive Effectiveness* (Cambridge, Mass.: Harvard University Press, 1954), p. 30.
5. The authors regard organization as does Glover who tersely writes, "Organization is an instrument of management. . . ." John G. Glover, *Fundamentals of Professional Management* (New York: Simmons-Boardman Publishing Corp., 1958), p. 199.
6. Some interesting dimensions of this possibility are set forth in Harold J. Leavitt, *Managerial Psychology* (Chicago: University of Chicago Press, 1958), pp. 274-290.
7. Edmund Learned, David N. Ulrich, and Donald R. Booz, *Executive Action* (Boston: Harvard University Press, 1951), p. 199.

8. ALLEN, *op. cit.*, pp. 327-330.
9. A brief but analytical summary of "classical organization theory" appears in JAMES G. MARCH and HERBERT A. SIMON, *Organizations* (New York: John Wiley & Sons, Inc., 1958), pp. 12-33; and a selected representation of views on "modern organizational theory" is compiled in MASON HAIRE (ed.), *Modern Organizational Theory* (New York: John Wiley & Sons, Inc., 1959).
10. The profile of administrative principles as a subject for analysis is complicated by the fact that, as Simon writes, "It is a fatal defect of the current principles of administration that, like proverbs, they occur in pairs. For almost every principle one can find an equally plausible and acceptable contradictory principle." HERBERT A. SIMON, *Administrative Behavior* (2nd ed.; The Macmillan Company, 1958), p. 20. Quoted with the permission of The Macmillan Co.
11. LUTHER GULICK, "Notes on the Theory of Organization" in LUTHER GULICK and L. URWICK (eds.), *Papers on the Science of Administration* (New York: Institute of Public Administration, Columbia University, 1937), pp. 15-30.
12. This series of steps in the grading of duties according to measures of authority and the concomitant responsibility is known as the *scalar chain*. JAMES D. MOONEY and ALAN C. REILEY, *The Principles of Organization* (New York: Harper & Brothers, Publishers, 1939), pp. 14-15.
13. A comprehensive philosophy of decentralization is succinctly expressed as "Ten Guiding Principles" in RALPH J. CORDINER, *New Frontiers for Professional Managers* (New York: McGraw-Hill Book Company, Inc., 1956), pp. 50-52.
14. A compilation of excerpts from widely representative authorities on line and staff organization has been brought together by LEPAWSKY, *op. cit.*, pp. 289-321.
15. A complete analysis of the staff in the managerial process is presented by ROBERT C. SAMPSON, *The Staff Role in Management* (New York: Harper & Brothers, Publishers, 1955); and a succinct differentiation from "line" is given in WILBERT E. MOORE, *The Conduct of the Corporation* (New York: Random House, 1962), pp. 133-136.
16. See Chapter XIX of this book for a treatment of control and for references on the subject.
17. For a presentation of the bonds of organization concept, attention is invited to E. WIGHT BAKKE, *Bonds of Organization* (New York: Harper & Brothers, Publishers, 1950).

CHAPTER 11

Timing and Surprise

> "There is a right time to do everything. It is the point at which receptivity for the step will be highest (or opposition, the lowest). The strategic administrator, always interested in the best possible results, will try to gauge his actions accordingly. In other words, he will endeavor to time them. There are many timing stratagems available for use by the administrator. Especially important is surprise."

IT HAS LONG BEEN said that there is a right time to do everything. Shakespeare immortalized this bit of ancient wisdom in famous verse:

> There is a tide in the affairs of men,
> Which, taken at the flood, leads on to fortune;
> Omitted, all the voyage of their life
> Is bound in shallows and miseries.[1]

To draw this beautiful gem of human expression and sentiment into a discussion of something as mundane and practical as administration may border on the profane. And yet it must be done, for nowhere else is the philosophy of timing —a matter of incalculable significance to good administration—so aptly set forth.

There is a right time to do everything. It is the point at which receptivity for the step will be highest (or opposition, the lowest). The strategic administrator, always interested in

254

the best possible results, will try to gauge his actions accordingly. In other words, he will endeavor to time them.[2]

Probably no more difficult task exists in the field of administration than right timing.[3] Two problems bedevil the executive in his efforts: one is the recognition of the optimum point and the other is the ability to move at this time. A discussion of these difficulties may, in a superficial sense, suggest the material presented in the chapter on opportunity; timing is involved in the use of opportunity. But timing and the exploitation of opportunity must not be confused. They are quite different. The former connotes a more or less regular function of the strategic administrator, the almost continual process of synchronizing his actions with circumstance; whereas the latter means seizing and making the most of a special situation.

Recognition of Optimum Point of Time

Unfortunately, the optimum moment or period for deciding or acting does not usually call itself to the attention of the administrator. It is for him to recognize it. And this is often not a simple task. Optimum points of time have no classical features for which the executive can look, and frequently they are obscured by the dynamics of the situation.

Short Duration

The recognition of the exactly optimum point of time to act in any situation is probably not often accomplished by the administrator. The point may be of short or merely fleeting duration. Examples are easy to envisage. The most profitable market for a planned product may last only until potentially strong competitors come to realize the profit opportunities in it. The company president whose sanction the administrator has been waiting to obtain for a favored project may be in a completely friendly mood for merely a few days after a signal victory over certain opposition on the board of directors. The employees under the administrator's supervision whose pay he wishes to cut may be sufficiently worried about getting other jobs during just the darkest month of the winter.

Preoccupation with Other Matters

Another condition which may make it difficult for the administrator to recognize the precisely optimum point in time is his preoccupation with tasks other than the one awaiting action. The work pattern of the administrator rarely consists of undivided attention to one project. In any given period he generally has under way a number of "jobs," routine or special, and, to make matters even more distracting, he usually has them at different stages of completion. In short, his span of attention may be at once so broad and so fragmented that his sensitivity to the existence of the most propitious moment at which to advance a given project may be deadened. Furthermore, the most opportune moments for two or more actions may appear simultaneously, or nearly so, so that the effort to effectuate one may confuse the administrator as to the presence of the other or others.

Human Failure

There is always human fraility as a barrier to the recognition of the best time to act. It may be that the administrator is not an alert and analytical individual, at least momentarily.[4] Executives obtain their positions in many ways. Although it is undoubtedly true that the majority are somehow selected on the basis of such qualities as imagination, breadth of vision and judgment, some with relatively low quotients in these qualities do gain office. The latter may lack the capacity to analyze situations, and they may not be able to detect the most propitious moment for action.

That recognition of the best possible time to do something

is not assured in the milieu of administration is apparent. Yet this fact should not cause the strategically minded to lose interest in timing. It seldom happens that the precisely optimum point is but an isolated spot in the situation. More often it is a central point around which progressively less favorable—but still favorable—zones of time extend as concentric areas. The practical implication is obvious.

The Zone of Compromise

If he does not locate the best time at which to do something, the administrator can at least find a better, rather than worse period, in which to undertake it. There are grounds for the suspicion that this alternate choice is the common practice in administration. The experienced executive, disillusioned with fine efforts to be exact, seasoned in compromise and beset with work, often makes his move under conditions which are but generally favorable. Examples of this compromise action are apparent throughout business and industry in inventory accumulation and liquidation, in production schedules, and even in employment rosters. Tersely speaking, one can find little other reason for the temporary miscalculation of needs and markets and for the constant necessity of adjustment in quantitative aspects of operation. At the same time it must be remembered that timing is not a mathematical art and that it is better to approximate the temporal target than to miss it far.

There is, however, a possible trap for the unwary administrator who operates on the theory that it is satisfactory to make his moves anytime circumstances are generally favorable. The danger exists in case his action involves dealings with another individual or individuals rather than a set of non-human factors. The rational human being, by way of illustration the president of a corporation, reaches a certain climax in his receptivity to proposal or imposition. But, since business is a very dynamic field of life with many and varying influences on him who manages it, the probability is that he will not long be on this dead center but rather usually in the process of advancing toward it or retreating from it. Now, the danger to the administrator becomes more apparent. If he makes his move to win the acquiescence or support of the chief executive when the chief executive is moving up to his pinnacle of receptivity, the action will seem unusually wise and proper to this official, for it will complement his movement. If he advances his project when the president is moving away from a climax of receptivity, he may not only fail to attain his end but, and here is the danger, also draw from the president more than ordinary opposition, criticism, rancor and general negative reaction, since the action may appear to the chief executive to be a deliberate obstacle to *his* movement.

Mobility at Optimum Point

The dynamic administrator usually can and does sense when the time is *somewhat* favorable.[5] By so doing he comes face to face with the second problem noted, his ability to act at this time. In an administrative Utopia, the executive would be free to take action whenever he considered it wise. Occasionally in the real world, he may for a while enjoy such freedom. But the odds of administrative life are against any such sanguine condition occurring often or lasting long. There are simply too many restrictive influences. Prominent among the conditions or factors that limit the freedom of the administrator to act when he thinks he should are his fears, personal commitments, loyalties, position in the administrative hierarchy, reputation with the company, underestimation of his power position, respect for the policies and rules of the organization, principles, morals, and legal restraints.

No doubt each of these "ties that bind" could serve as a

subject for lengthy discourse. However, they are not mutually exclusive in every instance. For example, personal commitments and loyalties, although amenable to distinction, are closely related in vital aspects. Furthermore, the guide lines to greater rather than lesser freedom to act at any time are not limited in their applicability to any one of the circumstances that bind the administrator. It seems reasonable, therefore, that one should attack the problem by discussing principles of general implication rather than narrow ideas or devices for negating one specific restraining influence.

Preparation

A significant principle which the administrator should follow, if he would be free to do the right thing at the right time, is concerned with his being prepared. The duration of the best time to act may not be long. It may be so short that he will not be able to prepare for the desired action once the auspicious period has appeared. Few courses of action can be taken effectively without preparation. The unprepared administrator is often kept from making his move at the optimum moment simply because he is not ready to do so. He may not know the facts of the case sufficiently well to risk action; his plans may be incomplete; he may not have built up the necessary following to support his innovation; he may have failed to motivate or organize his followers to do the work which his action will cause to fall on them; he may not have conditioned his superiors for the step forward; and he may have neglected to develop alternative courses of action or routes of retreat if his action fails.

An example is to be found in the case of the ambitious but unready manager of the research and development department of a household appliance manufacturing firm who long has waited to get from his president's office the decision to produce a heat pump. A conjuncture of fortuitous circumstances occurs. The loudest opponent of the proposal on the board of directors dies. The trade association of heat pump manufacturers reports that in the year just completed the heat pump has enjoyed phenomenal customer acceptance. The company has recently been informed by Washington that it is to be granted a large contract for the manufacture of humidifying equipment, a product line assumed by the company at the strong recommendation of the manager of research and development. Clearly, now is the time for him to come forth with the heat pump and try to obtain presidential endorsement. The source of much of the effective opposition is gone; the market for heat pumps is known to be good; and the president is happy over the new business for which, in a sense, the manager is responsible. But the manager is not prepared. His staff has not agreed upon the best type of heat pump and has not developed definitive engineering plans for one nor an estimate of its cost of production, and the market research office, with whom he has been feuding, has not completed a requested market survey and sales forecast. Clearly the manager is not free to present his case to the president because he is not ready to do so; he is fettered by his lack of preparation. His timing is bad.

If the lack of preparation were simply to result in tying up the administrator at a time when he should act, the loss might be written off as merely an opportune time passed. Negative implications go deeper. It may be that the temptation of the favorable situation induces the manager of research to present his case without being fully ready to do so. Uninformed and uncertain, he may cause the president to lose a measure of confidence in him, and he may place himself in a position from which it will be difficult to operate with this official in the future. Failing to obtain the sanction of the president for his project, he will be likely to lose some of his standing with his associates, especially his subordinates, who were interested in it as proponents or opponents. Defeat can elicit scorn from both friend and foe, and the lesson implicit here is just as pertinent to situations involving other individuals than the administrator's top superior, e.g., colleagues, subordinates, customers.

The immobility which unpreparedness can impose may be particularly costly to a subordinate administrator upon whom his chief depends to a special degree. The top executive of an organization is also not a free agent in all matters. Often he may strongly want something done but finds it impolitic to proceed to initiate it by order. He may, therefore, be forced to rely upon a subordinate as sufficiently sensitive, intelligent, and motivated to come forth at the right moment with the desired action. If the subordinate acts at the wrong time or fails to act, the chief executive's natural disappointment may be unusually keen, because he may have been suffering both from the frustration of not being able to do directly what he wants and from the fear that his subordinate will not initiate it.

The Image of Dependability

The administrator who would be free to make his moves at opportune times might well follow another principle. He should endeavor to acquire and maintain in the eyes of those with whom he works and deals an image of himself as one who can be depended upon. This is not a difficult task and does not require any Machiavellian tactics. A few relatively simple steps can contribute much to the creation of such an image. The administrator should do a little more than is expected of him in his job. Probably only few people do this, and so doing it will give him a mark of distinction, favorable at least to his superiors. He should also meticulously endeavor not to make foolish or unethical promises to his associates which it would be unwise to keep, and he should with equal care exert himself to honor all his commitments to his associates. In this connection, he should remember that it is almost as important to keep his word with his subordinates and contacts outside the organization as with his superiors. Those who are below him in the hierarchy of the company family or outside the organization or department are impressionable; they, too, talk; and, since they are likely to be quite numerous, they can do much to help build him a reputation for trustworthiness. To round out his image of dependability, he should rarely make requests from his superiors which he is not sure they will grant; he should not give orders to subordinates for which he does not have sound hope of satisfactory compliance; and he should not make promises to vendors, customers, and other outsiders which he is not reasonably certain he can fill. Such restraint will increase his "percentage of wins," and so he will come to be known as a man who gets what he goes after. People will regard him as a person of good judgment. These three qualities, distinction as a hard worker, reliability, and judgment, are the ingredients which make the image of dependability.

Now how is all this related to the freedom basic to good timing? In any organization, there is a strong desire on the part of its personnel to trust. Much of the reason lies in the fact that trusting makes them feel more secure, that it relieves them of a degree of worry, and that it lifts a measure of work from their shoulders. The desire to trust predisposes them toward the dependable man in their midst, since he can be trusted. They will tend more readily to have faith in him. Being trusted, he will be relatively free to proceed at the auspicious time without arousing suspicion, requiring inquisitive approval, or being denied his goal.

Freedom from Binding Commitment

Freedom to move when the time is right demands, however, more than being prepared and possessing the reputation of dependability. The administrator must also be free of commitment which can make it impossible, or extremely difficult, for him to act when he judges the time propitious. Such commitment is really of four types. One may be described as over-commitment. It may be the result of any of a large category of involvements, among which figure as likely possibilities other assignments for the department or company, outside business deals, social activities, political connections, and personal ties. Obviously a given individual, no matter what the catholicity of his interests, the degree of his vigor and vision and the level of his general intelligence, has limits of attention and effort beyond which he will not go or is incapable of extending himself, at least with reasonable efficiency and lack of overweighing repercussions. Whether or not the majority of administrators are completely committed is here a moot question. The important issue facing the individual administrator is a certain evaluation and ranking of commitments so that he will always have time and energy to push the more important matters under his organizational cognizance when the occasion is ripe to advance them. Of course, this is easier said than done, especially if the administrator takes all his commitments seriously and if his superiors, because of their faith in him or lack of faith in others, load him with work. At first glance, it appears that the less serious and industrious, and hence less valued, officials in the administrative hierarchy have the most freedom properly to time their action. Fortunately, this is probably not often true, since they are less likely than "good" administrators to be prepared and to enjoy the confidence of superiors and other associates.

There is a second type of commitment which can prove most restrictive to the administrator who desires to time an action correctly. It may be described as "role identification." In the passage of time, many hard working and intelligent executives come to play a *particular* role in organizational life. Described in the vernacular, some of these roles are that of trusted lieutenant, informal leader, fire-ball, operator, plodder, yeoman, yes-man, loyal-opposition, professional critic, cutthroat, opportunist, contemplative, fellow traveler, Casper Milquetoast, and bull-of-the-woods. It may be argued successfully that all or most of these roles are necessary to give an organization operational balance. Be this as it may, the sorry effect on correct timing is to be seen in the fact that the administrator's superiors and other associates come to expect him to stay in that role and that, therefore, when he must shake himself free of it, even temporarily, to take action at the right time, they are likely to be surprised and in their surprise neither understanding nor cooperative. An example of this is the case in which the so-called "operator," often actually the dynamic individual who knows how to get things done and who proceeds to do them, decides it is time for him to slow up, study some department or company problem, and recommend or make changes in same. Staff members, company eggheads, and even his fellow operators are aroused at this new creature in their ranks and are prone to block his efforts as being inappropriate.

Closely related to the commitment inherent in organizational role identification is a more subtle type of shackle. It is often inadvertently placed upon the administrator by an official of the department or company above the administrator's immediate superior. This higher executive may for a variety of reasons circumvent an immediate superior and go directly to the subordinate administrator with a hint, request, or order to do something. Quite generally, this will be an assignment over and above his regular work and may even be unknown to his intermediate superior. In the meantime, circumstances may so converge that the time appears for the administrator to get on with a task directly related to his own office. He then faces a dilemma: Shall he attempt to proceed with the higher official's project or shall he turn from it to his own work? This is not an easy question to answer. If he does the former, he may please the higher official but fail to discharge properly his recognized organizational duties, and thus he may incur the displeasure of his by-passed immediate superior. If he takes the latter course he runs the risk of disappointing higher authority, frequently a dangerous thing to do.

Diverse strategies present themselves as the means of meeting this double commitment. The administrator, pulled in two directions, might well try his best to do both jobs if he feels it his duty to do so. Moreover, this would seem to be intelligent action if he believes that the assignment from above is a special entrustment which will not happen often. Or it would appear to be the wisest if he believes advancement in the organization demands that he "overprove" himself for a while. Should he see the situation as continually exerting unduly restrictive pressure on the performance of his own work, then he might best inform the higher official regretfully that he cannot do the special assignments from above since their discharge precludes his keeping his own work up to schedule. Any other course of action when he is trapped more or less permanently under two bosses can be disastrous. It may so involve the administrator that he cannot do his own work at the right time and, hence, failing in a measure to perform properly in the eyes of the immediate superior who supervises him, come to be rated by him as an inept performer.

A final commitment which can tie the hands of an administrator when the time comes to act is a strong personal alliance with or affection for some one, within or without the organization, whose interests demand that the action not be taken now. A good illustration of this type of commitment may be seen in the problem of firing, retiring, or otherwise getting rid of senior employees. There are few administrators of any rank in American business or industry who have not at some time had to face this frequently unpleasant task. A common form of the situation develops when the administrator sees it possible to employ at a given time a much needed and awaited specialist, e.g., a research engineer, but, in order to do this under the budget, finds it necessary to sever from the payroll an old practical mechanic who for many years helped him with ideas for making new mechanical devices. It would seem that this is an instance in which one strategic course is overwhelmingly to be preferred. The administrator, when he first learns that to hire he must reduce present personnel, should take steps to discharge his personal obligations to the senior employee by making fair provision for him. This may range all the way from psychological preparation for severance to aid in obtaining good retirement terms or employment elsewhere. It is good for both his own morals and morale that he keep faith; it is likewise good for his reputation in the organization and for the morale of his staff and workers. This course of action is probably the best way to handle most commitments of loyalty and affection which may prevent one as an administrator from acting when the time is right.

It is clear that wise administrative timing requires freedom to act when temporal circumstances are favorable. The administrator will often face real difficulties in trying to follow this strategic pattern of administration. His chances to succeed, however, seem greater if he prepares himself for the main chance, develops for himself the image of dependability, and avoids the wrong commitments.

Some Timing Stratagems

The foregoing treatment of certain problems in timing has contained a few suggestions for appropriate action. The subject of timing techniques can probably not be covered most scientifically except by reducing the frame of reference to a particular company or department. However, it is important; a few further general ideas as to stratagems follow.[6]

Employment of Productive Communication Pipelines

One fruitful way in which to help assure better timing is for the administrator to have and use productive two-way communication pipelines with the individual, people, office, organization, or other entity with whom he wishes to synchronize some action. The incoming pipeline assumes great significance in timing. Only infrequently can an administrator know too much about circumstances bearing on the proper timing of his planned decision or action. These circumstances cast their shadows before them and do much, thereby, to signal the state of readiness in which the administrator must be in order to move timely. On the other hand, the necessity for "hitting the target" with decision or action at the appropriate time argues for good transmission facilities. Regardless, however, of which pipeline—incoming or outgoing—is of primary importance, there are two kinds of communication channels: the formal, those provided for in the organizational plan; and the informal, those that are superimposed as the formal prove inadequate to certain individuals or groups within the company.

As far as timing strategy is concerned, the administrator will generally be more concerned with the incoming pipeline. The strategic administrator interested in getting better timing information should first evaluate the effectiveness of the formal channels as to the speed by which information moves through them and as to the truth of it. If he finds something significant lacking in their operation, he should then seek to tap or establish extra-channels. Since he cannot with much hope of sympathy or support parade the argument of his own ignorance as an explanation for pulling the switch in some action too early or of delaying when he should have pulled it, he may at times go quite far in tapping and creating new channels. And so administrators are seen cultivating friendships with persons working at pivotal places in the organization, even supernumeraries, who are in a position to observe; demanding special report treatment from subordinates; inveigling themselves into routing schedules for memoranda and other correspondence; entertaining subordinates, colleagues, superiors, customers, government officials, and journalists; employing department or company spies; and even resorting to downright pilfering of information forbidden to them.

Quite apart from the question of how far an administrator can properly go in seeking information not furnished him by regular channels, there are several politic considerations which he should bear in mind when straying afield for further information. His enthusiasm may lead him to make acquaintances or commitments which will later be troublesome, as social contact with an ambitious clerk or promise of promotional help to an inept subordinate.[7] He may make a nuisance out of himself by demanding to know things which people have neither the time nor inclination to tell him. He may come into the possession of dangerous information such as confidential or misleading data which will cause him to act prematurely or delay too long, to be made a target for exploitation by others who want to know it or learn how he obtained it, to become a guilty party by association, or to be drafted as a "patsy" upon whom someone may put the blame for a leak in information. And it is even possible that he may be caught as a thief of reports, plans, letters, or other records and dealt with accordingly by those in a position to discipline him or otherwise make him pay for his indiscretion and wrongdoing.

Resort to Waiting

Waiting, as well as getting more and better information, can be a stratagem helpful to good timing.[8] There are various possible definitions of waiting, but all center about the concept of abstaining from the action in question. The abstention may be either a period of inaction or action; but, whichever it is, the importance of waiting must not be underestimated. It gives the administrator time better to prepare, if necessary, for the auspicious period. Through waiting, he may be prevented from premature action and, in a sense, disciplined for more subtlety in the future. Moreover, if he has nearly exhausted or used up completely the store of goodwill which his associates have had for him, he may find that waiting will provide the opportunity for them to develop a new store of friendly attitude toward him and his maneuvers, from which he may draw at a later date. Nor must one forget that waiting is a device which can be used to lead the opposition to make a move. Not knowing for certain when he will act, the opposition may do something, either in frustration or in an effort to force his hand, which will reveal its nature or intentions and, thus, help the administrator chose the best time to proceed. Here is certainly good support for the contention that business administrators need careful indoctrination in business ethics, for the issue of when deliberate waiting becomes wilful deceit may well arise.

Another word or two in respect to the nature of waiting seems in order. The point of whether it be in the form of inaction or action is of significance. Absence of action on the part of the administrator—and this means generally his devotion to routine duties, for it is rarely that he can and would be doing nothing—may signal one of two things to those who are watching him: admission of disinterest or defeat, or possession of some sly plan which he will hasten to put into effect when the timing is right. The administrator should try to ascertain which of these interpretations his opposition makes of his inaction, since each may dictate a different timing. Similarly to inaction, a pattern of action may herald one of two things to the opposition. It may convince them that he is about to make his move. Or it may, especially if it contains one or more relatively ambitious projects, persuade the opposition that he has abandoned the move in question or at least is off on some other course, the taking of which will preclude early movement in the opposed direction. It is apparent that to "dash about and do things" while waiting the opportune time for taking another and more desired action can confuse the opposition and, thereby, give the administrator more temporal leeway.

Use of the Phase Timing Device

Somewhat related to waiting in the category of timing maneuvers is phase timing. This is well illustrated in phase planning, a type of planning by stages with provision for each successive step forward dependent upon some degree of accomplishment in the previous stage. Phase timing is not confined, however, to planning; it can be used in almost all aspects of administration, since it simply means breaking proposed action into parts and trying to find the most propitious time to take each. The theory is certainly sound; to find the optimum time for a smaller step may be easier than to locate it for a larger move. But in practice certain dangers arise in the use of phase timing. For one thing, in order to act the administrator must make several decisions rather than a single one, and so he has more than one chance to be wrong in timing. Of course, this inherent risk can be considered partially balanced by the risk in the alternative action of making one big decision which, if taken at the wrong time, could bring total disaster to the project.

However all this may be, phase timing contains yet another danger, and this is a much less well recognized peril. It occurs because the sum total of several small correct timings does not necessarily assure that the timing of the total action is correct. Clarification of this thought can be gained from a consideration of the case of a district manager of a chain of shoe stores who wishes to make all the retail units under his supervision self-service stores. He knows that the top echelon of the company is lukewarm to the change and accordingly moves cautiously, waiting for favorable times and never asking at any one occasion for permission to convert more than one store. He succeeds in getting a number of permissions because at the time of each request the president of the company is not alarmed by it or is otherwise favorably disposed. Then the district manager decides to ask that all the remaining clerk-operated stores be changed over to self-service units. Forces of opposition appear. The president, previously occupied with the job of introducing a higher priced line of shoes, is now aware of the implications of wide scale self-service; his board of directors, who were involved in a proxy fight just settled, become aroused at what appears to be a major change in company policy; and the stockholders of the company see that the operations under the existing retail scheme are showing an increasingly handsome profit. The sales manager finds his project to convert all the stores to a new way of merchandising turned down. Correct in his timing of successive smaller steps, he was incorrect in timing his over-all project. The administrator who would time his actions by its phases should not become overconfident from earlier small successes.

Reliance upon Formula Timing

The subject of stratagems in timing is a broad one. The consideration of one more device, especially since it is quite unique in nature, may therefore be justified. For want of a better description, it may be termed formula timing. In essence it consists of "pegging" action to some other event. For example, the sales manager may decide that he will ask for an increase of two additional salesmen in his staff each time the sales of his existing sales force rises ten per cent.

The illustration suggestions that formula timing is characterized by rhythmic action. Although this is often the case, it is not necessarily true in all instances. Formula timing may involve but one action, as is seen in the instance of the head accountant who decides to ask for the creation of an accounts payable division in his office as soon as the existing treasurer of the company retires.

Rhythmic, or one-occasion, formula timing has considerable merit in the fact that it commits the user to act at a pre-determined and definite time. Even though the chosen moment for action may not be the best that possibly could be selected, it is a fixed factor in the administrator's plan of forward movement and, therefore, a certainty around which he can make specific plans. The commitment inherent in formula timing has still another advantage. It calls for more or less automatic action, so that once he has decided upon the formula, the administrator will not be plagued with the necessity for further timing decision. This may be an advantage of very great weight to the executive who is inclined to worry over his timing, to vacillate in decision making, or to be overworked.

Formula timing does not necessarily mean hitching planned action to isolated events; an administrator may implement it in quite a different manner. He may seek both the definite and automatic benefits it confers by associating himself with some individual, clique or other group, within or without the organization, whose action pattern calls for steps to be taken at times also right for his desired movements. The administrator's modus operandi here is obvious; he will act when his associates act. The peculiar merit of this type of formula timing is twofold. First, the administrator has the advantage of another's judgment as to the right time. Second, he has the corollary political advantage of the protection which union can afford him. He may be able to reach his goal under the combined strength of himself and associates or simply ride to success in their train. One sees a portrayal of this rather singular manifestation of formula timing, and a suggestion of its unique rewards, in the instance of the general office manager of an advertising firm who requisitions some new equipment each time the dynamic, highly successful, and hence favored new accounts department puts in to have its suite remodeled in the most modern decor to suggest more dynamism.

Action to Structure Time

These ideas as to stratagems in timing all start with a premise that the administrator is somehow a complete slave of circumstances—that the best he can do is to accommodate himself to them by ferreting out the right time to act and remaining free to be able to do so. The strategic administrator knows better. He is aware of the fact that an intelligent executive can do several things to make the best, or at least a generally favorable time, appear. In fact such steps, which create the condition in advance of the act, are probably the most calculating of all the timing strategies.[9] He will certainly realize the influence of judiciously dropped hints that now is the time to act. Such hints may be made at places quite far distant in organizational terms from the person or persons he wishes to sway, for frequently people will believe more easily that which they hear from relatively disinterested people. Thus the president of the company lets his bank president know at a bridge party that the organization is now ready to expand, with the expectation that the latter official will reflect this favorable view when the finance committee of the company approaches him as to new financing possibilities. The alert administrator will also recognize the powerful influence he can exert on a pivotal party or parties by constant, even though politic, reiteration of demands or recommendations to them. Even the greatest doubter is not wholly immune to constant psychological bombardment; this is one of the salient laws of propaganda.

In addition to these two ways in which an administrator can influence the time at which receptivity will be the highest or opposition the lowest, he has in his portfolio a further weapon which may raise an issue of ethics. This is the creation of a situation in which his desired action *must* be taken. No matter what the position of the administrator in the hierarchy of administration, he does have some potential for embarrassing or otherwise forcing the company into action at a particular time. He can accomplish this by intentional commitment of the organization to action out of which it does not dare extricate itself, or by deliberately doing something wrong or omitting something so that the company will be compelled to take corrective remedies in the form of the steps he desires at the time he prefers. The use of this technique is pointed up in the case of the sales engineer for a plastics company who decides to push this company into changing the nature of a product as soon as possible. He agrees with the chief purchasing agent of a large industrial customer that the present specifications of a certain plastic are wrong and that the specifications prepared by the laboratories of the customer company are to be preferred at once. This mouse-trapping of one's own organization can be a highly dangerous career risk. Dismissal or other punitive action may follow, but neither the danger nor possible unethical connotation of the procedure seems to rule it out. It is a device rather commonly used by administrators to force their department's or company's hand.

Surprise

One of the less well understood stratagems of administration is surprise.[10] In an action sense the concept connotes unexpectedness or suddenness. There is clearly a consideration of time in surprise, and it will therefore be discussed in the same frame of reference as timing.

General Rationale

The technique of surprise can be used by the administrator for at least three major purposes. In their broadest expression, these may be listed as follows: (1) to catch off guard the opposition to some course of action so that it cannot get set for effective blocking; (2) to attain a degree of support for the step advanced through the appeal to natural interest in unexpected innovation; and (3) to deepen a permitted or created crisis so that it can better serve the administrator's aims. Each has its own peculiar pattern of strategic possibilities, repercussions, and dangers.

To Catch Opposition in a Less Defensive Posture

The administrator utilizes surprise most commonly as a means of catching opposition off-guard. Opposition means individuals, groups, or organizations who oppose the administrator's proposed step, may potentially oppose it, or are simply in need of a degree of selling which the administrator cannot or does not wish to undertake by more conventional means. In order to use surprise most effectively for this end, the administrator should see to it that the greatest degree of secrecy is maintained. He should realize that surprise is most effective as an overwhelming device when it is so unexpected that the act is accomplished even before the opposition suspects that anything is happening. Only when it is this secret can it catch the opposition in the weakest possible condition of defenselessness. Any warning whatsoever may give the opposition time to erect some defense or at least to become psychologically braced against the sudden movement. One of the truths which administrators in any organization must always remember is that there is rarely such thing as a little leak of information. There is just a leak, and the information out will be blown up and passed about just as fast as the organizational gossip mechanism can function.

The philosophy of strategy which supports surprise as a shock weapon is sound. In the almost "perpetual battle" between the administrator and all those with whom he must contend to get his way, it is generally true that he who takes the offensive stands the better chance of winning. Just as possession is said to be nine-tenths of the law, so the deed is the major portion of successful action. Once done, it tends to have a claim to continued existence and justification merely because it has been done. The counterattack of the opposition now finds that the defender has arguments and circumstances on his side.

An illustration will sketch this reasoning sharply. A newcomer to a company is elected its president. He realizes that there is the more or less natural resentment among the organizational personnel at his quick elevation; and he understands that he is not the focus of all personnel loyalties. Therefore, he is worried about his ability to push through a major reorganizational change such as decentralization of equipment repair by the usually good democratic devices of seeking advice and recommendation as to how and when from his subordinate administrators. So he decides to stun his opposition into comparative ineffectiveness. He moves suddenly to order the change into effect; discharges a goodly portion of the central repair staff, sending the remainder out to field locations as local repair managers; and appoints one of the administrative team he brought with him as central office coordinator of equipment repair. What can those of his staff do who would have tried to advise him against such a move, suggested substitute measures, or even openly refused to cooperate in instituting the change? Their immediate opportunity to resist is past. The change is a fact. Now they must attack an established feature and policy of the company. This is plain resistance and those who engage in it are asking for discipline! The opposition has been surprised and thrust into the position in which, if they wish to resist, they must do so as open enemies. They have been outgeneralled by the maneuver of surprise.

To Attract by Unexpected Innovation

The second use of surprise appeals to the more or less natural attraction which something new and unexpected has for people. The origin of this attraction is probably to be found partly in the human instinct of curiosity and desire for adventure. Doubtlessly, these feelings account for much of the initial attraction of a surprise innovation. Let it be assumed that the new president also has this line of thought in mind when he chooses to resort to surprise to confound and confuse his enemies by issuing suddenly the order to decentralize. He reasons that substantial numbers of his staff and employees will want to see how decentralized repair works, enjoy seeing the status quo shaken up, and desire to make the acquaintance of the newly assigned repair managers. He is counting on the fact that, having attracted this much attention to his new system, he will have won at least a measure of potential support for it. Some will see merit in it; some will be inclined to be for it simply because it represents a sudden newness in their lives; some will enjoy the chagrin and hurt of those adversely affected by it; some will be proud of their elevation to better positions brought about by the reorganization; some will be happy to see their friends in positions of higher dignity and pay; and some will applaud the boldness and astuteness of the sudden change and of the man responsible. And he may well be correct in his hope that these people will act as leaven to the whole mass of company personnel and cause it to rise to support more or less fully his new system.

Of course, the fearful administrator may feel that a surprise innovation can bring just the opposite result, and that it can lay the basis for much greater opposition than already exists. This pessimism may be well founded and his direst expectations come true. But the chances are greater that the result will be good, since most people want to follow the "shiny new band wagon" once it has pulled out on the street. At any rate, the administrator who would be dynamic and resort to strategy must be prepared to take reasonable risks, for in gamesmanship the opponent can win; and to use surprise to gain support through doing something new is in itself not an unreasonable risk.

To Enhance the Potential of a Chosen Crisis

An administrator not infrequently allows a crisis to develop or moves to induce one in company affairs so that he may use resulting confusion and demand for action as a means of accomplishing some purpose. This objective may be that of diverting attention from another development, bringing about a situation which will require solution by a measure he believes necessary, or making an opportunity for him to assume a leadership role. Surprise can play a significant part in deepening a crisis. It can add an element of unexpectedness to the situation demanding immediate or drastic action, and thus increase the degree of its urgency. This may seem so obvious as scarcely to merit mention. However, the subject cannot be dismissed so lightly, for the use of surprise to shake the organization still further may bring dangerous repercussions. It may so startle the rank and file of the department or company that morale will be badly shaken. It may so alarm them and the administrator's own colleagues that he will not be able to furnish the solution since they, in their astonishment, may feel it necessary to turn to higher executives or other plans for salvation. And it may persuade the higher officialdom of the company that, in order to prevent a recurrence of such a sudden development, further controls must be instituted—controls which might be binding to a free-wheeling administrator, as may well be the one who permits and induces crises for his own purposes.

There is an even more dangerous possible repercussion in using the sudden, unforeseen crisis. The administrator should weigh it carefully before he commits himself to the surprise technique in crises formation. Exactly as the element of surprise can increase the sense of urgency in a crisis, it can also result in a degree of blame being attached to the administrator under whose laissez-faire policy or influence the crisis develops. If anything is certain about people in a crisis, it is that many among them will seek someone to blame. The intensity of this search is frequently in direct proportion to how much they feel disturbed by the crisis. Nor are they always very objective in their figurative pointing of fingers. The administrator who desires the crisis situation may prove to be the most convenient victim in sight and he may, therefore, end up with the blame for the very situation he helped bring about. This back-fire effect is most likely if the administrator happens to be at the top of the company ladder or well up it so that his area of responsibility and duty is sufficiently broad to bring him within the spectrum of blame. Conversely, the administrator whose position in the organization is such that the responsibility for the crisis cannot be laid at his door stands a lesser chance of being his own victim.

Reverse Surprise Strategy

Occasionally, the crises-minded administrator may turn against surprise and deliberately seek to keep the critical situation from being unexpected. His action may be dictated by the fear of backlash. But it may also be a reflection of his conviction that some warning of the approaching crisis may pre-condition people in the organization to favor his solution and leadership at the critical time. Is it not natural for people in a crisis situation to turn for advice and aid to the one who has been warning them that it was impending? It is not always impossible to be a hero in one's own nation, especially if he has prepared his public to see him in this role.

Rules of Surprise

It is thus apparent that surprise can be used for different purposes in administration. As is true in the case of all tools, there are proper and improper ways to employ it. The proper use may perhaps best be described by what can be termed the *rules of surprise.*

1. The administrator should be on his guard against unethical conduct in employing the technique of surprise. As in the use of timing devices in general, its utilization can easily degenerate into mere cunning and trickery.
2. In all cases, he should weigh the negative effects that it may have upon the health and other welfare of those affected. This is no less than his moral duty.
3. The administrator should not often resort to the use of surprise, otherwise its effect may be lost. Those whom he wants to influence by it will come to expect surprises and thus to grow immune to their influence.
4. He should try to gauge how much surprise is needed. Too little will not significantly pave his way and too much may derail him by influencing his superiors to take measures which will curtail him in his future administrative ambitions and operations.
5. Deep in his mind, he should always carry the old adage that a secret shared is a secret lost. If he would use the weapon of surprise, the administrator should keep his own confidence and apprise not one person more than necessary as to his strategy or the developing situation.
6. He should prepare himself for being surprised, for his associates whom he has handled through sudden and unexpected action may either learn from him the value of the technique or use it on him in a spirit of revenge.

A further word of warning is in order: surprise is truly a delicate instrument in the crib of administrative tools. Adherence to a set of rules cannot give complete assurance as to its wise use. There is always the possibility of the exceptional circumstance which no rule fits or whose influence negates the effect of cautious procedure. The strategic administrator, therefore, should give thought to other courses of action against the possibility that he may be surprised by the failure of surprise to work.

Conclusion

The administrator lives and works in a world of reality. He is constantly faced with the necessity for deciding when to act. If he makes the right decision as to optimum point of time and if he is free to act at this time, his chances of successful performance are much greater. He may be the best intentioned and most informed person imaginable, but if his timing is wrong he will find some of his planned actions doomed to failure.

There are many timing stratagems available for use by the administrator.[11] Among these are better channels of information, waiting, phase timing, formula timing, and self influence of timing. Surprise is especially important. Its possibilities are great, the patterns of its use varied, and the risks in its use dangerous. The administrator who would be strategic must employ one or more of these stratagems upon occasions, but he should take care that he does not outmaneuver himself.

BUSINESS SITUATIONS FOR ROLE-PLAYING

SITUATION XI

Timing and Surprise

THE SOLAK CLOTHING COMPANY

A. Scene. A large distributor of men's clothing and consisting of five stores in a mid-western city. The President has called in the Director of Public Relations to discuss a merger which has been "in the air."

B. Players.

1. President: Mr. Wilfred T. Throckmorton, an urbane but decisive executive, who secretly holds people in more or less contempt.

2. Director of Public Relations: Mr. Edward T. Phillips, an organizational man with a strong bent and liking for strategy.

C. Situation.

1. The President informs him that a secret agreement has been worked out to merge with one of their dynamic competitors.

2. Although such a proposal has been discussed at various executive meetings during the past month, the decision comes as a surprise to the Director of Public Relations.

3. Furthermore, Mr. Throckmorton reminds Mr. Phillips that several key officials, especially the Controller and Sales Manager, have been very outspoken against the merger, which is now a "fait accompli."

4. It is 3 p.m. The President outlines three possible courses of action:
    a. Let the news "leak out" into the organization.
    b. Take the initiative to "sell" the opponents slowly.
    c. Announce the merger immediately.

D. Assignment.

1. Select two players to act out the strategy to be taken and, if possible, choose individuals who have strong notions as to which basic course to take.

2. Have the group engage in a general postmortem discussion of strategic possibilities.

NOTES

1. SHAKESPEARE, *Julius Caesar*, Act IV, Scene iii, Lines 219-222.

2. The significance of timing to success in administration is well expressed by Copeland who states, ". . . in business management maximum effectiveness . . . is attained when executive action is keenly timed. In meeting the perils and hazards of an ever changing environment, proficiency in timing is a particularly valuable administrative asset." MELVIN T. COPELAND, *The Executive at Work* (Cambridge, Mass.: Harvard University Press, 1952), p. 143.

3. The literature of business administration seems to give little attention to the subject of timing as a political factor. A survey of 183 books in the fields of business organization, management, and personnel administration revealed less than ten publications which even referred directly to the subject.

4. The recognition of the optimum point of time requires keen sensitivity on the part of the administrator since "when to act," as Dennison puts it, is a political question, that is, one which must take into grave consideration the opinions of others. HENRY DENNISON, *Organization Engineering* (New York: McGraw-Hill Book Company, Inc., 1931), p. 36.

5. It is interesting to note that Copeland suspects timing sense to be almost an innate attribute. *Op. cit.*, p. 143.

6. A number of useful timing stratagems are suggested by Newman in connection with planning. However, they do have, as even apparent in his discussion, more or less general applicability. WILLIAM H. NEWMAN, *Administrative Action* (Englewood Cliffs, N.J.: Prentice-Hall, Inc., 1951), pp. 110-118.

7. This would be quite contrary to the good sense reflected in Parson's idea of insulation from reciprocities of a particularistic nature. TALCOTT PARSONS, *The Social System* (Glencoe, Illinois: The Free Press, 1951), p. 317.

8. Waiting should not be confused with the strategy of forbearance which Samstag describes, for waiting involves principally delay in decision and/or action whereas forbearance implies toleration of some undesired condition. See NICHOLAS SAMSTAG, "Strategy" in *The Engineering of Consent* (Norman, Oklahoma: University of Oklahoma Press, 1955), pp. 104-106.

9. *Ibid.*, p. 103.

10. One of the rare literary recognitions of surprise as a stratagem is that of Samstag; and he touches upon it only very briefly. *Ibid.*, pp. 108-109.
11. This fact is stressed by Samstag who proclaims that timing strategy pervades the world and is indeed ubiquitous. *Ibid.*, p. 103.

But, regardless of the timing strategy utilized by the administrator, he should remember that "The right solution at the wrong time is no better than the wrong solution at the right time." See Louis A. Allen, *The Management Profession* (New York: McGraw-Hill Book Company, 1964), p. 257.

CHAPTER **12**

Administrative Excesses and Irrelevancies

> "The actions of the administrator are not always of
> justifiable relation to his purpose and set course. One
> may define as excessive or irrelevant those things in
> administration—policies, methods, procedures, habits
> and symbols—which have relatively little or no bear-
> ing on the attainment of organizational objectives.
> Their study may not only reveal or emphasize areas of
> wasted energy and other resources but also suggest
> administrative stratagems of significance."

THE ADMINISTRATOR is a human being. He can, therefore, be
expected to act as one. This means that his actions will not
always be of justifiable relationship to his purpose or set
course. Exactly at what point his actions become excessive
or irrelevant is a question to make even the most scientific
students quail. Inability to categorize them with precision
into adequate or excessive, relevant or irrelevant, should not
deter one from examining closely those steps of the executive
which manifestly go further than necessary to his aim or
direction of movement or which are not significantly related
to them. Their study may not only reveal or emphasize areas
of wasted time, energy and other resources[1] but also suggest administrative stratagems of significance.

One may define as excessive or irrelevant those things in
administration—policies, methods, procedures, habits, and

symbols—which have *relatively little* or no bearing on the attainment of organizational aims. If the basic aims of business under the free enterprise system are to protect investment, make profit and discharge certain social responsibilities to employee, community and nation, all those actions of the business administrator that have little, if any, identifiable relationship to these objectives must be regarded as pitfalls.[2] The excessive and irrelevant will be treated within this frame of reference.

Excessive and irrelevant practices may be classified into four groups to avoid the monotony of numerous sub-headings. For want of better descriptive terminology and in a slightly facetious tone, these can be termed: Inordinate Concern with Human Relations, Over-Conformity, Executive Jitterbugging, and Exaggeration of the Hero Role.

Inordinate Concern with Human Relations

Many a late twentieth century American executive, were he to express himself in frank and embittered terms on the general subject of human relations, might state that no aspect of administration has been pushed so far out of proportion as human relations. He might even profess to see that there is a "cult of human relaters." What has happened? At the risk of exaggerating, one may venture the opinion that human relations knowledge and skills have somehow come to take the place of good administration. The necessity to distinguish between the two immediately arises.

Human Relations in Proper Perspective

By human relations is meant a dynamic social reality: in general terms, the way in which people associating with one another treat each other; and in business connotation, the way that superiors treat subordinates. Administration, on the other hand, may be defined as the mobilization and use of resources, human and material, to accomplish a purpose. It is sophomoric to point out that the treatment of people within the organization is less than the totality of administration.[3] And there is no implication here that labor is to be treated as a commodity, or that the individual is not entitled to the treatment his natural dignity and merit deserve.[4] The correct inference to be drawn is simply that the part is less than the whole, and that, therefore, human relations expertise is not to be confused with administration.[5]

Yet certain forces, at work for years, have obscured this distinction and seem to have reversed in the minds of many people, and even of some administrators, the position of administration and human relations. Today, there is a clearly discernible tendency on the part of large numbers, to consider that the business (or other employing entity) exists primarily for the good of those it employs. This means that these extremists expect good treatment from the administrator to be the prime consideration. Unfortunately, even executive ranks have become infected, by the general educative process or by the exigencies of their job, with this same belief. As a result, administrators are observed treating their people either unilaterally or in response to demand from "the help," in ways which have little clear relation to the operation of the business toward its primary goals. Examples are numerous: according work time privileges for which there is little need, such as frequent and prolonged absences from bench or desk; allowing extensive socializing during working hours; consulting with subordinates and other associates who are unable to contribute anything but whose opinion is asked in the interest of maintaining the fiction of democratic procedure; tolerating employee impudence to customers and superiors alike; giving suggestions instead of orders; and carefully refraining from direct and concise criticism of unsatisfactory work. Three questions arise as to this topsy-turvy condition in administration: "What has brought it about?"; "What is its significance?"; "How can an administrator cope with it?"

Why the Great Concern with Human Relations?

There are many influences behind the great concern with human relations that marks modern administration. Certainly one is the development of ethical patterns of conduct. Closely related, although not the same, is the drive long evident in Western civilization for more humanitarian treatment of people. The process of democratization which has rather thoroughly destroyed traditional social strata also must be given proper credit, for it has resulted in a widespread feeling of equalitarianism among Americans and others who are pledged to freedom as a way of life. Moreover, there must be cited the influence of the educational system and educative forces that have made the vast majority of people literate, aware of their rights, and vociferous in defending them. And then too, effective association, especially in the field of labor, has given millions new courage to demand proper and even "plush carpet" treatment. Finally, it is necessary to recognize that the tremendous increase in man's ability to support himself economically has made him much more independent. All in all, the forces of history seem to be, and for some time to have been, forming a conjuncture in favor of the follower.

What Is the Significance of Overemphasis on Human Relations?

Now it would be foolish, if not downright dishonest, to deny the wonderful good which these forces alone and in combination have brought the individual and those dependent upon him. On the credit side, one must list for the individual greater recognition, respect, freedom, reward, and security. Unhappily, forces for good may also bring some undesirable results, and this is the gist of the line of thought being developed here with respect to the overemphasis on human relations in administration. The very forces that have given the individual recognition and so much else also seem to have given him a somewhat inflated feeling of his own worth and ability to demand. The administrator has often yielded. Not only has he been outnumbered and outpressured to do so, but under his urge to succeed—itself a product in part of these forces—he has frequently seen it expedient to treat people too well.

When one speaks of treating people in the organization "too well," he is stepping out dangerously far. Many may contend that it is impossible to give anyone too good treatment. Such is the popular belief that all, regardless of virtue and effort, are entitled not only to the good life but to the best life. Yet, the administrator and his organization can pay a high price for over-concession to human relations. It can mean an unbalanced orientation in the whole administrative performance—a looking toward only the welfare and pleasure of personnel rather than the enduring health of the organization which employs them. It can mean individual decisions made in their interest at an exorbitant cost to the company or department. It can mean the creation of an administrative environment without adequate leadership, since everyone is "brought in on the act." And finally, it can create among the organizational family the general idea that the company exists to be exploited.

These negative results of the soft approach to human relations might well be viewed in the light of the sobering fact that the company's capacity to continue to furnish even something less than ideal employment depends upon its ability to produce good products at a fair return. Otherwise, there will be neither the customers to buy nor the investors to put more capital into it. Those who love too much the slogan of "Everybody should have the best under all circumstances" would do well to recognize the basic truth of the free enterprise system.

How Can the Administrator Avoid Overemphasis on Human Relations?

Fortunately, there are steps which the worried administrator can take to avoid overemphasis on human relations. As a step of prime importance, he can make certain that he knows what is meant by *proper* human relations. If he does not, he must seek both a general and a specific comprehension. The general understanding concerns the essentials of good human relations everywhere and in all situations. It demands that he acquaint himself with the fact of the dignity of man and the pattern of ethical behavior which this dignity dictates the executive follow in all his dealings with his fellowman, including his employees. Unless the administrator is so oriented, he may be inclined to judge his treatment of people according to relative standards, that is, as the expediency of the administrative situation demands.

In terms of specific understanding, he should endeavor, through an analysis of his personal prejudices, to make certain that his own approach to the handling of people is not beclouded by emotional considerations. This is not an easy task, because the administrator as a human being will have been conditioned by his own training and experiences to certain beliefs regarding the proper treatment of other people. In the effort to define human relations, as in all social studies, it is hard for the student to divorce himself from the subject. But unless he can, he will likely tend to see proper human relations not as they should be, but as his subjective viewpoint demands.

Getting a clear view of what his human relations should be is for the administrator essentially just basic orientation. In itself, it is not enough. He needs other brakes on himself and certainly restraints on the demands which others make of him. Therefore, he must proceed from orientation to policy and practice. There are literally dozens of useful measures he can adopt and take in an effort to assure correct relations with his followers and other associates. However, the thought here is concerned only with the avoidance of too great concern for their attitude and well-being at the expense of legitimate organizational goals. The steps by which this can be done, and done fairly, are fewer.

The administrator can do much to avoid becoming over-sentimental about his subordinates and their welfare, and to prevent the development of exorbitant expectations of him on their part, by constantly endeavoring to honor the contract nexus of employment. The best way he can do this is to set up clear and reasonable standards of performance and to insist upon their accomplishment. It may be assumed that by and large employees, high or low, know deeply in their consciousness that they must do a certain amount of work for their salary or wage. In general, too, people wish to know what is expected of them as members of their organization, for this knowledge contributes to the desired feelings of belonging and of security. These two facts make it relatively easier for the executive to establish standards which he expects them to attain. Such standards can be a real safeguard against devolution of the department or company from an efficiently functioning unit of production to simply a "nice place to work." On the one hand, they are a constant reminder to him that his people have a measurable obligation to him and the organization; and the degree to which they discharge it can greatly influence his attitude toward them. Unless he is a truly foolish administrator, he will want something from his employees for what he gives them. Here is a potentially strong brake on sentimental human relations. On the other hand, the existence of work standards, clearly set forth and known to be demanded by management as a minimum, can have a modifying influence on any tendency of subordinates to demand treatment unreasonably soft. These standards are a real reminder to them that to receive they must produce.

Closely allied to standards as a measure for keeping human relations with subordinates on a sensible keel is the curtailment of social intimacy with them. This implies specifically three restraints: that the administrator limit his intimate association with subordinates; that he confine a tendency he may have to over-confide in them; and that he curb any exaggerated curiosity which he may entertain concerning them as individuals. The practice of these restraints will keep him far enough removed from his subordinates so that, everything else being equal, he can view them with objectivity. There is no suggestion here that the administrator become a snob, disdainful of himself as a feeling creature and contemptuous of those about him as human beings.[6] Such a role would confer little of the mantle of leadership on him in this age of democracy and humanitarianism and could well border on the unethical. But he simply must not get too close to them. If he does, his sympathy for their weaknesses, ambitions, hopes, fears and problems, as well as his affection for them as associates and friends, may lead him to be more concerned about "coddling" them than running the organization efficiently.

The administrator, moreover, must also live with his equals and superiors. He can overemphasize human relations with these people and groups, just as he can with those below him. He can treat them too well; act soft in his dealings with them to the detriment of organizational welfare; and in general oversentimentalize his relations with them. How to associate with them in such manner as not to impair the efficient discharge of his duties as an executive is not always easy. All men need friends, and they commonly find them among those of their own ilk with whom they toil. So administrators are likely to view some of their fellows as friends, a perspective which can blind objective judgment because of the emotions involved. Then too, many administrators especially want to please their superiors, for they value dearly recognition, praise, and promotion. The result can be an effort to maintain the proper relations with "topside" at the expense of more relevant tasks in the organization and sometimes even at the expense of loyalty to others in the department or company who also deserve it.

The administrator can enhance the possibility of good balance in his human relations with equals and superiors through at least two means. One is self-control in the expenditure of his time and effort. Just as he should set up standards of work performance for his subordinates so that both they and he can see the line separating the proper from the excessive in treatment demanded and given, so he must impose on himself a philosophy of work in the organization. And this philosophy should be that the discharge of his duties as an administrator for the company, in the main, takes priority over the obligations of mere association with fellow administrators and over the desire to fawn on superiors. The administrator who views his life in and with the organization in this light will have much less opportunity to worry about "treating his friends and bosses well." He will simply be too busy.

The second means available to the administrator in the interest of maintaining reasonable balance in human relations with equals and superiors is quite different. As well known, the pattern of treatment which one person shows others is not only the result of his attitude toward them but also of their attitude toward and, hence, demands on, him. It is accordingly necessary for the administrator to seek some measure of self-protection against imposition. Perhaps one of the best measures is for the executive to let it be known that he can be pushed only so far. Actually, this is a reputation not difficult to acquire. In most cases it demands that the administrator should occasionally refuse to be pushed, become incensed, and even strike back regardless of where the chips may fall. Most of the members of management probably prefer peace, and desire to be known as good fellows. They are rather easily shaken by strong reaction on the part of a colleague and, should he show his temper and teeth a few times, they are likely to come to regard him as a person with whom it is well not to trifle. Even his superiors can be so educated, especially if they value his services highly.

Doubtlessly, the direction of the discussion will seem of brutal import to some, especially in this age and culture which places a high premium on "togetherness" and "getting along with each other." Yet nothing could be further from its intent than the desire to convey any impression that kindness is out of place in human relations. The core of good human relations is the Golden Rule of treating others as one himself would be treated, and so kindness is of the essence of proper human relations. But it is possible to be "too kind," that is, to be too willing to give subordinate, colleague, or superior anything he wants, regardless of his just deserts and the good of the group to which he belongs. It is against human relations of the excessively soft type here implied that argument is directed.

All sensible administrators will realize the possible need and desirability of exception to man-made principles and rules. Therefore, it should be pointed out that in the treatment of individuals or particular groups within a company there may be occasions when it is necessary for the administrator to step outside the bounds of proper human relations and do much better. One such is the situation which demands unusual charitable consideration, as the case of a faithful older employee who needs more personal recognition from the administrator, since he has come to fear the competition of younger employees. Another is the situation involving a capable but shy and uncertain individual who needs more than an ordinary show of administrative confidence to be retained on the job and properly trained. A still further situation justifying exception to the norm of sensible human relations appears in regard to the misdirected individual who for some reason is prejudiced against the administrator, department, or company and who needs double reassurance that he is not in the camp of the enemy. This is a very common problem in business organizations today, since there are so many influences working to make the employer and his managerial staff falsely appear to be exploiters of the employees. No doubt, there are many other circumstances which call for better than normally reasonable treatment of people.

There is another aspect of the overemphasis of human relations which must be mentioned. All the fine intentions and rules possible to keep human relations as a part and not the totality of administration can come to naught if those who demand better than fair and sensible treatment have some peculiar strength to obtain it. Such power may be obtained from many sources, among which three are most common: shortage in the employment market, favored protection by government, and membership in professional or labor organizations. In the United States, these three factors more often than not do conspire in effect to give the "other fellow" a stronger position in human relations. About all the rational administrator can do when faced with the phenomenon of power able to impose upon him is to make certain that he knows his own power position, and then to proceed from it with whatever skill he has but according to ethical principles. Even though he goes down to defeat and is forced to yield concessions in his human relations far beyond that which is right and reasonable, he will have added to his stature as a person who will stand his ground. He may, by so doing, reduce the frequency and intensity of future raids on his goodwill and kindness.

Over-Conformity

Many administrators, like the majority of people, desire relative peace, quiet, and safety. Their immediate goal is to run their organizations smoothly. In fact, some weak executives see this as their ultimate objective and will even allow their organizations to perform poorly and eventually fail rather than do anything which might disturb the status quo. One of the favorite weapons of these static executives is conformity. When confronted with the possibility of innovation, no matter how promising, or even with the proven necessity for change, they will drag out the red herring of precedent, policies, rules, and regulations to prove that the new step should not be taken, since it does not conform to the accepted pattern of operation. All too often, they will even attempt to apply "the law" out of context and, in effect, pervert its deep intent.[7]

To make matters worse, the administrator who conforms to protect his pleasant existence is often not a mild person who can be persuaded to abandon his reluctance to change or who can be easily circumvented in actual practice. In general demeanor often pleasant and placid, he can sometimes exhibit great energy, nimbleness, and tenacity in defending his negative position, such is his fear of change. Then too, he can prove an effective blocking force precisely because, doing little other than performing the routine jobs of administration, he has had time to analyze and plan for the defense of his position. In charity to the confirmed conformist, attention must be called to the fact that development of bureaucracy in business administration brings the requirement for more and more conformity.[8]

If the over-conforming administrator were merely an individual without support in the department or company, his obstructive tendencies, under the guise of "adherence to the law," might not be too significant. But he often draws considerable support from various directions. Some of his less imaginative subordinates will see in him an honorable man who treats all alike. Among his equals there will be a number who will interpret his devotion to conformity as a sign that he is solid and to be trusted. Even an occasional conservative superior will appreciate him as a man who takes few risks and, hence, who is not likely to cost the organization money or cause it embarrassment.

Correction of Personal Tendency to Over-Conform

There are two problems arising from the excessive use of conformity as an administrative tool. The first belongs to the executive who is guilty of doing so. For him, the question is, "What can I do to correct my tendency to seek cover in conformity when confronted with the possibility of innovation?" The second problem is that of the dynamic administrator who finds himself under or otherwise associated with the timid executive. His question is very simply stated, "How can I perform successfully with this roadblock in the way?" These are two quite different problems and require separate analysis.

The administrator who worries about his own habitual resort to conformity when confronted with a situation suggesting the need or desirability of innovation is well on the way to solving his own problem. The fact of his concern indicates that he is aware of his weakness, and awareness is the first major step in the correction of many types of faults. Of course, mere correct self-analysis is not enough. The worrisome executive needs the courage of his conviction. This he can find in certain truths, which he should add to his philosophy of administration. One is that policies, rules, regulations, and standard methods and procedures are developed and instituted by an organization because adherence to them is believed to be a good general guarantee of efficiency and safety. But no complex of guide lines can fit every situation. There will be circumstances demanding exception to almost any man-made dictum. A second truth is that many of those in a position to judge the administrator's behavior—stockholders, the board of directors, higher executives if any, colleagues, and subordinates—will at times expect the executive to make exceptions and will honor him for doing so. Such occasions may be instances presenting a real opportunity to show charity and kindness, to improve public relations, to gain an impressive advantage over competition, to make an unusual profit, and to turn a seeming defeat into victory. In this connection, the administrator should remember, too, that certain members of the organization may always be interested primarily in winning and not in rule-keeping, and that the very higher authority responsible for the "rules" may himself, on special occasion, desire them broken. And finally, the administrator should bring into his philosophy of administration recognition of a truth with implications of self-interest. It is simply that, while accomplishment in company or department interest is generally the surest way to get ahead in the organization, opportunities for accomplishment frequently demand departure from the accepted norms of operation.

Awareness of his woodenness, accompanied with full recognition that exceptions to rules are necessary, that there are those in the company who will support his breaking them, and that his own career may depend upon his doing so, would seem to generate enough assurance that an administrator will not commit the error of over-conformity. Such is, unfortunately, not the case. A strange wedding of circumstances sometimes occurs and, in effect, prevents him from taking the dynamic course. These circumstances are unrelated, except that they may appear in the life or personality of a given executive. One is early education and training in conservative attitudes and actions—such effective education and training that the administrator is always under great self-pressure to obey the rules even when he knows better. The other is plain laziness, no matter what its cause. Where conservatism and indolence are combined in one person, one often sees the slavishly conforming administrator.

Living and Working with an Over-Conformist

To solve his own problem the over-conforming administrator has principally but to deal with himself. The executive who must live and function with him has a manifold headache. He must "get along" at least to the extent that the organization demands internal peace. He must do his own job, even though the over-conformist in effect makes this more difficult. And last, but not by any means least, he must provide an extra measure of initiative, alertness, and industry to compensate for the rigidity and unresponsiveness of the over-conformist. This task can be particularly onerous when the wooden executive happens to be the administrator's superior, for then there is, combined with its intrinsic difficulty, the need for the special political approach by the administrator to prevent the superior from reacting against the informal leadership.

Clearly, successful performance in association with the over-conforming executive demands skillful strategy. In order of difficulty, the task of getting along with him is probably the easiest. As continuously underlined with regard to all administrative behavior patterns, the administrator should follow ethical principles when dealing with the over-conformist no matter what the temptation may be to handle him by trickery. Moral conduct has its own reason, and in this, as in all strategies, it needs no further justification. However, it has a peculiarly specific importance in living with the over-conforming executive. Since he has high respect for rules, he may be expected often to judge all conduct which disturbs him on the basis of the highest rules he knows, those of morality. He may commonly suspect chicanery or dishonor in any innovation proposed.

In addition to treating him with impeccable fairness and honesty, the strategic administrator who would try to live peacefully with the over-conformist can increase his chances of doing so by using certain specific techniques. Insofar as good dynamic leadership will permit, he should join the staid incumbent in the strict observance and defense of all rules, and thus create an identity of interests with him. Since the over-conformist is likely to be easily alarmed by the unusual, the dynamic administrator should be careful not to disturb him unnecessarily either by surprise, exaggeration, or ambition. Above all else, the aggressive administrator should endeavor to show him respect. This may be a hard thing to do, for there is commonly the urge to disdain, if not openly criticize, the official who, by his love of the word "No," appears to stand in the way of progress. These techniques should make it reasonably possible to live in peace with the over-conformist, since they can contribute substantially to his feeling of security.

The dynamic administrator must be strategic in his effort to do his own job well despite the hindrance of another executive, perhaps his superior, who lives unimaginatively by the book. The most obvious course available to him is to proceed with his own duties, asking only when absolutely necessary for the advice, concurrence, or permission of the rule-minded associate. Another course is for the dynamic administrator to associate himself with power centers in the organization that give him sufficient influence to do his work in spite of any blocking efforts by the defensive executive. This is not to suggest that the more imaginative go over the head of the less imaginative administrator. It is rather to imply that such identification with powerful entities, cliques, and leaders in the organization will help the arch-conservative executive to see his more lively associate as a member to respect in the administrative family. From this respect, perhaps only very indirectly generated by fear, may come a greater measure of understanding and toleration of the dynamic administrator's job.

Equally effective, but more subtle than either of these two courses of action, is a process which may be called conversion. It is basically the education of the less visionary by the more visionary executive to show him the real nature of the latter's job. As is true of all educational efforts, the process is best undertaken when preceded by a careful analysis of the one to be converted. Without preconceived notions, the dynamic administrator should carefully study the administrator who appears wedded to regulations to determine (1) if he really is as conforming as he appears; (2) whether or not he is educible; and (3) how he can be reached. Should his estimate of the situation be favorable, he then can proceed to teach the static executive. He must be willing to take different approaches. Certainly patience and tact will be generally useful, for the undynamic administrator may well be confused, misguided, stubborn, and proud. However, there will be times when stronger approaches, such as impetuosity and harshness, may be dictated, since it is quite possible that he may be too slow or too stubborn to be reached otherwise. Whatever approach is used, the dynamic administrator should remember that almost every contact, direct or indirect, with the subject of his educating effort can be used to condition him a bit further. Conversion is building a new attitude, and big structures are commonly built with small stones.

An illustration may be taken to demonstrate the complexity of the conversion process as here described. The branch manager of a utility company has a difficult problem. He clearly sees the necessity for helping create and maintain a good public image of the monopoly he represents, so he plunges into civic affairs in his district. Money is needed to carry on this extra-book activity; he requisitions the necessary funds from the company controller who, however, happens to be a strict constructionist as far as company operations are concerned. Nothing in stated company policies recognizes the need for expenditures on civic affairs. He cites this fact to the anxious branch manager, and turns down his request for money. But this executive is determined to put the company into civic affairs. He, therefore, considers the problem of educating the controller to their importance. (Perhaps he sees no other means of removing him as a roadblock.) He knows from experience that the controller lives by the book, but he feels that this individual's attitude can be changed, and he is rather certain that his Achilles heel is his desire to be promoted to the presidency of the utility company. He gently hints to the controller, and then with increasing tempo reminds him, in one way or another that a friendly public could be a big help to his ambition to become president. After a passage of time, but without specific preparation, the branch manager invites him to deliver the main address on Old Settlers Day at the County Fair. The controller, now less unfriendly to civic affairs, is influenced to accept, delivers the address, and is treated with honor. Perhaps one may hope that he understands better the branch manager's job and will approve his request for funds. If not, the branch manager can continue the teaching process. If there is a limit to the extent that a dynamic administrator can influence another executive in an organization, it is probably set only by the exhaustion of the former's desires, energy, and ingenuity.

Working out a rapprochement with the over-conforming administrator and trying to do one's own work properly despite his obstruction are but two answers to the dynamic executive's question, "How can I perform successfully with this roadblock in the way?" A third answer is required, and it deals with the stratagems by which the dynamic executive can contribute to the leadership which the company needs but does not get from the static office holder. Of course, the argument may be advanced that this degree of leadership is no concern of the more active executive. Yet, this is no real answer, since circumstances often saddle the meritorious administrator with the leadership duties shirked by the less dynamic executive. Among these circumstances are a feeling of chagrin and even moral responsibility by the former at the way affairs are handled, realization by the former that the organization needs his extra effort, the necessity in self-interest for this more imaginative and courageous person to help fill the gap, expectations of others in the company that he who has the "get up and go" will carry the load of leadership, and the placement by top authority of trust in the dynamic executive to propose and effect innovation.

The vital administrator caught in this position may pay a considerable price in doing that which organizationally is not his, and he will often need to exercise the utmost in political skill in shouldering the burden successfully. As a prime difficulty, he may expect the over-conforming associate to resent intrusion into his legitimate field of operation. A good device here is to implant in the mind of the reluctant party, as far as this can be done ethically, the idea that he is the innovator, and, if possible, to get him to order the dynamic administrator to undertake the new course of action. Often the effective use of this device demands the book-bound official be shown that the proposed innovation is in his self-interest and that it is valuable to the organization (in fairness, the fact must be recognized that the strictly conforming executive may be completely loyal to company objectives). It may also require a sense of timing, so that enough time is left between hints for the official to absorb the proposal into his consciousness as his own.

A further unpleasant and dangerous reaction may arise in

the form of resentment against the dynamic executive by others in the organization who consider him an ambitious man. Failing to understand that the formal leader is not functioning as a real leader, they see the one who assumes the burden as an interloper and usurper of power. Feeling of this type is dangerous not only to the prestige of the imaginative and willing administrator, but it also serves, with a sort of backlash effect, to throw more of the company family into the train of the static executive. What defense is there against such resentment? No doubt the general reputation of the dynamic individual as a fair and honorable person is a good shield. But it must exist to be effective, and it can be worn out by constant criticism. It seems that the executive acting as the informal leader can best protect himself by a general stance of honor. This means not seizing the limelight from the static executive, refraining from openly criticising him or belittling him, informing him as far as organizationally feasible of any intended action which may appear to infringe upon his legitimate organizational domain, and as far as possible sharing with him any honor that may come from successful innovation. Constant adherence to these norms of fair play will help liquidate the feeling that the hard working, alert, and forward looking administrator is infected with the disease of over-ambition.

As an added hazard for the administrator who tries to furnish the much needed leadership that should be supplied by someone else, there is the danger of failing. Any new or unusual course of action may not succeed, and he who takes it may suffer from the reflection of its failure. Yet the chances of failure in such action taken by the dynamic administrator attempting to fill the breech can be unusually high. He may be moving into strange fields; some in the organization, including the static executive, may oppose him; and, especially if he is a subordinate, he may not know the nuances of higher operation as well as he should. Here, then, arises a real need for analytical judgment. The informal leader assuming leadership in a particular innovation should carefully weigh his chances of not succeeding, and, if they are great, either not undertake it or do so with all necessary reservations having been communicated, at least upward, in the organization.

A word of caution! Much has been said about over-conformity, and the impression may have been given that conformity itself, or even allegiance to the organization,[9] is suspect. Nothing could be further from the intention of this presentation. Conformity as a norm of administrative procedure is absolutely necessary to the good functioning of any organization. Policies, rules, regulations, precedent, and standard ways of doing things are the basis for organizational self-discipline, without which there would be company or department anarchy. All that has been said is based on the assumption that it is possible to confine administration too closely within the limits of the book. And the purpose has been to suggest, in the broadest generalities, ways of coping with this administrative weakness.

Executive Jitterbugging

The position of the administrator requires an individual with the ability to do things. This means that the administrator must possess, no matter what other attributes are necessary, a good measure of energy and imagination. These are the characteristics which in fact more than anything else make him a doer. However, they do not guarantee that he will either conserve his ability or maintain a calm demeanor in his work. Business and industry, as well as other fields of activity, are replete with examples of executives who, in the vernacular, simply cannot remain calm or stand still.[10] The very qualities which make it possible for them to administer also cause them to turn to many excessive and irrelevant outlets. They can be observed doing far more than is necessary to accomplish their functions. Brought to mild frenzy by the excitement of action, anticipation of victory, frustration over indecision or slowness, and worry over possible failure, they are pushed into expression and action for the sake of expression and action. In a sense, they are the liveliest of dancers, endeavoring to attune their motions to all the noise and music they can hear. They are truly executive jitterbugs. Certainly, they lack what has been called the quality of "mellowness."[11]

This exaggerated responsiveness of the administrator to the varied stimuli that play upon him takes many forms. They may be identified as executive exhortation, multiple assignment, over-direction, immoderate supervision, premature insistence on evidence of accomplishment, detail hypnosis, unnecessary decision, over-concentration on work, and even over-indulgence in recreation.

Executive Exhortation

One of the common excesses or irrelevancies in administrative behavior is executive exhortation. The eager administrator, a victim of his own ardency and anxiety, feels himself driven to talk about his pet project or problem. He searches for an audience and, since he is in a position of some influence, usually finds one. Embarked upon his subject, he quickly picks up enthusiasm, loses much of his sense of proportion, and is off on an executive sermon.

In itself, the executive exhortation may seem to be nothing more or less than a psychological ventilation. If this were all, it would deserve little attention. However, the executive exhortation has inherent dangers. The mention of a few will illustrate their proportion. The jittery administrator may talk too much in the sense that he reveals secrets and confidences he should keep. He may lose leadership stature in the eyes of his listeners by appearing too concerned. He may, by the length and intensity of his remarks if they are in the nature of criticism, appear to overcriticize either those to whom he is speaking or about whom he is holding forth, and overcriticism can create many wrong impressions about him.[12] He may confuse them, especially if they are subordinates, as to his desires and directions, especially when the executive sermon is delivered at a meeting whose prime purpose is to assign them some duty. He may frustrate them if he "takes off on a preaching mission" when they have approached him for advice, decision, or approval. He may so over-do his remarks that he wastes his own time, the time of others, and, in effect, contributes to delay in the very thing about which he is excited. Not the least among the dangers of executive exhortation is the possibility that indulgence in it will make the indulger appear a bore.[13]

The subject could be dropped at this point since the discussion here is of administrative pitfalls. However, it would not be fair analysis to do so, for administrative exhortation has possibilities for constructive use by the strategic administrator. It must not always be viewed as an administrative excess. Among its constructive possibilities are its use to emphasize a view, to overwhelm opposition, to criticize or praise, to launch trial balloons, and to stimulate. No mention is included of the most obvious of all uses—to blow off steam. This omission may be proper since the type of discussion here branded as executive exhortation is a degree of preaching beyond that which is necessary for self-ventilation (the concept of executive "jitterbugging," as used throughout this discussion, is intended to exclude reasonable activities of the administrator to relieve his pressures by an expression of his enthusiasm and concern).

Multiple Assignment of Duties

The excitable administrator may further show his uneasiness by assigning the same duties to more than one party.

The multiple assignment of duties reflects specifically his worry over the possibility that they may not be discharged properly. This is not the most perilous form of administrative jitterbugging. Perhaps its greatest potential danger lies in the field of morale. Especially the first party to whom the duties are assigned may feel, upon learning that another has been given the same job, that he is not completely trusted by the administrator. Of course, there are other unpleasant possibilities. The two or more parties may clash in their efforts to do the job and enmities may be thus created. Or each party may simply lie down on the job and assume that the others will come through, with the result that it simply does not get done. Sometimes, to be certain, the dangers can be balanced by the double assurance of accomplishment proceeding from two or more assignments of the same thing.

Over-Direction

Not totally unconnected with multiple assignment is over-direction. Some nervous executives are inclined to repeat directions or to make them too detailed. This super-effort to assure himself that the work will be done as he wishes is a tempting procedure for the very conscientious person. It can, however, have some appreciable negative repercussions. Most important is the cumulative deadening effect upon initiative. Some minor repercussions are the possibility of giving contradictory orders or impressions with successive directions, and the equal possibility of making the order too inflexible by specifying details closely.

Immoderate Supervision

The arduous executive may indulge his nervousness by too much supervision. This immoderate course may manifest itself in many ways: requiring numerous appraisals of needs and progress; frequent visits and inspection trips to work sites; constantly observing performance; indulging in frequent criticism, suggestion and praise of subordinates; and sending many interim reports to superiors. Over-supervision can defeat the purpose of supervision by strangling action. The supervised may react either by playing games with the administrator to please him or by losing the spark of self-confidence which is nurtured in allowing a subordinate to be on his own.

Premature Insistence on Evidence of Accomplishment

Another excess of nervous administration, but perhaps also classifiable as over-supervision, is premature insistence on evidence of accomplishment. So anxious does the executive become, that he demands proof of progress too soon. The results can be disastrous. The operating party may be forced to do things inimical to the project simply in order to satisfy the administrator that something is being done; or he may be driven to fakery. In extreme cases, the party assigned to do the work may despair and give up, because the premature demands of the superior come to appear as standards impossible of accomplishment.

Detail Hypnosis

The executive infected with a case of Terpsichorean nerves often becomes over-concerned with details. Such is his interest and anxiety that he watches carefully the minutia of each proposal, plan, project, and action to see that everything is done correctly. Since details are more frequent features than major aspects, he will see more of them and, therefore, run the danger of hypnotizing himself with their importance. He may even come to mistake their proper accomplishment for major objectives. Then too, since details are more commonly overlooked than big things, he may lose sight of real values and progress and turn his attention to assuring himself that the details are not overlooked. This concentration on details is obviously not to be desired, as it consumes too much time, energy, and money and diverts the administrator from his real job of total accomplishment.[14]

Unnecessary Decision

Many an administrator commits an excess which may be described as unnecessary decision. Every situation does not demand that a decision be made, and certainly does not require that the particular administrator decide. This is a fact of organizational life which can scarcely be overemphasized to the over-eager executive who wants to do something about everything.[15] Unnecessary decision can have restraining influence on his subsequent performance and on company interests through the commitment it involves. When the executive makes a decision, he binds himself and his organization to some course. But the pursuit of it may be expensive in resources, and it may be costly in an indirect sense that it prevents him and the organization from moving in a different direction.

Over-Concentration on Work

Then there is the executive who is guilty of the excess of too much work. For many reasons, he works super-intensely at his job and also takes on more and more commitments. He fails to realize that his energy is sustained and his activities balanced by relaxation and engagement in pursuits outside the frame of reference of his work.[16] Concentrated attention on work can lead to over-fatigue and all the evils it brings.

Over-Indulgence in Recreation

Not the least of the excesses and irrelevancies of very spirited and competitive administrators is the tendency on the part of some of them to over-indulge in recreation. One sees such individuals playing eighteen holes of golf on a hot July afternoon, religiously batting about the elusive handball after a hard day's work, rushing to the beaches of Florida to cavort in the sand and night-clubs, living-it-up at evening social affairs, frantically pursuing hobbies, and otherwise behaving as individuals without other care or strain. The effects on the administrator can be physical, moral, and mental depletion. The human physique, character, and mind are not inexhaustible resources. Challenged and used too much, they figuratively burn themselves up. The executive who overexerts himself under the guise of recreation is likely to be engaged in a process of speedy self-consumption having little to do with success on his job. Moreover, his very over-indulgence in fun may serve to demean him in the minds of his associates. The mantle of playboy is one which sub-ordinates and many others are especially willing to award the executive.

The Strategy of Self-Restraint

Are there any stratagems or principles of strategy which can be called up to restrain executive jitterbugging or to mitigate its effects? There must be many, but they seem to add up to self-discipline by the offending administrator. A personal appraisal of the use of time and energy may be taken as an approach to this self-discipline. Interestingly enough, he who asks himself seriously the question, "How do I spend my day and energy?", may well come to enjoy answering it. He can find in the answer the way to a more successful and pleasant life.

Associating with the Nervous Administrator

As far as living with an administrator of the species *Jitterbugensis* is concerned, a calmer executive can find something of real value in the excesses and irrelevancies of his colleague. On the one hand, he can help his own chances of successful administrative performance. He can get an education in what not to do and, thus, avoid the pitfalls into which his colleague falls. On the other hand, he can expect an enhancement of his stature as an administrator in the company to proceed from the mere fact of favorable contrast in the eyes of his associates between his calm and reasonable approach and the excitable and exaggerated assault techniques of his eager colleague. Moreover, gratuitous competitive advantages may accrue to him from the indiscreet revelations and movements of the jitterbug, although they should not be followed up if it is unethical to do so.

Probably the most serious problem faced by the calm administrator in associating with the eager executive is to protect himself against infection with the disease of anxiety and excitement. Running in circles and spinning wheels is contagious. It provides a strong appeal for emulation, if for no other reason than that it gives the impression of a real leader at work. The administrator who would keep a more rational pattern of behavior should always ask himself, "What is this jitterbug accomplishing by his prolific words and motions?"

Exaggeration of the Hero Role

A hero is an individual who accomplishes an act of a very unusual nature, or performs an act of any nature in a superlative manner, and who is recognized for the remarkable character or virtue of the deed.[17] The position of the administrator presents a real opportunity for the emergence of a hero. To be effective, it demands uncommon acts and outstanding performance; and its incumbent, occupying an elevated position in the hierarchy of the group, is therefore easily observable in his extraordinary behavior. So favorable is administratorship to heroic stature that any executive may be tempted, at least occasionally, to consider himself as a hero. There is little danger to self or good administration in this bit of conceit; in fact, it may be a constructive factor of self-reward which can motivate the administrator to further effort.

Unhappily, some administrators seem obsessed with the idea of their own supreme importance—a condition which is encouraged by the common human desire for enhancement of essential ego. This exaggerated self-evaluation in the fertile climate of administratorship can convince the administrator that he really is of heroic proportions destined for heroic things. Even this might not result in anything particularly inimical to good administration; it might in fact impel the executive toward really dynamic leadership. The trouble is, however, that the executive who identifies himself strongly and generally with the heroic role often tries to live and act like a hero. He allows his desire for personal enhancement to get out of hand.[18] He is inclined to engage in excesses and irrelevancies to live up to his own great image of himself.

Assumption of Credit and Rejection of Blame

A common practice of the Olympic administrator is to attempt to take credit for all that is accomplished in the organization and to disclaim all that fails. An example is found in the case of the sales manager who proudly thumps his own chest each time the monthly quota is reached or surpassed but who blames the credit department for its conservative policy whenever sales fall below this point. The practice here illustrated becomes increasingly detrimental to the administrator's standing with his associates, especially his fellow administrators, since as members of management they know him well. Subordinates, superiors, and outsiders may not be as easily offended by his supreme conceit because they are further removed from him. In fact, outsiders may be quite susceptible to his claims and antics; they are so far from the scene that he may appear to them to be the only real leader in the organization.

Intense Drive for Publicity

Coupled with the hero's effort to monopolize the credit for all creditable accomplishments and to reject the blame for other results is often an inordinate desire for publicity. The egotistical sales manager probably will not be content with his own personal boasting; he will want much more publicity. The hero-centered administrator seeks public notice both as a source of personal gratification and as a means of further building himself up in the eyes of the public.

But publicity seeking is a heady game; each success may whet the executive's appetite for more public adulation. In his continual effort to hear his name, see his face, and read his praises, he can go so far that he destroys the hero image his publics hold of him. He can, in fact, make himself known to both those within and without the company as primarily a publicity hound. And there is still a greater danger. The publicity hungry administrator may come to believe all that the press, radio, television, trade associations, and civic groups say about him, so that, hypnotized by public acclaim, he sees himself far wiser and better and much more loved and respected than he is in reality. The stage is now set for real administrative blunders, since the administrator's consequent feeling of power may lead him grievously to overplay his hand. The sales manager, certain that his own position is impregnable and his worth beyond question, demands that the head of the credit department, who will not approve sales to poor credit risks, be discharged. The credit manager, himself a man of great influence in company affairs, reacts strongly, becomes the implacable enemy of the egotistical sales manager, and proceeds henceforth to oppose him whenever the opportunity arises.

Insistence upon Symbols

Sometimes the pedestal bound administrator may indulge his passion for recognition as a hero by more innocuous means. He may insist upon symbols which will suggest his heroic stature. These are many and varied. They include such diverse things as imposing titles; a striking office with elaborate accoutrements; more than enough personal assistance from private secretaries, administrative assistants, and public relations men; elaborate means of transportation; obsequious treatment from those around him and especially in his public appearances; association only with prominent people; and identification with some extreme of living, either lavish consumption or spartan fare. Indulgence in such status symbols alone may not be cause for too much alarm. However, when it is added to credit-grabbing and publicity-seeking, it can become highly detrimental to the prestige of the administrator with those who know him. It gives tangible evidence to them of his ambitions to be identified as much more than ordinary man.

Heroes Can Be Useful

There is no denying that the self-hero oriented administrator can do much for his organization. He is frequently a necessary remedy for the sluggish company or department which has been in the rut of sleepy performance for so long that both its members and the outside public have come to accept it as mediocre by nature. His pyrotechnics of self-acclaim, his driving efforts to justify himself, the spirit of do-or-die which he exhibits, and the concentration on publicity for himself and organization can prove exactly the tonic needed by the drowsy, spiritless organization. In short, he who sees himself as a hero can, through that fact, come to be a great leader and a real hero.

Again the Strategy of Self-Restraint

The important rule for the Olympus bewitched administrator to observe is that of self-restraint. Each achievement and the public acclaim it brings are likely to spur him on to still further efforts and claims. His positive response to the powerful stimulus of success can prove costly to him. By the heavy demands on his time, energy and health, it may make him neglect the ordinary responsibilities and duties of his office. And yet their successful discharge is more often than not the basic criteria by which he is judged when he is called to an accounting for his stewardship. Unfortunately, such an accounting may be demanded either by his enemies, for example, when the credit manager is made executive vice president; or at a time when the administrator's heroic deeds are no longer remembered.

So the sales manager is headed for real trouble. In the past, he has tried so hard to perform miracles that he has concentrated on selling unproven distributors in new African nations at the expense of servicing his tried and true, infinitely more significant Canadian market. Yet a prime responsibility and duty of his office is to maintain existing profitable markets. He will probably be judged at fault, if not a failure. This line of thought needs no more laboring. Somehow, he who would be a hero, whether selfishly in his own interest or altruistically in the interests of the organization, must restrain his offensive tactics sufficiently so that he can do the "ordinary" things expected of him. If he does not so attend to his defenses, he may be successfully attacked. He has proved himself a poor administrator in terms of his basic assignment simply because he tried to be a super-man.

Self-restraint is essential for another reason also. If the administrator tries too hard to act like a hero, he may appear simply to be strutting. The consequent effect on his associate's attitude toward him may be bad, especially if it results in their constantly *laughing at* him. No expression of criticism is more dangerous to leadership status than laughter at the leader's efforts and manner. It is the epitome of disdain and becomes highly infectious, signifying a relegation of the administrator to the category of buffoonery. Once his associates have so classified him, his most heroic efforts may be insufficient to regain even the image of simply acceptable leadership.

In the more rarified atmosphere of the administrator's life, it can be quite difficult to practice self-restraint of hero tendencies. The momentum of success, as has been said, is electric. Therefore, a wise precaution for the administrator to take is constantly to evaluate two things about himself: the quality of his performance as a routine administrator and the tone of public reaction to his statements, proposals, and accomplishments. This evaluation requires basically just good common sense and keen sensitivity, but the pressure of work may make it very difficult or impossible for him to see himself and his own work truly. Therefore, he should find in those with whom he associates some who possess the capacity to analyze, the courage to criticize him objectively, and the goodwill to help protect himself from himself. From these advisers, he can get some of the guidance so necessary to balance. Upon occasion when big decisions or projects are contemplated, he may well supplement the advice of his own coterie and call in professional consultants. The administrator, impelled toward heroic achievement, needs help in practicing the restraint necessary to keep him from "going over-board."

While on the subject of advisers, it may be well to note the special influence of the public relations officer. At times this official, necessary as he is in large organizations, may himself be somewhat culpable in the matter of administrative pseudo-deification. It may be his early success in placing the administrator before the public favorably, if not his Machiavellian intent, that first suggests to the administrator the glories of the heroic stance and the possibilities of achieving heroic stature. It may be the public relations officer's devotion to duty that brings the constant public acclaim which eventually completely seduces the administrator into a life of hero behavior and which maintains him in it. Whatever the case, the administrator should at times take a good look at the work of his public relations representative and, if necessary, check him in his enthusiasm. A pertinent question for the administrator to ask himself might well be, "Am I seeing myself in a magic mirror held up before me by my loyal public relations officer?"

Surviving with a Hero

Nothing has been said, as yet, about the problem of the more balanced administrator in living with the extremely conceited one. Quite obviously, the endeavor of the egotistical executive to take credit to himself, to seek public attention, and to live like a godling can be most annoying to another official in many ways. Once the latter has become convinced that his colleague really wants to be a hero and is operating toward this end, he should analyze the value of this ambitious person to the company and to his career. If he concludes that the hero bound character is doing more good than harm in both directions, he may rationally decide to tolerate him. If his conclusion is contrary, then he will be wise to take measures of self-protection and, should his judgment and conscience so dictate, steps to balance or counteract the bad effects on the company or department concerned. This is all just common sense. Perhaps a more difficult thing for the balanced administrator to do is to guard himself against emulating the hero-oriented executive. The temptation can be great, for such emulation may seem necessary to get the rewards being showered on the hero or, in fact, simply to compete with him. Strangely enough, the failure of one administrator to exercise self-restraint may bring another (or others) to forsake it.

To try to make oneself a hero, when his role is that of administrator, is not an uncommon human failing. Such is human hypnosis with self that it may be almost an un-realized effort. But intentional or not, it has its serious implications when carried too far.

Conclusion

The path of the administrator is rarely smooth. It almost always has its pitfalls, and among these are some created by the administrator himself. These we may call his excesses and irrelevancies. To write of them is not the surest route to popularity. Many of them are matters of degree, and differences do exist, even among thinking and honorable men, as to the point at which the adequate and appropriate ends and the undue and unrelated begins.

The analysis presented in the foregoing pages is not comprehensive, for so many are the vagaries and unpredict-abilities of human behavior that only the most imprudent man would lay claim to their full description in even a field as specialized as administration. Perhaps enough has been said to warn of their influnce in diverting the administrator from organizational goals and even from his own best interests.[19]

BUSINESS SITUATIONS FOR ROLE-PLAYING

SITUATION XII

Administrative Excesses and Irrelevancies

THE PLANCHETZ COMPANY

A. Scene.   A securities brokerage firm having twenty-seven offices throughout the United States. The executive lounge in the local office after all their colleagues have left for the day. The Resident Partner and the firm's Personnel Director are discussing the behavior of the Head Bookkeeper of the local office.

B. Players.

1. Resident Partner: Mr. Percival Petronius, an affable but astute financier and administrator, who understands the significance of adherence to bureaucratic rules in a financial house but who is also "customer conscious."

2. Personnel Director: Mr. Silas Pagaduan, an efficient bureaucrat from the central office in New York City, who finds it difficult to understand why a local office should not be content with the administrators he helps select for it.

C. Situation.

1. The Head Bookkeeper, Mr. Phineas St. John, has become a problem in that he treats all customers who have dealings with him on a strict "book basis." He allows no interpretation of the procedural manual the central office provides local bookkeepers; he treats rather pre-emptorily any customer who has a special problem; and he invariably seeks refuge from a complaining customer in quoting a company regulation which does not permit him to exercise judgment in the case.

2. Just this morning, a highly reliable customer with a large and active stock account complained to the Resident Partner that the Head Bookkeeper had demanded he pay up a net debt balance before closing hours rather than wait to do it until the next day, which technically is one day past the due date.

3. The Resident Partner has asked the Director of Personnel, who happens to be in the city, to stop for a while after closing time to discuss the situation and help him plan corrective action.

D. Assignment.

1. Make an effort to choose players with some knowledge of the stock market.

2. When their performance is finished, have the group participate in developing on the blackboard a sensible formula for the Head Bookkeeper's correction and subsequent control.

NOTES

1. Some constructive suggestions for avoiding excessive use of energy and time are set forth in JAMES T. McCAY, *The Management of Time* (Englewood Cliffs, N.J.: Prentice-Hall, Inc., 1959).

2. Certain of these pitfalls are discussed with a strong psychological tone, under the title of "Hazards of Leadership" in ORDWAY TEAD, *The Art of Leadership* (New York: McGraw-Hill Book Company, Inc., 1935).

3. For a comment on the place of human relations in management, see PETER F. DRUCKER, *The Practice of Management* (New York: Harper & Brothers, Publishers, 1954), p. 280.

4. The authors are inclined to agree with McNair who puts this view strongly. "The sum of the matter is this. It is not that the human relations concept is wrong; it is simply that we have blown it up too big. . . ." MALCOLM P. McNAIR, "A Dissenting Voice on Human Relations in Industry" in W. LLOYD WARNER and NORMAN H. MARTIN (eds.), *Industrial Man: Businessmen and Business Organizations* (New York: Harper & Brothers, Publishers, 1959), p. 339.

5. *Ibid.*, p. 338.

6. The possibility and wisdom of generally and strongly restraining personal feelings by group leaders is questioned by FRANKLYN S. HAIMAN, *Group Leadership and Democratic Action* (Boston: Houghton Mifflin Company, 1951), pp. 122-124.

7. It should be remembered that any precedent, policy, rule, or regulation may mean a quite different thing to one administrator than to another. Not only may it be communicated to each differently but ". . . the communicant rarely can function in response to a communique without first transforming it into a more personalized form of experience." EUGENE L. HARTLEY and RUTH E. HARTLEY, *Fundamentals of Social Psychology* (New York: Alfred A. Knopf, 1959), p. 127.

8. MELVILLE DALTON, *Men Who Manage* (New York: John Wiley & Sons, Inc., 1959), p. 268.

9. Extreme allegiance to the company or department should not be mistaken for over-conformity. An administrator, or other employee, could be most devoted to the organization and yet not necessarily live narrowly by its dicta.

A most provocative treatment of super-allegiance and self-submergence to the organization is presented in WIL- LIAM H. WHYTE, JR., *The Organization Man* (New York: Simon and Schuster, Inc., 1956).

10. Tead seems to identify the quality of "sheer busyness" as an emotional instability. "There is . . . an emotional impulse to be ceaselessly and nervously active—an excess of sheer busyness—accompanied by an inability to concentrate long on any task." TEAD, *op. cit.,* p. 219.

11. The significance of mellowness is underlined by Haiman. "Vitality without mellowness can be exceedingly ineffective. Those who advocate that good leaders are children at heart do not thereby advocate that children should become our leaders. Exuberance must be tempered with maturity and patience, energy must be conserved and channeled into purposeful activities." HAIMAN, *op. cit.,* p. 127.

12. Useful guidelines for effective criticism are advanced in LYNDE C. STECKLE, *The Man in Management* (New York: Harper & Brothers, Publishers, 1958), pp. 116-126.

13. ". . . we all know persons of whom it may truly be said that the more they talk the more undesirable they become. Apparently, a great quantity of talk without some degree of quality is not enough to make a leader." HAIMAN, *op. cit.,* p. 13.

14. MARSHALL EDWARD DIMOCK, *The Executive in Action* (New York: Harper & Brothers, Publishers, 1945), p. 202.

15. "The fine art of executive decision consists in not deciding questions that are not now pertinent, in not deciding prematurely, in not making decisions that cannot be made effective, and in not making decisions that others should make." CHESTER I. BARNARD, *The Functions of the Executive* (Cambridge, Mass.: Harvard University Press, 1956), p. 194.

16. Burleigh Gardner, "What Makes Successful and Unsuccessful Executives" in FREMONT A. SHULL, JR. (ed.), *Selected Readings in Management* (Homewood, Ill.: Richard D. Irwin, Inc., 1958), p. 319.

17. A challenging analysis of the hero and the hero role is undertaken by EUGENE E. JENNINGS, *An Anatomy of Leadership: Princes, Heroes, and Supermen* (New York: Harper & Brothers, Publishers, 1960), pp. 70-121.

18. TEAD, *op. cit.,* p. 215.

19. Insight into the behavior patterns of business leaders is given by Editors of Fortune, *The Executive Life* (Garden City, N.Y.: Doubleday & Company, Inc., 1956); and in

Osborn Elliott, *Men at the Top* (New York: Harper & Brothers, Publishers, 1959).

Some hints for avoiding administrative excesses and irrelevancies are contained in Fred DeArmond, *The Executive at Work* (Englewood Cliffs, N.J.: Prentice-Hall, Inc., 1958).

It should be remembered that the temptation to conserve leadership capacity and creativity by the establishment of more rules and by the vigorous enforcement of rules in general can have the opposite result. As Argyris states, "The organization can be rigidified, individuals may spend too much time 'covering themselves,' and this hampers teamwork." Chris Argyris, *Interpersonal Competence and Organizational Effectiveness* (Homewood, Ill.: Richard D. Irwin, Inc., 1962), p. 31.

The organized approach is more likely to yield the breakthrough—and to do so in shorter time—than the unorganized course of decision and action which, by its very nature, has so many administrative excesses and irrelevancies. Organized effort, then, would seem to be one profitable way of avoiding these wastes. This line of thought is partly suggested by J. M. Juran, *Managerial Breakthrough* (New York: McGraw-Hill Book Company, 1964), p. 17.

CHAPTER **13**

Democracy in Administration

> "Democracy is probably found in all types of administration. Few individuals will continually make their own decisions completely and alone. Man's fear is too great; his desire for association and support is too strong; and his capacity is too limited. Unhappily for the precise student . . . there is no one type of administration which can be described as 'democratic administration.' There are rather only administrations using democratic practices."

ADMINISTRATION as a dynamic social reality cannot escape the influence of the beliefs and philosophies of the environment in which it is practiced. In no respect is this general truth better illustrated than in the pressure which democratic ideas and ideals exert upon the management of business organizations in the United States. Administrators and employees alike, commonly attune to the popular conviction that the individual has both the ability and right to participate in the government of whatever association he joins, generally bring to the American company a measure of demand for democratic administration. Rare indeed is the company which does not accede in some degree.[1]

The concept of democratic administration in business is not as easy to define as might be expected. The nature of democracy itself has been a subject for bitter debate by philosophers and political theorists down through the centuries. When the idea of democracy is introduced into the milieu of business, conceptual analysis becomes even more difficult. Then too, American business has not had much experience with democratic administration. Traditionally engaged in great competition, companies generally have relied upon autocratic management for the certainty and quickness of decision essential to survival. Managerial practice in American business, therefore, has not yielded the full body of experience and knowledge necessary to the objective definition of democratic administration.

However, if one is to discuss the subject, he must somehow define the concept. For want of a better definition, the thought may be advanced as a practical text that democratic administration in business means some determinative involvement, in making decisions for management purposes, of individuals who would not so participate in the process under autocratic administration.[2] This seems to be an acceptable definition because it reflects the essence of democracy, which is self-government.

Democratic administration, as practiced by American business, has certain characteristics. An enumeration of some of them may shed light on definition. Certainly, one outstanding attribute is relativity. Business democracy assumes many forms and degrees varying with organization, managerial personnel, time, and place. And so democratic administration in some companies is nothing more than occasional executive discussion with a worker, and in other companies it reaches the heights of employee representation on policy committees. Another characteristic is a profound difference from political democracy. In American business administration, supreme power to make management decisions basically stems from property rights and is presumed to lie with ownership, and this ownership seriously limits the democratic base. In contrast, political sovereignty is assumed to rest with the people in general. Still another characteristic of democratic business administration in the United States is particularistic participation. Rarely is the whole "body politic," in the sense of all employees, involved in the making of every, or even any, decision. Even though management often, and loudly, subscribes to the desirability of mass involvement, in actual usage democracy is generally practiced on a selective basis with a few qualified or politically strategic members of the company family involved.[3]

Perspective

Often a subject for discussion and probably a growing feature of American culture, democracy in administration is harder to pin down in concrete forms than to describe in generality. What are the major democratic practices in administration? Are they stereotyped, or do they assume different manifestations with time, place, department, or company? Can one state that a practice is in essence democratic, or must he recognize that it is the use to which a technique is put that imparts an element of democracy to it? In addition to the more obvious democratic practices, are there subtle and less well identified types? Is it not true that certain kinds of administrative behavior are commonly mistaken for democratic procedures? These and perhaps other questions suggest the difficulty of precisely identifying, describing, classifying, and analyzing the forms of democratic behavior in management.

Autocracy, i.e., unilateral decision making by the superior, may be assumed to be the norm of administration. It is then possible to proceed logically to attempt to isolate specific democratic practices through arranging and discussing them by the successively greater degree of involvement in decision making which each permits. Although this tack will not assure the inclusion of every conceivable involvement technique, it will at least lend a much needed element of coherence to the presentation.

But before such course is taken certain matters of perspective must be considered. Participation in decision making may occur at any point in the process and may be of varying influence on the ultimate decision. Both the menial janitor whose opinion is asked by the president in the building elevator and the three vice presidents assembled in his office to vote do take part in the process. Neither the stage at which they enter the picture nor the degree to which they affect the conclusion can deny the fact that each is involved in decision making. If one is not guided by this understanding as he wends his way through the complexities of administrative democracy, he is likely to make the common error of identifying as democratic practice only advanced and high level involvement in decision making.

Such mis-identification might bring a number of serious consequences. It could tremendously narrow the scope of investigation by the elimination from consideration of many practices that are in nature truly democratic. In fact, most of the democratic practices in administration are probably of such insignificance to decision making that they would be overlooked in this high-handed approach. After all, democratic practices, which are the exception to the norm of administration, often do not occupy pivotal positions in its discharge. Moreover, the exclusive viewpoint of administrative democracy could becloud a real democratic trend in the evolution of the management pattern. It might well be that forces in a certain company or department are moving toward much more involvement of subordinates in administration but that, timid and cautious for the time being, top management permits only relatively insignificant roles to them. Finally, a disregard for early or small participation in decision making could lead the student of administration to the fallacious judgment that democracy in administration is conspicuous for the rarity of its occurrence. It is probably true that major roles in final decision making are comparatively infrequent, even in contemporary American business administration.

It may be wise to forestall any plunge into specific enumeration until still another clarifying fact about democracy in administration is understood. The frame of reference in which democracy has developed throughout the Western world has seen it appear as a freeing of those in positions of inferior power and status. Perhaps this is the only true meaning of democratization. Yet, one must add a certain other connotation to it in his treatment of business administration. In this area, he commonly sees examples of equals, whom he may in academic parlance term *colleagues*, being brought into decision making. Is this not democratic practice also? The answer must be in the affirmative, since democratic administration certainly includes the idea of involving more members of the organizational family in the making of decisions. The privilege may be claimed, therefore, of including in a treatment of democratic practices anything which brings either subordinates or *equals* into decision making.

An interesting by-product of qualification is that it reveals the need for further attention to perspective. Thus far it has been strongly implied that democracy in management signifies the participation of more people in it. However, democratic administration has another dimension, that of more extensive and intensive involvement by those subordinates and equals already participating in administration. It is just as truly an expression of democracy to allow five such people to participate in making ten decisions as it is to call in ten people to make five decisions. Of course, there does exist prejudice on the part of students of administration to consider democratization as simply the pulling of more people into decision making, and this prejudice may be reflected in these pages.

Delegation of Duty and Authority[4]

One may find in delegation of duty and authority the first departure from administrative autocracy,[5] and the most primitive type of democracy in administration. The sharing of duties is inherent in the practical fact of organization, and, therefore, the sharing of authority to make possible their discharge. No doubt it could be argued strongly that sharing work and power with associates does not connote any element of democracy whatsoever in management. The contention might well run along the line that democracy consists in the freedom which associates have to determine the course of management and that delegation of work with some power per se does not confer any such freedom. And, in a facetious manner, the argument could continue to the effect that, if sharing the burden constitutes in itself a democratic step, then the ownership and use of slaves in older days was democratic administration!

Yet a good case can be made to prove that delegation of duties and authority can generate democracy in effect, if not in intent. Few delegations, however well-defined, will cover all the situations which will demand decision making by the subordinate. There will almost always be problems and issues, even though very insignificant, which the higher administrator could or did not anticipate and provide for in his instructions. To do his job satisfactorily the subordinate may be constrained on occasion, therefore, to make a decision. At least, he may be asked for and venture his opinion should he himself not decide but instead take the unexpected situation to the superior for settlement. In either case, the subordinate obviously will be participating in the decision making process, and so will be fulfilling a democratic promise inherent in delegation. Of course, he could act otherwise, and not seize the opportunity of his chance freedom to decide.

If he is a weakling or a strict constructionist of directions given him, he may fail to decide on his own or even to give his superior an opinion. However, it is not very likely that such an extremely negative individual would long be considered a desirable employee by the dynamic administrator.

The democratic potential of delegation may be made clearer by the illustration of the newly founded power tool manufacturing company. It is a company of moderate size and employs some 300 people. The president is the chief stockholder but, in his efforts to organize, finance and launch the enterprise, he discovers that he will need help to run it. Whereupon, he appoints a general manager and three department heads. The former is to function as the president's executive officer and the latter as managers of the office, shop and sales departments, respectively. The president is a man of action, prizing swift and concise decision and steps; he, therefore, has no particular thought of or desire for the democratic in management. But democracy to a degree shows itself, for its seeds are embedded in the fact of delegation. It soon makes its appearance. The president is off on one of the innumerable trips incident to the opening of a new business. A crisis arises in the jurisdiction of the shop manager. A foreman strikes a worker; prompt action is necessary. The shop manager decides to suspend the supervisor, and takes the case to the general manager who not only concurs but fires the foreman. Upon his return, the chief executive permits the discharge to stand. Neither manager had been given any direction as to what to do in such a case. Perhaps the possibility of foreman trouble had never even occurred to the hard-pressed president. But each manager did make a decision, and the president allowed it to stand. Here one sees a manifestation of the potential for democracy which is inherent in delegation. It may be described as *accidental* freedom to participate in management.

A certain word of warning, however, seems in order. The

administrator should not hypnotize himself into believing that mere delegation of duty and authority constitutes a major direct concession to democracy in management. Delegation may simply make possible a measure of such involvement. In fact, it may even increase the need for democratic administration. Delegation is basically a process of decentralization,[6] and the control function may demand that subordinates be brought more into decision making simply because the job of administration is fragmentized. Then too, it should not be forgotten that delegation gives the recipients a taste of power and independence, so that their appetites for participation in management may be whetted. It may thus transpire that delegation, far from solving the problem of democratizing administration, will generate more pressure for democratic practices.

Consultation as a Democratic Practice

In the minds of certain authorities, delegation does not seem to figure in the category of democratic practices. They begin with consultation as the simplest expression of administrative democracy.[7] Whether or not their starting point is correct, certainly consultation (in the sense of seeking information, opinions and advice from others) is a democratic procedure. Consultation may assume several forms. It may be personal or impersonal, oral or written, informal or formal, and politic or elicitive. There are so many implications in each of these classifications that it is necessary to consider them separately.

Personal versus Impersonal Consultation

Everyone who has held an administrative position has at some time sought facts and reactions from his colleagues or subordinates. In some cases, he will probably have gone directly to individuals or groups and asked them for their knowledge and views. This direct approach means that he has personally confronted them, that he has not relied upon any go-betweens to solicit their expression. This is personal consultation. In other cases, the administrator will have availed himself of the services of a second party to get the information, opinions, and judgments of his associates. An example is seen in the case of a president who has assigned a staff assistant, subordinate administrator, or an outside professional service to canvass individuals or groups in his organization. He has used impersonal consultation.

Neither personal nor impersonal consultation is to be preferred exclusively. Conditions may demand that one or the other be used. In general, it will be safer for the strong administrator to use the personal approach. In his strength, he will not be as easily swayed by what he hears nor will he be as fearful of the consequences of not taking the advice he receives.

But regardless of the relative safety of personal versus impersonal consultations, there are at least three circumstances which clearly suggest certain advantages of the former. If the administrator wishes to establish a greater personal rapprochement with his people, he will avoid go-betweens and use direct contact to build understanding, sympathy, and loyalty. The general manager who "condescends" to talk to the ribbon clerk about the colors of ribbon to stock has an obvious chance to convert her to closer followership. The avenues of flattery and education are open to him. Of perhaps equal advantage with the rapprochement equation is the gain in accuracy to be had from personal consultation in the situation where the administration wants to know the real attitudes of his people toward the organization as a whole, his administration, or a specific subject. Intermediaries may be unfriendly to the administrator or prejudiced against the views of the interviewed and, therefore, his resort to them as canvassers could result in his getting colored, distorted, or even false impressions. In fact, he may be given an untrue picture by his intermediaries simply because they are incapable of sensing and interpreting the opinions and advice they gather. There may be a third advantage in utilizing personal consultation. Decision making sometimes tends to have a feverish and exciting influence on the administrator ultimately responsible for it. Personal contact takes time; by its greater degree of laboriousness it compels the administrator to slow up the process of deciding. In the time he wins by the personal canvassing of feelings, opinions and advice, he has more opportunity to consider and weigh, and to reach a more realistic view.

Still the arguments are not all on the side of personal consultation. Impersonal canvassing is clearly to be preferred if the administrator wishes to remain aloof, which may be the case when he is endeavoring to build up a reputation as a leader with many interests. Again, impersonal consultation may be peculiarly advantageous when the administrator does not wish to add impetus to demand for more democracy in administration. By staying away from his colleagues and subordinates, he avoids democratic involvement, which feeds and grows upon itself. Still another circumstance in which impersonality is to be desired should not be overlooked. Reference is had to the case wherein the administrator wishes to draw criticism away from himself or to build up the organizational stature of some assistant or assistants. By assigning these individuals to the job of soliciting information, opinions and advice, he does not involve himself directly, and whatever respect is engendered in them by the consultation more naturally is directed to the intermediary.

Oral and Written Consultation: an Independent Dichotomy

There is a temptation to identify the oral with the personal and the written with the impersonal technique of consultation. An administrator or his representative can solicit expression of fact, view or recommendation via the spoken or via the written word. Realization of this obvious fact should dispel any tendency to go far with this erroneous equation. Yet even such understanding may not erase all doubt as to the relationship of the written communication to the personal factor in consultation. Some people may continue to entertain the conviction that a degree of closeness in contact is lost by consulting people in writing; whereas others may continue to feel that a written communication is actually more intimate. This latter identity, which appears to be the more subtle, probably is most common in situations wherein those being consulted are not accustomed to receiving many written communications.

The administrator would be unwise to see the oral and written techniques of consultation as simply an artificial dichotomy. Regardless of what their true relation to other procedures may be, each does offer the possibility of special strategic uses. Oral consultation permits of an easier and more comprehensive exchange. It frees him of the restriction which the mere physical burden of written communication imposes upon those who use it, since talking is generally easier than writing. It facilitates the flow and counterflow of ideas because the administrator engaged in the discussion is immediately poised to pursue and develop any subject which the conversation raises. In short, it may be argued that oral consultation gives the administrator a means of tapping the "consultee" in both greater depth and breadth. In contrast, consultation through writing is believed to offer more in the way of control. The administrator can ask specifically for what he wants to know and, by requesting no more, protect himself in goodly measure against the embarrassment of being told things he does not wish to hear. Then too, a written communication, since it automatically records that which is set down, requires that the administrator who initiates it and the person who replies to it each exercise especial care in what he says to the other.

The strategy-minded executive should remember that the consultation process, which is generally a two way action of asking and receiving, can use both the oral and written vehicle in any one instance. The administrator can write to those whom he wishes to consult and request them to report orally; or he can orally ask for a written response. This *mestizo* arrangement may be used in the interest of economy of time and effort; or it may provide a means by which the administrator can obtain some desired result, such as more or less formality, in either asking for or getting the reaction of those whom he consults. A danger is inherent in the use of the two methods of communication for one instance of consultation. It lies in the possibility that those consulted may infer wrongly from the form of communication the administrator uses in consulting them. If he approaches them orally, they may, for example, not take him quite as seriously or literally as he intends. If he writes them seeking their knowledge, feelings and ideas, they may overestimate his intention and either freeze in response or exaggerate their reply because they believe he considers their response of great import. Unfortunately, the human predilection for misinterpretation is as present in business administration as anywhere.

A Complex Category: Informal and Formal Consultation

Informal and formal techniques are more difficult to describe than the oral and written as distinct methods of consultation. Their distinction may be suggested by an over-simplified observation: the informal method is characterized by casualness and the formal by a structured approach. The administrator who desires to use the informal approach tends by action and statement to keep his consultation effort from appearing to be part of a structured plan or campaign to get information, opinion, and advice. One sees this method used in the case of the department head who occasionally asks his secretaries late in the day as the torment of office work subsides what they think of the company as a place to work or how they view the subject of electric office equipment. The informal method endeavors to put people at their ease in the interest of desired response by keeping them from any feeling that they are being "pumped" as a part of an organized effort or grandiose scheme. On the contrary, the executive who elects the formal procedure plans his consultation as a campaign and brands the canvassing as significant and scientific. The personnel manager who asks for a rating of all secretaries by their immediate supervisors, who lets the secretaries know this, and who provides the supervisors with forms, instructions, and deadlines is truly illustrating the application of the formal method.

Possibilities of strategic advantages are vaguely suggested in this brief characterization of informal and formal consultation. They need to be brought into clearer focus. It can be easily seen that the informal approach has a certain soporific implication, in that casualness of contact disarms those being consulted or at least does not unduly alarm them. Just as apparent is the fact that the formal method has great potential for emphasizing the seriousness of and exactitude expected from the consultation. As a pivotal thought, it should be remembered that the strategic administrator here, as elsewhere, ought to be careful of making himself completely predictable or of creating a wrong image of himself. The executive who always uses the friendly, non-rhythmic, and unschematic technique of consultation may eventually be surprised to learn that his people regard him as basically just a hale-fellow well met. Or the administrator who uses the more blunt attack to learn what his colleagues and subordinates know and think may be equally amazed in the passage of time to learn that they look upon him as an unfeeling and efficient, if human, electronic brain. The analytical administrator will sense these perils and, imbued with the philosophy that the good administrator generally cannot afford sameness of operational pattern or stereotyped image, will at times use the informal and at times the formal technique.

Consultation for Divergent Purposes: The Politic and the Elicitive

Does the administrator really want to know that which he learns in consultation? The answer to this rhetorical question raises the specter of still another classification of consultation practices. It may be called the politic versus the elicitive. In the former, the administrator has little, if any, interest in the things which his consultation may reveal. In the latter method, he really desires to learn something, even though it may not be the apparent objective of his effort. Probably every administrator resorts to each from time to time. Moreover, the two are not always separated in practice, for both may be used in the same instance. This is to say that the administrator in a given instance may be pursuing some ulterior motive as well as trying to learn something.

Perhaps politic consultation does not really belong in this discussion, which is supposed to deal with democratic practices in administration. It may have little to do with broadening the decision making process. Yet it is one half of a dichotomy of consultation methods which are, except for the politic, all democratic practices. This fact and the difficulty of treating the subject elsewhere are taken to justify its inclusion here.

Politic consultation may serve one or more of several purposes. The strategic executive may simply wish to let off steam by talking to some one. He may wish to appear polite to his colleagues and subordinates, or he may want them to feel that he notices and appreciates them. Perhaps he believes they need a chance to relieve themselves of certain feelings and ideas. So the wise administrator stops and talks with them as he meets them, calls them to his office for a meeting, invites them to a social function, asks for a written report, or in some other way consults with them. His action reflects the truth of the old axiom that communication has purposes other than imparting and getting facts. Unfortunately, many people fail to realize this fact, and so they may view politic consultation as somewhat dishonorable.

The issues of consultative supervision and consultative direction may be raised in connection with the politic form of consultation. The former invites the employees to discuss matters affecting them;[8] the latter consults the people responsible for executing an instruction before issuance of the order.[9] By their very nature they invite the administrator to use them for purposes other than just obtaining information. They are excellent devices for all kinds of political purposes, and are so used.

The administrator who consults for reasons other than eliciting something from the consulted should be aware of two facts. One is significant because of its relation to his reputation. People tend to be alarmed and repelled by any practice on the part of their leader which smacks of insincerity. Their reaction is probably attributable to the feeling of insecurity which insincere leadership generates. Now, the administrator who consults with his associates but who is not really interested in what they tell him can come to be considered insincere. It is easy to imagine the typical reaction to this executive as running something like this, "Oh, the boss just likes to talk. He thinks that he is fooling us, but we know he doesn't give a hang for what we think." Fortunately, there is a stance which can be taken by the administrator engaged in politic consultation to protect himself against such negative reaction. He should neither by word nor implication lead his people to believe that he intends to act on what they tell him. And to this respect for a principle of honor, he should add whatever positive measures fit his personality and position, for example, the maintenance of an attitude of serious interest when talking to them, a show of lightheartedness or humor, and certainly the utmost respect for their confidences and thoughts.

But it has been said that there are two facts of special significance to the administrator who uses politic consultation. The second has to do with a certain peculiarity of procedure often necessary for the best results. Politic is much more likely than elicitive consultation to have as its objective a matter of emotional or sentimental import. It must, therefore, usually be conducted in an atmosphere of greater freedom and spontaneity. Emotional and sentimental values are easily lost in the artificiality of structure. The old time office manager learns this when he first tackles the problem of improving his human relations. At a management conference, he has heard a noted speaker emphasize the necessity for showing interest in employees as individuals. Whereupon he returns to his job fired with the determination to do just this with his group. He arranges a schedule of personal interviews with his secretaries, informs them well in advance, furnishes them with a list of questions that he may ask them, and requests each to be prepared to discuss these among other things. In general, they become apprehensive over the very formality of his approach, and speculation grows among them as to what he really intends to accomplish. They prepare themselves for an ordeal and, in so doing, condition themselves against that free interchange of heart and mind which can do so much to establish the good rapprochement between superior and subordinate and so much to make the subordinate feel understood, appreciated, and wanted. The office manager well might have approached his group less formally. Instead of arranging a schedule of personal interviews with every worker, it would have been wiser for him to have talked with each woman as he met her in the course of the work day.

Quite a different set of strategic actions are significant in the use of elicitive consultation. Here, as previously said, the purpose is to learn something from the consulted. Whatever the methodology used, it must be designed to draw forth information, feelings, judgments, advice, recommendations, or anything else sought. So the six rules of personal interview are applicable. They need but enumeration, for their significance is quite obvious. First, the consultor must be clear in his own mind as to what he wants to learn, otherwise he will not be able to direct the consultation to the desired objective. Second, he must make every effort to learn the motivational forces at work in the mind of the consulted, for only by appreciation of them can he hope to get the most pertinent response. Third, he must provide an environment which keeps the consultation, oral or written, free from distractions which will throw it "off the track." It may be noted that distractions can work on the administrator as well as the consulted, and that they may vary all the way from a noisy room with people running in and out to concern over the fact that more important work is being delayed by the interview, questionnaire, or report. Fourth, the administrator must give those he wishes to consult assurance, if such appears necessary, that there is no danger to them in speaking frankly and honestly, for fear can freeze response. Fifth, he must endeavor at all times to avoid any appearance of trickery in handling the consultation, since nothing will cause the consulted to react more negatively both during and after consultation than the feeling that they have been cozened or seduced into revealing their feelings and thoughts. And sixth, he must keep his part of the consultation process in a frame of reference the consulted understands, otherwise they will not know what he wants. Here is seen particularly the necessity for proper vocabulary, for an understanding of the cultural level of the consulted, and for an appreciation of their status within the organization.

It seems necessary to reiterate, before leaving the subject, that consultation is a democratic practice in administration.[10] Sight of this fact may have been lost in the analysis of consultation from the viewpoint of strategy. One need but remind himself that the essence of democracy in administration is to bring more people into decision making or the same people more into the process.

Institutionalized Democracy[11]

Some students of administration are inclined to see as real democratic practices only those efforts at democracy which are integral features of the management process. Their conviction is that, unless the practice represents a definite commitment by the company regularly to use some democratic method, it is not deserving of recognition. They limit their concepts of administrative democracy to that which is institutionalized. This view may be accepted as another basis for classifying democratic practices. The category of the institutionalized encompasses a wide range of democratic features, among which figure prominently general or group meetings such as yearly assemblies of employees, monthly staff and management conferences, standing committees, established grievance procedures, formalized suggestion programs, required counseling interviews, mandatory self-rating, scheduled group review of performance, actual open-door policy, and regular resort to internal attitude and opinion surveys.

The Common Element

The strategic implications of institutionalized democratic practices are amenable to collective discussion. They have a common characteristic. It can be called "commitment." Moreover, the dynamic use of democracy in management may perhaps be portrayed more clearly by the bold strokes of generality than by devotion to the numerous specifics which would require inclusion were one to attempt to show it by analyzing each of the regular democratic procedures.

The company or department which considers one or more democratic practices as part and parcel of its administrative behavior is more or less bound to it. The tie can be a particularly strong one. After all, democracy is generally considered to be a "good thing" and he who practices it, one of good will and liberal bent. Should the administrator wish to modify or abandon a democratic practice, he will face the not inconsiderable risk of seriously losing face with his subordinates and harming their morale. There seems to be a tendency on the part of American employees to consider autocracy as a sort of primitive organizational evil and to see any managerial retreat from democracy as a serious step backwards. One may suspect, therefore, that it is more difficult to curtail existing and established democracy in administration than to tolerate and support it. So the *negative* implications of commitment to democracy will be discussed first.

Retreat from Commitment

The administrator confronted with the problem of retreating from a democratic position may turn to one or more protective techniques. A simple device seems high on the list. It is to allow and encourage the democratic practice in question so that all will be able to experience or see its shortcomings. In a sense, this is a conditioning technique. The peculiar merit lies in the fact that it is largely a self-conditioning process. The administrator, therefore, can expect to avoid the stigma of having attacked democracy.

The operation of this self-conditioning may be seen in the case of the company with the suggestion program in effect for a year which has produced only trivial proposals. The president and the committee are sick of going through motions; he wants to drop the whole suggestion system, but he is afraid of reaction at this date. He, therefore, decides to let it continue for a year more to demonstrate to all its useless-ness. Of course, there is always the chance that the continued practice may in the words of the school teacher "prove per-fect." The practice, allowed to demonstrate its own short-comings, may turn out as far as the rank and file are con-cerned to be quite desirable. Such is the calculated risk in retaining the practice. The alert and analytical executive should always take this into consideration before deciding to keep the practice longer. In fairness to the democratic proc-esses, one may turn in the somewhat different direction and venture the thought that, if the suggestion program proves satisfactory to the employees, perhaps the administrator was wrong in thinking the organization were better rid of it.

Another protective technique which promises much is the employment of a democratic process as a means of reaching the decision to modify or abandon a democratic practice. The potential is obvious: opposition can be disarmed by enlisting its support. There comes to mind, for example, the appoint-ment of a committee with full employee representation to consider whether or not the self-rating procedure should be dropped. Naturally, resort to any democratic procedure for decision making is somewhat of a gamble, since the decision recommended or reached may go against the wishes of management. This is not to endorse administrative seduction or sand-bagging through the technique of appearing to use the democratic approach. However, the administrator who tackles his problem of using freedom to retreat from a free-dom has available a perfectly legitimate stratagem. He can see to it that all the facts of the case are made known to those whom he calls to participate with him in reaching decision. It may come as a surprise that this discourse which has so honored downright realism should now suggest a procedure which depends for its success upon the good judgment and good will of the rank and file of company or department employees. It is believed, however, that any cross section of the American masses has a substantial measure of ability to discern and of social decency to do the right thing. The presentation, directly or indirectly, of all the facts about self-rating, therefore, has a fair chance of drawing from the committee objective support for the administrator's proposal to jettison it.

In their effort to get rid of an unwanted democratic practice to which they are committed, some administrators will turn to what may be called the "freeze out" technique. The gist of this technique is to ignore the practice with the thought that sooner or later the participants, sensing the hopelessness of their efforts, will grow tired of meaningless motions and recommendations and will themselves become willing to abandon the practice. A democratic practice can be ignored in a number of ways: by paying little, if any, real attention to its recommendations and other actions, by failing to give it adequate financial support, by not allowing time for it, and by various slights such as not assigning it adequate space, publicity, and clerical services. The skeptic may step in here and argue that, if the administrator is determined to kill the practice by inattention, he might just as well decisively order its abolition. There can be, however, a definite value in keeping the practice but allowing it to die. The procedure will at least avoid for the administrator the head-on clash with the proponents of the practice and provide a period during which they can be slowly educated away from it.

Making Institutionalized Practices Work

But commitment to democratic practices has *positive* implications also. The problem of retreating from it, although the more involved, is probably of less real significance in this day of democratization than is the problem of making institutionalized practices work. The administration pledged to them must have undertaken them for one of three reasons: the conviction that they were intrinsically worthwhile, the feeling that their adoption would head off worse demands and developments, or the overwhelming pressure of superior force demanding their adoption. Common sense demands that practices adopted for the first of these reasons should be given the full support of administration.

The possibility exists, however, that administrators who have introduced and/or sanctioned democratic practices as a preventative may be reluctant to support them because they do not see their yielding any direct contribution to operation. This natural reaction can be risky. Not only can it defeat the purpose of prevention, since inadequate support may cause the inefficient conduct of the democratic processes, but it also may argue for greater democracy simply because the lesser does not work well. An illustration may bring this danger into clearer focus. An open-door policy is adopted by the president of a bank to head off what he believes will be the demand for a junior board of directors. He is a busy man and, after a few months of spending hours in conversing with his subordinates at what he considers to be the expense of his usual administrative duties, he decides to see them only after banking hours. He thus withdraws a measure of support from the preventive practice. Not all his subordinates who want to talk to him can get to see him. As a result, the ventilation advantage of the open-door policy is not fully realized, and the demand for the junior board persists. It may be that various subordinates who were not concerned much about participation in management are now stirred up and begin to think about the whole matter of democracy. Their combination with the original proponents of the junior board may well produce a movement to have something more than a junior board, for example, a monthly open forum at which the president is expected to be available for public query and discussion.

To be certain, the big question as to positive strategy in institutionalized democratic practices arises with regard to the management's support of a procedure forced upon it. The case of a grievance procedure which unions won in a long battle with a tool and die company is to the point. The general manager of the firm, noting that much company time is being used in the procedure and smarting under his defeat by the union, does everything in his power to block the procedure. He gives the grievance committee the worst possible space for its meetings, he lets it be known that there will be no clerical help available, he urges his supervisors to be legalistic, and in general he gives only the minimum support required by the union contract. It is conceivable that he may, if the union is in a comparatively weak bargaining position, win his battle to make ineffective the established democratic procedure of handling grievances. On the other hand, and this is a real likelihood, he may, by refusing the support necessary to the efficient operation of the procedure, create a situation of continual unrest within the company and strife with the union. At times, it may be wiser for administration to lend its full cooperation and aid to democratic practices forced upon it. Administrative efficiency and profitable operation seem to have little place for the expression of resentment about water that has passed irrevocably over the dam.

The Special Case of Committees

The committee in itself is neither of a democratic nor autocratic nature.[12] It is simply one among the many devices available to management for use in performing its various functions. However, the committee as a device is peculiarly well adapted to the democratic purpose. It is a superior means of involving more people, or the same people more, in decision making, if for no other reason than that it can accommodate more than one person and that it can be assigned particular duties.

The committee as a democratic device has become so common in American companies that it requires special consideration in this treatment of democracy.[13] Committees are seen everywhere in the business world, trying to carry on one or more of a wide variety of organizational functions.[14] In practical terms, a committee may be defined as two or more people associated for some purpose toward which they function as an organizational entity. Because multiple-person committees are more in line with democratic philosophy, this definition overlooks the fact that a committee may be but one person to whom some charge is entrusted.

There are two distinct types of committees: the temporary committee, which has the life span necessary to the accomplishment of its purpose, and the standing committee, which is a permanent feature of the organization. Either may exist for one or more of five general purposes: to study or give advice and recommendations; to perform some specific task requiring joint work; to reach and communicate a specific conclusion; to provide an opportunity for mutual consultation by and cross-fertilization of members and those whom they represent; and to serve any of several indirect and politic ends. But, no matter what their type or purpose, in actual business management they provide a widely used mechanism by which more people are involved in decision making or the same people are involved more in it.[15]

There is no universal agreement among business administrators as to the usefulness of committees, although they are appropriate on all levels of management.[16] No doubt this difference of opinion is partly attributable to varying individual experiences with the committee device. At times the experience can be rewarding to the executive's performance and feelings; at times it can be frustrating, if not downright harrowing. No one knows which result is most typical. However, for various reasons, perhaps principally their slowness and indecision, committees seem to come in for a considerable measure of adverse criticism. This reaction is often expressed in such bitter terms as, "If you don't want to get something done, give it to a committee to do." Such negative views should not deter the administrator from considering objectively the employment of committees. He may, even if he is relatively unacquainted with their use or even if he is acutely conscious of their adverse criticism, take courage from the fact that they are an ordinary administrative tool in a wide range of American business concerns.

Gains from Committee Action

Whatever the case, the executive may expect his strategic ability to be challenged at times by his use of or relations with committees in his administrative orbit. Should he be thinking of forming a committee to assist him in some way, he would do well to weigh the pros and cons. The committee and its use has certain merits. The committee can constitute a positive token of democratic inclination, and the executive who uses it may thereby enhance his reputation as a forward-minded individual. It can bring together people of varying views and ability, and so its product may be better than that possible by individual endeavor. Resort to a committee may give the administrator a greater reputation for seriousness of purpose and comprehensiveness of effort, since it suggests that he is trying to supplement his own ability and work. The administrator who seeks to escape a measure of responsibility, or to prevent the responsibility for a decision or act from falling heavily upon someone else, may do so by assigning the task to a committee so that more than one will share the burden.

These are only four of the better known merits of committee and committee action. There are others, too, that deserve mention. The administrator who is considering the employment of a committee should remember that it is the stalling device par excellence. In hyperbolic terms, there is practically no amount of time which a committee cannot waste by trying to meet and by meeting. In effect, its slowness can even be used to kill a project through delaying action until it is useless or until the necessary outside interest in and support for it are no longer forthcoming. Then too, the executive should note that he can employ a committee to call attention away from a course he wishes to follow, by assigning it some other project which will occupy the attention of the committee members if they are the people from whom he wishes to insulate his actions, or which will divert the curiosity of others whom he wishes to keep in ignorance. Also, the committee assignment as such can be used as a method of keeping busy an individual or group which might, if time and energy were available, engage in activities injurious to the administrator or the organization. Furthermore, it should not be forgotten that the committee vehicle is a fine communication center, and an excellent means of educating some one or more of its members.[17] Ideas planted and developed in it frequently convert members and get around the organization via representatives on committees. And finally, the administrator will sometimes discover committee assignment to be a means of recognizing people whom he wishes to reward or motivate.

The Negative Side

It is clear that the administrator can find quite a case for the appointment of a committee or the assignment of a job to one. But all is not on the asset side of the ledger. The committeee has disadvantages, and its use can be costly. Immediately, there comes to mind the fact of its more or less inherent slowness and expensiveness in salaries of members if in nothing else. To choose members and to get them appointed may take time, but this is only a beginning. Then organization of the committee, meeting times and places, and agenda enter the picture. And after all this, committee action itself tends to move less fast than individual operation. Different views must be expressed, debated, and reconciled if possible into some agreement or conclusion; and communications prepared and sent.

Although ponderosity is ordinarily cited as its prime defect, the committee device and its utilization can be charged with other demerits. One individual or clique may dominate the committee proceedings and conclusions so that its work is neither that of compromise nor integration.[18] And then there is always the possibility that its ultimate work, whether cross-fertilization, advice, plan, decision or completed action project, will represent a compromise of views and skills somewhat less in nature and value than the most capable and best oriented individual could produce. The influence of the most competent or best-willed person can be lost in the committee. The committee, furthermore, may encourage irresponsibility among its members, because they can hide in the group and they may, therefore, tend to be less considerate, scrupulous, and decisive than an individual as an organizational unit.[19] Still an additional potential drawback of the committee is the fact that it may prove a source of opposition to the administrator who uses it, should he not accept its work or should there be a strong minority whose views are not included in the end product which the executive accepts. It is frequently worse to ask for group help and then ignore it, than it is to carry the whole burden alone. As a capstone to this listing of some of the negative features and implications of the committee, which the administrator should consider in evaluating it, is the possibility that he or his organization may come to depend upon it too much. After all, the employment of committees can be tempting not only to the hard pressed, lazy, or fearful executive but also to almost any administrator, since it promises so much. The evil of over-dependence upon committee support may be long run in the sense that it can engender for the administration the habit of slothful and reluctant decision and action.

Selecting Committee Members

Let it be supposed that an administrator does not have a standing committee to which to turn and that he must appoint a committee. Now he faces a whole new category of problems. First and foremost, he must determine the basis for committee composition. Shall he choose his friends, his enemies, people with common or divergent views, some of all these, representation from each department, a mixture of influential and uninfluential individuals? Or shall he pick just those who he believes are best fitted for the assignment at hand? It will often be desirable for him to choose politically, as well as objectively on the basis of competency and virtue. If he does not use both bases, he may find that either the committee will not function properly or that the organization will get more repercussions than the gains from committee usage will justify. This is not to argue that the administrator should never select committee members on the basis of capacity and character alone, or for that matter exclusively on the basis of any of the lesser criteria. The total end he has in mind must be the determining factor. One sees here a good illustration of the contention that the best administration requires a synthesis of the knowledge, skills, and wisdom which the executive possesses.

In selecting the members of a committee, the administrator should, however, always be guided by the basic principle that the mere fact of association will not assure the successful work of any committee. Ten men brought together, no matter how well intentioned, who know little or nothing about a given subject will know in conjunction no more about it than one. If competent work is expected from a committee, it must be composed of able people or at least its membership must represent a sum total of ability sufficient unto the task. This consideration at times may make it necessary, even for the most strategic of administrators, to ignore all considerations of political representation in appointing committee members.

Living with the Committee

When the administrator has his committee, he must live with it. One of his most difficult tasks may come to be the maintenance of a sufficient feeling of urgency on the part of the committee so that it will continue to function effectively. By its very nature committee membership is rarely a full time job for administrative personnel, and so the members, committed to other tasks of their own within the organization, often consider it not more than secondary duty. Then too, and this is especially true of the standing type, the committee may be expected to function only occasionally. The result of these two forces can be a lackadaisical attitude on the part of the members as such and the committee as a whole, an attitude which can express itself in only the minimum group performance. This poor committee morale may suffer still further deterioration if the membership develops the feeling that management does not care about its work anyway.

A definite pattern of positive conduct on the part of the administrator with respect to a committee, or a system of committees, seems in order if he would keep it alive and lively.[20] Certainly, he should see that the committee is properly organized with an assignment, a chairman, a meeting schedule, and a place to meet. Above all else, he should regularly recognize the committee's existence. This can be done in many ways, but one easy manner is to require periodical reports, even if brief, and to return them to the committee with evidence of their having been perused. It is probably a rarity that an administrator cannot find some aspect of a committee's work to accept, and acceptance of a committee's effort is the surest way to give it a feeling of pride and significance. In addition to these means of recognizing a committee, the alert executive can find many incidental ways to bring it into the limelight, for example, by furnishing it an operating budget, including it in published charts of organization and other company publications, and mentioning it in public utterances. Upon occasion, and this may be very time consuming if he has a whole array of committees, the administrator might well cap his whole committee recognition process by himself attending one or more of its meetings or inviting it to meet with him. The gist of this train of thought is that committees, to be kept vital and vigorous in their work, must be made to feel needed.

But there is a quite opposite side to this living with a committee. The administrator may find a committee embarrassing to him because it is too active, its work unsatisfactory, or its performance unfriendly to his or organizational interests. Each of these sources of embarrassment suggests a particular strategy for its handling. If the committee is too active, the administrator can slow it down by private instructions to its chairman or other leading members, by ignoring some of its work, by giving it too much to do, or by replacing it with a number of committees each having a portion of the original task to perform but none having the combination of energetic individuals who comprised the original committee. If the work of the committee is not satisfactory, a reprimand to the chairman or committee as a whole may be adequate; and, in other cases, it may be necessary to have the chairman replaced or to change the composition of the committee. When this more drastic action is required but the administrator feels it impolitic to "discharge" the chairman or members, he can resort to the legitimate fiction of relieving them and giving others a share of and chance at the extra duty which often committee work is in reality.

Sometimes the committee, especially if it feels itself in a sufficiently strong position to challenge the administrator, may do things unfriendly to him. For example, it may send him recommendations or plans but publish them without his permission, or it may commit him to some decision by announcing a popular finding or suggestion before he has time to take an official view on it. It is in this situation that the administrator really must tread with caution. The committee may be of his creation and its members of his choosing. If he disbands it, he may appear to be backing down from a position or to be running out on part of his team. If the committee is an entity neither of his creation nor staffing, any adverse action which he takes against it may appear to be a stab at a predecessor, a colleague, or a pressure group which caused it to be brought into being. Unless the committee grows intolerable and liquidation is evidently necessary, the administrator might best try to handle it through observing its actions closely and moving promptly to block any unfriendly steps by it. To do this, he should maintain close relations with it, requiring frequent reports, consulting often with the chairman, and meeting with the group upon occasion. If he knows the committee to be deceitful, he should give wide publicity to all its moves so that when it changes course, to circumvent or to persecute him, its chicanery will be apparent.

Supplying Specific Committee Needs

The preceding thought may have painted a picture of company or department committees as blacksheep engaging in one of two extremes, either too little or unsatisfactory work, or excessive activity. The contrary is probably true.

The majority of committees in American business concerns may be expected to go about their business with considerable balance and efficiency, because they are made up for the most part of trustworthy employees. They deserve, therefore, the positive cooperation and full support of management. To function properly, they need a number of considerations from the administrator under whom they operate. Above all else, they need enough time in which to do their work. Not all administrators seem to realize this simple fact. Often an official appoints a committee and, failing to realize that its members have their own jobs, expects them to subordinate other duties. This blind and imposing approach may succeed occasionally; yet if continually practiced, especially with respect to the same personnel, it cannot fail to have its telling effect upon morale and upon the smooth functioning of the organization. Closely connected with the element of time is the wisdom of spreading committee assignments in the interests of morale and over-all operational efficiency. Habitually to assign the same individuals to committees may not only make them disgruntled with the burden of work but also lead others in the organization to believe that these people are the favorites of management. Of course, it must be realized that in every company or department the number of able and willing people is likely to be limited and the administrator, pressed to get things done, may frequently be tempted or practically forced to place them on committees.

Certain resources should be made available to committees. The time for meetings and other work should normally be at company expense, for otherwise committee duty, by depriving an employee of his own free time, will become detested and something to avoid. Furthermore, a place should be provided for committee functions, and it should be as private as possible. Group action does not flourish in an environment of noise and interruption. Some provision should be made for necessary stenographic and clerical aid.

In addition to these more prosaic considerations, and possibly of greater significance, the administrator owes his committees clear instructions as to what he expects of them in terms of objectives, procedures, and deadlines. Many committees are appointed and seek to function without being quite sure as to one or more of these basic facts.

Rewarding Committee Members

The strategic administrator who sees value in committee assistance should want to create and maintain among his people a desire to serve on committees. This is simply to assure his own future convenience. All the considerations of support mentioned will favor this attitude, but he may well go even further to court it. After all, they are largely designed to assure the proper functioning of committees. To win and keep his employees friendly to committees, he can do much by rewarding those of them who satisfactorily serve on committees. This reward can be granted in one or more of several forms: giving weight to committee activities in rating employee performance and determining salary raises and promotion; paying extra compensation, especially for extensive overtime devotion to committee work; giving committee members some special recognition or status, for example, mention in organizational reports; and providing them social entertainment such as luncheons, dinners, and tickets to prized events.

What about Dormant Committees?

Proportion dictates that the subject of committees be pursued no further. Yet one issue still demands comment. How about the maintenance in a company or department of a number of committees which either do not function or do so very rarely and then perhaps insignificantly? Should the administrator move to get rid of them? Perhaps the executive who sees organizational components as justifiable only in their direct contribution to or use for effective administration may wish to purge the organization of useless committees just for his own peace of mind. Apart from this desire and the possible necessity for clearing the deck so that new committees or positions can be created, there are certain ends which can be served by their retention. One is to maintain a façade of democracy, a procedure which may be ethically questionable. The other is to use assignment, even to inactive or rather meaningless committees, as a form of recognition and approval for other good and faithful service or as a stimulus for further constructive work.

An Evaluation

Democracy is probably found in all types of administration. Few individuals will continually make all their own decisions completely and alone. Man's fear is too great; his desire for association and support are too strong; and his capacity is too limited. Democratic practices, if only slight, are at times to be found in the behavior pattern of even the most autocratic administrator. Moreover, one may expect more and more democracy in the management of American companies, because the social order in which they live is friendly to the development of individual potential and rife with the feeling of equalitarianism.

A sound brief for democratic administration can be built. The defense of democratic practices in management is not, as some people seem to believe, just a concession to an historical trend which elevates the individual. There are a number of valid advantages to management which can be gained by the participation of more people or the greater participation of the same people in the decision making process. To make the affirmative case as simple as possible, only the four principal arguments need be cited.

The Pooling of Intelligence and Conscience

A major contention, and an oft repeated line, in favor of democratic managerial practices stems from the idea that two heads are better than one.[21] In other words, democratic administration is presented as a means of mobilizing and enlisting the brains and conscience of other people in the organization. This is an irrefutable contention, if one does not make the mistake of going too far. It should not suggest that intelligent and virtuous administration is possible only with democratic procedures. If the administrator or administration is sufficiently able and properly principled, the mere fact of bringing more people into the act, or the same people deeper into it, may add little to the intrinsic quality of decision making. The cause of democracy, in the sense that it is a means of providing additives, is best advanced by stating that in many cases subordinates and colleagues can contribute something to decision making which the administrator by himself cannot give, at least under the circumstances in which he finds himself.

One sees the "pooling-of-intelligence-and-conscience" advantage of democracy in situations of prime import as well as in routine or insignificant problems. The daily administrative life of a hypothetical dairy manager is illustrative. This individual, a Scandinavian by descent and a product of the best in agriculture training, is faced with declining sales for milk. He knows the dairy business from end to end, but he cannot hit upon a more productive marketing formula. In desperation, he calls all his drivers in for a general meeting to discuss the matter with them. Several of them are oldtimers who have repeatedly been asked by restaurant people on their routes to sell them bulk milk early in the day. The drivers advise the manager that each delivery truck could carry a number of multiple gallon containers, and that it would be little work to set these off at anxious restaurants.

He realizes that his drivers have hit upon a large untapped market, and so he moves to exploit it. Here the company family has contributed to a decision of major significance. But this same manager is more or less often beset by smaller headaches and here, too, he discovers that his associates can help him choose the proper course. The dairy company is approached for a donation to a local church building fund. The manager feels it is the company's civic duty to contribute, but its established policy does not permit the company to do so either directly from its own funds or indirectly by employee solicitation. He consults with his standing committee on community relations. On it is one young man who from previous experience with fund raising suggests a type of employee solicitation by a club formed for the purpose. The manager, sensing both the fund raising and politic possibilities of such a club, grasps the suggestion as a figurative life saver. He has just seen that democracy can contribute even to small decisions, and that from joint thought there may come better product.

Identification with the Good

Another argument for democratic administration is that democratic practices identify the practitioner with certain values highly regarded by Western society. Among these are the humility to seek the help of others, recognition of individual worth, belief in equality, and faith in numbers of people. The relation of democracy to each is obvious. The administrator in seeking the aid of others, particularly those below him, clearly demonstrates that humbleness on the part of the leader which Americans so dearly love. To trust other people for advice and guidance is truly to recognize the capacity and dignity of individuals. Bringing others into decision making, and especially letting them have a real voice in the matter, certainly implies some feeling of equality. The mere fact of group and mass involvement suggests faith in numbers.

The "identification-with-the-good" argument holds that the administrator and his administration is strengthened thereby. His employees, it is said, will respect him the more for it and will be motivated by it toward better performance individually and on teams. His colleagues and superiors, it is contended, will find him to be a man who can get along with people and who can marshall support when necessary. The outside public, it is virtually shouted, will see him as a forward-looking individual, symbolic of his and the organization's devotion to progress in human relations and management.

Mitigation of Pressures

The proponents of democracy in administration advance, as a still further affirmative issue, the older argument that democratic administration is a way of "sharing responsibility." This argument, as stated, is completely fallacious. Responsibility cannot be shared; it is obligation and as such cannot be detached in any measure from the position of administratorship. The contention, therefore, must be modified. It can be legitimately restated to express the idea that democratic practices are ways by which the administrator can attempt to protect himself against certain undesirable pressures. One is the mere burden of work; the use of a committee to work up a recommended decision or plan may be a defense against irksomeness, diversion and fatigue. A second is negative criticism; the employment of a self-rating system may avoid a concentration of criticism on the administrator as the rater. A third pressure against which democratic practices can defend the administrator is that which comes from constant isolation in public view; resort to grievance procedures for settling certain personnel problems can divert attention away from the administration by getting him out of the limelight.

The fact that an administrator cannot share his responsibility does not keep certain executives from trying to do so. One often sees a company or department official attempting to push off onto colleagues or subordinates the task of deciding and, if his decision and action proves wrong, to lay the blame for the error on them. At times this shirking procedure unfortunately seems to get results. How often is an administrator heard to say something like this: "Well, the group wanted it, and so we're stuck with it. There's nothing I can do." In reality, the administrator who feels this way is not shedding responsibility; he is attempting to avoid it, a step he can take with success only because neither superior authority nor any of his "publics" is sufficiently interested or strong to pin the responsibility back on him.

Democratic Containment

An argument in favor of democratic management, but more elusive than any of the three cited, may be described as that of "democratic containment." It runs in an interesting vein. Most organizations have potential extremists who can cause administration embarrassment and trouble by their actions. These extremists may simply be people with too much energy and too many ideas who are continually trying to do something. They are inclined to act at times just for the sake of action. Such extremists may be held within the bounds of reasonable activity by involving them in democratic institutions and processes. The idea may be advanced somewhat facetiously that the committee is an ideal prison for these culprits, since it is admirably suited to absorb their energies and temper their ideas while at the same time permitting them to do constructive work. But all extremists are not just energetic and imaginative people; they are often misguided or antagonistic individuals or groups. Democratic involvement can be an excellent way of curbing their obstructive tendencies by including them with other people in the task of management. The apparent recognition and faith placed in them by such action, as well as the restraining, guiding and educating influence of others in the democratic process, may straighten them out.

Motivational Influence

A final point which can be strongly advanced to support democratic administration is its "motivational effect" on members of the organization. There is probably little doubt but that people play better for the team on which they feel wanted. Opportunity to participate in decision making can certainly generate a feeling of welcome. Of course, the executive who uses democratic practices for motivational purposes should beware of overplaying his hand; if he permits or encourages too much employee participation in management he may lose some of his power to win obedience and, in effect, a measure of his ability to motivate.

Less Pleasant Things about Democracy

Of course, these arguments, effective as they may be in support of democratic practices in administration, do not tell the whole story. There are definite limitations on the use of democracy in management. Quite obviously, it can yield little in areas in which technical knowledge and competence are demanded. A problem involving the determination of stresses and strains in constructing a railway overpass is not amenable to democratic decision. This needs definite answer, and it must come from an engineering elite. In situations requiring fast decision and action, democratic processes seem also to have little place. Democracy connotes deliberation, and deliberation takes time which is not then available. A flood damages a railway bridge at midnight.

The division superintendent must act at once. He orders the nearest section gang to the spot. There simply is no time to consult with other divisional officials to decide who shall take over the job of emergency repair. Even more serious in many cases than these two limitations on democracy is one which is not commonly mentioned. It is the limitation inherent in the situation where those available for assignment to democratic procedures are not sufficiently capable or trustworthy to participate. Such a situation is especially likely to exist if the organizational family is made up largely of people of low culture levels or of extremely antagonistic people who do not understand the situation or who simply will not cooperate.

The negative side of democratic administration, then, includes certain limits on the scope of its use. But it also must list several specific disadvantages and dangers, most of which have been cited so often that they need no exposition.[22] Such points as democracy's slowness and cumbersomeness have been labored *ad nauseam* in regard to particular democratic practices, and the consequent expense has received almost equal attention. There is, however, one potential drawback which is not the most pleasant thing for the administrator to admit. It is the danger, suggested in the analysis of committee usage, that the use of democratic practices will eventually undermine the ability and desire of the executive to make his own decisions. Depending on others, he may become an organizational cripple. The extent to which democracy in management so undermines effective administration is unknown, but deduction from the nature of man argues that the peril is real. Man is a creature of habits and he generally feels safer in and relying on a group.

The organization may also become a headless group as a result of its democratic practices. A major role of the leader is to constitute a repository of responsibility, a focal point toward which all who are members of or deal with the organization can turn with confidence, praise, or blame. If democratic practices are carried to extreme limits, they can, in effect, so diffuse responsibility that responsibility cannot be located. The result will probably be paralysis of indecision, or at least serious frustration and confusion among the members of the organizational family. Here is obviously a further potential demerit of democracy in administration.

Conclusion

There is a trend in American business administration to permit, introduce, foster, and use democratic practices. In simplest terms this means to bring more members of the organization into decision making or, as seems less commonly appreciated, to bring further into decision making those already involved in it. It signifies, therefore, wider or deeper participation of the company or department family in management. Sometimes, the fact of democratic administration is overlooked by observers, since they are searching for a large measure of such participation. But democratic administration is a matter of degree and any sharing of decision making, no matter how slight the influence of the unusual participant in it, is democratic administration.

Unhappily for the precise student or administrator who places great value on the niceties of clean-cut categorization, there is no one type of administration which can be described as "democratic administration." There are rather only administrations using democratic practices. For want of better terminology, they may be called democratic administrations. Among these practices, the use of any one or combination of which does raise the administrator out of the ranks of pure autocracy, are support of subordinates in unexpected decision situations, consultation, and institutionalized democratic procedures. Each of these is a fertile field for strategic action; but, since American business administrators appear to have a strong affinity for committee action as an outlet for their democratic predilections, committees stand out as a special subject for investigation.

The question as to whether democracy in administration is an aid or hindrance to the attainment of organizational goals probably cannot be answered in terms of generality.[23] Proof lies in the fact that American businessmen take various attitudes, friendly and unfriendly, toward it, and in the corollary fact that the use of democratic techniques varies widely from company to company in the United States. Certainly, there are administrative situations in which it seems absolutely necessary to resort to democracy, some in which democracy offers something, and still others in which any form of further involvement of people would be distinctly unwarranted. The wise administrator should weigh democratic practices in the light of his particular administrative situation, but always with the thought that freedom to participate in the decisions affecting his group is a common aspiration of Western man and that permitting him to do so can be a means of recognizing his dignity as a human being.

BUSINESS SITUATIONS FOR ROLE-PLAYING

Situation XIII

Democracy in Administration

OGASIO BROTHERS, INC.

A. Scene.   A candy making firm in the business since 1892. The three members of the Executive Committee are at a dinner in the home of the senior member, who is President of the company. They are attempting to lay out the broad outlines of a plan to relax the general autocratic pattern of company administration.

B. Players.   1. President: Mr. Jacob Galileo, the elder son of the founder of the company and a family-trained administrator of great good will toward all but with relatively little knowledge of democratic practices in management.

2. Operations and Sales Manager: Mr. Mario Galileo, grandson of the founder, who unlike his uncle has had the advantage of a fine education in business administration at Montcalm University.

3. Controller: Mr. J. Thornton Thompson, a C.P.A. who some years ago was employed away from a public accounting firm with whom he had been connected for a decade.

C. Situation.   The Ogasio firm until recently functioned peacefully and quietly, making and selling at good profit high quality candy. By 1950 it had reached its present organizational dimensions of four factories and eighty-seven retail outlets. Ogasio products have always been sold only through company owned and operated stores.

In the last decade, the home office in Chicago, which holds a tight rein over all operations, has been beset with high turnover in supervisory and intermediate management personnel. Higher salaries and bonus payments have failed to stabilize this personnel picture.

Moreover, sales have been falling for the last six years. The executive committee has wracked its collective intelligence for sales stimulation ideas, but it has exhausted its potential. It is greatly disappointed that so few suggestions are being received from supervisors and subordinate executives.

In mild desperation, the other two members are flirting with the suggestion of Mr. Mario Galileo that a new spirit can be generated in the company by bringing lower officials more into management decision making.

D. Assignment. 1. Ask for volunteers to play the roles of President and Operations and Sales Manager, but select, if one is present in the group, an accountant to take the part of the Controller.

2. Ask the group to criticize the "plan for democracy" worked out by the Executive Committee in its presentation, considering both its short- and long-term implications.

NOTES

1. Tead is, in fact, emphatic on the need for democracy. ORDWAY TEAD, *The Art of Administration* (New York: McGraw-Hill Book Company, Inc., 1951), p. 73.
2. It is easier to describe democracy as a polar concept. Haiman does this in a succinct manner. He states, "Authoritarianism is based upon the assumption that the leader knows better than others what should be done and should direct the behavior of the group accordingly. Democracy is based upon the assumption that the group has the right and capacity to make its own decisions, and that the leader's function is to help it do so in the best way possible." FRANKLYN S. HAIMAN, *Group Leadership and Democratic Action* (Boston: Houghton Mifflin Company, 1951), p. 47.
3. Some authorities go much further and define democracy in industry as involving all employed by the organization. See E. F. L. BRECH, *Management: Its Nature and Significance* (3rd ed.; London: Sir Isaac Pitman & Sons, Ltd., 1946), p. 142.
4. Whether or not delegation of duty and authority is actually democratic practice is, of course, open to question. However, the extreme necessity of this delegation to successful management is not. The case for delegation is outlined in MARSHALL EDWARD DIMOCK, *The Executive in Action* (New York: Harper & Brothers, Publishers, 1945), pp. 174-180. The process and methods of delegation are analyzed in LOUIS A. ALLEN, *Management and Organization* (New York: McGraw-Hill Book Company, Inc., 1958), pp. 114-155.
5. For a certain identification of delegation with transfer, consult ALVIN BROWN, *Organization: A Formulation of Principle* (New York: Hibbert Printing Company, 1945), p. 29.
6. The process of delegation, with attention to the psychological factors, is discussed in DONALD A. LAIRD and ELEANOR

C. LAIRD, *The Techniques of Delegating* (New York: McGraw-Hill Book Company, Inc., 1957).

7. Consultation, which was described by Yoder nearly a decade ago as the staff function having the widest recognition, is also a practice extensively used by line administrators. The authors employ the concept in its generic sense, that is, to mean both staff and line consultation. See DALE YODER, *Personnel Principles and Policies* (New York: Prentice-Hall, Inc., 1952), p. 25.

8. ALLEN, *op. cit.*, pp. 143-144.

9. WILLIAM H. NEWMAN, *Administrative Action: The Techniques of Organization and Management* (Englewood Cliffs, N.J.: Prentice-Hall, Inc., 1951), pp. 384-388.

10. Of course, as Urwick points out in discussing government and leadership, the act of consultation can become very burdensome, and overwhelming engagement in it can result in subordinates being left to coordinate themselves. LYNDALL F. URWICK, *The Pattern of Management* (Minneapolis: University of Minnesota Press, 1956), p. 70.

11. *Institutionalized* democracy is not to be confused with the concept of *institutional* democracy advanced by Commons and discussed by Knowles. They use *institutional* democracy to designate a middle ground between the absolute powers of management and the various proposals to surrender management to employees or the government. See JOHN R. COMMONS, *Industrial Goodwill* (New York: McGraw-Hill Book Company, Inc., 1919), p. 36; and WILLIAM H. KNOWLES, *Personnel Management: A Human Relations Approach* (New York: American Book Company, 1955), p. 288.

12. It is the conviction of Urwick that committees are frequently tyrannical. L. URWICK, *Committees in Organization.* Reprinted from *British Management Review* (London: Management Journals, Ltd., n.d.), p. 4.

13. Attention is invited to the fact that the study of organization practice by the American Management Association devoted very considerable attention to committees. ERNEST DALE, *Planning and Developing the Company Organization Structure.* Research Report No. 20. (New York: *American Management Association*, 1952), pp. 83-97.

One of the larger experimental investigations into committee action and behavior is that which was launched by the Laboratory of Social Relations at Harvard University in 1947. A summary of its findings on committee functions and mechanics is quoted in JOHN M. PFIFFNER and FRANK

P. SHERWOOD, *Administrative Organization* (Englewood Cliffs, N.J.: Prentice-Hall, Inc., 1960), pp. 166-167.

14. This is not to imply that the committee has degenerated into little more than a low level administrative device. Quite to the contrary, the committee is today seen employed at all levels of management. The executive committee is an illustration of its more noble role. An interesting description of the functioning of the executive committee is that of W. H. Mylander, "Management by Executive Committee" in HAROLD KOONTZ and CYRIL O'DONNELL (eds.), *Readings in Management* (New York: McGraw-Hill Book Company, Inc., 1959), pp. 140-153.

15. The use of committees is treated at some length in NEWMAN, *op. cit.*, pp. 217-236.

16. PAUL E. HOLDEN, LOUNSBURY S. FISH, and HUBERT L. SMITH, *Top-Management Organization and Control* (New York: McGraw-Hill Book Company, Inc., 1951), p. 59.

17. The committee has been cited as a device for coaching "lieutenants." MELVIN T. COPELAND, *The Executive at Work* (Cambridge, Mass.: Harvard University Press, 1952), p. 55.

It has been said that committees are basically integrating devices to effect agreement. ORDWAY TEAD, *Democratic Administration* (New York: Association Press, 1945), p. 31.

18. RALPH CURRIER DAVIS, *The Fundamentals of Top Management* (New York: Harper & Brothers, Publishers, 1951), p. 483.

19. L. URWICK, *The Elements of Administration* (New York: Harper & Brothers, Publishers, n.d.), p. 72.

20. Attention to the operating problems of committees is given in HAROLD J. LEAVITT, *Managerial Psychology* (Chicago: University of Chicago Press, 1958), pp. 216-232.

See also the interesting enumeration of principles for effective committee work ventured by AUDREY R. TRECKER and HARLEIGH B. TRECKER, *Committee Common Sense* (New York: Whiteside, Inc. and William Morrow & Company, Inc., 1954), pp. 145-156.

21. A prominent industrialist, Mr. William B. Given, Jr., President of the American Brake Shoe Company, uniquely called attention to this view shortly after the close of World War II in his book *Bottom-Up Management* (New York: Harper & Brothers, Publishers, 1949).

22. In his handling of what he calls "democratic difficulties," Tead includes both certain limits to and particular perils in the use of democracy in administration. ORDWAY TEAD, *The*

Art of Administration (New York: McGraw-Hill Book Company, Inc., 1951), pp. 83-89.

23. For a review of the dilemmas of leadership in the democratic process, see CHESTER I. BARNARD, *Organization and Management* (Cambridge, Mass.: Harvard University Press, 1952), pp. 24-50.

But there are some fairly certain positive results of democratic leadership which stand as clear advantages. One is the development of a ". . . structural framework for achieving productive activity and experiences that serve to unite [the members of the organization] in common endeavor." Quotation from EUGENE EMERSON JENNINGS, *The Executive: Autocrat, Bureaucrat, Democrat* (New York: Harper & Row, Publishers, 1962), p. 221.

A concluding note on the attitude of the effective professional manager toward democracy seems in order. Allen puts it succinctly when, in speaking of the professional manager, he declares, "He uses autocratic and democratic methods both, as the situation requires." LOUIS A. ALLEN, *The Management Profession* (New York: McGraw-Hill Book Company, 1964), p. 243.

CHAPTER **14**

Communication: The Indispensable Nexus

"Without fear of exaggerating, the analyst of administration can describe communication as one of the
most significant and complex aspects of contemporary
business administration. Business organizations are
basically groups of people associated in the pursuit
of special tasks, each of which is expected to contribute something to the final product. To work together toward the common goal of product output,
they must communicate in order to coordinate and
integrate their thought and activity."

NO ORGANIZATION, whether business, labor, political, military,
social or religious, can function without the passage of
ideas among its members. The pattern of organizational
effort is division of labor, with each member attempting to
perform only a part of the total effort required to accomplish
the goals of the organization. Nowhere is this better illustrated than in the case of the usual American business concern
or its department. Competition and cost are here the com-
pelling forces. They make efficiency essential to survival and
success, and so they demand that the work of the company
or department be carefully broken down to secure the advantages of specialization. A company or any of its larger
components may be seen as a group of individuals each of
which, engaged in his own special job, is performing a part

371

of the whole task of the organization. But their activity would be little more than anarchy were they not given orders and directions from above, were they unable to convey notions and feelings to colleagues and receive ideas from them, were they incapable of ordering and directing subordinates, and were they not able to pass up to superiors that which superiors should know. Indeed, successful group operation, as clearly seen in business administration, demands a veritable communication network.

The Essence of the Process

Communication is variously defined.[1] The gist of most simple definitions is the conveyance of ideas. (The word "idea" is here used in the broad sense to mean, as Descartes and Locke held, ". . . that which one thinks, feels, or fancies. . . ."[2])

This does not imply, however, that communication is merely the *sending out* of messages nor that simplicity is a general attribute of the process.[3] Quite to the contrary, the conveyance of ideas is one of the most complex aspects of human relations. It involves a veritable host of considerations on each side of the equation—that of the sender and that of the receiver—as well as a formidable number in the area of obstructing and facilitating circumstances which frequently lies between the parties to the communication. The strategic administrator appreciates the perplexing character of communication and is inclined to view it as one of his big problems. Yet true to his nature, he sees it not only as a difficulty demanding solution but as a potential source of many opportunities. It is safe to assume, therefore, that the alert executive is vitally interested in a thorough understanding of the process of communication and that this requires an understanding of its salient characteristics.

Interactive in Nature

Communication is usually interaction among organisms and takes the form of stimulation and response.[4] It is, therefore, generally a matter of both reciprocation and alternation. This suggests that communication is to be seen as a two-way process. The business administrator, in view of his experience with communiques that invoke no reply or other apparent response, may wish to quarrel with such a doctrinaire view. If the social psychologist were prone to argue with him, which would probably not be certain for even he seems at times willing to admit that communication is only *usually* a two-way avenue, he could point out to the administrator that generally what appears to be no response is in fact a negative reaction—which is just as truly a response as positive reaction. The critical business administrator may console himself with the fact that a communication to be truly a communication need not be successful in terms of what he wants it to accomplish.[5] And he may take even further support from the fact that two-way communication is sometimes held to exist only when the recipient talks back.[6]

Numerous Purposes

High in significance among the characteristics of communication is the fact that it is carried on for one or more of a formidable array of purposes. One may summarize these as some sixteen general objectives: to establish rapprochement, to indulge the gregarious instinct, to learn, to elicit reaction and feedback, to explain and educate, to condition and/or convert, to order, to give directions, to win compliance, to prevent, refute or otherwise negate adverse criticism, to attack opposition, to stall, to slow down or speed up thought or action, to divert consideration away from a subject, to turn attention onto new subjects, to confuse, to call attention to the communicator, and to spotlight the communicant. It is obvious that not all of these objectives are mutually exclusive. There is overlapping or intertwining of at least two types. It is easy to see that the reaching of certain of these objectives can involve the pursuit of another. For example, an individual or organization may have "to explain and educate" in order "to condition and/or convert." It is also rather apparent that a given effort to transmit ideas may have more than one purpose. A case in point is the communication from the administrator which contains both an order to do something and directions as to how it shall be done.

The administrator may take good profit from a certain philosophical pondering of the multi-purpose nature of communication. A more complete comprehension of the numerous ends to be served by communication may open up for him a wider vista as to its use. Whereas in the days of his provincialism he looked upon it as largely a device for sending down orders and directions and getting back reports, he may in his new enlightenment, for example, come to understand that it is also a powerful means of preventing unfriendly criticism and attack or of calling attention to himself. Even more significant than the influence on his horizons may be the effect this awakening can have upon the thought and care he gives his efforts to get his ideas across. If he brings himself to a true appreciation of the possibilities inherent in communication, then he may take more pains with his communicative processes. The suspicion is warranted that administrators are often slipshod in talking, writing and otherwise communicating, precisely because they do not realize fully the potential of better communication.

Almost Unlimited Means

Well up in the scale of importance is another characteristic. Communication can be conducted by many means. It is commonly thought to be a matter for the spoken or the written word. To be certain, these two means of communication are perhaps of most importance and do undoubtedly receive prime attention from students of administration. Their overwhelming significance, however, should not becloud the existence of potent non-verbal ways of transmitting ideas. Among these, for example, are demeanor and manner, action, reaction, audio and visual vehicles, and the very subtle forms of empathy.[7] Communication, then, includes a wide range of activity and device; in fact, there seems almost no limit to the means of communication. All that an interchange needs to qualify as communication is an exchange of symbols between the sender and receiver which is meaningful.[8] The administrator who thinks of it as no more than talking to people, writing letters and other documents, and receiving oral or written reports overlooks much that is useful and effective. How prevalent this oversight is in American business probably no one knows. Yet, more or less particularistic observation lends support to the conclusion that it is all too common.

Voluntary or Involuntary

Communication, at least on the sending side of the process, may be voluntary or involuntary. This attribute appears to be less well appreciated in literature on the subject than are some of its other characteristics. Voluntary communication begins with a conscious decision to convey an idea of some nature. It is further distinguished by an element of exclusiveness in that it is directed at some individual or group. A simple example of voluntary communication is a letter or other written document addressed to a specific recipient or a remark made directly to another person or assembly of people. Involuntary communication, on the other hand, is the transmission of an idea without the decision of the communicator.[9] It is, in a sense, an unrealized by-product of the voluntary form, or of some unrelated action on the part of a person or entity in itself not intended as a transmitting effort. The by-product subtype of involuntary communication is seen in the case of the administrator who regularly shouts orders at his employees. He succeeds in getting his orders across in direct communication but he also, quite unintentionally, may succeed in giving his people the idea that he is a bully, an insecure person, or both. The unrelated action subtype of involuntary communication is manifested, for example, in the frequent results of the day to day performance of his duties by the administrator. He may work hard, attending strictly to his own responsibilities with no intention of impressing any of his publics, and yet, by his industry, bring his superiors to see him as a valuable person worth watching for promotion or his colleagues to regard him as an eager beaver interested primarily in furthering his own career.

Whether or not involuntary is more likely to convey different ideas to different people than voluntary communication is an intriguing academic question. Sufficient data is probably not available to substantiate a conclusion in either direction. However, reason supports the belief that in one respect the involuntary transmission of ideas is more perilous. Should the recipient interpret the voluntary communication in a sense other than the communicator intended, the latter has a better chance of correcting the impression, since he knows what and how he communicated. On the contrary, if the recipient misinterprets the involuntary transmission, the communicator is in a much less favorable position for corrective endeavor, because he may not realize, at least for awhile, that he has "broadcast any message." The executive can save himself real headaches if he appreciates this greater danger, for his cognizance of it may cause him to be more careful in the pattern and tone of his behavior in general.

Organizational Universality

Still a further attribute of communication is its universality in the organization. Everyone in the company or department, if analysis be confined to the sphere of business, is a broadcasting and a receiving unit. He senses and thinks and, sensing and thinking, he develops ideas and the desire to express them. As a subordinate, colleague or superior, he is required to report, share knowledge, give or receive orders and directions, or engage in any one of the many other communication actions necessary to satisfy intra-personal, person to group, or group to group relations. As the object of observation by others, he involuntarily transmits ideas to them, and, observing them, he involuntarily receives ideas. In other words, no member of an organization can escape communicating, unless, of course, he is a complete recluse. Even then he may communicate his own image as a museum piece via the involuntary pattern. The implication of this general involvement in the communication process to the administrator is obvious. Since he commands per force in the form of his organization a communication complex, it behooves him to consider the matter of communication as something more than should be entrusted to chance or even good clerks and efficient secretaries.

Motivational Influence

The temptation to continue presenting characteristics of communication can be overcome by presenting a given feature as a final attribute. It seems logical to select as this characteristic the fact that communication, whether seen as both sending and receiving ideas or more narrowly as either of these aspects, does have a stimulative effect on those who engage in it. To transmit, the sender must do something; to receive, the recipient, even if on a more passive level, must also exert some effort. Such acts are the result of the fact of communication. But this is quite obvious. There are both more definite and more subtly energizing effects of communication upon those involved. The communicator must often make the decision to communicate, and this may motivate him, especially if he is strategy-minded, to study carefully the situation as to the wisdom of communicating at all, the form his communication should take, the steps necessary either to protect himself or his organization from any negative repercussions, and the stratagems useful to exploit in his own or their interest any positive implications from his communicating action. So communication can be seen as a possible powerful stimulant to analytical thinking on the part of the first party to the process. If the subject of the stimulative influence of communication on him were to be pursued further, it would be necessary to point out that not only does it make him think but it also makes him act, since much of his thought will be meaningless unless corresponding and effectuating steps are subsequently taken.

Yet the sender is not the only party motivated, for the receiver also is influenced to thought and action by his involvement in the communicative nexus. He must consciously or unconsciously accept or resist the message. If he accepts it, he may be influenced to do no more than acknowledge it. Indeed the strategist knows that acknowledging it itself is often the very step demanded by the situation, since it may give the receiver time, further burden or confuse the sender, or forestall decision making. The receiver may be motivated beyond mere acknowledgment to more definitely positive or negative action and so react either as the sender wanted him to do or in opposition to the sender's intent. Interestingly, the motivational influence of communication may be more intense on the receiver than on the communicator precisely because the latter has taken the initiative and thus forced the receiver into accommodating thought and maneuver.

In practice, the stimulating effect of communication goes

further than motivating the two parties to the process into single sets of reactions. Communication is self-generating. An original communication can become the stimulus for further communication, and further communication may breed still more communication. If one were to speak facetiously, he could declare that the growth limiting factors seem to be conspicuous for their absence in the biological make-up of communication. A simple spoken word, a short letter, an unintended example are often the tiny acorns from which mighty forests of words and paper grow.

The dimensions of this self-generating potential of communication are seen in the situation of the newly appointed safety engineer who writes a simple memo to department heads requesting a report on their efforts to insure the safety of employees during working hours. The department heads, feeling that his appointment reflects serious concern topside regarding industrial accidents and disease, generally reply in great detail. The safety engineer is overwhelmed by the size of their reports and the diversity of their practices but, seeing the need of standardization and fearing repercussions from his unilateral imposition of a general safety code, he calls all department heads together for a safety conference. At this meeting, each department head stoutly defends his own safety practices. The safety engineer adds the minutes of the meeting to his already voluminous file of reports from the departments. He next decides it is politic to send a complete copy of the file to each department head as well as to his own superiors in the company. Now well sowed, the seeds really begin to grow. Numerous interchanges spring up between all parties in all directions. Finally, the safety engineer recommends the appointment of a committee of department heads to work with him in writing a safety manual. This project alone will require another great round of communication. The general manager's approval for the creation of such a committee must be obtained. Then the potential members must be notified; meeting schedules worked out; and agenda prepared. Each meeting will produce piles of minutes, and these will be distributed for study prior to the next meeting. Finally, a draft manual is gotten up. By this time, the verbal and paper forest has grown to the sapling stage. But much lies ahead. The draft must be distributed to all parties concerned, reviewed, and corrected. All of this feeds the forest of paper and words. This illustration, although much simplified as to actual interchange of communication, demonstrates the extent to which a given communication can grow in terms of interchange. What started out as a more or less innocent request for information by the safety engineer became a generative force of considerable magnitude.

In summary, communication is a phenomenon of five identifiable characteristics. It is interactive in nature; it has many purposes; it boasts of unlimited means; it may be voluntary or involuntary, especially on the part of the originator; it is a universal feature in all organizations; and it may prove itself a motivating force for thought and action.

Selecting the Media

There is an appropriate medium for conveying any idea or ideas to be transmitted in that it, above all others, promises most in helping attain the aims of the communication. The selection of this means is an important and difficult task.[10] It is important because best results depend upon it, and difficult because there are so many diverse and specific media of communication from which to select. Possible media vary with the field of activity, but a sample listing of those available in business administration alone will suggest their wide range. The business executive who ponders the question of the most suitable communication vehicle must select from among the following and many more: demeanor, action, reaction, hint, conversation, symbolic audio and symbolic visual tool, telephone call, telegram, teletype, intercom, public address system, speech or lecture, press announcement, radio or television release, movies and film strip, letter, memorandum, bulletin, circular, pamphlet, newsletter, job instruction, payroll insert, manual, handbook, personal interview, meeting, and management or training conference. In actual practice, of course, the problem of selection may not involve such a wide choice, for the organization may already be committed to a certain communication device or complex of devices. It is very likely that, once this commitment has been made, subsequent messages will be conveyed via it.[11] Be this as it may, no formula exists for choosing the precisely correct medium, but a number of principles do point the way to correct selection.

Selection, a Significant Step

Communication should be regarded as one of the most significant steps in any administrative decision, plan, or action in which it is required.[12] This principle, so prosaic sounding upon initial reading, is basic to the choice of the proper communication medium. It carries a guarantee of adequate attention to communication techniques, and it warns against a common failing on the part of many administrators in the form of a self-hypnotic concentration on the "job proper" with little regard for the transmission and receipt of ideas that are inadvertently or intentionally involved. Oddly enough, this self-hypnotic attitude seems least likely early in the work. At that time, the administrator is prone to pay special attention to the matter of communication, because he wishes to maintain a degree of secrecy regarding his plans and movements, because he needs to obtain the approval and support of others in the organization for it, or simply because he is enthusiastic over his project. But he may be expected sooner or later to grow progressively more preoccupied with whatever he is doing, and as time passes he allows it to absorb so much of his energies and attention that he disregards or forgets others and ceases to think actively about the pipelines to them. When he reaches the climatic effort and the "job proper" lies before him apparently done, he often in a figurative sense walks away from it saying, "Well, that's that."

The administrator who brings the direct action component of a task to successful completion with progressively less concern for communication may be reflecting physical or mental exhaustion or just plain ignorance as to the significance of interim and final communication. He may think that, since he has worked so long and hard with the task, everyone else concerned is properly acquainted with it. At best, he may communicate his decision, submit his plan, or report on his action in some perfunctory manner. The disregard for proper communication methods occasioned by preoccupation and exhaustion with the core of the task at hand can be very costly. If an unclear, untimely, undignified, or other medium improper to the occasion or subject is used, an untrue picture of what is intended or has transpired may be given, an opportunity to sell it may be lost, or a downright unfriendly attitude toward it may be engendered. It is often not enough for the administrator to take wise decision, draw up intelligent plans, and see projects through efficiently. They appear to people as they are communicated to them and, to the extent and in the light that the administrator wants them to be known, he had best concern himself with the medium of their description.

Timeliness

Communication must be timely,[13] and this is a second guiding principle in the selection of the medium. Those to whom the idea or ideas are to be conveyed are as much a variable in the communicating process as those who initiate the message. To have the best chance of influencing them as desired, the communication should reach them at the time when they are most receptive. For example, employees may be most attentive to directions early in the day when the pressure of work has not yet pushed them into defensive attitudes against further assignment or interfered with freedom of thought and action. Colleagues may be more receptive to an appeal for their assistance just before a holiday when the spirit of camaraderie is greatest. Superiors may be most permissive just after the treasurer has reported a profitable earnings period. These examples could be multiplied ad infinitum to illustrate the truth that it is not just the message, but also when it is sent, that counts.

What has the timing element to do with the choice of the medium of communicating? The point of most favorable receptivity may be immediate, soon, or later. Each medium has its own particular potential with respect to timing. A smile to express approval can be given instantaneously; a telephone call to discuss a matter takes a little longer; a letter granting permission consumes still more time; a personal visit to sell an idea may require weeks to arrange; a departmental report may demand months of preparation; and a procedural manual may consume years in research and writing. The implication here is that the strategic administrator, having in mind the great significance of getting his idea or ideas to the desired place at the propitious moment, must choose a means of transmission sufficiently fast or slow to get there at this time.

This line of thought may give the unintended impression that timing is a matter of one approach and that, therefore, it demands only one choice from among available media. The truth is that correct timing can involve sequential choices of media, simply because the administrator finds it necessary to communicate more than once. The chief of research attending a cocktail party suggests in a friendly conversation with the president of the company the desirability of building a modern laboratory building, believing that the top executive is now in a somewhat friendly mood. Four days later, proceeding on the assumption that the president has not forgotten his remarks, the chief of research dispatches a lengthy memorandum outlining his proposal regarding the new facility. Two months later but still well before "budget time," he calls the president to arrange a personal interview to discuss the building. This recitation of hypothetical events suggests that correct timing can require more than one choice of media and the selection of a different medium each time.

Attention to Objectives

To choose the most appropriate medium, the administrator must heed another principle. Not all media of communication are equally suitable for each of the numerous objectives of communicating, and, therefore, the strategic administrator will endeavor to match media with objectives. Certain circumstances may stand in the way of his doing this. The pressure of time, the lack of money, personnel and other resources, his own inability to write or speak, customs and regulations of his organization, and a host of other barriers may exist. Once clear in his own mind as to which medium or complex of media will best serve his purposes, he can proceed in one of two ways. First, he can attempt to liquidate these roadblocks, although this in itself may incur at least other waves of communication. The chief of the systems section wishes to formalize sales procedures into a manual. This will cost a considerable amount. He, therefore, seeks the support of the sales manager and, with his endorsement, prepares a special funds request to the treasurer, who in turn must get the approval of the budget committee, which again in turn must make a recommendation to the president who responds by calling in the systems chief for a conference on the matter. The insistent chief may, before the matter is resolved, be tempted to doubt the wisdom of his proposal to communicate procedures via the manual, although he may eventually succeed in getting the necessary funds. Should the strategic administrator decide not to attempt to publish a manual, he could fall back on the second way of handling the communication situation with roadblocks. It is the age-old strategy of substituting for the ideal course of action the next best one. In the example, it could be resort to the orderly summarization in circular letters of existing directives on sales procedures.

Respect for the Human Factor

Somewhat akin to the principle of selecting media in view of the communication objectives sought is the tenet that the medium should fit the peculiarities and interrelationships of the two human factors in the equation, namely, the sender and the receiver.[14] As far as the sender is concerned, it must be remembered that individuals differ in their ability to use different media. This is especially true with respect to the broader categories of media, for example, the written and the oral. It would seem common sense for the sender to use that communication vehicle with which he is most able to express himself. But there is even a bit more to the relation of the sender to the type of media. Each sender is seen as a particular personality by the receiver, and this fact, the strategic sender will find, may have quite diverse influences on his selection of communication techniques. If the sender wishes to "stay in character," he will find it necessary to use that medium which reflects the image the receiver has of him. And so the hail-fellow-well-met may choose to convey his message at a golf-club cocktail party attended by the one with whom he would communicate, whereas the formal and precise person may deem it best to write a careful letter. On the other hand, if the sender desires to "step out of character," as might be the case for example, were he anxious to emphasize some point, he can go to some medium not generally associated with him. The warm friendly individual could send a legalistic and impersonal letter, and the cold and bureaucratic person could resort to intimate conversation.

Yet the peculiarities of the receiver are probably of more importance in the selection of the communication medium than are those of the sender. After all, the sender has a reason, in his desire to convey ideas, to adapt himself to various media. The receiver not only may lack any desire to accommodate his reactions to the sender's choice but he is totally helpless to do anything about it once the sender has "dispatched" his message. Apparently then, the medium chosen is generally to be seen as a fixed stimulus to reaction by the recipient of the communication. He may react favorably or unfavorably, and his positive or negative reaction may be of varying degrees. Certainly, the strategic communicator will want to consider carefully the possible influence the type of communication medium will have on the receiver. And so, he will choose, for example, the well prepared periodical report in dealing with a distant superior who is a careful and objective administrator but the personal Christmas greeting in attempting to establish closer personal rapprochement with subordinates.

Resources

The administrator should choose the medium or combination of media which he is able to use. A communication device has little value in itself, and its employment requires that the executive have the necessary resources to put it to work effectively. These are the personal ability, the time, the money and the physical facilities to handle it. The warning implicit in this last guiding principle for selecting the best medium seems necessary. The administrator may be under strong influences to pick unwisely. His company or departments may have commitments to other media, his superiors may not like the one which is best, his training may lead him to more archaic or radical vehicles, and fad and fashion may becloud his judgment. Truly, the executive should remember that in the end no consideration is as likely to be the basis for judging his success or failure as much as is the outcome of his effort. Therefore, he should take unto himself the medium which he can successfully make work or for whose success he has the greatest chance.

Mechanics of Communication

Once decision has been made by the administrator as to the type of communication medium circumstances demand, he faces the challenge of using it most wisely. To the strategic executive, this means the consideration of many things, and certainly they include prominently the quantitative aspects of the message, its accuracy, frequency of communication, appeal to emotions, format, procedure of preparation, routing and delivery, and means of influencing recipients to react as desired. These are not mutually exclusive subjects, even though it is necessary to discuss each separately in an effort to point up its nature, significance, and strategic handling.

Quantitative Aspects

A matter of prime importance in the actual use of any medium of communication is how much to include in it. There is an optimum amount to say in any communication. In terms of broadest generality, it is that amount which conveys the message and obtains the desired reaction, no less and no more. The administrator who contemplates communicating with someone has a delicate task to delimit how much to say. After all, the adequacy of communication can in the main only be measured in the mind of the recipient.[15] Moreover, there are a number of forces which may lead the sender to include more than is necessary. Enthusiasm over an idea being advanced or an accomplishment being reported upon is among these. Over-eagerness to tell all because of an intense desire to win approval or support, or to injure another, is also conducive to "liberality in content." Fear may enter the picture, for some individuals cannot bear the pressure of carrying a dangerous secret or risk alone. And then finally, there is just the plain factor of ignorance, which causes the administrator to convey more than is necessary simply because he does not realize the importance of proper dimension of subject matter or cannot determine it.

The strategic administrator should be on his guard against over-expansive messages. Too much conveyed can obscure the gist of the message, so that the receiver will fail to get it, or it can make the message so difficult for the receiver to understand that he will grow impatient with the sender or otherwise react negatively toward him. But this is by no means the only danger in saying too much. There is also the possibility that ideas will be conveyed which the administrator, for his own welfare in the organization or for organizational interests, should not give. Knowledge is said to be power, and there are times when, and things about which, certain knowledge may give an inferior, colleague, superior, or other associate the capacity to do harm to the communicating administrator or the entity he represents. Then too, the administrator who is prone to be somewhat loquacious should be sensitive to the danger of overstepping that which is ethical. Every executive at times certainly comes into information which is actually none of his concern and which, if repeated, can seriously injure others. Should he divulge it, he may be indulging in nothing more than pernicious gossip.

To guard against saying too much in his communications, the administrator should ask himself five questions before he communicates. What is the main purpose of my communication? Do I have collateral aims and, if so, what are they and should they be sought in this effort at communication? Is there anything extraneous in the planned message? Does it include ideas which will unnecessarily place me or my organization in jeopardy? Am I including anything which violates ethical principles and honor? Certainly the administrator has no time to engage in an academic analysis every time he wishes to communicate. These questions and the positive implications for wise and proper communicating which their consideration carries can constitute points of reference. If the executive will from time to time check his communications against them, he should be able to make them established norms of his administrative behavior or, at least, he will make himself conscious of the fact that there are things which should not be told to others.

Of course, this matter of right dimensions in message content has an insufficiency aspect also. Administrators at times simply do not convey enough to those with whom they are communicating. As in loquacious communication, the reasons may be various. They may be the tendency to regard communication as a necessary evil; an overestimation of the intelligence, orientation, and knowledge possessed by the receiver; a lack of understanding by the administrator himself of the subject upon which he is communicating; fear of the consequences of saying more; and general laziness and irresponsibility. The element of time itself may account for much of the inadequacy in message content. The administrator, under the sheer pressure of work, may be sketchy in his messages.

Saying too little in a communication can be costly to the administrator. It may generate the need for further communication, and this procedure can be time consuming and expensive to both the sender and receiver. It can be especially irritating to the receiver, since he is as a rule initially blameless. Inadequate messages can make the sender and his organization appear careless, inept, uninformed, unprepared, or plain stupid in the eyes of the receiver, a particularly dangerous result if the latter happens to be an important superior or customer. But the greatest cost may be in lost opportunity. The recipient may make a negative decision on the basis of too little information. A company president, at best perhaps not too favorably disposed toward a new sales campaign proposal, may reject it summarily because it is not well explained or substantiated. Even if the recipient's attitude and other circumstances are favorable at the time the inadequate communication is submitted, they or some part of them may change for the worse by the time the communication can be supplemented or resubmitted. The president, in the glow of self-satisfaction over praise from his board of directors for a profitable year just reported, may be receptive to the proposal for a new sales effort. But, feeling that he must know more about it, he returns the plan to the sales manager for further elaboration. By the time this official has the necessary research undertaken, analyzed and written into the plan, the president is back in his usual conservative mood and either turns down the proposal or approves it with conditions. The administrator who does not make his initial communication sufficiently full may get no second good chance.

A measure of specific self-discipline, in addition to attention to general work habits, is necessary for the administrator to insure the adequacy of content in his communications. First of all, he should force himself to regard proper communication as a prime requisite to successful administration. Then, he should school himself to the conviction that the recipients of his communications know less rather than more about the subject. Next, he should make himself a master of the subject upon which he communicates, or rely upon someone else to provide the data and ideas to be conveyed. And finally, he should estimate the danger involved in communicating enough and weigh it against the gain to be had from doing so. The self-discipline necessary to send a full-bodied message is probably as difficult as the self-restraint essential to keep from saying too much. There is a marked tendency on the part of many administrators, busy as they are with a wide variety of duties, to economize effort in directions where economy seems possible. One such is communication, if for no other reason than that it commonly is not clearly seen as a step in operations.

In considering the issue of the amount of subject matter essential to a good communication the question arises as to which is generally preferable, the long or short communication. Contemporary American business administration tends to favor the briefer communication, for speed is a keynote to its management behavior pattern and success. Thus, company executives are commonly expected by their superiors to make letters short and to the point, to prepare succinct summaries of long reports, and to be concise in conference discussion. Proper as this emphasis on brevity may be to modern management, it must not be forgotten that the content of a communication, like all other aspects of the message, must be tailored to circumstances. There are situations which demand sheer length and volume of content. Some more common instances are the existence of department policies which call for only one communication as, for example, a year-end report; circumstances in which the recipient is very poorly informed of the subject or in which it is deemed necessary to direct him carefully; conditions that require recipient be given the flattery which lengthy communication may carry; and situations which dictate the wisdom of having many specifics on record. The strategic administrator will be devoted to short and concise communication, but he will not be hypnotized by it to the exclusion of the occasional need for the quantity message.

Accuracy[16]

One of the more difficult problems which the administrator must face in the mechanics of communication is that of saying or writing exactly that which he wishes to express. Inadequate ability to use the language, lack of time to prepare communications and to edit and polish them, ignorance as to facts, and clerical and secretarial errors are but a few of the more or less ordinary factors that may result in inaccuracies creeping into a communication. Their liquidation probably requires no deep stratagems. Should his inability to express himself keep him from being as accurate as possible, the administrator should endeavor to improve himself by some educative process. The administrator ought never feel himself too old to learn communication skills. Should open study embarrass him, he may resort to self-study or private tutoring. Inadequate time can be a most serious impediment to communication accuracy, for the hard pressed administrator may neither be able to devote more time to communication nor be able to obtain any trustworthy help to assist him adequately in it. Caught in this dilemma, it would seem that the best he can do is to keep his communications as few as possible and to make every effort to check those he does send. Ignorance of facts is a common source of communication inaccuracies. There is no one formula for protection against it. About all that the administrator can do in this regard is to refrain from including in his statements that which he does not know, to make it clear when he is expressing gossip, opinion or conjecture, and to attempt to avail himself of whatever superior knowledge or research facilities it is feasible for him to tap. Clerical and secretarial errors are best handled by simply not tolerating them. The busy administrator, by virtue of his very involvement in so much other work, may not have time to check all tabulations, typing, and the host of mechanical things that office staff members do in getting out communications. But he can occasionally scrutinize some of them and, when he finds an error, move decisively to have it corrected and to use it as an object lesson that he will not allow carelessness.

To be sure, these may be the least serious aspects of inaccuracy. There may be much more powerful forces at work to distort the truth.[17] One is the selfishness or ambition of the sender which leads him deliberately to prevaricate. The strategic administrator will realize that dishonesty in communications, completely objectionable on moral grounds, is an almost certain way to lay the basis for future trouble. An administrator can usually, at least in the long run, do his best when he enjoys the trust of those with whom he associates, but this trust will neither be given nor maintained by them if they discover him to be untruthful. And discover him they usually will sooner or later, for few men can successfully prevaricate over any great period of time. The administrator will find it wise, even as a matter of policy, to tell the truth. If he feels that it is unwise or dishonorable to do so, the best thing he can do is to refrain from expressing himself on the subject.

Another powerful force for inaccuracy is the pressure of third parties on the communicator to distort the truth. This pressure is probably not unusual, even if ethically questionable, in companies and departments, for the simple reason that third parties in the business concern, as in most organizations, may gain by enlisting the support of an administrator through pressing him to make false statements or give false impressions to second parties. Random illustrations point out the variety of these third parties and their influence. A union steward, who causes a shop superintendent unwarranted trouble by agitating the workers, asks him for a favorable recommendation to the works manager of another division of the company. A fellow department head, seeking an enlargement of his travel allotment, urges an administrator, who needs his constant cooperation in research matters, to put in for an equally exaggerated amount of travel funds. A lazy superior who wants to impress the president of the company with the effectiveness of his assistance to subordinates lets it be known to his subordinates that their favorable comments in the presence of the president at social events is expected.

Has the pressured administrator any real protection against the undue influence being exerted upon him to tell that which is not true? There are a number of courses which he can try. He can endeavor to ignore the pressure by such devices as appearing not to understand what is wanted, or by staying away as much and as far as possible from the person or persons exerting it. He can take notice of the desires of the third party, but either stall until it is too late for his statements to serve the purpose of this person or simply fail to make the desired false communication. Or finally, he can reject the efforts of the third party to force him into falsehood. This may be done with varying degrees of subtlety or brutality, depending upon the effect which is needed and the power of the third party. One of the best protective techniques to be used, in case rejection is planned, is for the administrator to ask the pressuring party to request in writing that which he specially desires. Many connivers will not put their dishonorable requests in writing for fear of future repercussions against them. If they do, they give the pressured executive a written record which he can, if necessary, use against them.

Frequency of Communication

The number of times an administrator should communicate with a given individual or group on a subject or during a period is a significant issue in the mechanics of communication. Frequency of communication is itself a stratagem, and as such can be used in different ways to accomplish different purposes. Rare communication may help to keep the administrator in the outer zones of attention as far as the recipient is concerned, a result to be desired by the administrator who fears a superior or who wants to enjoy the greatest independence of existence and action. The export manager of a company which is primarily concerned with domestic sales may wish to remain quiet for fear that his president will decide to abolish his office or to bring it under the special services division as a subordinate entity. To be sure, there is a certain risk in trying to remain anonymous by not communicating more than is absolutely necessary. Protracted silence on the part of the administrator can result in his being relatively forgotten by those with power to give his activity greater support or to advance him in the organization, or it can even result in his eventually being considered of so little significance that his position becomes a candidate for downgrading or abolition in internal reorganization moves.

The range of frequency stratagems is broad, and its breadth is indicated by a pattern quite opposite to the silent course, that is, by numerous successive communications to call attention to the administrator himself, to his ideas, to some project he is pushing, or to his accomplishment. One of the rules of propaganda is to say a thing often, and so a number of more or less repetitive communications can be a powerful weapon of conversion. The general manager may not pay much heed to one letter requesting additional office space, but he may find it difficult to resist successive requests. Of course, there is a grave caution to be observed in resort to this multiple communication. It is so to convey the successive messages as not to stimulate the recipient to greater resistance. In other words, constant communicative hammering must have a degree of subtlety. This subtle approach can take one of several forms: scheduling each communication to reach the recipient at a time when conditions favor his receptivity to it; changing media so as to reduce the monotony and identification factor in the recipient's mind; altering the content of each succeeding communication in order to add to the whole case being presented and to give the appearance of the fresh approach; and feeding the recipient a bit more of the new and unpalatable each time to insure gradual absorption of it without serious reaction.

As a corollary strategy to the use of numerous and successive communications to influence the recipient in a given direction, the administrator has the possibility of uneven tempo in the build-up. At times, he may figuratively bombard the recipient with messages, and at other times he may use what the military term interdictory fire, that is, he may send just enough communications to keep the recipient aware of the subject of the communication barrage. The peculiar purpose to be served by varying the tempo is basically to gain the positive results of crescendo with a mounting pressure leading to a climax or a diminishing pressure moving away from it. It would appear, then, that change in speed of pressure application can be used at almost any place on the communication scale. It may be wise to start slowly and apply increasing pressure on the recipient, hit him hard at first and then diminish communications, or use one or more waves of mounting and receding messages.

The error of using too few or too many communications may be the reflection of the nature of the administrator himself. An especially unfortunate administrative situation develops when the weak or fearful executive communicates too often. Driven to gain the recognition necessary to shore up his strength and courage, he seizes opportunities to call himself and his to the attention of those whose support he craves, and this may mean the whole circle of his associates—

inferiors, equals, and superiors. So he becomes, in a figurative sense, a broadcasting unit, communicating in one way or another with all who will listen. Often he succeeds in making a nuisance of himself, and in revealing his own sense of insecurity. More importantly, he may by what he says or writes expose his ignorance or incompetence, and by his exaggeration of communication show a lack of political sense and plain good taste. As a rule good strategy dictates that the less than adequate executive use restraint in communication lest he reveal his deficiencies and fears.

The strong-minded administrator may be tempted to communicate too rarely. Convinced of the soundness of his ideas and record, he is sometimes inclined to believe that all sensible people to whom he makes even a token communication will appreciate them. So he drops a hint, enters an occasional conversation, writes a single letter, or drafts an infrequent report, in the belief that one communication effort is sufficient. Repercussions can be serious. Those who should learn of his thoughts, plans, and performance may not get to know them fully. And so the able executive is denied a large measure of the receptivity and support he deserves, simply because he refuses to bring his light completely out from under the bushel. The psychological effect of not being properly recognized or appreciated can be serious to the self-assured executive who thinks everyone knows of his merit. He may come to suffer anxiety and frustration and, feeling undervalued, he may finally leave the organization or, feeling inadequate and defeated, he may sink back into comparative inactivity and obscurity within his company or department. The lesson he has not learned is that those who should know of his virtue and of the quality of his ideas and performance cannot always be trusted to obtain the information for themselves; they often must be told of them by the administrator himself.

Successive communication of his own thought and attainments by the executive is not boasting, that verbal exercise so detested by many people. It is a basic necessity in many companies and subdivisions thereof because of their size and the complexity of their organizational pattern. But the administrator who must repeatedly tell of himself needs know and respect the limits of propriety in speaking of self. They differ a great deal with time, place, and associates as simple illustrations will suggest. The newly appointed executive will find that, while he could speak rather often and well of himself in his prior subordinate job, he now must tread softly until he proves himself. The dynamic salesman in a sales rally meeting can almost continuously boast of exceeding the quota, but when he serves as an instructor in the company's sales training program he may find it wise to communicate his accomplishments but once and then as the expected work of a good salesman.

Appeal to Emotions

The recipient of a communication does not always react rationally to the message he receives. His emotions often play a part in determining his response, and consequently he does at times respond to such forces as love, hate, and fear in a basically irrational fashion. The dynamic administrator is cognizant of this fact and will try to appeal, where he deems it otherwise strategic, to the recipient's emotions as well as to his mind.[18] How the emotional appeal is best attempted presents a very real question.

The first problem in considering the insertion of an emotional appeal is to decide whether it should set the tone of the whole communication or somehow be made to appear incidental to the rational. This problem, for example, arises in preparing a monthly safety bulletin on lost time accidents. Should the administrator pitch the message in terms of economic loss to the employee who does not get full compensation when off the job with the injury and to his company whose production quota drops, or should he aim it at human fear of personal suffering and disability? There are probably many determining factors in each such case. And yet one consideration appears to outweigh all the others, the potential of the appeal for accomplishing the desired end of the message. This may be a difficult philosophy for the American business administrator to accept. In general, American culture places a premium on reason and tends to belittle appeal to emotions as almost something underhanded. Yet the public relations manager and the advertising director well know the value of emotional appeal. The realistic administrator acknowledges the pre-eminence of reason, but he also understands the complexity of human nature. And so he does not overlook the possibility of successfully influencing another person or organizational unit by emotional rapprochement.

The use of emotional appeal in communication is not without certain risks. Emotions are hard to identify. Their manifestations vary greatly, and their degree at a given time is difficult to ascertain. Hence, the communicating administrator may err in selecting the particular emotional appeal he directs toward the recipient of his message. A case in point is the resort by a purchasing agent of a large company to the fear of a vendor that his plastics may no longer be bought unless he cuts price substantially. The purchasing agent, having in the past had his way with the vendor who always exhibited the greatest desire to obtain orders from the big company, does not know that the vendor really wants to get out of the business and therefore is not apprehensive of failure to secure orders. The cost to the communicator of his misappraisal of emotions which can be exploited may be very real. In the illustration at hand, the vendor may simply refuse to do business and leave the major company for an appreciable period of time without a reliable source. Here is one of the substantial risks of emotional appeal, namely, that emotions are mercurial phenomena and can, when wrongly challenged, cause the individual to behave in an unpredictable and explosive manner. As a result, the seemingly harmless effort to use them may set off repercussions far beyond anything justified by the possible gain to be had from recourse to them.

Emotional appeal is often the essence of the use of personal contact to gain business advantage. The administrator who likes to put matters on a personal basis often feels that somewhere in the great category of human emotions he can find a unique opening through which to exert his influence. Personal contact assumes a myriad of forms, ranging from such a simple nexus as a friendly greeting in a letter to the formal personal interview. The friendly business administrator may be tempted to rely upon it beyond its ability to produce desired results. The businessman is strongly motivated by economic considerations. How far he will ignore the possibility of economic gain in specific instances, in order to respond to a personal contact, is uncertain. Therefore, the strategic administrator who attempts the personal appeal should be prepared for its failure. He should be ready to proceed by another approach and this may be either another emotional or, as is more likely to be effective, the dollar-and-cents argument.

Format

The shape, size, and general arrangement of a communication can be called its format. The consideration of format is pertinent to both written and oral communications. This is an important fact for the administrator to realize; he may be inclined to feel that only written communications, since they can be restudied and since they are enduring, deserve attention as to format. The contention may be ventured that the dimensions and profile of oral communication is even more important because of the greater difficulty which the recipient may have in getting the intended message from one hearing than from reading the communication but once.

But perhaps the line of thought gets ahead of itself. The initial question regarding format could well be, "What is the correct form of a communication?" Obviously, this question can be answered only in broadest generalities because each medium of communication has its own rules of format and because even these norms may be adjusted by the strategist to the uses to which he puts the medium. In terms of principles, however, something can be said about the correct format of any medium in any circumstances. Certainly coherence, proportion, and emphasis are involved. Any communication must "stick together" to be most effective, not overplay one or some of its parts at the expense of others, but certainly emphasize something. If it does not do these things, it will at best be a conglomeration of more or less related ideas leading to no central impression.

Another principle underlying good format is recognition of the fact that all communications basically have a common anatomy. They all must have a beginning, a body, and an ending. The real strategist who contemplates this seemingly prosaic tenet should come to see appreciable significance in it. First of all, he should recognize that recipients of a communication may be cold to any message, in the sense that they may be neither cognizant of its coming nor interested in its receipt. From this appreciation he will proceed to do those things in the beginning of his communication which will predispose the recipient to receive the message. Second, his consideration of format anatomy should reteach him, if necessary, the very simple but highly significant lesson that a communication must have something to say. Interestingly enough, some communicators concentrate so heavily on setting the stage and summarizing that the body of the presentation is neglected or at least relegated to an appendix with the treatment that appendices all too commonly receive.

Finally, the strategic executive is reminded of the necessity for leaving the recipient of the communication with the right impression. The fact that there is an ending should remind him of the possibilities of such effective devices as summaries, conclusions, suggestions for further communication or action, and parting rapprochement.

Still a further principle of format is what may be known as respect for the mode of expression. Receptivity to a message is no doubt partly the result of the style of the communication. Among the stylistic features are matters of English and expression,[19] typography, pictorial items such as photographs, graphs and charts, page arrangement, enumeration, and even addresses for further correspondence. A number of these features seem related only to written communications but, carefully considered, most of them appear to be pertinent to both the written and spoken word. In regard to strictly oral communication, the administrator may by a little deeper thought add to this list other items as diverse as formality of his appearance, the beauty of surroundings in which the oral communication is made, and sounds in the nature of the communicator's voice or even background music. The important thing about communication style is that it appeals to as many senses as possible, so that the chances of the message succeeding are greatest. This might be interpreted as arguing that the ideal form of communication is one which combines both written and oral components.

In connection with the matter of style, there arises the interesting, if at times wondrous, subject of the *plain talk* thesis and movement[20] that has as its objective the reduction of verbal communication to a level of great simplicity. The movement is the essence of what has been described as prose engineering which is said to be "an attempt to provide a sort of pidgin English by which we can intercommunicate over the gaps."[21] Perhaps one of the defects in this drive toward simplicity of expression is the failure to realize that simplicity is the product of many other factors than little words and brief sentences. It is the result of "discipline and organization of thought, intellectual courage, and many other attributes more hard won than by short words and sentences."[22]

Preparation of the Communication

Although communication is at times spontaneous or involuntary and, therefore, cannot always be preceded by specific aforethought, it normally is sufficiently deliberate to permit of some preparation. The administrator, bearing in mind that much of the impression people entertain of him and his organization is a direct reflection of what and how he communicates, should give all the attention circumstances permit to preparing his message. It is almost axiomatic that he make an estimate of the situation and then structure his communication to its peculiarities. There are several difficulties which he may encounter in doing so, each of which suggests particular strategic action. One is a shortage of time; he may either begin to prepare too late, or unexpected circumstances may intrude and take up a portion of the time he could have spent in getting ready. The administrator, caught in this not uncommon trap, can extricate himself with a minimum of ill result by converting his intended communication into a shorter or more simple message to be followed, if necessary, by a fuller message. The point here is that it is better to send a less complex communication which time will permit to be prepared well than to convey a hasty and slipshod effort. Under certain circumstances, he might take the more logical course of holding back transmission until he has had time to prepare thoroughly, but this action carries the risk of undue delay in view of what the message is expected to accomplish and the risk of helping create in the minds of others an image of the communicator as a procrastinator.

A second difficulty that may present itself in the preparation of a communication is lack of knowledge as to the facts
of the subject, the intended recipient, his expectations and
prejudices, and the possible action of the intermediate people
and offices through which the communication must pass.
Here is clearly an investigative problem. The collection of
facts often begins with listening, commonly a neglected
phase of communication.[23] Should he have the ability to do
so and should his time and other resources permit, the communicating executive might go further and find the implied
research a most instructive personal experience. But at best
the question of alternative uses of energy will remain, and
decision may have to be made on resort to others for assistance in getting the necessary data. If the administrator decides and/or finds it possible to employ others to help him,
he should take steps to insure that they report the truth to
him. This necessitates his taking one or both of two precautions. He must select his "researchers" with care as to
their alertness, analytical ability and veracity; and upon receiving their reports he should apply whatever tests are
available, if only his own good common sense, to their
objectivity.

The employment of others, especially members of the
organization, to investigate the facts of a given subject or
situation can result in what may be known as "discovery
embarrassment." These individuals previously unaware of
certain unpleasant things in the organization or of problems
and plans which should remain secret, may learn of them in
their research. It is quite possible, therefore, that the executive's use of assistance in getting the information essential to
a planned communication may indirectly be contributing to
revelations which can mean trouble to him. The leak may be
harmful to some of his associates who will react against him
and who will enlist others to do so; it may be injurious to
company or department interests; or it can, if it yields nega-

tive facts about him or his work, harm him directly. Quite possibly, the uncovering of hidden facts may have all these results.

For example, the chief accountant assigns two accounting clerks to get the facts on an unusually high expense account which a salesman has submitted. These two energetic young men discover that most of the salesmen have been rather liberal in spending company money, and inadvertently they make this known to the whole accounting office, whereupon the sales personnel turns on this office in force. Top management, learning of the situation and the disclosure, is embarrassed by the bad publicity proceeding therefrom; and the chief accountant himself is shamed by what amounts to a revelation of his own inefficiency in not discovering the overexpenditure pattern sooner.

Often the administrator is in full possession of the facts of the case and does not need any research assistance. This does not, however, obviate the necessity for any and all aid. The task of actually writing or structuring the communication in all its details remains to be undertaken. The executive may have neither the opportunity nor ability to do this work, and so he must call in technicians. These individuals may be his own office secretaries or, at the other extreme, representatives of highly specialized commercial services. But whatever their position in the range of communication specialists, they are essentially craftsmen. The ultimate responsibility for the quality of finished communication rests with the administrator, no matter what degree of reliance he places on his own secretary, staff, and other subordinates or upon the outside help of promotional, public relations, and advertising experts.

The possession of this responsibility dictates that the administrator should definitely remain in command of the preparation process. This is not to argue that he should interfere in the work of the skilled personnel doing the job as the whim to do so strikes him, but it does mean that he should take part whenever he feels it necessary in the interest of getting the type of communication he has decided to be best. At times such interference, even though it may involve nothing more than a suggestion to a secretary as to a matter of punctuation or to a commercial artist as to a color, is difficult to effectuate. Many who prepare communications for others, not unnaturally perhaps, tend to develop a keen sense of possessiveness toward the project at hand and come to resent any interference, even from the person who employs them to do the job. Unfortunately upon occasion, the administrator inadvertently contributes to their sense of independence and untouchability by his manifest ignorance of communication techniques and by his repeated reliance upon their judgment. It is not uncommon to see a situation in which the communication technician unduly influences the communication by proceeding to change it as he wishes and by resisting suggestions and orders from his principal. This might not be so serious were the technician commonly not more interested in the final style of the communication than in its message. The possibility of technicians becoming dangerously headstrong confirms the wisdom of definite action by the administrator to establish his authority over those who assist him in communication. Perhaps his best strategy is to give the technicians a clear picture of what he wants and, while exhibiting the greatest confidence in them through a minimum of interference with their work, to move firmly and decisively against them when and if they refuse to do as he wishes. Such action will do much to remind them who is in command.

A last difficulty for the administrator in the preparation of his communications has to do with corrections in the final form. More often than not, there is a degree of urgency about a given communication. Just before sending it or otherwise delivering the message, the administrator may take a last look at it to see that it is proper in substance and mechanics. To his consternation, he may discover a major error in fact, statement, rhetoric, or some other feature. What is to be done? Pressure to get it out urges him to send it without alteration or with only perfunctory correction. Good sense and perhaps fear argue otherwise. A sound criterion upon which to decide to deliver the message as it is or to withhold it for proper alteration is the relative cost of each course to all parties concerned. The administrator should make this decision, for it is a matter of his responsibility. If he decides properly, the merit will be his; if wrongly, the blame likewise will be assignable to him. He must, therefore, be careful not to be overwhelmed by others who have assisted him in the preparation procedure and who are so tired or proud of their handiwork that they urge him to use the communication despite its deficiencies.

Routing and Delivery

A communication can be sent to one or more destinations. The situational factors should be determinative. Clearly the case for transmitting the message to one destination is in the main that of greater secrecy and minimum side repercussions. But a variety of purposes may be served by transmitting it to multiple destinations. All who need be informed or persuaded are covered, and, especially if each receives it at about the same time, no one or clique of recipients can use superior knowledge as the basis for inimical comment or action. If simultaneous reaction in various quarters or of a massive nature is sought, obviously communications to a number of parties can help provide the requisite general stimulus. The conveyance of such matters as opinions, recommendations, requisitions, and warnings to two or more recipients can be a method of assurance that they have been made, for numerous records will thereby be brought into being. More subtle than any of these three possible uses of multiple distribution is one which may be described as "prodding." The communicator transmits messages to different parties to ascertain the nature and depth of group feeling toward him or some subject in which he is interested.

However, the sending of a communication to more than one party necessitates two decisions as to procedure. One has to do with timing. To prevent unfriendly individuals from receiving information earlier than others and to protect himself against charges of showing favoritism, the administrator may find it necessary to dispatch his communication so that it will be received simultaneously by all intended recipients. On the other hand, he may find it strategic to send copies of it on some priority schedule so that certain individuals whom he wishes to honor, whom he wants to receive it sooner so that they may have more time to ponder it, or whom he trusts to use it to desired advantage, will have the message earlier.

The other procedural decision which must be taken in multiple distribution of a communication concerns the degree of sameness necessary in each message. To be sure, the assumption underlying multiple distribution is that the *same* communication will be addressed to more than one party. However, in practice it may be wise to vary modestly some feature of the communication, e.g., its format, length or method of delivery, to fit a particular destination. A department chief in a stamping company might simply call the shop superintendent and tell him the final figures on a month's production but write in a formal letter the same data with more details to the vice president in charge of production. The delicate consideration involved here is how far an administrator can go in changing a communication and still keep it basically the same message. An error of judgment on this point can be embarrassing to him, because it may result in what is thought to be the same message eliciting different reactions. The embarrassment can be particularly keen when two or more recipients get together and discover or conclude that they have been told different things.

Once the number of addressees has been determined, and this is as true of an oral as of a written communication, the question of routing arises. Basically, there are five routes[24] available for the transmission of any message regardless of whether it is to be directed upward, downward, or laterally in the organization.[25] *First*, it can be dispatched directly to its final destination, which means passage through no intermediate hands. The expected merits of this direct route are those of speed and integrity of message, for it avoids the time consumed by the forwarding process and escapes the numerous changes which intermediate individuals and offices can make in a communication sent through them.[26]

Second, the communication can be dispatched "through channels," which means that it will be routed through some established communication hierarchy, usually the chain of command.[27] This route is generally preferred by the organization as a whole for the very reason that it respects chain of command by informing in order of responsibility and authority all who should know, and thus contributes to the smooth functioning and status quo of the organizational structure. It is not always so clearly to the advantage of the communicator, however. In a very real sense, he is at the mercy of the "communication channel forwarding stations" who have the power to act against the interests of the communication in that they may delay sending it on or even lose it; in that they may by summarizing, editing, or endorsing it in certain ways actually disguise or alter its contents; and in that they may use the information it carries as a basis for prejudicing other parties against the communicator or as a springboard for otherwise attacking him.

The administrator who suspects or knows that intermediaries are mistreating his communication can take protective action. To speed up transmittal, he can state upon originally entrusting it to them that it is to reach its destination by a certain time. Such warning can be given by classifying the communication high in whatever handling priority scheme is used or by advance notice to the possibly recalcitrant intermediaries that speed is expected. Should such preparatory steps not get the desired response in promptness, then the administrator can resort to the technique of checking with the intended recipient as to whether or not he has received the communication. If he has not, and especially if he is an important and powerful personage, the fact can be used as grounds for checking on and stimulating the movement of the communication through channels. In this connection, dropping the name of the addressee and hinting at his anxiety and possible feeling of displeasure over the slowness of the forwarding agents can be a real prodding device.

Yet delay in moving the communication forward may not be the major worry of the administrator who fears the channels through which it must pass. He may see much more danger in their somehow changing its content or influencing negatively the reaction of the recipient to it. Fortunately, there are very potent stratagems at his disposal to eliminate or mitigate this peril. The administrator can announce more or less widely what he has said in the communication at the time he formally dispatches the message or while it is in transit. In so doing he relys upon public knowledge to tie the hands of intermediate meddlers. He can dispatch copies as a matter of record directly to other individuals and offices, with the thought that their existence will constitute a brake on manipulation or chicanery in the communication channels. To be certain of the truth getting through, the executive can also dispatch the communication over more than one route, e.g., a letter through the line chain of command and an oral conversation with a leading staff official. In cases of extreme concern over possible changes in the message during the forwarding process, the sender can make his fear known to the addressee and ask for the privilege of communicating with him directly. The obvious danger in this procedure is that the request may reveal to the recipient some deficiency in the sender's internal relations, ideas, or performance. If none of these precautionary steps promise or give adequate protection to the integrity of the message, the administrator may await its receipt by the one to whom he has sent it and then, through subsequent communication with him, check to see what ideas he has drawn from it. An effective step in this connection is to seek a conference with the recipient to discuss something that was to have been conveyed by the communication.

The *third* route by which a communication can be sent is characterized by indirection. It involves transmitting the message to some party as the apparent final recipient with the hope that he will see that it gets to the ultimate destination for which it is really intended. An illustration may bring this route into better focus. The head of the training department desires to obtain two more instructors for a foreman training project. He knows that the president of the company must give final approval to his request, but he feels it unwise to approach him with the requisition. However, the executive vice president is particularly sympathetic to training activities, so the department head directs his request to this official, trusting that he will either act for the president or present the case in such manner to the president that he will react favorably. A caution or two are in order. The official whose influence is being sought may, especially if the administrator turns to him repeatedly, come to consider himself as being imposed upon and to resent the administrator. Moreover, if this official makes, or influences his superior to make, a favorable decision in response to the administrator's communication and it turns out to be a serious mistake, he may react especially strongly against the communicator. For example, if the executive vice president gets permission for the employment of the additional instructors and if the foreman development project proves a costly failure, he is likely to reflect the blame he receives in a much lower estimate of the administrator who petitioned him.

The *fourth* communication route is also one of indirection. It may be described as the "public broadcast." The communicator makes a pronouncement to some "public," e.g., stockholders meeting, employees assembly, professional institute, civic gathering, or press conference. The message is calculated to reach the intended recipient via public demand that he support the communicator's views, and at times it may have the effect of committing the recipient to the communicator's views because of its successful appeal to a public's opinion, judgment, or interest. A hypothetical case is easy to imagine. At a press conference with representatives of farm periodicals, the president of a farm implement manufacturing company portrays the advantages of a mechanical cotton picker, the production of which the board of directors has consistently opposed. The president wants his belief in the implement to be transmitted strongly to the objecting directors, and so he enlists the agricultural press, which he believes to favor farm mechanization, as a route over which to express himself influentially to the board. The choice of this route is not without risk to the administrator. Not only may the press present his views untactfully or incorrectly, but his superiors may react strongly against him for his endeavor to commit them when they do not wish to be committed.

The *final* communication route is difficult to describe, but it is well known as the "grape-vine." The message is dropped in the hope that someone or a chain of intermediaries will pick it up and carry it to the desired destination. This route differs from the others that use intermediaries in that the communicator neither formally recognizes nor acknowledges their existence or transmittal activities. He remains disassociated with the messengers and assumes no responsibility for the communication. The grape-vine route is calculated to provide the administrator with a high degree of insulation against unfavorable reaction to his communication and to leave him in a position from which he can move as the success or failure of the communication suggests.[28] The administrator, however, might be well advised to bear in mind that resort to the grape-vine route is in certain cases tantamount to the unethical practice of rumor-mongering and that, if he is detected planting stories or rumors, he may be seriously criticized or disciplined by his organization and his associates.

Whether the routing is direct, through channels, more obliquely via an influential intercessor, overheard by public announcement, or by the grape-vine, the problem of delivery remains. It is one thing in the case of written communications and quite a different thing in regard to the oral.[29] Written communications can be entrusted to a messenger, mailed, sent electrically or electronically, or carried personally. In general, organizational custom and rules as well as the exigencies of the particular situation will be controlling. However, there is something special to be said in favor of personal delivery. The written communication at best carries a degree of coldness and inflexibility. It can do little to argue for itself beyond the formal thoughts and sentiments it expresses. But, if its originator carries it to its destination, he may be able by his personality and exposition to make it seem of more or less significance, whichever is desired, and to pave the way for the particular reaction he desires. Of course, the administrator who delivers his own written communication may have to pay a price. The procedure is time and effort consuming. Furthermore, if the message has unpleasant connotations or results, he may draw to himself as he delivers it, or subsequently, a measure of the negative reaction it generates.

The truly strategic administrator is always on the lookout for possible corollary benefits from any action he takes. There do appear two such which can accrue to the executive who "walks his written communication." The surest is the opportunity to learn more about organizational affairs, for the process of personal delivery normally means more contacts with other members of the organization as well as the chance to talk with them. A less certain, but equally significant, indirect advantage is the opening that such contacts and ancillary conversation gives the administrator to sell others on his ideas and himself generally. It is probably true that one of the great "competitive edges" a member of a company or department can get is closer communication with his associates. This gives him greater sensitivity to what is and what can be done.

The delivery of an oral communication may be effected in person or by a representative. It is direct when the sender himself speaks to the receiver, and indirect when he entrusts a representative to talk for him. This classification of the ways of delivering an oral message should not be confused with the general concepts of direct and indirect routing, since delivery is the action of moving the communication over a given route but an oral message can be routed via any of the five avenues described. The two forms of oral delivery have their own peculiar merits. Speaking directly to the recipient provides an opportunity for using the force of personality, for observing the reactions of the recipient, and for exercising a high degree of flexibility since the communicator can change his approach and thought as the developing personal contact permits and requires.[30] The indirect oral communication, on the other hand, makes it possible for the communicator to inform a recipient but at the same time to stay away from him. And in this fact alone the administrator can find several strategic advantages. He can inform the recipient of his displeasure without confronting him and so run less danger of creating a personal rift; he can send, as it were, advance and subtle notice of desire or intent to do something without making a real commitment to it; he can let others carry the message and by so doing also educate them in the ideas carried; and, aware of the positive response to social approval, he can, by expressing to the intermediate parties his faith in and praise of the ultimate recipient, motivate this person to desired thought or action.

The administrator should remember, however, that indirect oral communication can get away from his control and cause him trouble. The carrier of the message may distort its content and connotation, so that it becomes something quite different from its original form. There seems to be a particular tendency for intermediaries to blow up a message out of proportion to its intention, and so to gratify some of their proclivities for personal recognition and sensationalism. The best safeguard for the communicating administrator in this respect is to give the message to intermediaries who can be depended upon to deliver it truly, and to present its contents to them clearly so that they will not carry mistaken ideas.

The trouble that "unreliable messengers" can cause may be mild in comparison with the repercussions of that unintended communication which an administrator can inadvertently initiate in casual conversation or gossip. Here matters can really get out of control. The executive may not be quite certain as to who has heard his remarks, and he can rarely be sure as to exactly what they have heard, whether they will repeat it, and, if so, what they will say to others. Clearly, the administrator must choose his associates and guard his tongue with an eye to security.

Maintenance of Secrecy

Administrators differ greatly in their attitude toward keeping communications secret.[31] Some executives are most open in their handling of messages received and sent, and at times even seem to extend themselves to disseminate the content. At the opposite extreme are executives with an almost pathological fear of anyone's seeing or hearing their communications. The strategy-oriented administrator will realize that the degree of secrecy desirable varies with circumstances, and he will neither hesitate to keep hidden that which conditions require be kept quiet nor to make widely public that which conditions demand be open knowledge. In general, however, he will identify himself with the middle of the road and neither hide nor publicize the information he sends and receives. This approach has several advantages: it tends to give him greater peace of mind because he does not feel constrained to take either extreme course; it helps avoid offense to his associates who might be irritated or insulted by his efforts to keep things from them or by his frenzy to tell all; and it leaves him in a control position from which he may, with the minimum of injury to public relations and to his standard office procedures for handling communications, move toward greater secrecy or more openness.

The techniques for insuring secrecy are numerous and belong to a special field of study. It does appear, though, that the executive with no particular training or experience in matters of security can take at least two steps to keep his communications within the limits of the ordinary confidence desired. Most importantly, he can surround himself with trustworthy people, and especially with faithful and discreet clerks and secretaries, for office employees almost of necessity must know something of most communications. Of but slightly less significance is the matter of office facilities and rules. The office of the administrator is normally a dynamic social entity with much going and coming of people, rumor and counter-rumor, pressure and counter-pressure to get things done, and general disturbance to those who work there. Information may leak out somehow in the general milieu of operation. It is essential, therefore, that the office be properly equipped and arranged so that the lack of adequate physical facilities will not contribute to this "natural leakage." It is necessary also that rules of proper office procedure be laid down and enforced by the administrator so that human error or frailty will be less likely to result in a drain on security.

A bothersome incidental problem arises when the administrator learns that one of his staff has already divulged classified information. If the offense is serious enough he may be inclined to discharge the untrustworthy person, and rightly so because his continued employment in the office could be worrisome or dangerous. Yet, there are times when this step may be risky. If discharged, the individual may reveal still more on the secret subject. Moreover, the fact of his discharge may suggest to others in the organization that the administrator has not been properly running his office. Finally, the discharge may make the administrator seem heartless or at least unobjective, since in many cases he cannot, due to the demand for continued secrecy, indicate why he fired the unreliable individual. Faced with the dilemma of having to keep the employee who should be let go, the administrator may have to resort to methods of educating him to greater security consciousness or isolate him from the stream of communication.

Influencing Desired Reaction

The end purpose of a communication is to influence the recipient into a desired attitude, decision, or action. Therefore, the strategic executive should so handle his communications as to enhance chances of evoking desired reaction. The reactions sought are of course varied. The first reaction desired is often simply to get the recipient to take note of the communication, that is, to look at it, read it, or listen to it.

Unless it obtains this result, the communication will probably fail, except insofar as its preparation may cause the sender to think and insofar as its dispatch puts the sender on record as having sent it. The next reaction wanted is commonly some acknowledgment from the recipient that he has received the communication. This will assure the sender and make it possible for him to base future strategy on the knowledge that the message has reached the addressee; in a subtle way, it may also commit the recipient to peruse the communication. Categorically, reactions wanted subsequent to these two may take one of three forms: positive response in that the receiver approves that which is presented to him; negative response in that he disapproves it; and neutral response in that the recipient gives no clear indication of his final reaction.

While it is difficult to identify and describe the various stratagems by which an administrator can bring about desired reactions through the act of communication, each situation presents a particular problem. Strategic approaches to the recipient can be designed to meet it, and they are especially important in view of the fact that the recipient may have any one of three possible "reception attitudes": friendly, laissez-faire, or hostile.[32] Some of the stratagems are listed below:

1. *Call upon the recipient's sense of loyalty and duty.* The communicator attempts to arouse in the receiver a feeling of obligation to self, to a second party or parties, to the organization, or to the subject or purpose of the communication. *Example:* The sender telephones to a fellow administrator requesting his cooperation in a crash assignment just received from the plant superintendent and reminds this colleague of the several times the superintendent has helped them both.

2. *Use praise.* Most individuals respond favorably to praise. The administrator can often, by judicious expression of appreciation of the receiver, his work or something else

dear to him, arouse him to friendly reaction to whatever is included in the communication. *Example:* A top chain store manager, in an oral appeal to the supervisor of his meat department for better arrangement and display of merchandise, passes on to him a letter of commendation from the president of the company lauding the meat department for the best total sales effort of any one department in the chain.

3. *Appeal to the desire for identification with the "big and the bold."* This strategy is a potent device to enlist support for the objective of a communication. It attempts to appeal to two deeply-embedded human qualities, the desire for recognition and the desire to belong. People like to be on the band wagon of success. *Example:* The president of a small company, having insufficient administrative staff, wants to use his department heads on a company project not under the cognizance of any one of them. He assembles them, describes the project in oracular terms as potentially the most valuable opportunity the organization has ever had, and then invites them to participate in it.

4. *Stimulate self-interest.* The communicator may assume that people appreciate something more than life presently affords them. He has a chance of affecting their judgment by giving them hope of enhanced reward for effort and service. *Example:* A credit manager, determined to cut charge account losses, sends a circular memorandum to all his account supervisors promising an extra week's vacation to the one whose acceptance list shows the fewest delinquent accounts for the year.

5. *Arouse an element of fear.*[33] Few people can tolerate danger without fear. A communicating executive can within the bounds of morality and decency indicate in the communication that improper response to it would prove unfriendly to the best interests of the recipient. *Example:* The manager of an automobile lamp factory places a payroll insert in each check envelope by which he points out that, if labor costs continue to mount because of loafing on the job, the company will be forced into further automation.

6. *Use a communication barrage.* This means figuratively to bombard the addressee with communications, either of the same type or of different types, so that pressure of constant

suggestion, order, direction, request, or report will wear down his resistance until he either gives in from sheer weariness at being urged or becomes convinced that the course the sender seeks is the correct one. *Example:* A supervisory engineer wants an appointment to a graduate institute, but the personnel manager is not disposed to approve his leaving for the required six weeks. Consequently, the ambitious engineer supplements his initial application for leave of absence with a telephone appeal, a personal visit, and the written intercession of the production manager and the chief of engineering research.

7. *Make the desired course of action easy.* Many times the person who receives a communication fails to act as the sender desires because of the work involved in doing so. Some recipients would do what is wanted if it were made easy for them. The strategic executive often can make profitable use of laziness and inertia by showing in his communication how the request can be granted or the proposal carried out. *Example:* A branch bank manager seeks to increase the services of his unit. He proposes by formal letter to the indolent first vice president that his branch be given a drive-in facility, and he includes a plan for an ingenious location of the driveway and tellers' windows because the ground space is limited.

8. *Use surprise.* Some people have a tendency to agree with ideas and propositions submitted to them as more or less of a surprise. Perhaps they are unable quickly to marshal their forces of good judgment and, not knowing immediately what to do, take the course of least resistance in the form of responding as the administrator's startling message indicates they should. *Example:* A shop foreman in an automobile bumper manufacturing company rushes into the office of the works superintendent with a new plan for routing the bumpers through a bottleneck on the production line, and this official is pushed into accepting the idea for an expensive tryout.

9. *Employ procedural tactics.* At times the sender can control the response of the recipient by making it procedurally impossible for him to do otherwise. A familiar device used to influence him is to introduce into the communication some procedural requirement which the receiver cannot

ignore. *Example:* An office manager wants a written acknowledgment by each of the large number of secretaries and clerks under her supervision of their having seen a new regulation; she circulates a copy of the regulation with an attached typed list of employee names, and requires that each employee sign opposite her name before she passes the document on to another person.

10. *Give orders and directions with as little bossing connotation as possible.* The more an individual is bossed, the more his thought takes place within the "bossing-pattern." The cumulative result can be opposition to the person doing the bossing and to the orders and directions he communicates.[34] *Example:* A foreman always orders his men in a conciliatory manner, saying, "I suggest we try this." And so his men usually follow his orders, feeling that they are not commanded.

And so it is apparent that the communicating administrator is not simply a hapless individual with no more power than that of expressing himself. He can, as these strategic courses indicate, definitely impose a measure of his will on those to whom he transmits a message. Care must be taken to recognize the ethical issues which arise out of misuse of the stratagems just suggested.

Can the Administrator Trust His Own Communication Strategy?

No matter how resourceful the communicator may be, he cannot in most instances be certain as to the effect of his communication. There is always the possibility of attrition from entropy, "a term which suggests the degree of ignorance, chaos and randomness in a system,"[35] and especially from a type known as "noise entropy" which arises from errors and distortions in the communication system.[36] The thinking executive will understand that the answer to entropy is organization. Fortunately too, there are forces which cause people to resist ignorance, chaos, and randomness. The behavior incentive for pushing toward equilibrium and stability is known as homeostasis.[37] The administrator also can find some comfort in the new field of cybernetics, the study of control and communication, wherein the concept of feedback figures prominently.[38] Feedback has been defined by the sociologist as the "observation by the communicator of the effect of the communication."[39] It connotes in administration a circular pattern[40] of information flow, reaction, and new information flowback. Of course, the administrator must bear in mind the sociological fact that differences in organization of companies and departments encourage varying degrees in the efficiency of feedback.[41]

The Strategy of Reception

The administrator is not correctly seen as a mere sender of communications. He is also a receiver of messages. To discuss his administrative stratagems in the communication function without touching upon his role as a recipient would be decidedly remiss.

Control through Reputation

The receipt of communications is a continuous and significant function of administration. The executive, therefore, will find it to his advantage to have determinative influence over the number and nature of the messages which he receives. One of the best control devices by which the administrator can assure the receipt of desired communications is to establish a reputation as a definite type of recipient. A few matching pairs will be illustrative. If the strategic executive wishes to receive all, many and varied communications, he will attempt to be seen as a highly approachable person. Should he not want to be bothered with insignificant communications and should he be unwilling to tolerate poorly prepared ones, he will endeavor to appear meticulous, formal, and distant. In case he desires to receive only communications that are objective, he will strive to gain the reputation as a person who tolerates only the truthful and factual.

Whatever attitude the situation demands that the administrator have toward accepting communications, he will have less trouble maintaining it and getting people to conform to it if he creates an image of himself as a person who *insists* upon receiving *that* type of communication. When people, even superiors at times, know what a person requires and will tolerate, they tend to behave accordingly. It is often easier, and generally more pleasant, to conform to a person's wishes than it is to violate them. Furthermore, the response to an individual's image may become more or less automatic, since people grow to associate a certain way of doing things with him. So the executive who consistently demands to hear all will probably not be insulated by his subordinates against the flood of messages. The administrator who makes himself known as an executive hard to approach will probably get fewer and better prepared messages than the one who is thought to be receptive to almost any form of communication, and vice versa. The executive that establishes himself as an administrator who will listen to no rumor mongering, unsubstantiated criticism, colored information, or false reports generally will receive less of these objectionable communications than one that lets himself be typed as a person who avidly grasps every scrap of information coming his way.

Yet the establishment of his stance as a particular type of communication recipient will probably not solve all the administrator's reception problems. Obviously he is not likely to receive exactly the kind of communication he wants and in the preferred form and at the desired time. To approximate this general result, he can lay down rules for his subordinates, for example, that he wants a short report on certain subjects on the last business day of each month. Upon occasion he will likewise be compelled to press his equals and superiors for such communications as are necessary to the proper discharge of his responsibilities. If his equals are reluctant or negligent in communicating with him, he can resort to the policy of negative reciprocation and curtail or neglect his messages to them. If appropriate data is not received from his superiors, he can make an effort to secure the information for himself, perhaps by associating with pivotal people or by other means. Failure to receive appropriate communications from superiors may be indicative of their lack of confidence in him or some other serious deficiency in relationship. Basically the administrator should overcome the problem through the use of his ingenuity and industry to win and maintain such confidence with his superiors that he is entrusted with the information pertinent to the functioning of his office, to his leadership, and to his welfare.

Defense against Unwanted Communication

There are occasions when the strategic administrator will be concerned with something almost the reverse of getting the right communication, and they are the times when he does not wish to receive any communication from a particular person, office, or organization. Circumstances may make the administrator totally unreceptive. He may wish to ignore someone in order to humble or discipline him. Pressure of work may make it unwise or impossible for him to respond correctly to the communication. The most logical course for the administrator who does not want to receive a communication is to refuse to receive it—neither look at it, read it, nor listen to it. To do this may be difficult, since the sender by and large has enough freedom to prepare the message and to try to get it into the administrator's hands. Chances are that the administrator does not have an opportunity to refuse receptance until the communication is at hand, and then refusal raises the unpleasant and possibly dangerous technique of late outright rejection. Should the communique be coming up from a subordinate, and especially if it contains a complaint or supplication, the administrator's action may be seen as "back-turning"—a step destructive of good morale. If the message is from a superior, rejection may be considered insubordination and result in a loss of standing with the superior, in disciplinary action, or discharge. If the communique comes from an equal, rejection may weaken ties of friendship and respect or lay the grounds for subsequent retaliatory action.

Rejection of the message by an administrator is a perilous defense against the unwanted communication. The strategic administrator usually will search for other ways to protect himself against it. He may find that a cold and formal attitude toward any comunication will be adequate. He may discover effective techniques in department or company rules which specify that all but certain types of communications are to be routed for final decision to a subordinate. He may have recourse to such stratagems as being absent from his office or avoiding particular people at times when he expects unwanted communication to be likely. Of a more complicated nature is a certain source selection which some administrators make as a technique of insulating themselves against unwanted messages. It involves seeking out communications only from sources sympathetic to him. This action may be a deliberate step or an unconscious surrender to the attraction of sympathy.[42] Regardless of what means he takes to protect himself against undesired communication, he should remember that there is always the possibility of the message reaching him and that, therefore, he should be prepared for the consequences of its receipt.

Precipitate and Negative Reaction

The problem of getting the "right communications" by no means includes all the reception difficulties of the administrator. Another difficulty which deserves prominent mention is that of guarding himself against his own precipitate reaction to a communication. To avoid making the wrong response, the administrator can take two steps. He can read or listen to the communication with utmost care so that he will be sure of the ideas it conveys; and then, if the subject is large, the communication complicated, the message of high import as to eventual decision, or the sender of great relative power in the organization, the administrator, putting it aside for a while, can contemplate its meaning and subsequently restudy it, with consultative assistance if necessary.

In some cases the administrator will be forced by circumstances to ignore or otherwise respond negatively to a communication. An important question for the official in this position, who wants to maintain the good human relations, is how to reject all or part of a message and still generate minimum friction and ill will. Above all else, he should be courteous in his receipt of a communication. Negative replies are often more acceptable when expressed in a polite vein, and politeness here often is best expressed by adequate explanation of the rejection or disapproval.

Time is said to be a device for taking the sting out of unpleasant acts. This old axiom suggests that the administrator can reply in the negative to a communication with less likelihood of rancorous reaction from the sender if he takes an appreciable period to give his answer. Hope eventually may wane in the expectant communicator and he may become more conditioned to the possibility of ill news. But note two exceptions to delayed reply. One is a matter of tactics; there are times when swift and decisive response by the recipient will produce the least inimical results. They may be situations in which the sender is not yet fully prepared to fight back or situations in which the sender respects the recipient for the promptness and precision of his answer, even though he may not agree with it. The other exception to the deliberate handling of a communication is a matter of ethics. Quite possibly, the sender may have a right to a quick answer and even may suffer serious loss if he does not get it.

Should the administrator decide to use the delaying technique, he has an excellent means at hand. He can seize the device of further communication with the sender; the possibilities of stalling in this manner are great. The further communication process can include requests for resubmission of the original communication in different forms or at a future time, for elaboration of one or more points, and for analysis and presentation of corollary subjects. It can entertain time consuming argument over any or all points in the original communication. The strategic recipient will be able to involve the sender in a veritable communication orgy should he engineer separate exchanges in each request and argument. If this pattern of delay proves impossible or too difficult to develop, the receiving administrator can turn to the more unimaginative and simple technique of taking a substantial amount of time to react to a message. In case explanation for the delay is deemed necessary, he may with truth be able to refer to the pressure of his duties or the necessity for referring the matter to others for advice or approval.

Referral of Communication

The referral of a communication by the executive who receives it to others for comment, analysis, advice, approval, disapproval, or other action raises some interesting implications of strategy. Not only can it serve as a delaying tactic but it also is a way of accomplishing several other purposes. The administrator can diffuse culpability for whatever action is taken on the communication by the democratic step of seeking and abiding by the advice, recommendations, or votes of those to whom he submits it for perusal. He can subtly flatter these people by the respect for their knowledge and trust in their judgment implied by his turning to them. With an eye toward eventual trouble from the sender, he can, by using the communication to alert and convert his associates to the ideas, plans and attainments of this communicator, prepare them as allies for future battles. Of real importance also is the fact that the communication may be passed on to non-addressees to get them to do the work its reply requires or which some project it initiates will necessitate. To the hard pressed executive, this shifting of part of the burden of responding to communications can be providential.

However, the strategic executive should guard against the trouble referral can bring if the communication and its study by others reveals to them weaknesses in his administration or leads them to react against his wishes. Such an outcome can be especially serious if those to whom he referred it are his superiors or others with the power to move against him effectively. They may use the information to injure him and his interests, and they are probably in a position to do so. This danger is illustrated in the example of a very busy dispatcher for a trucking company who refers a series of written complaints from contract customers to his immediate supervisor and to certain other dispatchers senior to him for their advice. They all study the complaints and conclude that his timing and supervision of movement has been less than satisfactory. In thus seeking the help of others in handling a communication, he has actually placed himself in their hands.

Obtaining Sufficient Correct Information

Each of these problems and stratagems incidental to the receiving of a communication by an administrator is of significance in the practical world of business, but there is probably one reception problem and set of corresponding solutions which concern many contemporary business administrators more than all the rest. It is that of getting sufficient correct information. Various factors and developments account for this. Companies and departments are larger than ever before and, with their expanding areas of activity, they present a subject about which there is so much more to know. Their organizational structure tends to grow broader and more intricate, and the administrator finds himself further and further from sources of information. He is also increasingly at the mercy of the ever more numerous intermediaries in communication channels. The leadership pattern affects the amount and kind of message content. Subordinate officials tend more or less to be leader centered and, hence, to reflect in their communications what they believe he wants or what they think makes them appear most favorable.[43] Inferiors are better educated, more economically secure, and bolder in their new found sense of social equality, and so they often do not feel constrained to report to their administrator. Fellow administrators are frequently caught up in the competitive battle for personal advancement, and, therefore, they often keep their knowledge away from their colleague or misinform him. Superiors grow more distant not only with the expansion in the size of the business but also with the development of a class of professional managers.

What can the administrator do to assure his coming into possession of enough true information about matters of organizational import? One general rule points the way to substantial assurance of being properly informed. It is for the administrator to locate himself or trusted associates at the bottleneck or bottlenecks through which the most pertinent information flows and which are least security-minded. This task varies greatly in nature and difficulty. In some instances, it will be primarily one of establishing social contact, superficial friendship, or political alliance with a confiding executive, chatty secretary, or eager-to-please supernumerary. At times, it may be a much harder thing to do and require the administrator to prove his ability to work industriously, fast and intelligently, so that he will be noticed by his superiors and appointed to projects and positions in leaky bottleneck locations. The gist of the *law of informational location* is that the administrator who wants to know more of organizational matters may, with hope of good results, search out and locate himself in the right organizational spots. This implies a perfectly honorable course of action, provided he resorts to neither bribery nor other unethical coercion to locate himself.

Conclusion

The length of this chapter suggests the dimensions of the topic of communication. Without fear of overstatement, communication can be described as one of the most significant and complex aspects of contemporary business administration. The transmission and reception of ideas is the life blood of management, and without these communication activities no company or department can be made to function. Business organizations are basically groups of people associated together in the pursuit of special tasks, each of which is expected to contribute something to the attainment of the organizational goals. When every individual member of the company or department is seen as a specialist and when every sub-group is likewise so regarded, the overwhelming significance of communication is evident. They must communicate in order to coordinate and integrate their thought and activity toward the common objectives.

Communication is much more, however, than an organizational necessity which in its imperativeness will more or less naturally take care of itself. It is rather a task that requires the most politic approach and the most skilled methodology. Hence, it must be analyzed as to its essential nature; then, in terms of the dynamics of the particular situation demanding communication, the media and mechanics of properly undertaking the task are to be chosen and implemented.

Commonly, administrators and students of administration, especially in the field of business, overlook the role of the executive as a recipient of communications. Their point of reference seems to be primarily that of the transmitter. The administrator who would use to the full the strategic possibilities of his position should not make this mistake. If he does, he is missing a real opportunity to improve his administrative performance and incidentally advance his own interests. Much influence and control can be exerted through reception stratagems.

BUSINESS SITUATIONS FOR ROLE-PLAYING

SITUATION XIV

Communication: The Indispensable Nexus

THE PRONTEX COMPANY

A. Scene.

A medium size job manufacturer of plastic items. The Office of the Plant Manager who is in conference with the Production Control Manager and the Chief Inspector.

B. Players.

1. Plant Manager: Mr. Thomas Q. Smith, an able, alert and industrious executive, whose present main concern is getting the wheels oiled in preparation for an expected large job.

2. Production Control Manager: Mr. William Z. Jones, a hard-driving man in a demanding job, who is almost obsessed with getting those "____" orders out the back door.

3. Chief Inspector: Mr. John X Brown, capable and technically well suited for his position, but

more concerned with quality than shipments and delivery schedules.

Situation.

1. All three men are company-minded and normal cooperation prevails among them, except for some needling by Mr. Brown to the effect that Production Control does not allow for adequate inspection, and by Mr. Jones that over-inspection is the normal procedure.

2. Recently too many shipments that were to have been rushed have been late because of delay in the Inspection Department, by which they were not given warranted priority over regular production. Extra efforts throughout the plant have been negated by this failure. Mr. Smith feels that there is a communication breakdown involved.

3. Since demand for fast deliveries is expected to grow more common, a satisfactory means of communication must be established before the situation becomes critical.

Assignment.

1. Assign individuals to fill the roles of the three characters and establish a method to resolve the situation.

2. Require the group, by prior assignments, to submit typical forms which might be used as part of the solution.

3. Have the group criticize the solution evolved by the players and the forms submitted. If time does not permit both, choose a few of the forms after the group session and introduce them at the next meeting.

NOTES

1. For a succinct but comprehensive view of the nature of communication, see EUGENE L. HARTLEY and RUTH E. HARTLEY, *Fundamentals of Social Psychology* (New York: Alfred A. Knopf, 1959), pp. 16-35.

2. *A New English Dictionary of Historical Principles* (Oxford: Clarendon Press, 1901), V, p. 17 (I).
3. The complexity of the administrative communication process is suggested by Redfield who identifies five elements in it: a communicator, an act of transmission, a message, a communicatee, and a response. CHARLES E. REDFIELD, *Communication in Management: The Theory and Practice of Administrative Communications* (Rev. ed.; Chicago: University of Chicago Press, 1958), p. 5.
4. HARTLEY and HARTLEY, *op. cit.*, p. 31.
5. However, there seems to be a tendency in some recent literature on business communication to define the process of communication in terms of its success. For example, Merrihue apparently defines communication as it *should be practiced* in business. He writes, "In this context, communication may perhaps best be defined as 'any initiated behavior on the part of the sender which conveys the desired meaning to the receiver and causes desired response behavior from the receiver.'" WILLARD V. MERRIHUE, *Managing by Communication* (New York: McGraw-Hill Book Company, Inc. 1960), p. 16.
6. HAROLD J. LEAVITT, *Managerial Psychology* (Chicago: University of Chicago Press, 1958), pp. 120-126.
7. The terms "audio, audio-visual, and visual" appear to have two divergent meanings in the semantics of communication. Some authors use them to designate respectively the three broad classifications into which they place all communication media; others apply the terms more narrowly, as do the authors, to mean devices such as music, sound film strips, and graphic material that appeal specifically to the ear and eye.
8. ROBERT DUBIN, *The World of Work: Industrial Society and Human Relations* (Englewood Cliffs, N.J.: Prentice-Hall, Inc., © 1958), p. 336.
9. Hartley and Hartley add another element to the concept of involuntary communication. They insist that the reaction it invokes must be congruent with the state of the individual being observed, else no communication of any type has taken place. HARTLEY and HARTLEY, *op. cit.*, p. 33.
10. Fitzgerald puts the problem of selection very clearly. STEPHEN E. FITZGERALD, *Communicating Ideas to the Public* (New York: Funk & Wagnalls Company, 1950), pp. 91-92, as quoted in Redfield, *op. cit.*, p. 70.
11. REDFIELD, *op. cit.*, p. 71.

12. "The importance of communication is not confined to the individual. It is the force that enables groups to cohere. In interpersonal relations it performs functions similar to those of cement, mortar, glue, or the charges of a magnetic field. Not only do small informal associations depend upon it for their continued existence, but every formal organization, every industrial unit, every governmental body functions effectively only when it communicates with ease and facility." Hartley and Hartley, *op. cit.*, p. 23.

13. Redfield recognizes this fact when he writes, "The same message will be received or responded to differently by different individuals and groups at different times. Even in an emergency one dare not overlook the situational and technical aspects of timing." *Op. cit.*, p. 38.

14. Merrihue, *op. cit.*, p. 241; Sune Carlson, *Executive Behavior* (Stockholm: Strombergs, 1951), pp. 77-93.

15. Suggested by Redfield, *op. cit.*, p. 36.

16. In his comments on avoiding some of the common barriers to communication, Jones manifests a strong interest in accuracy. Manley Howe Jones, *Executive Decision Making* (Homewood, Ill.: Richard D. Irwin, Inc., 1957), pp. 181-189.

17. *Ibid.*, pp. 186-187.

18. The importance of considering emotions is advanced by Roethlisberger who, however, emphasizes the term "sentiment." F. J. Roethlisberger, *Management and Morale* (Cambridge, Mass.: Harvard University Press, 1946), pp. 104-108.

19. "Ten Rules for Clear English" are set down by R. W. Bell, "Form, Style and Expression" in Cecil Chisholm (ed.), *Communication in Industry* (London: Business Publications, Ltd. in association with B. T. Botsford, Ltd., 1955), pp. 88-91.

20. For an exposition of this plain talk view, see Rudolf Flesch, *The Art of Plain Talk* (New York: Harper & Brothers, Publishers, 1946); and *The Art of Readable Writing* (New York: Harper & Brothers, Publishers, 1949).

21. William H. Whyte, Jr., and the Editors of Fortune, *Is Anybody Listening?* (New York: Simon and Schuster, Inc., 1952), p. 79.

22. *Ibid.*, p. 80.

23. The subject of listening is discussed in Lynde C. Steckle, *The Man in Management* (Harper & Brothers, Publishers, 1958), pp. 70-82; and in Roethlisberger, *op. cit.*, pp. 101-102, 107.

24. Bakke defines the communication route as ". . . the line of persons within the organization through whom it passes either in process of elaboration from its origin or in the process of transmission from initiator to recipient." By elaboration he means making the message going upward more generalized and the message going downward more particularized. E. WIGHT BAKKE, *Bonds of Organization* (New York: Harper & Brothers, Publishers, 1950), p. 81.

25. Redfield identifies these three possible directions of communication. *Op. cit.*, pp. 18-36.

26. For a succinct comment on the filtering barrier in the communication process, see RENSIS LIKERT, "A Motivational Approach to a Modified Theory of Organization and Management" in MASON HAIRE (ed.), *Modern Organization Theory* (New York: John Wiley & Sons, Inc., 1959), p. 195.

27. "Official communication in the organization generally follows the flow of organization authority." DUBIN, *op. cit.*, p. 339.

28. Some hints for using the grapevine are contained in KEITH DAVIS, "Making Constructive Use of the Grapevine" in FREMONT A. SHULL, JR., *Selected Readings in Management* (Homewood, Ill.: Richard D. Irwin, Inc., 1958), pp. 297-306.

29. Merrihue gives a review of the oral and written categories of communication. *Op. cit.*, pp. 164-193.

30. "Face-to-face communication is most often a matter of informal contact while the work is in progress." LOUIS A. ALLEN, *Management and Organization* (New York: McGraw-Hill Book Company, Inc., 1958), p. 144.

31. However, there seems to be a degree of "natural" secrecy in companies. "There is always an inherent tendency in the organization toward a barrier of secrecy created, at the outset, by formal organization and/or directive leadership and/or management controls. This tendency is reinforced by pseudo-human relations and communication programs." CHRIS ARGYRIS, *Personality and Organization* (New York: Harper & Brothers, Publishers, 1957), p. 158.

32. Suggested by JOHN G. GLOVER, *Fundamentals of Professional Management* (Rev. ed.: New York: Simmons-Boardman Publishing Corp., 1958), pp. 166-167.

33. The authors are aware of the fact that the use of fear in motivation is commonly frowned upon. They see it, however, as a legitimate expression of the antithesis of reward. Certainly fear is used widely as an incentive on all employment levels, down to the lowest. Whyte holds that piece

rates find their support in the reward-punishment theory of motivation. WILLIAM FOOTE WHYTE, *Money and Motivation* (New York: Harper & Brothers, Publishers, 1955), p. 194.

A treatment of the feeling of uncertainty, anxiety and apprehension that may beset the executive in his central position is given by EUGENE EMERSON JENNINGS, *The Executive: Autocrat, Bureaucrat, Democrat* (New York: Harper & Row, Publishers, 1962), pp. 235-66. Interestingly, he terms his chapter on the subject "Neurocrat and the Flexible Executive."

34. MARY PARKER FOLLETT, "The Giving of Orders" in HENRY C. METCALF and L. URWICK (eds.), *Dynamic Administration: The Collected Papers of Mary Parker Follett* (New York: Harper & Brothers, Publishers, 1940), p. 57.

35. JOHN M. PFIFFNER and FRANK P. SHERWOOD, *Administrative Organization* (Englewood Cliffs, N.J.: Prentice-Hall, Inc., 1960), p. 297.

36. *Ibid.*, p. 297; LEAVITT, *op. cit.*, pp. 119-121.

37. PFIFFNER and SHERWOOD, *op. cit.*, p. 298.

38. *Ibid.*, pp. 298-299.

39. HARTLEY and HARTLEY, *op. cit.*, p. 30.

40. PFIFFNER and SHERWOOD, *op. cit.*, p. 299.

41. ROBERT K. MERTON, *Social Theory and Social Structure* (Rev. ed.; Glencoe, Ill.: The Free Press, 1957), p. 320.

42. An interesting comment on the choice of sources of information is found in MASON HAIRE, *Psychology in Management* (New York: McGraw-Hill Book Company, Inc., 1956), pp. 78-84.

Regardless of what particular sources of information the administrator selects, he would be wise to pay attention to the advice of Allen who asserts, "Information will be most meaningful if each manager is provided with data that apply specifically to his own accountability." LOUIS A. ALLEN, *The Management Profession* (New York: McGraw-Hill Book Company, 1964), p. 335.

43. In his treatment of the dependence of supervisors upon the leader, Argyris too lends support to this view. CHRIS ARGYRIS, *Executive Leadership* (Harper & Brothers, Publishers, 1953), pp. 46-48.

CHAPTER 15

Luck: A Variable in Success

> "The belief in luck is an ancient faith of all peoples. Generally it has been a trust in something mystical; fortune has been seen as a gift or a burden, as it were, from the gods. In a modern objective analysis of human behavior, luck signifies circumstances which are recognized as or believed to be uncontrollable and, in fact, circumstances that are often unexpected. Luck cannot be overlooked in a discussion of administrative strategy since it is often a determinant of decision and action."

ONE OF THE BEST illustrated truths of human behavior is that man is not completely the master of his own course. With respect to matters high or low, each individual is compelled or overwhelmingly induced at times to surrender himself to circumstances beyond his control or which he believes to be so. He is the occasional beneficiary or victim of fortune.[1]

The terms "fortune" and "luck" signify one and the same factor. The essence of the meaning is uncontrollable circumstance. In current American parlance, it seems that luck is the more commonly used term, possessing a somewhat less mystical connotation. But each term is quite appropriate and signifies *circumstance or circumstances beyond the control of the individual or group concerned, or considered by these entities to be beyond his or its control.*

Luck is not to be confused with opportunity, which is nothing more or less than a situation that can be used to advantage. Such a situation can be ignored, utilized partially, or fully exploited. Even more, it can be in part or whole the product of the very individual or group to whom it is pertinent, that is, it can be made. But always in luck there is found the element of gratuity and even more of outside thrust—for luck is circumstance, to a degree, forced upon the individual or the group. Good or bad, it is something which just happens. This does not deny that good luck can come in the form of opportunity—a shape in which it frequently appears.

The Significance of Luck

To be certain, not all luck is strongly impelling. Good fortune may appear merely as opportunity; and ill fortune, as a stumbling block or problem. In fact, the element of luck may be so unpretentious in making itself known that the leader may fail to sense or recognize it. Perhaps he is too busy or by nature and training not sufficiently sensitive.

Yet, regardless of the force with which it makes itself known, luck is a real factor in shaping the success or failure of the administrator. He can sometimes ignore it, but he can never eliminate it. The frame of reference in which he, as the leader, lives and operates contains so many determinative influnces, singly and in combination with each other, that he is, in a sense, helpless before some of them. It is impossible for him to operate as a completely independent agent. Luck will catch him sooner or later.[2]

As a matter of reality, the administrator within the organizational milieu is probably more subject to luck, or at least will experience it more, than the non-leader, because the work of leadership extends the field for decision and action and because, as a more dynamic endeavor, it introduces additional variables. Although the leader is not to be seen as a creature of fate, helplessly buffeted this way and that by the caprices of life, yet it is true that the accident of luck—good and bad—is more likely to happen to him.

It is impossible, in view of the everpresent possibility of luck, to rule out fortune as a component in leadership. Unfortunately, the science and art of administration give little place in their literature to a consideration of this factor. The truth is that scholarly research and productivity in the field of management, through its preoccupation with structured and the structuring of situations, has de facto discouraged consideration of luck.

Luck, an Overlooked Factor in Leadership

The specific reasons for the literary neglect of fortune as a factor in leadership are several in number. The first finds its genesis in the importance that the free enterprise philosophy has placed upon industriousness and the other personal virtues which make it possible for an individual to get ahead. The prevailing attitude in the relatively free economy characteristic of much of the Western World since the Industrial Revolution has been that success demands initiative, hardwork, and thrift. So strongly entrenched has been this rationale that such a gratuitous thing as luck has been considered, if not almost an immoral expectation, at least something sought or depended upon only by leaders of the more romantic or speculative breed.

Luck has also been the victim of the appearance of scientific management. As organizations grew larger and more complex in the last one-half of the nineteenth century and the first years of the twentieth, students of management and managers themselves, particularly in the field of business and industry, energetically revolted against the hit and miss, somewhat too intuitive management which had sufficed for so many years in administration of simpler organizations and activities. Once having glimpsed the possibilities of objective judgment based on fact, these individuals, whose historical task it was to carry forth the development of administration as a science and art, tended to disregard "mere luck" as something unworthy of their mission. The significance of fortune was lost in the adoration of fact. Here then is a second reason for the scant attention given luck in literature on administration and decision making.

Closely allied to its loss in the hypnosis of scientific management is still another depressant helping to keep fortune obscured in the study of and publications on leadership. This factor is the immeasurability of luck. In a day and age of growing dependence on and allegiance to quantitative methodology this attribute is well nigh fatal. Fortune is frequently unpredictable as to occurrence, often incapable of translation into figures, and not uncommonly a rather nebulous and slippery phenomenon. It is not of the substance upon which mathematics, formula, and computers can feed. Not being grist for their mill, it is, in practice, too often disregarded by their devotees.

A final reason for the insignificant place assigned to luck in the study of administration and decision making is found in the hero complex that is inevitable to leadership thinking either by leaders themselves or by analysts of leadership. The hero is one who performs unique acts or ordinary acts in a unique manner. Leaders are prone sooner or later to see themselves as unusual performers—doing great deeds or not-so-great deeds in a great fashion, even though many of their decisions and actions actually are trivial or usual in essence and manner.[3] Commonly they attribute what they consider to be their outstanding performance to their own virtues and come to regard themselves as heroes more or less. Students of leadership tend, it seems, to fall into the same cult of self-approval through identification with their subject.

Neither the leader nor the analysts can be expected, therefore, to attribute much of success in leadership to what they are tempted to class as "blind chance." To give fortune its due somehow limits the possibility of self-acclaim and undercuts the formation and maintenance of the hero image endemic in leadership.

Sources of Luck

A treatment of luck and the role it plays in administration demands, in the beginning, a consideration of the sources of fortune. The significance of an examination of these sources far transcends the mere servicing of academic completeness. To know the sources of good fortune should prove an important strategic asset to the leader, helping him, in deciding or acting, to place and time his choice of alternatives so as to draw upon fortuitous knowledge, facilities, and/or support. To be aware of the sources of ill fortune ought prove also a valuable strategic asset; it should enable the administrator at least to reduce the possibility of negative variables influencing his manner of decision and action as well as the alternative chosen.

The Necessity for Decision

For the administrator, who is constantly identified throughout this book as a leader, a prime source of fortune is the necessity for decision. The pressure which this necessity exerts on him provides gratuitous motivation—or at least a gratuitous incentive—for him to decide or to get otherwise involved in the problem. To be certain, this motivation may turn out to be ill luck if it leads him to undertake a decision which is not properly his, to make an unwise decision, or to reach a decision in an impolitic manner. Yet, the administrator will not be likely to enjoy the possible fruits of good fortune inherent in a decision demanding situation itself unless he makes some commitment to it, even if this commitment be nothing more than a degree of association with the situation and/or the process of deciding. After all, luck generally shines most brightly on him who seizes opportunity or lingers in its shadow.

Good luck in the form of gratuitous motivation to participate in the solution of some problem from which gain to the individual and/or his organization may flow often appears first as something unpleasant. From the point of view of the individual, this is well illustrated in the case of the young sales executive with growing family responsibilities who, because of inexperience in selling or employment with the wrong company, is not making a sufficient income to meet his financial obligations. Compelled by dire economic necessity, he decides to seek more remunerative employment and, perhaps in real discouragement and even fear, he resigns his position and obtains another which turns out to be much more rewarding in compensation. So often do circumstances demand the cutting of ties that it is common for successful men to make some such remark as "The best thing that ever happened to me was to be forced to leave *that* job" or "To drop *that* line of products was the smartest thing the company ever did."

Random Matching

It sometimes happens, whether by the design of a kind Providence or by chance itself, that a given situation falling under the jurisdiction of a particular administrator will contain requirements which this individual through his own and/or organization's capacities is peculiarly well able to meet. The fortuitous match of needs and means can bring results that will redound to the benefit of administrator and organization alike. Although the match is not always the result of chance, it is certain to be such at times because of the almost limitless combinations into which the variables of given complex of capabilities and problems group themselves or are grouped.

A hospital administrator is appointed to the presidency of a financially ailing small midwestern hospital. The needs of the institution are for imaginative and dynamic leadership by an individual committed to the practical concept that running a hospital is basically a business proposition. Moreover, the area from which the hospital can draw is one of some egalitarian attitude. In general, the population mix believes that all who want hospital treatment and can afford the cost should be allowed to have such care. Obviously, the situation which the new president faces is almost "tailor-made" for his promotional ability and bent. There is in this confrontation of task and administrator a most promising combination of problem and problem-solver.

Realism demands recognition of the fact that mismatch of situation requirements and administrative strengths may occur as often as the more favorable juxtaposition described above. When mismatch happens in a specific case, the results can be anything but positive to one or all concerned. Of course, the optimist may take the view that, in the longer run, the mismatch of problem and problem-solver can produce some good effects. Among these, he will mention, no doubt, a realization by the wise and conscientious mismatched administrator of the fact that he is not adequate to all tasks and that he must strengthen both his own capacity and/or his organizational resource base. If he is organizationally oriented, the optimist may also point out that the organization, observing the mismatch and perhaps suffering from the unsuccessful efforts of its administrator to handle the situation, may take steps to insulate itself against the type of situation its administration cannot handle or steps to strengthen its administrative capacity.

Nothing in the line of thought above on random matching as a source of luck—good or bad—is intended to deny the fact that the match of the problem and problem-solving capacity at a given place and time is often the result of objective analysis, or to disregard the fact that the mismatch of these variables at a given place and time is commonly the outcome of improper analysis. Considered decision and action is very frequently responsible for either success or failure in meeting a problem. The factor of luck here described is only that of randomness—the combining of needs and resources by circumstances beyond what is controllable or what the administrator and/or his organization believe controllable.

The ingredient of randomness may appear only as one determining element in the match or mismatch. The midwestern hospital certainly does canvass the field for the type of president it wants. The individual who accepted the presidency surely weighs the advantages and disadvantages of the position. Appointment and acceptance are conscious actions over which each party had control—and to this extent the good match of job and administrator is not the result of chance alone. But luck does enter the picture, for the regional feeling that all people should be eligible for hospital care is a circumstance beyond either the control of the hospital or of the president. And so here is seen luck as an influence in the successful match of need and resources, since the new president is imbued with the egalitarian health philosophy that holds for general hospital admission and treatment.

Association as a Source of Luck

Neither the organization, his department thereof, nor the administrator himself can choose all those with whom he associates. His life, and more specifically his administrative decisions and actions, will bring him into contacts which are not selected by his superiors or himself. If luck is properly definable as circumstance beyond the control of the individual or his organization—or considered to be beyond control by them—then it follows that these unselected contacts properly can be called sources of luck. The influences which they, singly or collectively, have upon the administrator and, through him, upon his entity are the significant manifestations of luck. If the influences further the purpose or welfare of the administrator, his organization, or both, they may be classified as good fortune; if they are unfriendly to this purpose or welfare, they may be considered as ill fortune.

These uncontrollable contacts—or contacts held to be uncontrollable—may have one or more of three types of influences on the administrator and/or the entity he represents. First, they may, by their attitude toward his own or his organization's image, views, services or products, add to his and so indirectly to his organization's vigor to promote them or determination to change them. To do this, the contacts must either endorse them or take a negative stand which, by its antagonizing of the administrator and even perhaps his superiors, confirms him or the "higher-ups" in commitment to these ends.

Illustrations are easy to conjure up. The manager of a business records division of a publishing house who has sponsored the production of new kinds of inventory control forms, in an effort to expand the market for them, is forced to canvass a number of stationery jobbers. These jobbers like the new forms and his explanation of their use, so they express great enthusiasm for them by placing sizable trial orders. The manager, reflecting this feeling, proceeds to obtain permission from his president to expand the production and to push the sale of the product.

A somewhat different example will serve to illustrate the fact that the influence of contacts may be the type of luck which strengthens the determination to change views, services, or products. A chemical company, interested in developing a deodorizing chemical for commercial busses and trucks, experiments with a jasmine scented product and attempts to sell it to several municipal transit commissions. The reaction of these first customers, who do buy some for trial, is so negative as to reinforce a somewhat vague feeling which the president of the chemical company long had entertained to the whole concept of motor exhaust deodorizing chemicals.

It should be borne in mind that the energizing effect of chance contacts on the leadership hierarchy, whether it be positive or negative, may prove to be in inverse relation to the echelon of organizational command it first strikes. The manager of the business records division, already having committed himself and considerable of the company's resources to the publication of the new inventory record forms, may be doubly motivated by the enthusiastic reception the initial sales effort meets. He not only feels himself proud in his own decision and action but is also anxious to show himself justified to his superiors. The president of the chemical company, being the top executive, may not be quite so concerned over the reaction to the deodorizer—even though it was negative. His power position may make him less sensitive to the success or failure of one corporate effort.

A second type of influence which chance contact with others may have upon the administrator is that of encouraging traumatic change in decision. In a sense, this effect could be classified as an extreme form of the invigorating or devigorating influence described in the paragraphs above. But it deserves its own categorization because of its definitely determinative role. A successful medical doctor, somewhat restricted in creative opportunity by his specialty, becomes lured into business by the substantial opportunities for social service—and monetary gain—to be had in the "nursing home" business. In his spare time, he investigates the field and purchases a somewhat run-down home which he believes can be operated to his satisfaction by some superficial repairs and a change of managerial staff. Shortly after he takes over the project, he is summoned by a representative of the county department of health, from whose office his lawyer has already obtained a license for the home. To his surprise, this county official insists on certain expensive repairs, amounting almost to the total reconstruction of the building. The doctor is so dejected by the specter of tremendous expense that he backs away from the whole concept of entering the nursing home field and quickly sells the nursing home he has purchased.

One of the more intriguing features of this traumatic influence is the fact that the administrator may never quite be certain as to whether it was good or bad luck. Generally, he is immediately so happy, or at least relieved, to have learned of the crucial fact or reaction from the contact that he becomes somewhat euphoristic. Then too, he may be either so ashamed of almost having made a mistake, or, if the contact supports the direction in which he is moving, so pleased with his own astuteness that he becomes rather subjective about the whole matter.

However, these first two influences of chance association, one corroboratory and the other traumatic, are directive in nature. They serve to steer the administrator and those whom he represents into a right or wrong path. There is quite a different form of lucky influence to be found in some chance associations. This third influence is in the nature of what may be termed "resource revelation." Someone met at a social affair, a politician or government official met at a civic function, a professional met at a convention, a banker met in a conference over company finances—uncontrolled contacts such as these and many more—may reveal ideas and resources to the administrator, especially the alert leader. A young college teacher of engineering, turned production consultant for a candy company, catches the eye of the chairman of the board of directors at a meeting of confection producers. He tells the highly placed official of his plans to develop a new extrusion machine, which so impresses the chairman that this individual expresses a personal interest in helping finance its development.

There is, it should be pointed out, at least one caution to be observed with respect to the resource revelation influence. Upon occasion, a chance contact, either not understanding what the administrator or his organization has in mind or being somewhat of a "professional big shot," may lead the administrator to believe that the idea is better than it really is in fact, that he—the contact—is really interested, that more financial aid than is actually available may be forthcoming, or other fallacious things. Unfortunate indeed is the person who is so seduced by one or more of these false impressions that he brings his associates or company to lend their support, financial or otherwise, on the hope that the outside contact is right and is willing to back the proposition. Colleagues and the organization have a way of not liking the administrator who raises costly false hopes.

Fads, Fashions and Secular Trends

A final source of luck can be lumped under the heading of fads, fashions, and secular trends. Of course, changes in demand for kind and for quantity of products and services, in this day and age of remarkably effective advertisement and sales promotion, are not always to be seen by the administrator, or even by his organization, as something which just happens. Certainly profit as well as non-profit organizations, through their educative efforts, do help determine what their publics desire.

Yet, to the executive of a department or total organization the market not infrequently appears, qualitatively and quantitatively, a fixed factor or a variable beyond significant influence, that is, a matter of fortune. It then becomes a market to be accepted or rejected. Many administrators, as for example, those in the highly profitable tool and die industry at the onslaught of World War II and those in booming non-profit activities, such as private colleges and universities under the GI privileges of post-World War II days, were most successful because of fortuitous markets for their organization's output. It cannot be denied that much success, particularly of leadership in a free enterprise society, can be attributed to demand conditions really beyond the control of the individual leader himself.

Actually, changes in demand, whether they be of a short run nature, such as that which proceeds from the appearance of fad, or of a longer run nature, such as that which comes from style or secular change, may also prove to be bad luck. This is generally due to the fact that the leader and his organization have pledged their resources to a previous fad, style, or secular change and cannot liquidate them fast or adequately enough, or obtain other resources sufficient to meet the new human vagary in demand. Hence, it is extremely important for organizational leadership to keep a weather eye out for an uncontrollable or apparently uncontrollable change in demand for its services or products and also develop financial resources or possible support against the time when a changing or changed market will demand new or more production.

Changes in fads, styles, and long time trends also take place in the field of science and technology. Here is an area in which luck can play a truly awesome role in determining the success or failure of organizational leadership. Often in the initial stages of such changes, the knowledge of the new discoveries and inventions concerned is a closely guarded secret or at least a fact recognized by few. As a result of this condition, the leader, whether his entity be in the public or private sector of society, can be building himself the basis for great achievement if he is in "on the know" or digging his grave, as it were, if he is not. The unexpected and stupendous World War II success of the German army and airforce with its mobile warfare, to which French military and political leadership had been deaf, is a dramatic example of what can happen to public fortune as a result of a change in science and technology. The collapse of the whole family of horse drawn vehicle industries in the United States as a result of the development of the horseless carriages is an illustration in the private sector of what can occur when the market changes, particularly in the proportions of a long run trend, and when leadership fails to appreciate a revolution in science and technology.

Living with and Using Luck

That luck exists in the form of circumstances which cannot be controlled or which they believe uncontrollable is an established fact and a reality which all administrators must face. Yet there seems to be no precise formula, even in this time of devotion to mathematics and the electronic computer, for living with fortune peaceably and for using it to advantage. About all that the administrator can do is to consider luck as a capricious friend and foe and to take a stance which will permit him to treat it as such.

A reasonable stance for the administrator to assume with respect to luck would appear to have at least five features. No one of these attributes is exclusive of the others, but they can be identified best by individual treatment.

Sensitivity to Environment

The strategic administrator who would live most comfortably with luck and get the most out of it should adopt as the first feature of his stance a keen sensitivity to his environment. The reason is manifest. The circumstance or circumstances which constitute luck emanate from some phase of the leader's environment. To know this environment, then, is to have a better chance of anticipating fortune or at least of noting early its twistings and turnings.

The task of remaining sensitive to environment is not a simple one. After all, a given administrator's environment generally consists of several different publics (groups oriented toward him), geographical areas, time periods, and socio-politico-economic situations. Moreover, he is often so taken up or harassed by the ordinary tasks and day to day problems of management that he has but limited time, energy, and imagination to use in studying and analyzing the many different environmental segments out of which changes in luck may come.

Yet there is a minimum assurance of sensitivity which he must maintain or run the risk of suffering unduly from uncontrollable—and often unexpected—circumstance. To maintain this assurance, at least four steps are necessary. One is to establish and keep operative good communication channels within the organization.[4] These channels should not only provide the administrator with the knowledge of uncontrollable change taking place within the organization but they also should serve to give him an indirect ear to the outside world, since some of what his subordinates, colleagues, and superiors learn of lucky or unlucky conditions in the outside world, will get up to him via these channels in the form of queries, complaints, reactions, reports, and the like.

Another step which the administrator must take to assure himself of minimum sensitivity to environment is to pay attention to what the various media of public communication are saying. In practice, this means to read widely in newspapers, periodicals—trade, professional and general, and pertinent books; and to listen to significant radio and television releases. The shadow of coming fortune as it may affect the administrator often casts itself ahead via public pronouncement, exposition, and comment.

A third step to keep in tune with environmental sectors out of which fortune may lunge is to move about personally in the places, during the times, and on the levels at which it is most likely to incubate. Personal acquaintance with influential people, on-the-ground observation of action underway, and first hand knowledge of problems and critical points can do much to arm the administrator to seize good fortune and buffet ill.

Finally, in those cases in which the environment is too remote or involved for the administrator to assay, in view of his time, energy and mental capacity to do so, he should resort to the use of advisors or advisory services. These exist in all fields of administration: business and industry, politics and government, education, defense, social service, and religion. The important rule to follow in choosing professional advice or a professional advisor is to learn its or his relative competence and peculiar prejudice. It is prudent for the administrator to assume that no advisor has the capacity to note, analyze, and communicate any environmental sector perfectly and without interjecting his own feelings and opinions.

Willingness to Take Unusual Risk

The willingness to take risks is a *sine qua non* of dynamic leadership, and another feature of a sensible stance toward luck. It obviously requires courage since the possibility of failure is often present in undertaking any task whose outcome depends upon human decision and limited resources. But to use luck, or even to insulate himself and his organization against it, may demand more than usual bravery on the part of the administrator. After all, the favorable or unfavorable circumstance which constitutes the parcel of fortune the administrator now faces may have fallen into his hands unexpectedly; it may be of a strange nature; and it may require for its exploitation or in the defense against it personal capacities and organizational treasures which the administrator may not possess or have available quickly or in sufficient quantity and quality. The danger in handling his luck, good or bad, may be greater, therefore, than the risk in administering the more ordinary problem that the administrator faces in his managerial routine.

From what sources shall he draw the courage necessary to undertake this additional risk? He should take stock of himself and his organizational connection. This is plain common sense, for his inventory well may reveal his power position to be greater than he believed in the first shock of worry or fear over "his luck." But of equal import to the generation of courage should be his hard-headed realization that it is necessary to take some chances in order to move himself and his entity toward desired goals. To feel that victory, more often than not, goes to the bold is a source of courage.

The Flexible Feature

A still further feature of the reasonable stance which the administrator should take toward luck is that of flexibility. Since luck is to be seen as something which cannot be controlled and which is frequently unexpected, at least in its specific form, it behooves the intelligent administrator so to position himself and resources as to be able to change the direction and intensity of his commitments. With respect to self, the matter is basically one of attitude. He should realize that events beyond his control, and often unanticipated, will occur. He should look upon them as inevitable for all practical purposes and be willing to change his goals, policies, and practices to save himself and his entity from the greatest harm and to gain the greatest advantage.

Above all else, this freewheeling frame of mind demands that the leader not take himself and that which he desires and does too seriously. Hypnosis with one's self as a hero, entrancement with one's goals as almost preordained objectives, and a love affair with one's policies and practices are most unfriendly to that leadership flexibility which the administrator must have if he is to synchronize his direction of self and organization with the ebb and flow of his fortune.

One of the finest cases in point of the inflexible stance and the consequent incapacity to take fortune by the forelock is to be seen in the automobile industry of the pre-1920 decade and early years of that decade. This industry was diffused among many producers. A substantial number were making and attempting to market huge cars. When smaller cars became practical with the development of more efficient engines and better designed bodies, the leadership of many of the companies making big automobiles was not able to change its views on the matter. Their eventual failure must have been due in appreciable degree to the refusal to change with the times. By the same token, the monumental achievements of the Ford Motor Company, the General Motors Corporation, and the Chrysler Corporation are undoubtedly to be attributed in part to the open-mindedness of their leadership with respect to change-dictating forces conceived to be beyond control.

Still, the flexibility necessary to withstand and utilize shifts in fortune requires more than objective attitude. It presupposes the capacity to withdraw and/or to commit resources as the tide changes. On the large and successful corporate level, this need is rather well met by the ability to tap the money market via stocks, bonds, short term securities, bank borrowing, and mercantile credit. But small businesses and especially new small concerns, as well as non-profit organizations, not uncommonly find it difficult, if not impossible, to maintain financial freedom as an ingredient of the over-all managerial flexibility necessary to deal with luck. It is well, therefore, for the administration of such organizations to have careful long-range financial planning, to protect credit ratings prudently, and to keep current operations on a sound financial basis. This practice is uniquely essential for all organizations of relatively low financial strength, since sources of finances for them tend to dry up in an almost geometric progression once such entities get into a financial bind. Not being financial "Rocks of Gibralter" to begin with, they are doubly suspect as investment and credit risks when fortune turns against them. Sadly enough, all too commonly the administrators of such organizations, enthusiastic over success for a period, tend to get careless financially. This tendency is especially true during the economic boom which, for many a leader and his entity, is the supreme lucky circumstance. A lurking tragedy can lie, as he may forget, in a subsequent economic recession—itself also a matter of fortune.

Maintenance of an Avenue of Retreat

Closely associated with the attribute of flexibility is the fourth feature of the proper leadership stance with respect to luck. It may be described as the maintenance of an avenue of retreat and was, in fact, strongly implied in the discussion of flexibility above. The strategic administrator will realize that retreat is a valuable device of leadership. He will understand that often it connotes intelligent decision and action and not fear or cowardliness; that in fact retreat, whether as a result of ill luck or considered administrative decision, may be a piece of truly strategic leadership.[5]

The strategic administrator uses retreat for two purposes, as far as luck is concerned. He resorts to it to conserve resource strength, and so he retreats in the form of curtailing expenditure in a certain direction, cutting back on total production volume or on output of a specific item, closing down a plant, or taking any of a numerous list of essential economy movements. He also utilizes retreat to gain time to estimate the new situation apparently being created by circumstances he believes or knows to be beyond his direction, and to gain time to regroup his and/or the organization's energy and other resources. It is during retreat for either or both of these purposes that good public relations become an extreme necessity in order to prevent, as far as possible, the development among one or more of the "publics" interested the impression that something is seriously wrong. Indeed, there are on record many cases in which clever public relations have made even forced retreat appear as a truly wise move of a dynamic, forward moving organization.

Development of Reputation as a Winner

A "political" attribute rounds out the quintet of features that comprises for the administrator a good stance toward luck. Since luck can play such havoc with the image of an administrator and, consequently, with the moral and material support he receives, it seems politic for him to develop his image as that of a winner. The possession of the winner's image will give him a "supply of support" that may enable him to withstand serious buffeting by fate. The publics who matter to him will be less inclined to desert him for some bad luck he suffers, believing that this is more or less an isolated incident and that the administrator, who generally conquers all obstacles, will come back strongly to master the onslaught of fortune.

It is not the function of this analysis to dissect the techniques by which an administrator makes himself appear a winner to his subordinates, colleagues, superiors, customers, clients, and other publics. But the temptation to emphasize one or two valuable guiding tenets is too strong to resist.

One is that the administrator should only rarely attempt to do that which he is unlikely to accomplish. More positively stated, the principle is that a leader should devote his energies to attempting rather surely possible tasks. Adherence to this common-sense rule of administration will make the leader seem to be one who succeeds almost always. To be certain, the rule is not an easy one to follow. Many parties, including subordinates, will press the administrator to undertake courses not likely to succeed. This pressure is often due to their ignorance of facts and to their belief that they will gain by the leader's more daring approach.

Another technique by which the winner image is created and maintained is really a phase of the first. It is restraint in asking superiors for things which superiors probably will not give and to confine upward bound petitions to requesting things which superiors are known to be willing to grant. The contribution of this technique to the winner image is in the form of identifying the administrator as a favored sub-leader. When bad luck comes to him, his department, the whole organization, and his followers will tend to have more faith in him than would otherwise be the case.

Is There a Lucky Leader?

Often it is heard said that a certain Mr. Morris is a lucky businessman, that the Reverend Reed is a lucky clergyman, that General Green is a lucky commander, and that Senator Simmons is a lucky politician. What really is meant by these popular classifications? One may assume with confidence the implication usually to be that these gentlemen are successful in most of the things, or at least the big things, they undertake, and that somehow they are so because of some special, almost mystical, quality which they possess.

The scientific essence of the query "Is there a lucky leader?" goes beyond this popular implication. It raises the issue as to whether or not some individuals—in this case leaders—enjoy an unusual amount of favorable gratuitous circumstances in their leadership.

Proof of the Lucky Leader's Existence

The conclusion that there are lucky leaders in the sense described seems tenable. A number of deductive arguments can be advanced in support of it. One is the statistical probability that favorable circumstances can multiply at one time and one situs and that the leader who holds the pertinent administrative seat at that time and place can be the recipient of them and their beneficial influence. In popular jargon, lightning does strike twice in the same place.

Another deductive support proceeds from the phenomenon of individual differences among people and continues with the reasoning that, since some are more alert and imaginative than others, they will be able to recognize and enjoy good fortune the more.

A final deductive underpinning of the view that there are lucky individuals is to be found in the thought that, since some leaders move about more than others—geographically, socially, and in areas of attention—they are more likely than others to be present at times and locales when circumstances are more favorable to them and their purposes.

An objection may be raised to the last argument along the line that it denies the previous "concentration of favorable circumstances" conclusion. However, there is nothing incompatible in holding to both conclusions. The fact that favorable circumstances—uncontrollable and sometimes unanticipated—tend to fall repeatedly on a particular leader in a particular organization does not mean that such circumstances cannot also follow an individual as he progresses from period of time to period of time and from place to place. In fact, some good inductive evidence seems to prove compatibility. Various leaders stay in a given organizational frame of reference and fortuitous and gratuitous circumstance after circumstance present themselves to them; whereas other leaders change positions often and are repeatedly blessed by such circumstances.

It probably is, in truth, quite impossible inductively to establish or deny the view that lucky leaders exist. An insurmountable obstacle appears in the form of the objective judgments which would be required before the counting process could proceed. Among these would be the value judgment as to what constitutes a good luck leader in terms of what really has been good for him and his organization, and the factual assignment of the proportions of the good results he has enjoyed among the two categories of the factors responsible for them: considered decision and action and conditions seen or assumed to be uncontrollable.

The Manufacture of Luck

Eminently successful administrators are sometimes heard to remark that they make or have created their own luck. By definition, this is an impossible accomplishment if luck is defined as uncontrollable circumstance or circumstance estimated to be beyond control. However, in a certain sense, the leader can make his own luck. This process involves the exertion by him of determinative influence on the sources of fortune. He may so administer his organization or conduct himself as to enhance or diminish the necessity for decision; by remaining in a given environment or by moving, he may increase or decrease his chances of getting a desired need and resource matching, although to the extent that he succeeds in so doing he eliminates a degree of randomness; he may change his pattern of association at least to insure more contacts with people who "think creatively and make things happen"; and, of course, by his own direct or indirect action, if its influence is great enough, he can help change fads and fashions and even to start and energize long-term change.

But the administrator who tries to make his own luck should bear in mind the significance of defining for himself, if not his organization, his own objectives in so doing. It is not—one may presume in most cases—just more uncontrolled circumstance or circumstances he seeks, but rather a particular type of fortune. "The wisest managers are aware that the rules of luck are almost as rigid as the rules of logic. Purposeful men . . . take chances, but always with a goal before them." [6]

The Wisdom of Assuming the Lucky Leader's Existence

As far as organizational welfare is concerned, it is probably wise to believe that there are lucky leaders. Superiors could do well, for a number of reasons, to attempt to employ good luck individuals as administrators. If there actually are administrators upon whom fortune shines, their appointment, *ceteris paribus*, obviously can be to the gain of the organization. If the appointing authority believes there to be such individuals and hires them as administrators, even though there are no such individuals as lucky people, advantage can accrue to the organization since this authority may place greater confidence in them and give them a larger measure of freedom to exercise their own unique capacities. If the lucky individuals are merely the successful ones, then the appointment of them to administrative posts can be wise for the organization because the traits that helped them succeed before may contribute to their success in the new positions. Inspired by *Pascal*, superiors should remember that "We do not know whether or not there are those upon whom Fortune smiles, but it is well, in choosing leaders, to act as if there are such people."

The Ill-Starred Leader

One occasionally is led to observe that a certain administrator is just plain unlucky. This view can be erroneous if it is the categorical identification of the simply unsuccessful official, particularly the grossly or continuingly unsuccessful, as being the victim of bad fortune. Or it can be correct if the line of deductive reasoning as presented to substantiate the existence of the good leader is true. Certainly, if the contention that probability can work to concentrate favorable uncontrollable circumstances is sound, then it is equally tenable to hold that probability can work to concentrate unfavorable circumstances of an uncontrollable nature. Certainly too, individual differences, just as they can produce some individuals more alert and imaginative, can produce other individuals too dull to sense an opportunity or danger thrust upon them. And then, of course, while various leaders move about and, in effect, find luck, others remain stationary and are not present when fortune smiles or, moving about, manage somehow to be on the scene repeatedly when it frowns.

It would appear good judgment not to select individuals known or seen to be unlucky for appointment to positions of leadership.[7] Whether unlucky leaders exist or not, an individual so categorized can do the organization, even if inadvertently, real harm. Should he be recognized as unlucky by those to be his subordinates, they may not give him the degree of effective followership he needs to do a proper job for the organization or the department to which he is assigned. Should he be classed as unlucky by his colleagues, they may look down upon him and their superiors who chose him and thus refuse, through lack of respect, to give both the new administrator and the superiors proper cooperation. Should the appointing authorities themselves feel him to be unlucky, they may be inclined, particularly when reverses become serious, to blame him for what unpleasant things happen and more readily to withdraw their support from him. And, of course, all this does not mention the external danger of choosing an unlucky individual as a leader. Customers, clients, vendors, voters, students, parishioners and even fans—any of the many external publics of the organization—may come to judge negatively the organization in its purposes, efforts, and products because of the association of the whole with the unfortunate part, that is, the unlucky leader.

The Suicide Man

These dangers are especially sharp when the unlucky individual is an extremely unfortunate person. The negative reaction of his publics and the organization's publics will tend to be even worse. More importantly he may come to regard himself as the target of the angry gods. The initial effect may be a behavior pattern on his part resulting in disregard of good luck. Losing confidence, he then may not be willing to undertake the innovations or move into the new ground opened to him gratuitously by circumstances over which he had no direction. But repeated failure may cause him to expect more failure. The least negative behavior which can then be expected is that he occupy himself with defensive stratagems to protect himself from the bad he feels is coming. The next downward step that can be anticipated is that he becomes in his own mind a convinced loser and so he grows incapable of even smart defensive tactics. He figuratively sits with his head bent, awaiting the axe. Yet neither of these career or organizational errors is as tragic as the ultimate in self-degradation into which some chronically unlucky leaders devolve. Reference is had to that which may be called, for lack of a better phrase, the *suicide* personality. This stage of devolvement from real leadership stature is reached when the administrator, so accustomed to bad luck and so expectant of its continuation, begins to assume it as a normal state of affairs and so administers and behaves personally in a manner to attract it.

A hypothetical example of the suicide leader may prove useful. A college dean employed on the basis that he complete his doctorate in a given period fails to do so and so his contract is terminated. He seeks and gains an appointment in a university abroad, at which, injudiciously endorsing a reform movement in government, he becomes *persona non grata* and is forced to resign. Next he returns to the United States and, after being unemployed for a period, obtains another appointment as a dean, a position which he gladly leaves in a few years because he finds his views or education to conflict with those of a number of trouble-causing young turks on his faculty. A friend of his undergraduate days, now a member of the board of regents of the state university system, steers him into an assignment as academic vice president of a new but large and bustling community college. Some years have gone by and this gentleman is now no longer physically young. But the serious defect in his make-up is really a determination on his part that, to survive, he must do nothing except routine administration. And so he rejects suggestions from subordinates and colleagues. He pleads inability and caution to his superiors. He even reacts unpleasantly to those in the organization who, on their own, attempt to institute needed change and challenging innovation. In short, his leadership pattern is not only extremely cautious but downright disastrous since he is holding back all forward movement of the college. He is committing career suicide and impairing seriously the institution by the cardinal sin of failing to recognize that the organization which does not move ahead moves backwards. His bad luck has made him believe it is safer to stay at the starting line and keep the other horses there.

The Luck Syndrome: Special Caution

The great danger to the leader in reliance on luck, either to bring good or bad results, resides in the possibility of self-hypnosis with it. The lucky leader may come to consider himself the favorite of fortune. This may be a strong factor in giving him the confidence and aggressive spirit necessary to mobilize followers and resources, to facilitate their working together, and to direct them toward a goal. Yet it may, on the negative side of the ledger, engender in the leader a conceit or feeling of super-confidence which makes him so sure of himself that he does not analyze, plan, and take other necessary sound steps toward good decision and action. It is as if he no longer needs to worry, for he has become mistake proof. On the other hand, the unlucky leader, depressed by the constant blows of unkind fortune, may degenerate as far as the figuratively suicidal stage. He can come to believe that there is just no use in trying, everything will go wrong anyway.

There are two types of luck syndromes. The real luck syndrome is an actual recurring of uncontrolled circumstances that come to bless or damm a certain individual. The pseudo-syndrome of luck is the imagined existence of such conditions. Which is most dangerous to the leader is probably an academic question, for each in hypnotic effect can be equally serious. If either is to be more feared, it is perhaps the pseudo-syndrome of bad luck. Here the leader imagines that, no matter what course he elects, he will not win. Its especial threat is its lack of reality. In the true bad-luck syndrome, the necessity for battling actual problems may introduce an element of balance, if not hope, into the decisions and actions of the leader. But, in the pseudo bad-luck syndrome, imagined ill-fortune works its negative effect on the mind of the leader almost untrammeled, because of the subtle effect of imagination uninterrupted by much reality. The victim becomes a leader who dwells in more perfect ill-fortune because pseudo bad luck, through its perfection, has few elements of motivation to struggle upward from it.

Conclusion

The truly strategy minded leader takes for granted that the factor of luck does exist and will influence his course of leadership.[8] He will identify fortune, if favorable to his aims and/or those of his entity, as something he calls a "good chance" or "fine opportunity"; he will see fortune of the opposite type as a "good warning" or "lesson." For practical purposes he will then proceed to make the most of his luck, realizing that it may be the force that gives him the edge over his competitors. The value he places on fortune may cause him to remain as an administrator in one organization or to move about from employer to employer. Still, whichever course he elects in this regard, he must pay heed to the dangers inherent in the fortune syndrome, lest he become in his own mind the fair-haired boy of fate or the perennial victim of bad luck.

BUSINESS SITUATIONS FOR ROLE PLAYING

SITUATION XV

Luck: A Variable in Success

THE NIGHTINGAILE NURSING HOMES, INC.

A. Scene.   A large and well financed Eastern chain of nursing homes. The four principal stockholders, all members of the eleven man board of directors, meeting in a special rump discussion at the home of the chairman of the board, the largest stockholder.

B. Players.   1. Chairman of the Board: Mr. N. J. Standard, a very busy individual well over sixty-four years of age, who owes his great financial success to being in the right place at the right time.

2. Youngest Member of the Board: Mr. Daniel A. Primo, a rising youthful genius widely ac-

claimed in financial circles, who is strongly indoctrinated in and loyal to quantitative methodology in decision making.

3. Conservative Director: Mr. S. Sylvester Smith, an arch-conservative in all his attitudes and decisions.

4. Trained and Experienced Hospital Administrator: Mr. Yancey Rockwaite, one of the first Ph.D's in hospital administration to graduate from a Big Ten university, who has inherited his stock unexpectedly from a long lost cousin of his mother.

C. Situation. 1. A conflict of opinion exists among these defacto manipulators of the corporation regarding the type of resident administrators to be hired as replacements when members of the present echelon of such managers retire.

2. The Chairman insists on picking successful nursing home managers whose records show them to be winners.

3. The Young Director favors selection by reputation for effective internal control and profit-per-bed record.

4. The Conservative Director is motivated principally by considerations of seniority and economy in salaries required.

5. In contrast, the Hospital Administrator insists, as a *sine qua non*, that the managers be professionally trained hospital administrators.

D. Assignment. 1. Direct class to elect from its members four individuals to assume the above roles, with greatest care given choice of the Chairman.

2. Have each of the four directors in dialogue format advance and defend clearly and vigorously his criteria for selection of local managers.

3. See to it that the Chairman opens the discussion with the importance of hiring "lucky"

individuals, and that the other role players emphasize what they call "more objective" bases of selection.

4. Invite the class to add comments and indicate by vote the majority view on best selection criteria.

NOTES

1. Throughout his famous work—*The Prince*—Machiavelli sees luck as having much more than an occasional influence. He identifies that which he calls *fortuna* as one of the two determinants of success, the other being *virtu* (capacity).
2. The view that it ". . . is practically impossible for an executive to eliminate luck . . ." is clearly stated in a book on the dynamics of management. See GEORGE S. ODIORNE, *How Managers Make Things Happen* (Englewood Cliffs, N.J.: Prentice-Hall, Inc., 1961), p. 167.
3. Sayles declares that actually ". . . the essence of management is not of heroic proportions. Rather, most managerial behavior is mundane—and frustrating." LEONARD R. SAYLES, *Managerial Behavior* (New York: McGraw-Hill Book Company, 1964), p. 260.
4. The literature on business management notes that internal communication systems are often not adequate either in structure or functioning. For example, Likert points out that ". . . the communication systems of most companies have serious flaws." RENSIS LIKERT, *New Patterns of Management* (New York: McGraw-Hill Book Company, 1961), p. 44.
5. A similar thought seems well expressed in the following quotation: "To call abandonment an 'opportunity' may come as a surprise. Yet planned, purposeful abandonment of the old and of the unrewarding is a prerequisite to successful pursuit of the new and highly promising. Above all, abandonment is the key to innovation—both because it frees the necessary resources and because it stimulates the search for the new that will replace the old." PETER F. DRUCKER, *Managing for Results* (New York: Harper & Row, Publishers, 1964), p. 143.
6. CHARLES D. FLORY (ed.), *Managers for Tomorrow* (New York: The New American Library, 1965), p. 91.
7. Napoleon placed great importance on the avoidance of

unlucky individuals, believing that unlucky men are "of no use as fighters." REES, L. W. B., *Fighting in the Air* (Washington, D.C.: Gibson Brothers, n.d.), p. 15.

8. Confidence in luck seems to be quite evident in the minds of great military leaders. Field-Marshall the Viscount Montgomery of Alamein writes, "No commander ever took greater care than Nelson to prepare against every possible contingency, but no one was ever so well able to recognize the moment when, everything having been done that reason can dictate, something must be left to chance or fate." LAW, BERNARD, *The Memoirs of Field-Marshall the Viscount Montgomery of Alamein* (Cleveland: The World Publishing Company, 1958), p. 316.

CHAPTER 16

Focus on Decision Making

> "Man is a political animal, living and working with many of his kind in the organizational framework. He needs, therefore, to consider their reactions to his decisions. Since decision making is his chief and highest leadership activity, it is a principal motive for his behavior in whatever leadership role he finds himself—that of supervisor, executive, manager or administrator."

THE MODERN study of administration, which began well along in the last century, boasts a succession of different areas of concentration. Subject after subject has held the stage prominently, if briefly. Then it has been pushed into the background in favor of some new hypnosis—not so much rejected as relegated to the growing accumulation of what man thought he already knew about the handling of people and things in the framework of an organization.

The Evolutionary Process

This subject inconstancy is traceable in quite general terms. Modern investigation of the administrative process centered first on efficiency in production. It drew the attention primarily of industrial engineers, some of whom published what are still classical works in the literature of administra-

469

tion. Soon, as history could have expected, scholarly interest broadened and, abandoning mesmerism with efficiency, evolved into an urge to identify and state the so-called "principles of management."

The search for principles, beginning in noteworthy proportions about the turn of the century, proved irresistible to both the academician and the practitioner of management. Although entering it somewhat warily, they soon were entranced with its possibilities. From their pens flowed many books and articles on the more or less basic propositions of administration as a generic field and of its processes and operational functions as particular areas. Out of their yearning to propound these observations probably came a substantial degree of the force behind the introduction of management courses and curricula into institutions of higher learning.

But general principles, in and of themselves, tend to be rather bare bones and, at best, carry no assurance of containing all the truth. In an effort to give accepted principles substance and life—as well as in an endeavor to dig ever deeper into human conduct for additional truths of administration—there developed, shortly after World War II and especially in United States academic circles concerned with the study of management, a fascination with two "scientific" ways of shoring up recognized tenets, revealing additional facts, and developing new assumptions. These are the *behavioral science* and *quantitative approaches.* Of incalculable assistance in the explanation of and even in the prediction of administrative behavior, each of these approaches has drawn its almost frenziedly loyal proponents and become, in a sense, the current subject of their concentration.

No doubt, the understanding of administration has been furthered by the changing pattern of concentration. This shifting has certainly meant the addition of facts and hypotheses to the general store of knowledge and belief, particularly about the specific area of preoccupation in vogue at the given time. Moreover, it has surely provided in each point of emphasis a new pinnacle from which to view existing positions, if in a somewhat different perspective; and, in so doing, it has facilitated that constant testing of the old which is necessary to scientific advance.

But these results are not the only contributions of the scholarly fickleness. There is another outcome the historian may consider of even more long-run significance. It is the fact that the successive preoccupations have constituted a forward moving pattern of thinking which has now brought the student of administration to a vital concern with its very essence, that is, with *decision making*.[1] This is neither to assert nor to deny that there has been evolution in the sense of a logical or predestined progression. The implication is rather that somehow the sequential attention to different subjects of special interest has exhausted their seduction, at least for the time being, and that the paramount dimension of the administrative process thus has become sufficiently exposed to attract its own investigation.

The General Hypnosis with Decision Making

There exists today, on both the academic and actual management fronts, a vital and rapidly expanding interest in decision making. Overwhelming evidence is at hand. Learned publications on decision making in both the macro and micro frames of reference are being generated in increasing numbers. An ever growing array of courses, conferences, and research projects dealing with matters and techniques of decision making is being offered by colleges and universities, business enterprises, and trade and professional groups. Throughout the world and in many languages, expressions such as "How to Make a Decision" or "How to Improve Decision Making" are becoming a part of usual and acceptable managerial jargon. Perhaps the fever of the times is most dramatically indicated by the appearance even of major novels devoted to decision situations.

Practical Interest in Decision Making

Of course, this interest in decision making cannot be explained adequately in terms alone of the simple facts that students of administration have grown tired of other more primitive aspects of their subject or that the managerial science and art have advanced to the discovery that decision making is the very essence of administration. There must be a number of practical reasons which also, and perhaps to a very forcible extent, are drawing attention to the decision problem.

One practical reason is the plain fact that the contemporary administrator, and most particularly he who holds a managerial post in business, is today beset in his decision making with a category of formidable variables unique in recent history. Whereas in the past those officials of the organization who had the power to make the significant decisions were either its owners or in close personal alliance through such ties as blood or marriage with the proprietorship, now most of the administrators of the company who must reach the important decisions are "hired managers." Here is seen the really big new tough class of variables in decision making.

The professional administrator employed by the concern but not of its ownership commonly faces four questions in his decision situations; and, in most cases, his reward or very survival as a member of the management of the organization depends upon deciding according to the right answers to these questions. The questions are: first, "Do my superiors want me to render a decision in this case?"; second, "What do they want me to decide?"; third, "How do they want me to make the decision?"; and fourth, "To what extent and in what way do they want to be associated with the decision, its making, and the commitments it implies?" But the right answers with which the decision maker must come up are frequently a function of his own interpretation and judgment of his superiors' desires in a particular decision situation. If the superiors are strategically minded individuals, that is, administrators who want decision making appropriate to each situation and who are unpredictable by formula, then the decision maker is indeed faced with real variables. And certainly, if he is a rational being, he will be most interested in learning more of the decision process so that he can increase his percentage of correct decisions and thus both his own and the organization's welfare.

Another practical explanation for the currently lively concern with decision making is the expanding size of organizations in all areas of human endeavor—business, professions, government, military affairs, religion, and education. Inherent in most large organizations are certain potential obstacles to ease in reaching the right decision. Among these are fragmentation of decision making power, contradiction in objectives, and complexity of communication. Certainly the classical village blacksmith faced no such hurdles in the operation of his shop, but mere size tends to implant hurdles in the way of the management of a large tire manufacturing firm of the mid-twentieth century whose employees number thousands, whose plants are multiple, and whose operational processes are broken down into many specialties. Simply because larger size renders decision making more difficult, or at least potentially harder, many of those who are concerned with directing the destiny of the big modern business corporation—or that of any other large organization—are now giving the decision process serious and increasing scrutiny.

Technological advance is a third practical cause of the burgeoning interest in decision making. As here used, technology means the combination of scientific knowledge and industrial arts. The successful operation, and even the continued existence, of many organizations—particularly business concerns—depends upon the development and application of ever more technology. There seems to be no other way by which they can meet the demands on them for mass handling and mass production at economical costs. Technology reduces the intimate connection the administrator had in more primitive times with the managing of people and resources and with the productive process itself. Therefore, it deprives him of much of the down-to-earth knowledge and feeling which he formerly used in making his decision. As if to put the decision maker on an even "tougher spot," technology may demand ever more important prudential decisions from the administrator, precisely because it cannot make such decisions and because it is often so costly. It may be said that the decision maker, especially in the world of business, is now entrapped by technology and that technology, in turn, is entrapped by him. And so the administrator in the organization which has a vital dependence upon technology is evidencing, of necessity, an increasing concern with the topic of how to make, and even live with, a decision.

The establishment, operation, maintenance, and expansion of all types of organizations are becoming progressively more costly throughout the world. This is probably the result of a historical combination of various factors, among which are the generally rising standard of living, the depletion of available natural resources, effective pressure groups such as labor unions and trade associations, government demands in taxation and in standards compliance, cold or hot war, and inflation. This factor of rising costs—whether it be found in an automobile manufacturing company, a unit of government, a medical practice, or a church organization—constitutes a fourth practical reason for the contemporary interest in decision making. Obviously, rising costs tend to make management in all types of enterprise more sensitive to error and so to decision making as an act in which the foundation for administrative error can be laid.

This attempt to establish the view that there are genuinely practical and weighty external reasons for the current interest and growing fixation with decision making is not intended to deny the probability that decision making, by its very nature, generates a degree of positive enthusiasm over its own study. Decision making is undoubtedly a somewhat charismatic or talent concept in all societies. After all, the quality of decisiveness is universally recognized as the prime attribute of leadership, and the leader is likely to be the respected (or feared) member of the group. It is logical, therefore, to expect that the characteristic which people value in the leader may become, as it were, a symbol and topic for their special consideration. The capacity of decision making to generate interest in itself would seem to be most potent in the democratic society, which by its emphasis upon equality frees all to dream of and seek success in the form of leadership stature.

The Concern of the Individual Administrator

Indeed, literature on administration, accumulating at an increasing rate since Taylor and Fayol and their predecessors of the Nineteenth Century published their classics, is now voluminous. It ranges from long and detailed analysis to brief and succinct shop manuals. Few indeed are the facets of the managerial function which cannot claim their extensive bibliography. And the topic of decision making is no exception. What, then, is the purpose of completing a treatise on *administrative strategy* with a discussion of decision making? Can this action be justified by the argument that it attempts to cover an overlooked side of administrative strategy, or that it endeavors to expand the existing treatment of a sub-topic of administrative dynamism, or that it seeks to present a new view on some point of strategy in leadership?

Relation of Decision to Administrative Behavior

The truth is that a specific aspect of administrative behavior has been neglected sorely by the literature on management in general and decision making in particular. The dedicated student of realism in organizational leadership recognizes that this facet is one of prime import in its deep implications to the discharge of the full administrative function. *The aspect overlooked is the reaction of the administrator in response to the motivational influence of the decision—to be made or already made.* And so, the purpose and, it is hoped, the justification for the treatment of decision making given here and in the ensuing terminal chapters of this work will be to deal in a descriptive, analytical, and at times even advisory, manner with that portion of the administrator's behavior pattern in his organization which is the result, direct or indirect, of the stimulus of decision on him.

The motivational force of the necessity for a decision is probably greater than that of a decision already made. That which demands decision commonly carries an element of fear with respect to choice of the right alternative and/or an element of hope for good results to flow from the alternative chosen. Both fear and hope are powerful motives. Although they may be generated by the decision already made with which the administrator must live, they are probably less in this case because of the greater element of certainty which it contains. "Decision . . . is a cut between past and future, an introduction of an essentially new strand into the emerging pattern of history."[2] When already made, the future, in a sense, can be more easily seen.

Throughout this analysis more attention will be devoted to the motivational impact of the situation requiring decision than to the decision already in existence. This concentration will have the value of recognizing the greater dynamic and of portraying the influence of the more significant dimension.

The "decision situation" is that complexus of circumstances which confronts the administrator with the demand that a decision be made relative to it. In its essence, it requires of him one or both of two things: first, that he decide whether or not he should make the decision; and second, if his conclusion is positive, that he marshal possible alternatives and choose the best from among them. This task can be simple or complex, pleasant or disturbing. But no matter what its nature, it is a motivating factor as far as the administrator facing the decision situation is concerned.

The motivational influence of the decision situation proceeds from a trilogy of causes. Basic is the fact that any type of decision making requires intellectual activity.[3] The decision maker cannot escape this activity, for he must make a judgment or judgments as to which alternative to choose. Should he contemplate escaping heavier consequences by "deciding not to decide," he will still have to make the judgment as to what to do.

Another source of motivational influence inherent in the decision situation is that it threatens the decision maker with commitment, since any decision he may reach will somehow obligate him to assume a certain attitude and often to take appropriate defensive or offensive political measures. Of course, commitment means the loss of a degree of administrative freedom. To the rational administrator, this is a matter of real concern—and it will cause him to think and/or act over and above the actual decision.

A final origin of motivational influence is the "coefficient of obligation" in the situation demanding decision. This means the mental and/or emotional pressure the situation exerts on the administrator to undertake the making of the decision. Four conditions, presently to be discussed, generate the sense of obligation: constitutional position, moral responsibility, public expectation, and emergency.[4] It is conceivable that a sufficiently insensitive, unmoral, and/or immoral administrator could resist the feeling, but even this possibility may be less when the situation is such that more than one of the obligatory conditions prevail.

In a brutal sense then, the administrator must be seen as the victim of the decision making requirement of his job. He is helpless to insulate himself completely against its stimulation. The need for decision making, and even more clearly the actual making of the decision, will force him to react somehow.

Of course, the degree of motivation exerted by the decision situation will vary with many factors. Among the more obivous are the power position of the administrator in the organization, his courage, and his interpretation of the situation in terms of danger and opportunity to himself and/ or his organization.

But there is one factor, quite subtle in essence, which should not be overlooked. It is the nature of the decision situation. If it is strictly a problem, that is, a situation whose dimensions are known, the motivational influence, especially on intellectual activity, may be less because it is only the solution which is needed. However, if the situation is more complex in that even the problem must be isolated, its stimulus, *ceteris paribus*, may be greater. Certainly more study and analysis will be needed. And, even after "the problem" has been uncovered, the motivational influence may be compounded. Enhanced stimulation may occur if the administrator is not sure that he has found the real problem or if he thinks he has unearthed one of such proportions that the decision to be taken promises to be unusually dangerous or peculiarly rich in opportunity. Also, a greater degree of stimulation may make itself felt if the administrator knows he has found the problem which has eluded others in the organization or if he thinks he is the only one available with the know-how to find the right solution. In fact, a strong degree of motivational influence flowing from the decision situation may cause the administrator, especially if he is strategy minded, to see and define even the problem in a manner advantageous to himself.

The skeptic may raise the question at this point as to whether or not the decision situation is really a sufficiently major influence in determining the behavior pattern of the administrator to warrant all this consideration. Clarification is to be found in the very facts of administrative life. It cannot be denied that the most important function of the administrator is to make necessary and wise decisions. This function is of the very essence of his leadership, and it is his leadership which should chart the course of the organization, or the portion thereof, for which he is responsible. Certainly that which calls for the highest act of leadership must be presumed to stimulate him as much as or more than any of his other myriad of tasks. It is in truth basic to everything else he does as a member of management.

The successful administrator is keenly attuned to the requirements and unique features of the situations calling for decision. He views each as a strategist,[5] doing that which *is most appropriate to it.* He is wary and bold, slow and fast, superficial and analytical as the realities of the problem demand. His pattern of behavior is nicely inconsistent, being characterized by backing and filling, by plunging directly ahead and by zigzagging. He endeavors, of course, to stay within the bounds of ethics, social decency, and the law so that he will have the assurance of followership, the protection of the moral shield, and a sufficient degree of peace of mind. His fears of failure and hopes of success—as well as the good of his organization—depend on nothing less than his acting as a "complete political creature" in his reaction to the decision-making stimulus. Clearly then, it shall be the controlling purpose of this treatment of decision making to mark, describe, and analyze his fulfillment of the essential political role which decisional motivation makes it his to perform.

Negative Influence of Decision Motivation

To be certain, the decision requirement of the situation can—and does at times—have unfortunate effects on the administrator. These results may be quite polar in nature, causing one individual to be highly excited and nervous and inducing another to freeze up. The first often will be seen engaging in many administrative excesses and irrelevancies in an effort to discharge his burdensome task of deciding. The second not infrequently will resort to or fall back into inaction, being too fearful or confused to react in any substantial measure. These may be extreme types but they are not uncommon in the ranks of management. And so they must be noted in any effort to portray the full picture of the administrative decision maker's political response.

The Profile of the Decision Making Process

Now it seems quite in order to launch a description of decision making as a process by defining its immediate goal or result—the decision itself. A decision is a course of action or inaction chosen to meet the requirements of a situation, popularly termed *the problem*. A vital element or characteristic already implied in previous paragraphs is the fact that the decision is forward looking. Jones puts this clearly in his statement, ". . . a decision . . . is a conclusion that a man has reached as to what he (or others) should do later . . ." [6]

Many authorities underscore the idea that a decision is one of a number of examined alternatives and that it is the one the decider considers the best. Although this view may be a bit sanguine in light of the fact that many individuals have neither the time nor ability to conceive and organize any considerable number of alternatives, it is probably not basically in error because even the busy or very slow individual knows that there are two courses from which to pick—the one he leans toward and any other. As to the decider choosing the alternative he considers best, there can be little argument if one is willing to accept, at times, rather extreme or weird value judgments.

Decision Making, an Intellectual Activity

Decision making is said to be an intellectual activity, because it requires selection from among alternatives. This is, of course, a minimum rationale for classifying it as an endeavor of the intellect. Certainly the necessity for imagination constitutes further proof. If imagination is defined as the capacity to, or the act of, marshalling one's intention and experience to envision the future, there can be no doubt of the vital role it plays in decision making. Decisions, although always taken at a moment of time, are designed with future consequences primarily in mind. So the future must be seen at least in generality, if the decision is to be properly oriented in terms of goals. Decision making, then, is intellectual because it calls for the use of both judgment and imagination. It could be argued successfully otherwise only were imagination to be classified as a component of judgment, perhaps a not altogether illogical categorization since the administrator should look into the future before he formulates alternatives and makes his choice of the one he ranks first.

The Logical Route

The true strategist in administration will be aware that there are various approaches to decision. While not mutually exclusive, each does suggest unique usefulness in particular situations. The most time honored in Western literature is that of logic. The concept of "logical" in the popular mind means a correct way of arriving at a conclusion. But it has a more specific meaning also—and that is reaching a conclusion by the principles of sound reasoning. In this sense, then, the logical approach to decision making may be either deductive or inductive, the former implying reasoning from the general to the particular and the latter from the particular to the general. In business decision making each is used, and no doubt combined in many instances, even though they are not identified. Some experts in the field appear to entertain a measure of agreement that the logical steps in decision making are as follows: (1) a feeling of doubt; (2) an analysis of the problematic situation; (3) the proposal of alternatives; and (4) the deductive treatment of these hypotheses.[7] The relationship of these steps to the purely deductive and purely inductive is of little practical concern to the executive, although in themselves they may be of great use.

Principle of Practical Rationality

It is easy to describe the decision making process in terms of a sequence of logical, or right thinking, steps. And it is pleasant to do so; the attraction of orderliness is strong. But the element of cost, monetary and other, seldom permits the decision maker, particularly when he is a member of an organization, to take a completely rational stand. He usually must be satisfied with something less than the perfect alternative. Examples are to be found at every level of decision making in all types of organizations. The shop foreman cannot pursue the wholly reasonable course and discharge a chronic troublemaker; he must recommend transfer to another gang because discharge would bring the union down upon him. The chief executive of a firm producing durable

goods cannot take the totally rational action of not permitting model changes for a decade; his competitors would
seek to capture the market by turning out new models and
availing themselves of the profitable advantages of style
differential and innovation appeal. The President and Congress of the United States must content themselves—and
the nation go along—with a degree of the possible national
military readiness as a basis for foreign policy, since the
clearly logical step of raising and maintaining a striking
force of such magnitude as the Communist world could not
dare to think of challenging would prove intolerable in
terms of taxes and other popular sacrifice. Clearly, the
decision maker must follow what may be called, for want
of a better term, the *Principle of Practical Rationality.*

Non-Logical Approaches

However, it may be conceded that the continuum beginning with the stage of confusion and uncertainty and ter-
minating in the verification of alternatives marks a certain
stereotype progression which is more or less commonly followed, if at times sketchily and rather unrecognizably, in
the decision process. Yet this is not to imply that every
decision eventually reached is always even the approximate
result of a logical mental exercise in the sense that it is
arrived at by general adherence to principles of right reason.
There are true non-logical approaches to decision making
occasioned by various influences operative on the decision
maker, such as ignorance, prejudice and concession to
expediency or downright necessity.

The non-logical approaches are at least five in number.
Common is the *emotional approach* which produces a decision reflecting the strong feeling or feelings of the decider;
it is here that such irrational and divergent elements as
affection, anger, hate, fear, jealousy, covetousness, and pride
get in "their influential licks." At times confused with the

emotional is the *psychological approach*. The stress is upon selecting the course of action or inaction which will evoke the least disapproval and the most approval. (Perhaps it would be preferable to identify this second approach as the *political*; still to do so might be to confuse the part with the whole, since it may be reiterated that the purpose of this chapter is to identify the decision maker in his political reaction to the built-in stimulus of the problem.) A third approach to decision making may be given the term *negotiational*; its essence is compromise, the conclusion reached not being either quite what the parties involved want or do not want. And then, of course, there is the *democratic approach*, which contemporarily finds especially staunch support from those convinced of the administrative advantages to be obtained from better human relations. It signifies the bringing of more people, or the same people more, into the decision process in determinative roles. In final order of enumeration, there may be cited the *mechanistic approach* which seeks to arrive at the right conclusion by the utilization of formula and/or mechanical devices. Currently, this avenue is being given much attention and appreciable adulation as something new and scientific. Simon constructs a category of "modern" techniques of decision making by listing operational research, electronic data processing, and heuristic problem solving—all of which have strongly mechanistic elements.[8] In fact, its proponents tend to see it not at all as a non-logical approach but rather as a way of enhancing the possibility of making logical decisions.

The Balance of Precedence and Inspiration

The necessity for choosing a course which falls short of the best in terms of facts and values should not be permitted to becloud the truth that the process of deciding must reflect what may be called historical sequence. There is an order—a precedence—in the affairs and beliefs of men and organizations which even rational compromise with facts and principles in a given situation, cannot deny. Among these prominently stand the irreducible minimum code of ethics to which the group subscribes and the other institutionalized principles and practices of the group and the larger community of which it recognizes itself as a really integral part.

On the other side of the picture is inspiration, which can balance the tendency to conform in decision making. "Decision," writes Shackle, ". . . is more than mere response to circumstances and contains an element which we may call inspiration, which brings essential novelty into the historical sequence of states of affairs." [9] This element does, as he suggests, render decision making something more than "a sequential calculus of human conduct." [10] It is satisfying to agree with his contention that choice and creative freedom are not illusory. A word of caution does, however, seem appropriate—and it is to the effect that the existence and positive influence of inspiration may be suffering progressive deterioration in face of the tremendous drive for conformity which today characterizes Western society and especially its United States sector.

Situs and Tempo of Decision Making: Preliminary Statement

The student of decision making should remember, regardless of the subtlety of its nature and of its balance, that the process is one of broad dimensions and varying speed. It embraces a wide range of administrative attitude and conduct; it moves slowly, moderately or rapidly. The logic minded students of the subject suggest the width in their division of the process into stages; [11] the diverse rates of speed in their implication that the demands of each stage may require a different amount of time. The non-logic minded students perform a similar function by their use of widely divergent approaches. An objective administrator may draw an important inference from this line of thought, namely: if he would be a master of decision making he must not look for the process in just his office or staff, or identify it with a given rate of decisiveness.

Indeed, no attempt to draw the profile of decision making even when oriented to organizational life, as it here is, would be complete without some specific word on the situs and tempo of the process. Decision making, although it often bears the connotation of a function reserved in large degree to individuals fairly high in the administrative hierarchy, is actually a duty which falls to all members of management. Jones eloquently declares, "Decision making is probably the most characteristic task of the executive. All executives, high and low, work on decisions constantly." [12] In tempo, a constantly changing rate pattern is usually the norm. And there seems to be little positive correlation between height on the management scale and speed with which decisions must be made. A slow, moderate, or frenzied pace may be quite appropriate strategically anywhere up or down the administrative ladder. The rate at any particular time may, in fact, be an indication of either the urgency of arriving at a conclusion or of the existence of more than one decision requiring situation at the moment and of the consequent simultaneous attention by a given administrator or administrative echelon to the multiple problem.

The Aura of Mystique

This concluding effort to bring the decision making process down to earth, as it were, may require a bit more rounding out. Reference is had to the need for dispelling, in some measure, the aura of mystique which to some appears to surround decision making and particularly to becloud the understanding of its analysis as set forth in scholarly studies. The mystique proceeds to a considerable extent, it may be reasonably assumed, from the vocabularly used. The choice of words smacks of philosophy and logic which, in this day and age of educational concentration on life adjustment, can appear as strange and elusive fields.

The reaction of the uninitiated tends to be negative. Consequently, for example, they back away from such terms as "premises" and "hypothesis," not realizing that these words meaning simply "supposition" are, as is true of many of their fellows, easily translated into common parlance. The retreat from vocabulary all too often probably induces them also to retire from a scientific consideration of the very subject of decision making. Unfortunately for these individuals, a whole new collection of strange terms is being introduced by the advanced analyst of decision as he embraces the tools of mathematics and of its subsidiaries—statistics and electronic computation. If the amateur and the unread are freightened by some of these old terms, they may indeed tend to panic when confronted with such verbiage as "distributional uncertainty variable" and "linear programming." Perhaps the solution is a matter of self-discipline. They must settle down and make a sincere effort to master the meanings of such, to them, exotic terms, before they write off the study of decision making as an exercise open only to professional scholars. It happens that the more formidable terms are truly reducible, in the main, to ordinary language and that their number is not legion.

The Ideal Decision Maker

The basic tone of this study is intended to be realistic—to set down what really happens or should transpire in a chosen segment of the administrator's behavior. The basic point of reference is the usual administrator and a portion of his usual behavior. However, it has been said truthfully that the ordinary can be comprehensible and measurable only when the ideal is understood. It seems appropriate, there-

fore, to devote some attention to the ideal decision maker—
the individual who consistently selects the best alternative—
and to attempt a short description of him.

Identity with Ideal Leader

The task could probably be avoided by repeating that
the best type of decision maker must have the attributes of
the best type of leader. Yet more concrete treatment seems
feasible because the subsequent chapters will refer upon
numerous occasions to what the "rational," the "dynamic,"
the "strategic," or the "good" decision maker would do in
view of this or that circumstance. Such reference can have
its truly cogent meaning only when the specifics of the
nature of the ideal decision maker are held clearly in mind
by both the writer and reader. The concept of ideal leadership, unless it has been recently considered, tends to evolve
into a blur of desirable qualities—a somewhat rosy subjective symbol of what the leader should be in the best of all
possible worlds. Man, it is suspected, all too often has the
tendency to forget the objective specifics of that which is
more reassuring to him.

High intelligence is undoubtedly one of the qualities the
decision maker must possess to rank as ideal. But what is
superior intellectual capacity? Intelligence is a composite of
various mental abilities, and so it can mean in particular
instances many things, depending upon the components,
their degree, the mix in which they are combined. It is safer,
therefore, in reference to the requirement of intelligence to
say that the ideal decision maker must possess a high
degree of a certain type of intelligence. This composite certainly must contain at least three components of real quality:
alertness, imagination, and judgment. The first ingredient is essential to recognition of the dynamics of the problem and the frame of reference in which it is to be handled;
the second is at least necessary to that mobilization of inten-

tion and experience which leads to the cognizance of the various alternatives; and the third is basic to the selection of that alternative which will best further the ends the decider seeks.

High intelligence by itself is not sufficient to guarantee that the decision maker will be ideal. The element of personal discipline is needed, and this must proceed from what loosely may be described as a *balanced personality*—another essential attribute of the "perfect decider." This concept, which students of pure psychology might reject as an invention of the lay mind, is of the total person as an individual so constituted by nature, training, and experience that he will have developed his own systems of values and goals and integrated them in a rational array with those of the organization he helps administer. The concept also implies an individual who, as a rule, will move with respect to each decision situation which confronts him in conformity with this hierarchy. Obviously, the balanced personalty will not be inclined to pursue radical or irrelevant courses nor will he often react solely as a creature of emotion.

The erroneous inference that the balanced personality is inflexible might be drawn from the explanation above. However, inflexibility is as foreign to this personality as is the erratic pattern. The balanced personality rests on two pillars which, taken together, do not permit inflexibility either as blind consistency or as ritualistic conformity. They are a broad view of job, organization, and life itself—a value oriented outlook; and the practical attitude that individual and organization should move forward to get things done— a goal-oriented feeling. The interplay of this duo of forces, although it gives balance, may not be friendly to reputation, for each tends to negate the tendency of the other to direct the individual consistently.

Where does all this leave that flash of inspiration and creativity which at times seems to move the administrator to marvelously correct decision? Surely some of the great decisions of organizations have sprung from the minds and hearts of their leaders in an almost magic manner.[13] Society recognizes the great worth of such conclusions in the expression of approbation "inspired decisions." No sensible enumeration or evaluation of the ideal decision maker's necessary attributes would presume to speak out against them. To do so would be to deny the possibility that random choice of alternatives may be correct, that intuition can be fruitful of right conclusion, that reasoning from insufficient evidence can yield results seemingly miraculous, or that even Divine Guidance can play a hand in pointing out the right course. A sound stand with respect to the inspired decision would seem to be one of receptivity and gratitude but not of reliance as a rule.

Then there is the characteristic of *courage*—still another trait basic to perfection in the decision maker. Courage, whether it be considered a quality of mind or character, is the quality which makes it possible for an individual to do what fear might otherwise block. Obviously, it is of prime importance to the decision maker. The process of making a decision is by its very nature quite capable of generating fear in the person who contemplates undertaking it. To make a decision means to incur the possibility of three types of danger quite apart from the loss of fluidity itself. Two of these flow from the fact that decision does mean, in essence, commitment by the decider to the status quo, to the introduction of a new element into the siuation, or to some completely new course. In any case, it signifies "taking a stand." This can be perilous to the decider or to those whom he represents either because it somehow threatens the interests of second parties or simply because it is now something on which they can more easily focus their attention because it has become formalized as a target. The other of the two dangers flowing from commitment is more subtle. Precisely because a decision may create and mobilize opposition to it and, therefore, to its maker, some or all of his friends, associates, assistants, and other supporters may move away from him in order to avoid the possibility of suffering a measure of the blame for it or of sharing other repercussions which may fall on him. More or less deserted, the decision maker can find himself standing alone or at least with lessened support. Here is truly a very real source of fear with which the decider may have to contend.

In all probability, situations exist which in their requirements do not contain for the decision maker any appreciable fear stimulus. They may be so bland in implication that there is little, if any, incipient opposition to be stirred up; the decision maker may be quite insensitive to any inherent danger; or he may be in such a favorable power position that he simply disregards, as it were, any possible fear excitement. This is not, however, adequate grounds for contending that need for courage on the part of the ideal decision maker is any less. After all, danger and consequent fear likely will arise somewhere in the galaxy of problems for which he must find the best solutions. Yet even more significant is the possibility of making the wrong decision—an eventuality always present and in itself a notable source of peril and fright to the decider. This third type of danger and source of disquiet—that of error—can be very great, especially when heavy organizational pressure is present as in the case of the strongly cost conscious business concern or department of a company. It certainly is no exaggeration to contend that the quality of courage must be included among the basic characteristics of the ideal maker of decisions.

To round out the enumeration of his traits one more attribute must be assigned the ideal decision maker. It is his *acceptance by the organization in which he discharges his decision function.* Acceptance of the individual by the organization means several different things. In a mild form, it is simple friendship; in a little stronger form, it is approval or agreement—either understood or expressed; in a still more vigorous form, it is outright effort, actual or ready, to help the member on his chosen course; and in its most pristine form, it is love. But, whatever its nature, organizational acceptance is essential to the best in decision making. The administrator or, for that matter, any other member of the firm, government, church, or military unit whose task it is to make decisions will be likely to be circumscribed in this function should he lack requisite acceptance by his organization. Part of this circumscription, which may make itself evident in conclusions somewhat inadequate to the requirements of the problems he must handle or even in avoiding or evading them completely, may be of a somewhat emotional character; the administrator, sensing himself to be not completely a part of the group, may hold back in vigor, boldness, and daring because he feels uncertain of the support his innovation will receive or because he does not believe the organization to merit "the best." A no less important reason for his partial decision effort may arise from the rational conviction that, if he decides as the situations demand, he may bring harm to himself, to those he wishes to protect in the organization, and to the organization itself, because others in the equity will not assume their proper share of the decision burden whether it be as bystanders, compilers, communicators, or implementors.

The question well may be raised at this point as to what degree of acceptance the decision maker needs in order to proceed ideally. The proper dimension depends somewhat upon his emotional make-up. Should he be an extremely sensitive individual who values social approval dearly, he well may need a high form of acceptance bordering even upon affection. On the other hand, should he be of the more callous ilk, he may have relatively little need for group support. The correct degree of acceptance depends also upon rational factors such as the decision maker's estimate of the help he will require in making, communicating, selling, and carrying out the alternative courses he chooses and his estimate of the protection he will need because of their effects on others either as the right or wrong decisions. It should be remembered, however, that in the last analysis the decision maker needs that degree of acceptance which he feels and thinks he should have. Acceptance by his organization has its true meaning as a motivating force only to the individual it motivates.

Behavior Pattern of Ideal Decision Maker

Directed by the traits which make him ideal, the ideal decision maker will follow the pattern of behavior they dictate. This pattern, properly described as idealistic, will evidence itself in five ways: (1) he will estimate the situation in its parts as well as its totality; (2) he will learn how far the environment can be modified and maintain personal adaptability; (3) he will be creative in proposing alternatives and in grasping new opportunities to meet the situation; (4) he will anticipate reactions of others in terms of expected results as well as in terms of calculated risks; and (5) he will remain withal flexible and committed to a multiple front strategy. The end result of this behavior pattern can be the choice of the best alternative in each situation.

As a final thought, it should be pointed out that the leader has two types of decisions to make. The basic distinction between them finds an expression in the language of Drucker who speaks of tactical and strategic decisions.[14] It also is reflected in the popularly used dichotomy of routine and dynamic decisions. The difference, however stated, is essentially the contrast of the more simple decision that is called for when the problem is known and the more difficult decision that is required when both the problem and its solution are unknown. The ideal decision maker, exhibiting the behavior pattern described above, also will understand and respect this distinction. And certainly, he will respond most vigorously and intelligently to the greater motivating influence of the two-dimensional decision situation.

Decision Obligations

The loud furor, in both academic circles and the ranks of administrators, about decision making may over-stimulate a particular member of an organization who is alert to current thinking and thought fads in management. Driven by strong desire to be a good leader, by intense ambition to get ahead, and/or by active fear of criticism and failure, he may see his optimum course of action as consisting of decision making, and so he may attempt to decide all, or at least most, of the situations demanding decision that come into his range of cognizance. In short, he is panicked, as it were, into deciding "right and left."

The strategic administrator should understand, as almost his basic principle in decision making, that he does not need to make every decision necessary in his organization. There are, in fact, only four types of situations when the burden of decision making rests squarely upon him as the particular leader. The most obvious is the *condition of legitimate assignment,* that is, the situation in which the charter, by-laws, or other constitutional vehicles place the responsibility of the particular decision on him. For example, the vice president in charge of personnel must approve or disapprove all requests for additional employees because the by-laws direct him to do so. An interesting question arises here as to the burden of decision making with respect to an established informal leader. If such a leader has consistently over a period of time arrogated to himself the making of decisions with respect to a particular subject, is he obligated to continue so to decide? This may be a problem for legitimate authority to ponder. But it should be remembered that constant tolerated usurpation of power may raise the presumption that the act is de facto permitted by the organization's constitution and that, therefore, it continues to be the informal leader's responsibility.

The next situation which imposes the responsibility for making a decision upon the administrator is one which involves *moral values*. It is the complexus in which the responsibility is properly his from the viewpoint of the moral law. To decline the duty of decision would be wrong, even though legally and otherwise he is not obligated to decide. An instance of such nature may be seen in the illustration of the office manager who accidentally discovers that the treasurer of the corporation is stealing from the employee pension fund. There is nothing in the organic documents of the company directing him to report the malfeasance of his colleagues. But moral considerations demand his reporting the crime. More often than not, of course, the moral obligation to decide is not so clear as in this simple case of theft.

A more subtle situation which places decision responsibility on the administrator is that of *public expectation*. It is one in which his followers or other publics expect him to make the decision. This can be an influence of great force, and it can be so strongly felt by the executive that he cannot ignore or avoid the burden it places upon him. The pressure of his personal pride, loyalty, respect and prestige, as well as the administrator's desire to assume or consume the role of leader for his public, put him in a position in which he must decide. The labor union official, for example, is frequently put in this position by the mass of people who follow him as one who can improve their lot.

The last condition placing the administrator on the deciding spot can be labelled *emergency*. An emergency here may be defined as something demanding urgent decision from the administrator since there is no one else to make the choice of solutions. The burden may descend upon him simply because he is the sole person present, because he is willing to decide, because he is the only one there with leadership stature, or because he is the only person at hand who knows how to make the decision. A complicated machine falters; the works manager cannot be located; the machine must be repaired or it will do irreparable damage to itself. So the section superintendent orders it stopped and calls in the manufacturer of the machine to make repairs. The superintendent is forced to reach a decision because he is the only official present. It should be remembered that he who seizes decision making in an emergency runs two risks: those of making himself a "hero or a bum." If a hero, he may well become the candidate for decision making in future emergencies. If a bum, he may suffer blame, disgrace, and even formal penalties.

Conclusion

Decision making—and its understanding—is the topic of prime significance in the present day study of management. It occupies this place partly because of a *de facto* evolutionary process and partly because, negatively expressed for emphasis, a combination of circumstances has turned it into an act of such practical significance as to endanger or even ruin in its wrong discharge, as never before, not only the career of the administrator but also the welfare and survival of the organization.

The necessity for reaching decisions as well as the decision reached are vital influences on administrative behavior. Singly or together, they constitute for the individual administrator a principal motivating force which determines the nature of his conduct as an administrator. They are at once the most immediate of his important action targets and the pivotal points of greatest danger to his leadership. In response to the stimulation of these decision factors—conclusions to be made and conclusions made—the rational administrator becomes a truly political creature. He decides to decide or not to decide; he concludes that action or inaction is dictated; and he takes these steps at varying rates of procedure.

The administrator can gain from a sound knowledge of the prerequisites for ideal decision making and of the circumstances under which a decision maker, even though he is less than a paragon of decision virtue, must undertake to make a decision. Such awareness will render him more of a realist by providing him standards against which he can measure his own decision making. And realism is the essence of success in all forms of administrative strategy, including its apex of decision making.

BUSINESS SITUATIONS FOR ROLE PLAYING

Situation XVI

Focus on Decision Making

THE HOMESIDE LUMBER COMPANY

A. Scene.　　A small city, family owned lumber company. A week end business conference in a luxury suite of a nearby river inn.

B. Players.　　1. President: Mr. O. Clement Ash, a recent M.B.A. graduate of the Harvard Graduate School of Business, who is the grandson of the founder of the company.

2. Chief Stockholder: Mr. Ansidine Q. Ash, a grand uncle of the President and a gentleman of the old school with a strong sense of civic pride and obligation toward his community.

3. Sales Manager: Mr. Stephen Oake, a second cousin of the President who, having inherited

his initial connection with Homeside, has earned his position by imagination and hard work.

C. Situation. 1. The local Board of Commerce has been pressing the President to head up an urban renewal advisory committee to the Mayor of the city.

2. Competition has been growing more intense, reflecting the aggressive sales promotion by two chain building supply companies which recently have "come to town."

3. The uncle, with his fortune assured, has a strong feeling of responsibility for community affairs, and he is inclined to believe that all the members of his clan should shoulder assignments in behalf of the city.

4. The cousin, now a "made-man," shares this same sense of social responsibility.

5. The pressure of competition is demanding more and more attention of the President to strictly business, and he is facing a serious personal decision as to the maintenance of the family image of community leadership.

D. Assignment. 1. Choose players to assume the discussion roles of the three members of the family and firm.

2. Have the President emphasize emotionally his present fatigue and psychological pull as between civic and company values.

3. Assign the players the task of debating the proper allocation of the President's time and energy and the task of reaching a decision on this issue, using either logical or non-logical decision processes.

4. Ask the class for comments.

NOTES

1. Simon goes even further, treating "decision making as synonymous with managing." HERBERT A. SIMON, *The New*

Science of Management Decision (New York: Harper & Row, Publishers, 1960), p. 1.

2. G. L. S. SHACKLE, *Decision, Order & Time in Human Affairs* (Cambridge, England: Cambridge University Press, 1961), p. 3.
3. R. W. MORRELL, *Managerial Decision-Making* (Milwaukee: The Bruce Publishing Company, 1960), p. 11.
4. C. T. HARDWICK and B. F. LANDUYT, *Administrative Strategy* (New York: Simmons-Boardman Publishing Company, 1961), pp. 464-466.
5. See *Ibid.* pp. 1-18, for a description of administrative strategy.
6. MANLEY HOWE JONES, *Executive Decision Making* (Homewood, Illinois: Richard D. Irwin, Inc., 1957), p. 5.
7. MORRELL, *op. cit.*, p. 89.
8. SIMON, *op. cit.*, p. 8.
9. SHACKLE, *op. cit.*, p. ix.
10. *Ibid.*
11. There are many versions of these stages, each varying somewhat more in arrangement and vocabulary than in substance. One of the more succinct presentations is found in Drucker, who uses the term "phases." PETER DRUCKER, *The Practice of Management* (New York: Harper & Brothers, Publishers, 1954), pp. 253-264.
12. JONES, *op. cit.*, p. 1.
13. Sloan gives intuition an important place in decision making, even though he recognizes that the great task behind business judgment is finding and acknowledging facts and circumstances. He declares, "The final act of business judgment is of course intuitive." ALFRED P. SLOAN, JR., *My Years with General Motors* (Garden City, New York: Doubleday & Company, Inc., 1964), p. xxiii.
14. DRUCKER, *op. cit.*, pp. 352-353.

CHAPTER 17

The Decision Arena: Entrance and
Speed of Movement

> "It is not the function of the administrator to take unto
> himself or his organizational entity the task of decision
> in every situation demanding decision. The question
> of deciding whether or not to decide is perhaps one
> of the most significant issues confronting the leader,
> for his very success—and that of his organization or
> unit thereof—may depend upon it. Moreover, there
> are no formulae in organizational life which specify
> the point at which the administrator should enter the
> decision arena or the wisdom of a particular rate of
> speed in reaching a conclusion therein. Proper strat-
> egy should be permitted to dictate the time of en-
> trance and the rate of movement in the choice of the
> correct alternative."

THE DECISION maker is to be viewed as a human being. This
laconic statement seems necessary in view of a pronounced
tendency to regard the process of reaching a decision as a
precise exercise in logical thought which carries with it a
consequential conformity of human behavior. Nothing could
be further from the truth. The administrator who faces the
task of making a decision is often possessed of feelings of
uncertainty as to whether the decision is properly his; he
often entertains doubts as to when to enter the process and
as to how fast to proceed in reaching the conclusion. He is
frequently seen turning this way and that, venturing and

retreating, in a reflection of his quandary about the "best thing to do" or in an effort to test out the ground ahead.

The Theory of Strategic Movement

To the individual concerned with making decisions, each decision becomes an objective. If he is an astute personage, he will subscribe knowingly or unknowingly to the strategic course. The theory of strategy holds that the wise individual will attempt to move in an *appropriate* manner with respect to an objective—that he will, in other words, attempt to handle the issue or problem in the light of the facts of the existing situation. As far as decision making is concerned, this means that the strategic leader will appraise the situation and determine his movements on the basis of its own peculiarities. And so he is seen in his proper conduct pattern of handling different decision situations in different manners. "This is the meaning of effective decision—the control of the changeable strategic factors, that is, the exercise of control at the right time, right place, right amount, and right form . . ."[1]

One should, of course, hasten to point out that nothing here is intended to suggest complete surrender by the decision maker to the dictates of mere pragmatism. There are dogmatic factors which even the most strategic administrator cannot ignore. Looming large among these are such demanding limitations as the stark truths that given premises lead straight to inevitable conclusions, that particular causes bring particular results, and that the basic principles of morality, social decency, and the law should be honored in every decision-making situation and these limitations are not to be considered irrelevant. Although not perhaps dynamic factors in a specific situation, they nonetheless are real elements in it. Then too, they actually constitute ground rules for decision making, and in particular the rules of ethical conduct bring an element of freedom which balances their curbing effect by introducing greater assurance of correct movement into and in the decision arena.

The Decision to Decide

The first question which the prospective decision maker must ask himself is simple of statement: "Why should I assume the task of deciding?" This is indeed a serious proposition. Decision making, as pointed out in the previous chapter, involves commitment to something—a point of view, a principle, an individual, a group, or a course of action. Commitment, it may be stressed again, is always the surrender of a measure of independence for a degree of bondage. Certainly the leader is well advised to consider carefully the meaning of his entrance into the decision making process in relation to his subsequent freedom to decide and to take the resulting necessary action. Moreover, he should be cautious about assuming the responsibility for or an important role in decision situations, because many that appear to be properly in his cognizance do not really belong to his realm of responsibility, and, if left untouched by him, will gravitate for decision to some other party or disintegrate of themselves under the influence of changing circumstance. The loss of freedom, as well as the burden of cost in energy, time, material, resources and mental torment, entailed in assuming the obligation for decision may be needless.

Some Guidelines: Moral Responsibility

Mere reference to the conditions under which the administrator is obligated to make a decision will not give him in many specific instances sufficiently clear grounds upon which to decide whether to decide. These conditions need to be translated into action guidelines designed to recognize the puissant realities of strategy. Fortunately, such guidelines are not hard to formulate. *One guideline is moral responsibility.* Obviously, this can be a complex consideration, for it involves drawing a distinction between what is ethically right and what is ethically wrong. Also, quite apart from the fine ethical questions which may arise, the distinction can be rendered difficult by forces that commonly tend to blunt moral sensitivity. In this connection, there may be mentioned the significance of the decision to be taken. The fact of its slight import may influence the leader to overlook moral obligation; and that of its great magnitude may cause him to feel unduly responsible. And then, of course, the added effect of such negative factors as fear, selfishness, and greed may be noted. Their presence, if strong enough, may cause administrators who are made too much of common clay to be less responsive to duty. Yet neither of these deadening influences should be allowed by the leader to dull his moral sense. For reasons of followership confidence, reputation for trustworthiness and peace of mind, no real compromise with the course of honor is to be tolerated. If the administrator's conscience and judgment convince him that the decision is his moral obligation, his action must be positive; if it does otherwise, he legitimately may refrain, everything else being equal, from making the decision.

Opportunity Inherent in Decision

Another guideline is the opportunity inherent in the decision to be made. Opportunity refers to the possibility of extracting something desirable from a situation or commitment concerning it. The administrator should weigh, in his consideration of whether or not to assume the decision burden, the chances that he can gain for his organization and/ or self something worthwhile by doing so. This is such an obviously rational course that it seems scarcely necessary of mention, and yet many an administrator passes up the grasping of a decision situation to himself because he is either just too sleepy, lazy, busy, or worried about consequent repercussions and costs.

In a poetic sense, it may be contended that the field of unmade decisions should represent for the administrator a rich territory to explore and prospect. What riches in opportunities may he find there? A number can be noted. First of all, the assumption of the task of deciding and the making of the decision can be a further identification with the role of leader. This role may mean greater security for the administrator in his position, since his followers, associates, and superiors will have less cause to question his courage and farsightedness.

The strengthening of hierarchal position is often especially necessary in modern-day organizations with their great internal competition and with their tendency progressively to employ better and better trained people. The superintendent of plant who has worked his way up and who now finds himself in company with many young and ambitious university trained industrial engineers may find it to his definite advantage to demonstrate his leadership capacity by deciding, for example, to fire certain inefficient foremen rather than tolerate their slovenly work until the ridiculousness of their output forces his superiors to act. The further identification with the leadership role that commitment to decision can bring means much also to the individual who desires to move up the organizational ladder. It is a well established principle in economics that product distinction can be and often is the basis for raising the market value of an item. And so it is with organizational personnel. He who is willing to make and who makes decisions, particularly when his colleagues stand back, is likely thereby to become identified as a leader and thus as an individual whom the organization will turn to when it needs someone for a higher position. The plant superintendent may be made general manager because, over the years, he has brought himself to the attention of his superiors by his decisiveness when others were quiescent or vacillating.

A second opportunity for the administrator which can frequently be found in decision making is precisely that of commiting by the decision either self, some individual or individuals in it, or the whole organization to a desired course of action. It is fallacious to assume, as is sometimes done in the classical approach to management, that all decisions taken by an organization to do this or that, to move here or there at a fast or slow pace, are made by individuals or groups who by the "constitution" of the organization are assigned this power. Subordinate individuals or groups, as well as those who, while equal or superior in the hierarchal ladder, do not have legitimately the power to decide, can by being bold and making the decision, or by boldly doing things leading up to it, so commit the organization that those entrusted with the decision must acquiesce in the one already made or decide as the insurgent element desires. The plant superintendent by forthwith firing his undesirable foremen can put the personnel office, who might not want anymore personnel turnover for the time, on the spot by a *fait accompli* with which it must go along.

What is perhaps the most common opportunity in decision making is rather less subtle than either further leadership role identification or forced commitment. It may be described as the "step forward." Progress toward goals, no matter how irrational the objectives or erratic the forward movement, is the normal action pattern of the organization and of its leaders. This progress is rarely possible as one straight and continuous movement from an established operational base. It more usually can be accomplished only in a series of steps, each one the result of a decision and the action based on it.[2] Therefore, the administrator should scrutinize the chance to make a decision to see whether or not it may now offer him another step toward a given goal being pursued by him and/or his organization. He frequently will find that the decision situation affords an opportunity for advancement in the goal direction; after all, many issues in administration can be solved only by what is called sequential decision or the "decision chain." [3] It may well be that the superintendent, who has become the illustration of this opportunity analysis, can find in the discharge of his lazy and inept foremen a forward step from which to act in getting rid of other inefficient supervisors. The opposition of a clique, for example, may be broken by and the general manager won over to the belief that the superintendent will tolerate no ineffective personnel.

Danger of Bypassing a Decision Task

Oftentimes, failure "to enter the decision arena" will allow someone else to make the decision. The full implications of this must be weighed by the reluctant administrator. *His evaluation of the danger to him personally or to his organizational entity of bypassing the decision task is a third so-called guideline for him.* If he feels that the action of another party in making the decision can remove the responsibility from his shoulders without costly repercussions in his direction, he may find it desirable to stay out of the picture. Yet this sanguine possibility is not always the case. It may well be that reluctance to make decision will precipitate the seizure of the decision making situation by some other person or group who, because of incompetence or animosity, will select an alternative course unfriendly at least to the leader who could have been the decider. Moreover, it may thrust into the hands of some actual or potential competitor within the organization an opportunity to gain a favored position over the reluctant leader, from which situs the competitor may advance his views and cause at the expense of the former. The refusal of the head of the engineering department to decide on whether or not to devote a portion of its scarce time and facilities to building a mock-up of an aluminum extruding machine may throw the matter into the hands of the head of the research department, who has always favored contracting out developmental engineering and who now decides to do so. Not only will this decision tend to downgrade the importance of the engineering department, but it may set a precedent dangerous to the growth of the engineering department, especially if the contracting firm does a good and economical job and thus proves the head of the research department to have been right.

The Cost of Deciding

To be certain, even the dynamic administrator, for reasons much more prosaic than the considerations just discussed under the concepts of morality, opportunity and political self-injury, may feel at times that it is imprudent to make a decision. Reference is made to the fact that a certain decision can be costly to make in terms of the effort necessary to reach it and/or in terms of the things which the decider must do consequentially to his having made it. Time, personnel, and facilities may have to be diverted, and additional outlay may be needed to add to the capacity of the leader or his staff. The whole matter becomes one of relative advantage, and *it is the judgment as to the cost factor which should serve as a fourth guiding tenet* to the hard pressed administrator who is in doubt about taking on the burden of another decision. One may envision, as an illustration, that the chief of market research in a large corporation whose office is fully committed to a domestic market forecast may choose to ignore the making of a decision to recommend certain action by the sales department in Africa. He may know that the requisite survey would prove very hard on his already fully employed office and nearly exhausted budget. Even decisions that would be of manifest advantage are sometimes too expensive to make.

Respect for Commitments Entered via Decision

Closely related to the factor of cost is the impossible burden which the commitment inherent in a decision can impose sometimes upon the decider. Not infrequently he who decides to do something finds that, having reached a decision, he is now saddled with an expected performance he cannot produce. The chary leader, therefore, should keep an eye to windward in the sense that he looks into this possibility. After all, it is one thing to have the honor and advantage of being bold and brave and astute enough to decide, but it is an equally or perhaps even more serious thing to plunge oneself or organization into an impossibility. Failure in a commitment can be very harmful; it can shake self-confidence; shatter the trust of followers, colleagues, and superiors; drain off effort and resources universally; and provide competitors or enemies within and without the organization both the opportunity to get ahead during the abortive attempt and to criticize adversely because of it. The market research chief might be politic to refrain from deciding upon a recommendation to study the African market if he knows that he cannot do a good job. The credit department, while he was diverted with the research, could prove that payment possibilities in the domestic market are infinitely better and, when he came up with his African study without a clear analysis of the credit standing of African distributors, at least bring derision on him. The strategic administrator should add to his list of guiding principles *this fifth admonition not to decide something which will fall into his lap to do but which he is sure he cannot accomplish.*

Sound Attitude Toward Fear

Then, of course, there is the matter of fear. Many a decision is left unmade or allowed to drift into the purview of someone else because a particular administrator is afraid to make it. This fear can proceed from previous disastrous experience in having "stuck his neck out." It also can come from organizational overtone which holds down democratic action and puts a premium on routine leadership, from lack of personal or group courage, and from the feeling that to make a decision would infringe upon another's prerogative or at least bring serious repercussions from other quarters.

A measure of fear is no doubt a very valuable attribute to the administrator; it provides him a certain self-control factor. Still it can be so overwhelming as to make it virtually impossible for him to be as dynamic in his decision-making functions as the leader is supposed to be. How one rids himself of such blocking fright is no doubt a question to be answered by specialists working in conjuncture—the psychologist, the sociologist, and the cleric. Common sense unsupported by expertise, however, can make two suggestions which, taken together, constitute the last guiding tenet for decision as to whether or not to decide. One is the fact that decision itself in reality can be only correct or incorrect, and that the chances of its being one or the other are generally about equal. Therefore, the fearful executive can take courage from his gambler's chance of doing the right thing in entering the arena and in the nature of the decision he takes. The other is the equally stark fact that many of one's group, and even of his enemies and competitors, like to avoid decision and are even themselves fearful of it, and so they may be expected to be much less antagonistic to his assuming leadership and making up his mind—and often theirs—than he may at first believe. All this is to develop the aforementioned final guiding rule as a capstone to the list: *let not the specter of fear loom too large as a barrier to decision*

*making, for there is a good chance that what is feared does
not exist, and at least in anything like its imagined gross
dimensions.*

Time of Entrance

The administrator who is to make a decision may enter the
process at one of a number of different times. These may be
identified as the precipitation, developmental, and climactic
stages. To be rational, his behavior should vary with the
stage, for each imposes different restrictions upon him and
also opens different opportunities to him. This is not to
imply that the stages are sharply distinguished one from
the other; rather they are roughly identifiable areas which,
although each shades into the next, call for and make possible different patterns of strategy.

At the Precipitation Stage

The precipitation stage of the decision-making process
refers to the period when the need for a decision first occurs.
Manifestly, it is not always possible for even the most awake
administrator to get in at the very beginning, since the
necessity for a decision may arise well before it is realized
by any of those who could conceivably make the decision.
However, he can adopt a general attitude and stance in his
organizational life which will enable him to be the first, or
among the first, to "get in on the act." This will require
above all else two things—a general alertness to everything
pertinent which concerns the organization or his part therein
and a thorough competence in the knowledge and judgmental skills necessary to decide on matters in this area.

There is no implication here that the leader must be a
veritable superman. Alterness is not the most common
human characteristic, and particularly it is not such in the
large bureaucratic organisms—the modern corporations and

huge government entities—which today employ the bulk of administrative personnel in the United States. All that is necessary in the way of alertness to beat one's competitors to the punch is relatively more sensitivity than they possess—and this may not be a great quantity, for the security rhythm and actual security of bureaucratic life do not seem friendly to human acuteness.

Gaining knowledge and judgment capacity also is probably circumscribed somewhat by the bureaucratic life, since its rules and regulations require more of the mechanical and less of the general comprehension and imagination essential to rounded ability to decide. This argues that the administrator who would early seize decision making by the forelock should determine to be both the specialist his bureaucratic assignment demands and a generalist who can recognize new situations and who is ready to decide in favor of or against innovation. It suggests that this leader orient himself basically through mastering his own job and that he further "his education" by reading, observing both in and around his area of organizational cognizance, maintaining contact with both the operational and staff personnel, keeping up on developments in the profession to which his position is related, and acquainting himself with the thinking and practices of others with positions elsewhere corresponding to his job.

The question may be raised as to why the administrator would want to enter early into the making of a decision. The truth is that there are a large number of reasons, among which stand prominently sense of duty, excitement over the possibilities the decision situation affords, desire to control the direction of the thinking by being in on the ground floor, and fear that someone else will be able to direct the thinking if he does not enter the process early. All of these, with the possible exception of the excitement factor, seem quite justifiable, and even it must not be completely castigated, because excitement is at times a good reason for action, furnishing as it does an outlet for normal constructive and honorable impulses and providing much of the "nerve fuel" necessary to carry the leader through to his final decision.

To be certain, no mention as yet has been made of the early plunge into decision making which comes from being compelled to swim or drown. Such a plunge may also be the result of one or more of several developments or exigencies: for example, insistence by the organization that the administrator in question make decisions on certain matters with dispatch; the painfully manifest responsibility of this administrator to decide; the pressure for decision when the only one who can or will decide happens to be this individual; and the manipulation, by other parties, of the administrator into a position in which he must for political considerations "get going" at once on reaching a decision.

During the Development Period

Entrance into decision making during the developmental stage may be the easiest, since the broadest spectrum of opportunity for entrance is then likely to be presented to the administrator. The development period should extend from the time those able to make a decision realize the necessity for one until the time all the facts are in and the other spade work is done for the conclusion. In actual life, the duration of this span depends upon the time and resources available to work on the decision as well as upon the intent of the directing mind with respect to coming to a well founded choice of alternatives. Also in reality, it may be expected that the developmental period will depend upon the significance of the decision to be taken, a fact which, if realized, may be reflected in the time, resources, and intent.

The strategic norm of conduct for the administrator who plans to take over the decision during the development span is to wait no longer than necessary to accomplish what he wishes to do by staying out. This is in recognition of the danger that someone else may become unmovable from the driver's seat in the meantime. Yet, the essence of strategy is to act as the situation demands, and so it may be prudent for the leader contemplating the making of the decision not to make any moves in that direction until he has had a chance to see and benefit by the errors of the person who is currently master-minding the process. This may require self-control by the dynamic administrator, because he, by nature, wants to get into the fray. It may also require careful interpretation in order to determine when the current "master-mind" has done everything he can, or at least enough to point the correct path to the waiting administrator. This line of thought may be vitalized by the illustration of the rather cautious central office purchasing agent who is watching his counterpart in a decentralized branch office move toward a decision to buy replacement machinery only at auction sales of bankrupt firms. The central office functionary, contemplating making a company decision in the matter, is leery of the thinking and experimenting of his titular subordinate, so he waits until the research, plans, and trial and error of this individual have gone far enough to reveal enough truth but not so far that he has made a decision for or against auction sales. Where is this point? Effective information channels used by the watching superior with patience and analytical judgment should reveal it.

Then too, there is here the issue of morality. The cautious administrator waiting, as it were, to jump in the right direction when his fellow executive's progress signals the right time may actually be somewhat of a pirate. How far one administrator honorably can let another pioneer the thinking and work toward a decision and then enter the process to take over the actual decision rendering must be left to conscience and the professional moralist. One may assume with safety, however, that, if the colleague in the given case is a subordinate, the administrator may with a greater degree and appearance of honesty move into the process at a time of his selection. The subordinate does represent an extension of the hand and mind of the superior and the subordinate's work may, with some justice, be viewed as an extension of or supplement to a course that is to be regarded as a superior endeavor of the organization.

At the Climax

Finally, as an entrance point into the decision melee, there is the climax, the moment when the decision is about to be made by someone else. Much that has been said of reason, subtlety, and caution with respect to the developmental entree is true, but generally in larger measure, of the "last minute plunge and grasp." An administrator, even though he is not indolent, fearful or blind to the situation, may wait for good reason until the decision is almost made by someone else. He may simply not have time to give the matter sufficient thought to get in any earlier. Being executive vice president, he is too busy with union negotiations on a new contract to study a proposal being pushed upon the president by a committee of senior employees for their retention as consultants after their retirement. He may not have been able to rise to a position in which he could legitimately venture the decision before this crucial moment; perhaps his authority at the time the making of a decision first became significant was not yet sufficiently strong in the organization to allow him to decide the matter. Nor should the political factor be forgotten; it may be of the utmost importance to an administrator to know what another leader in the organization would determine before he himself can move with greatest wisdom. An example of regard for the political element is seen in the case of the president of a commercial research laboratory who waits until the last possible moment before his leading scientist decides to reveal a world-shaking discovery, and then determines to reveal it himself as company publicity. The political consideration here illustrated is a common one—that of not deciding until it is certain that another is willing to make the same decision.

Rate of Speed in the Decision Process

Once in the decision arena, the die is cast and progress toward the conclusion which is the goal becomes an issue demanding attention. Procedural consideration will be required of the administrator as to how fast to proceed, or circumstances may determine the rate quite independent of his desires. Nevertheless, movement toward decision can be either too slow or too fast; by the same token, there is an optimum rate of movement in this direction. Since so much in reaching the proper decision from the viewpoint of both the administrator's and the organization's interests depends upon the speed with which the decision process takes place, it behooves the strategic executive to give careful attention to its rate of progress.

Slowness

A great deal is heard of slowness in decision making. In an age of "operation," such as now prevails in the United States, the emphasis is upon speed to reach conclusions. One may, therefore, properly turn his attention to the nature and implications of slowness. Yet a matter of semantics must first be resolved. Deliberateness in decision making does not necessarily connote slowness; it may simply suggest care.[4] The slowness here to be discussed is in the nature of too little speed—not too much thought, analysis, and evaluation.

Slowness in reaching a decision means a rate of progress

toward it which will cause it to be made too late for the effects desired. In extreme cases, a tardy decision may be too late to be applicable at all; the occasion for the decision may have passed. If the real estate office of an expanding company decides to bid on a piece of property which has been withdrawn from the market, the decision to make an offer on it is obviously useless as far as immediate acquisition is concerned. And still such inapplicable decisions continue to be forthcoming. The causes seem to be fourfold: the tardy decision of this extreme type is ground out simply because the decision-making machinery cannot stop, being relatively masterless as in situations of extreme bureaucracy; the decision maker is unaware that the reason for the decision no longer exists; or, aware of this fact, the decision maker believes it wise for internal political reasons to show that he has been on the job and so issues his conclusion; and, finally the decision maker wishes to go on record as having a certain attitude toward the problem or issue, even though it is no longer a demanding situation.

The administrator who makes an inapplicable decision or permits one to be rendered may lose little or much in opportunity to advance self and organizational interests. The magnitude of this intrinsic loss will obviously bear close relation to the significance of that which called for decision. However, there is generally an important extrinsic loss in all inapplicable decisions through their detraction from the leadership stature of the administrator. It is the cost of failure, and like all costs, if repeated enough or if alone of heavy enough proportions, this can become a staggering quantity. The leader who repeatedly makes the error of deciding "after the fact," or who once does so in a crucial situation, is very likely to be seen as a buffoon by his followers, a dullard by his colleagues, and an incompetent by his superiors, who are likely to feel that he is too costly to keep.

There are various degrees of slow movement in decision rendering, and some of the less slow rates are probably more common than the extreme situation just described. Mediocre progress toward the decision target may produce a result which, while applicable to the target, is not early enough to insure the "best possible results." What are some of these first class results missed by the leisurely decider? Certainly, one involves *primacy*; the decision maker and/or his organization can enhance strategic position by coming forth with the decision first or relatively earlier. The case of the slothful real estate office may again be introduced. It may be assumed that it has now learned somewhat the need for more speed, but still is not first with its offer on another property sought by its company. So, failing to make up its mind fast enough to insure the bid's hitting early, it now faces the growing value consciousness of the owner occasioned by other offers—it has lost an advantage of primacy.

But primacy is not the only best result lost by too leisurely deciding. Another concerns *responsiveness*. Two types of reactions are forthcoming to any decision—approval and disapproval—and either may proceed from any one or combination of the decision maker's three publics: internal, intermediate, and external. There is a time in every decision situation when approval will be highest and disapproval lowest. A slow decision, even if it hits the target before the problem or issue disappears, may well strike somewhat after this period of time. Fortunately for many slow-moving administrators, the zone of strong approval for many decisions is probably wide and the range of severe disapproval narrow.

The loss from dawdling which may accrue to the administrator and the organization he represents will, as in the case of the *ex post facto* decision, depend upon the situation. Even in identical situations, however, it may be just as heavy or even more serious as that proceeding from making a decision too late to apply. The totally inapplicable decision has at least one merit—negative as this may be; and it is the fact that such decision comes too late to commit the leader and his organization to action, even though it may express an intent. The approval lost and the disapproval avoided will not, since there is no commitment to action, prove as clear grounds for attack. This is not the case in the somewhat tardy decision; here there must be added to whatever loss the lateness may bring in terms of strategic advantage passed the fact that, since the moderately late decision has made a commitment to action, the forces of approval and disapproval can go to work on something tangible. It must be remembered that human beings and their organizations are often blamed more for what they do wrongly than for what they fail to do at all. The real estate office in the first case failed completely and at least did not erect for itself a continuing monument of inefficiency; in its second case, it did poorly something with which it must live. The point belabored here is that it is not necessarily safe to take comfort in the fact of being just moderately late, for a little success can be as dangerous as a big failure.

Excessive Speed

Naturally, the whole unpleasant story of rates of speed in decision making is not told by devotion to the subject of slowness. Decisions can also be made too fast. In concrete terms, this can connote several excesses in decision movement. Perhaps the most commonly identified is that of giving insufficient time to the things necessary to both good decision making and the best decision. In discussing the excessive speed category, these two concepts must be isolated for too great rapidity can affect each. Good decision making requires very often respect for political considerations. There may be the simple necessity to bow to internal public relations by informing certain individuals and subentities within the organization of what is to be decided and even of seeking their aid in deciding. In more serious dimensions, there may be a need to recognize potential opposition by actually preselling the anticipated decision to those within and without the organization who may oppose it. Whatever the situation, when the administrator moves too fast to give due attention to public relations, he may stir up a torrent of antagonism for himself and opposition to his plan. He may learn that the intrinsic worth of the decision by itself is not the only thing he must consider in reaching it. Still a good decision, apart from the requirements of its own proper making, has certain other demands on time; and when they are met too skimpily, the necessary fact finding and analysis may not be possible. The result can be something less than the best decision, that is, an injudicious judgment with all its ill consequences.

Another excess in speed of decision making has to do with the motivational influence of the decisional problem or issue upon the potential decision maker. In plain English, this means that the administrator reaches a decision before he has had time to feel the true proportions of the demand which the situation generates for a decision. Unseasonably early action of this type can yield bad fruit. It can produce a superficial conclusion far too simple, an intricate decision much too complex, or one too inappropriate in some other respect. The precipitate choice from among alternative courses is basically at fault because it fails to follow the ancient wisdom, especially honored in military circles, that the good leader first makes an estimate of the situation [5] and then chooses from among possible solutions. When the administrator rushes through decision making, he may not really understand what is needed, and even more probably he may not develop a consciousness of the various ways of providing it.[6]

The case of the energetic export manager of an American

sporting goods manufacturing company is a case in point. He receives assurances from one of his firm's vice presidents, who has just returned from a world tour which has taken him to the Philippines, that the market there is ripe for American basketball and track and field uniforms, even though the people are poor and reluctant to buy expensive uniforms which their primitive laundry practice of pounding will destroy almost as fast as it will cheaper Japanese uniforms. The export manager immediately decides to request the production department to make up a substantial quantity of black cotton uniforms, proceeding on the assumption that this dark color will help solve the laundry problem and thus meet potential objection to the purchase of the relatively higher priced American items. So anxious is he to proceed at the suggestion of his superior that he does not really take time to study the market. Hence, his decision proves quite erroneous. He did not realize that black is the color of mourning in the Philippine Islands and that athletic uniforms of this hue are not easily salable to Filipinos. In short, the export manager acted before he made a proper appraisal of the situation and before he investigated the possibilities of meeting the laundry problem otherwise.

A final form of the unwise lunge toward a conclusion is the hasty decision made without due regard for the power coefficient. In every set of circumstances requiring decision, a degree of power should be held by the leader who assumes the task. Power, as correctly defined, signifies the capacity to win compliance. The decision maker who would be a practical administrator had best appraise his power, if he is in doubt of it, before he decides. If he does not have the power, he may find himself committed to a view or action he cannot implement successfully, or at least he may lose leadership stature by a necessary subsequent act of power usurpation. The plea here is for the administrator to take enough time to ask himself the question, "Can I handle the commitment my decision will imply and can I stand the possible damage which making it will do me by creating bad feeling among my associates who may feel that I have overstepped the bounds of my legitimate power?"

Some dynamic leaders, at times in conformity with their own nature and philosophy of management and at other times in response to obvious opportunity or frustration at the blindness and delay of others, will rush into decisions which are not theirs to make within the bounds of organizational authority. At times this is a praiseworthy eagerness, for it can mean really effective leadership.[7] The maximization of utility in the decision-making process may be accomplished, under given circumstances, at a rapid pace. But, like all unorthodox action, it can or cannot be done politically. Certainly, the administrator who wants to continue his dynamic pattern of leadership is well advised not to be "caught out on the limb" too often or too seriously. His greatest asset is his ability to operate in the zone of power reflected from his constitutional power and/or flowing from nonconstitutional sources, and this can be done only if his organization allows him to act and react with a larger degree of independence than it normally gives its leaders. Should he habitually rush headlong into decisions on matters not under his purview in the organization, or should he make one of an extremely serious nature, he may find his necessary freedom curtailed because his superiors have come to distrust his discretion. Perhaps, therefore, the dynamic administrator should follow the stated long self-query above with a shorter summation question, "Am I really about to overstep *unduly* my power?"

The Subject of Primary Concern: Optimum Speed

To be sure, the good administrator should be concerned only secondarily with the excesses he may commit. He should think more positively, and be primarily interested in the right course to take. He ought, with respect to the proper rate of forward movement in decision making, do everything in his power to decide at the optimum speed—that which will avoid the pitfalls just treated and result in the best possible decision complex, including both process and alternative selected as the decision. No formula exists for the accomplishment of this task; the variables cannot be met by more than broad generalities. Yet there are at least three precautions which the administrator can take to enhance his chances of proceeding at the optimum tempo.

Preeminent among these in potential influence is concentration upon the demands of the situation, both as to the behavior pattern necessary in working out the decision and as to the essence of the decision itself. What this signifies in actual practice is for the administrator to use the so-called "open model" [8] approach to decision making, that is, to take enough time to survey and analyze the entire complex of circumstances surrounding him as a decision maker in the case. This practice should result in his disregard or at most his very prudential use of stereotyped decision approaches.

The division superintendent for a chain grocery company faces the question of whether or not to permit the opening of a new branch in an older suburb where there is still, however, considerable vacant land. The issue has been raised by a recommendation for such a branch received from a zone manager who barely substantiates his recommendation and who, anyway, is usually a bit radical in his views. The superintendent is hard pressed for time. Being of late middle age, he has been rather well sold on the potentialities of the consumer market survey, which has generally come up with the right answer for him in the past. He contacts the firm which normally does his surveys and employs it to conduct one such in the suburb. Within a few days, time being precious to the chain store official, the survey company manages to report its findings. They are negative and indicate that the residents do not feel the need for another supermarket. Consequently, the superintendent almost automatically disapproves the zone manager's request. But in this case, the survey gives a distorted picture; the scarcity of residential building sites in the city has induced a number of big builders quietly to buy up the vacant land in the suburb. There will be profitable business for another supermarket as soon as the new houses are built on them and occupied. What really has happened? The superintendent has not taken enough time to evaluate this particular request of the zone manager as an individual matter, to analyze the suburban situation as it really stands, and to do more than fall back on a procedure which had worked well before.

Of perhaps equal significance with the need for a healthy skepticism of accepted ways of arriving at decisions is the caution which holds that the leader should not let himself undertake the task of deciding unless he feels that he will be able to devote sufficient time to it. This is a direct corollary of the sound operational theorem that anything which is worth doing is worth doing well. Many forces may be at work urging the particular leader to undertake the decision: his habit of aggressive management; his pride; his realization that, if he does not decide the matter, no one will or at best some incompetent person will try; and the pressure of his superiors and other associates to get on with it. There is no recommendation here that the leader should not give in to one or more of these pressures; at times it may be wise to do so. There is rather intended the suggestion he weigh carefully his chances of making the right choice of alternatives in the time allotted and, if he feels that the time available will not permit him a reasonable chance to come up in the right manner with the right answer, that he decline. Should the pressure prove irresistible, then the best he can do is to let it be known that he may or may not make the proper decision properly. Of course, this warning would be wise only if the interests of his individual and company security, as well as of politic behavior, permit it. Such warning may be especially necessary to protect the decider in an environment which places great value on democratic procedures, for speed toward the decision target may necessitate that they be disregarded. As a buttress to his position already shored up by warning of possible failure, and in fact as the only course available in case circumstances preclude such a warning, the prospective decision maker might well anticipate attack from potential critics and try to block them by action extraneous to the decision making. Such action can be the cessation or concealment of other decisions and acts that may prove unpopular, the preparation of counterattacks on probable critics, and the adoption of a devil-may-care attitude, which can give the leader some of the invulnerability lesser men find in more courageous personalities.

A final caution which may help the administrator travel at the optimum rate toward his decision as an objective is the maintenance of close contact with sources of pertinent information, while at the same time preserving enough psychological distance from pressuring individuals and circumstance to enable him to think and proceed objectively. This is no mean task; it needs both sensitivity and insensitivity. How can an administrator, especially one caught in the fever and excitement of decision making, accomplish it? One technique is to use reliable channels of information so that rumor, half-truths, and inconsequential data are not constantly pouring in to disrupt mental and emotional progression toward the decision. Another is to insist upon discussing the decision or phases of it with one or more trustworthy associates. Nothing helps the tormented administrator to maintain correct forward movement much more than the opportunity to air views and, by doing so, to see his feelings and thoughts more clearly as that which must be rejected, modified, or accepted. And then there is always the technique of periodic seclusion. The leader, in the ferment of trying to find the most appropriate course, needs time to think by and for himself, away from the possibility of disturbance. Some may contend that the busy administrator just cannot find such privacy. Yet the day is a varied kaleidoscope even to the busiest leader, and in it he can almost always manage to draw away into himself for a while—if at no other time than on the trip to and from work or in the peace of the night when others slumber. Such techniques as these can help leaders maintain objectivity and sanity; no doubt the individual administrator can both refine their use and develop a goodly galaxy of other practical remedies.

Conclusion

There is an obvious false assumption in the treatment above of entrance into and speed in the decision making arena. It is that all decisions are important. This is, of course, quite contrary to fact. Many, perhaps most, decisions are of slight consequence to anyone, and most particularly to the leader who makes them or the organization he represents. Were they all of sufficient significance to deserve the attention here given decisions in general, the deciders would bog down under a hopeless burden and either resign their posts or end up in a mental asylum; and organizational behavior would, therefore, disintegrate into something resembling anarchy.

Yet, it has seemed necessary to assume that all decisions are major. Only such an assumption can generate sufficient concern for objective analysis of the subject; and it is only with regard to major decisions that such analysis is worthwhile. Moreover, had the myriad of hour-to-hour and day-to-day problems been considered as such they would have done nothing but clutter up the field of study, since most of them are made almost automatically or with little forethought.

Within the limits implied by this postscript refinement, strategy in decision making, as far as assuming the task of making the decision and as far as speed in reaching it are concerned, becomes more clearly the procedure dictated by common sense. After all, doing that which is appropriate to the facts of the case is more important in the situation demanding a decision of significance than in the problem requiring a conclusion of minor import. A formulistic or plain unrealistic solution of a minor problem can be afforded with less serious consequences to the administrator and his organization. In fact, it may be wise for the administrator's continued higher level performance as a leader—and indeed for the organization which should be interested in conserving his time and energy—if his strategic capacity is not tapped to solve every problem. Human creativity is a limited resource in the human organism.

BUSINESS SITUATIONS FOR ROLE PLAYING

Situation XVII

The Decision Arena: Entrance and Speed of Movement

THE MIRROR MOTOR CAR COMPANY

A. Scene.   A tertiary size manufacturer of passenger automobiles. A luncheon meeting of the office manager and the industrial relations director.

B. Players.   1. The Office Manager: Mr. Otis Regison, an old-fashioned office manager of the "chief-clerk" type, who simply cannot conceive of white collar workers as members of a labor organization and who, reflecting in large measure a marital alliance, always has considered himself a member of top management.

2. Industrial Relations Director: Mr. Terrence Paige, a well seasoned lawyer negotiator, who understands strategy and who has a good appreciation of the strong forces behind the unionization of white collar workers.

C. Situation. 1. A vigorous movement seems to be starting for the unionization of white collar workers.

2. The Office Manager, having access to the President who happens to be his brother-in-law and generally exercising considerable influence in the company management, stoutly advances the opinion that the company make no decision on its stand with respect to the movement as long as the drive produces no serious work interruption.

3. The Industrial Relations Director, assuming that the movement will be irresistible, urges an immediate company decision as to a basic policy of accommodating the new union. His influence in management is not as direct as that of the Office Manager.

4. Each is trying to persuade the other to his view for reasons of pride and unified front in an approaching consultation with the President and the Policy Committee.

D. Assignment. 1. Select a class member of demonstrated conservatism and union dislike to take the part of the Office Manager.

2. Invite a class volunteer, who signifies his sympathy with unions, to play the role of the Industrial Relations Director. If there are several volunteers, repeat the performance described below.

3. Have these two individuals attempt to persuade each other as to the proper time for entering the troublesome decision arena.

4. Request the class to make improvement suggestions if there is but one presentation; if

there is more than one, ask the class to contrast them as to strong and weak substantive and persuasive points.

NOTES

1. CHESTER I. BARNARD, *The Functions of the Executive* (Cambridge, Massachusetts: Harvard University Press, 1956), pp. 204-205.
2. Jones appears to recognize this fact, at least by strong implication, in speaking of the chief premises pertinent to each alternative. He declares that one of these premises ". . . would be some variant of the following statement: 'This alternative will serve as a means of achieving the goal resting on the step just above.' " MANLEY HOWE JONES, *Executive Decision Making* (Homewood, Illinois: Richard D. Irwin, Inc., 1957), p. 57.
3. IRWIN D. J. BROSS, *Design for Decision* (New York: The Macmillan Company, 1953), p. 132.
4. It should be borne in mind that, although modern research techniques and tools may make it possible to proceed faster toward the selection of the correct alternative, yet the fact that these techniques and tools encourage deeper and broader analysis is in turn a brake upon decision speed. After all, they make more study possible and feasible—and this well may take *time*. Mann's presentation of the possibilities of economic analysis for business decisions illustrates the countervailing effects of efficient research approaches on the rate at which the decisions may be made. ALAN S. MANN, *Economic Analysis for Business Decisions* (New York: McGraw-Hill Company, Inc., 1961).
5. For comment on the military concept of the "estimate of the situation," with reference to decision making, see WILLIAM H. NEWMAN and CHARLES E. SUMMER, JR., *The Process of Management* (Englewood Cliffs, N.J.: Prentice-Hall, Inc., 1961), pp. 257-258.
6. This is not to imply that "scientific decision making" will elicit the most support from a given public. A case to prove the opposite is apparent in the administration of the Department of Defense by Secretary Robert S. McNamara, who, more than any other Secretary of Defense, brought the scientific approach to matters of military logistics. Among his critics were some who seemed ". . . to end up talking bitterly about systems analysis, cost effectiveness studies, whiz kids, computers and other manifestations of

a scientific spirit . . ." which were said to be overriding the human factors. DANIEL SELEGMAN, "McNamara's Management Revolution," *Fortune.* LXXII: 118, July, 1965.

7. This fact, in a sense, offers support to the *expected utility maximization hypothesis.* The EUMH is described in ORVILLE BRIM et al., *Personality and Decision Processes* (Stanford: Stanford University Press, 1962), p. 203.

8. CHARLES Z. WILSON and MARCUS ALEXIS, "Basic Frameworks for Decisions," *Journal of the Academy of Management.* August, 1962.

CHAPTER 18

Contemplating the Substance
of the Decision

"Generally the decision maker has an interval of time
before he must choose from among the alternatives.
This can be a very valuable period. It provides him
with time to ponder the various alternatives and even
parts thereof. It is then that he has the opportunity
to weigh and accept or discard—to engage, as it were,
in a process of progressive selection by contemplating
many possible conclusions."

MOST SIGNIFICANT decisions are preceded by a period of
anticipation on the part of the decider. He generally knows
in advance that a decision is to be made. This knowledge
may come from his realization that a determination is
feasible, necessary, or inevitable; it may often result from
his having decided to decide. But whatever the source of
his sensitivity to impending decision, the time during which
he is conscious of the fact is in essence one of arousal. Then
it is that the decider can be said to have decision awareness.
The keenness of this cognizance will depend upon his
imaginative powers, that is, upon his capacity to envision
the future. If he has little capacity to see ahead, he may
think of the decision as simply a more or less necessary task.
Should he have great ability to peer into the future, he may
almost foretaste the decision and much that it portends.

To the strategy minded administrator, the period of
arousal presents real opportunity. It permits him to ponder

530

the *substance* of the decision to be taken—to determine its general nature as well as its specific characteristics. This is an especially valuable opportunity, since the decision maker not only must contemplate various data alternatives but also because he often will experience conflict in the pre-decision situation due to what has been described as the "simultaneous presence of at least two mutually incompatible response tendencies." [1]

The substance of a decision may be described as its essential import or as its gist. It is to be distinguished from what may be termed its objective, or procedural, aspects which deal with how it shall be issued, sold, implemented and in general handled. In short, the substance of a decision is that part of it which specifies what is to be done about what. Without it, the decision has no being.

Perspective

Much attention justifiably may be given the nature of the decision, since it is obviously a basic issue in every decision situation. The question here is stark: "What shall the substance of the decision be?" For every decision demanding situation, there is, at least in theory, an alternative most appropriate in intrinsic character. One can easily imagine a decision of this type: a determination by the general manager, who is alarmed by the growing volume of a competing company's sales, to add a sufficient number of salesmen to offset the competitor's marketing effort but not so many salesmen that individual commissions will be endangered. From the substantive viewpoint, the optimum decision is the one that meets all the content requirements of the situation. And these requirements not infrequently represent a wide spectrum. They may range, as here illustrated, from the obligation for aggressive action to the necessity for delicate balance in taking it.

Ideally, the administrator—or other decision maker—would spend his anticipating hours and days in the objective analysis and synthesis of pertinent principles and dynamics to arrive at the decision precisely correct in substance. Some administrators may do this in one or more of the conditions under which decisions are made—competitive, cooperative and neutral—[2]especially when they consider the matter for decisions of grave import. It may be assumed, however, in the absence of empirical data as to their conduct, that many administrators do not so intensely dedicate themselves to the problem. Either they do not appreciate the full significance and/or complexity of the decision to be taken or they are held back by some limitation on their ability to consider it, such as lack of necessary intellectual capacity, inadequate training and experience, shortage of time, and paucity of financial and other resources.

But, regardless of the actual preparation undertaken for reaching the right decision content, the decision maker does have available certain means which he can use to arrive at a better understanding as to what the decision should contain. Indeed a review of these will show that there are techniques and devices which even the relatively restricted administrator will find it possible to employ. It should be realized, of course, that the utilization of any one of these "weapons for assault on the screen of ignorance" demands, as a minimum for its real effectiveness, the serious intent of the would-be decision maker. He who does not care much what decision is made or who thinks he knows what should be decided without much further study will probably not resort to any measure of self-enlightenment beyond giving it lip service. Unfortunately, it appears that some administrators are so callous of consequences or sure of themselves that they all too often use some means of investigation and analysis just because it is the thing that many other administrators do.

The Superficial Estimate of the Situation

One of the simplest means of studying what should be the content of the decision is the *Superficial Estimate of the Situation*. This SES technique is a more or less primitive combination of the deductive and inductive processes. It involves no new gathering of data or advice, but rather consists of self-questioning by the decision maker along several lines without further digging into the matter. Although the number and character of the questions properly may be varied to meet special situations, there are six queries that would seem to constitute a stable core for the SES. They follow with brief comment:

1. *What is the prime purpose to be served by my impending decision?* This question justly deserves first place in the Superficial Estimate of the Situation, since the main objective is that which should be the controlling target for every total act of decision making. At any rate, necessity for making a decision generally presents the decision maker with the opportunity to attain or at least further one or more objectives, because he can choose from a variety of possible alternatives. The office manager, confronted with the resignation of a secretary, now has the opportunity to raise the efficiency of his office, to assure its continued smooth functioning, to save on salaries, to improve office morale, or to do a favor for a superior. And so he is faced with a veritable plethora of possible decisions: to employ a better secretary, to seek the same type of performer, to replace the resigned secretary with a less able person at lower pay, to elevate a deserving stenographer to the vacancy, or to hire the daughter of a friend of the general manager. Unfortunately, what decision to make may not be obvious at once to the office manager. He, and like him most decision makers, must make value judgments—and there is nothing in the given decision situation that automatically indicates which is the best decision to make.[3] Clearly a basic criterion in any value judgment must be the end to be served, and so the administrator, or other decision maker, can profitably devote his attention to an evaluation

of alternate objectives. By so doing, he will increase his chances of making the "right" decision.

2. *How completely should my decision cover the issue?* The problem which the decision maker faces may, and usually does, have several facets. Such a multi-sided problem is that of the chief of the systems and procedures section who has been given carte blanche authority to revamp the whole records keeping system. The task is a complex one. It involves the determination of the point at which to start, the respect to be paid precedent and the procedures to be retained, the particular type of new steps to be instituted, the costs involved, the timing of changeover, and even the mollification or other handling of opposition. Here, as in the case of all intricate problems, it may be wise or unwise to attempt to decide everything at once, that is, in a single decision. Circumstances, such as the pressure of other work and the desirability of total commitment, may argue for unitary determination; other conditions, such as the extreme complexity of the matters to be decided or the political feasability of phase decision, may point to the wisdom of deciding upon only certain aspects. All this is to imply strongly that the wise approach to the substance of a decision demands attention to how much of the subject situation should be covered, and that the SES should contain early in its hierarchy of questions a self-interrogation that will assure this attention. The strategy of decision making may make either a narrow or broad decision proper—and the decision maker should early determine which.

3. *What portion of the total decision complexus should I assume as my task?* This third question introduces into the Superficial Estimate of the Situation what is perhaps its most difficult element. Much of import to the decision maker and the organization he may represent depends upon what part of the decision he takes upon himself. By seizing the job of the entire decision, the decision maker may acquire fuller leadership stature, enhance the possibility of his control of subsequent decisions and actions, and prevent the delay and opposition which all too often characterize the discharge of diffused duty or responsibility. On the other hand, by side-stepping certain aspects of the decision, he may reduce the proportions of the work

involved, minimize the degree of blame for possible failure, and perhaps help assure a better decision since others, more able in various aspects of the matter, will participate in the determination of the end decision product.

These, and probably various other advantages and disadvantages of relative degrees of participation in making the whole decision, are very real and may have much to do with the success or failure of the decision maker and the entity he administers. This is quite clear in the case of both the office manager with the secretarial vacancy and the chief of the systems and procedures department with his mandate to reform record keeping. Should each have undertaken, for example, to decide both the new personnel necessary and the costs thereof, they could have sunk or swum on to better things. Had their decisions eventuated in much greater efficiency, they could have emerged as "heroes." But, had their decisions, even though made with the precision of the best unilateral approach, produced lowered efficiency at the same or higher costs, they could have come out, again in the delightful jargon of adolescence, as "bums." In view of the risk of such dire results, it might have been better for the office manager and the section chief to have insisted upon the personnel department setting the salaries of all new employees. The lesson here should be clear. He who would handle a decision situation has real reason to search his feelings and mind in order to weigh the question of how much or little of the decision task it is wise for him to take unto himself.

4. *How far do I want the decision to commit me?* By its very nature, decision means commitment. The decision maker—be he plain citizen, company supervisor or administrator, military officer, public servant, or churchman—by the very act of decision commits himself to something: a stand, an attitude, a pledge, or a course of action. The facts of significance to him here are the degree to which the decision impending will bind him and the measure to which he wants to be tied by it. It is conceivable that he may desire to be bound tightly, that is, to be so committed by it that freedom to decide and act further and in other directions is curtailed. This could be the case of the company president who decides to urge upon the board of

directors the building of a new building in Detroit so that funds will not be available to expand plant in Akron, where for some reason he does not want further facility development. Or it is also conceivable that the decision maker might want to remain free of any commitment by a decision. The general manager who decides to employ the services of a professional consultant to help solve a sales problem may not wish to create such a precedent that he will be constrained to seek expertise in making a subsequent decision. The implication of this line of reasoning to the SES seems clear. The decision maker, in his contemplating period, will need to take a hard look at what he ponders deciding in order to determine how it will influence his subsequent freedom. And the question designed to engage him in this effort may well be placed last in the SES, since it calls for a scrutiny of any conclusions already reached by the decision maker in his consideration of the previous three questions.

A case for the Superficial Estimate of the Situation is not difficult to make. First of all, it certainly can be contended with strength that the SES is better than no formal action in contemplating the substance of the decision to be taken. Self-query along definite lines does motivate the individual to marshall his feelings and knowledge and to engage in some thought on the matter. It would be a rare situation indeed were the person contemplating a determination on some matter to be totally neutral and uniformed on it. Moreover, the decision maker may be assumed in many cases to have even more than usual competence. He is often a professional specialist or leader who, because of his capacity, has been entrusted with or seizes the decision making function. The end product of attempting to focus on the problem or issue at stake, *ceteris paribus*, should give the decision maker a better chance of reaching the right conclusion than would mere acceptance at random or decision as convenient. After all, it may be presumed that some formal consideration of a problem is better than none.

The SES technique demands a minimum of the decision maker's time; this is a second point which may be advanced in its favor. He simply needs to gather together and to bring to bear on the decision to be made what he feels and knows of the subject. To be certain, the word "simply" is here to be interpreted as implying relativity. Although the SES approach to decision making may prove easy (as, for example, when the decision is a simple one to make and the maker's competence to reach it is high), it actually can be a real mental effort. The simplicity implied, then, signifies the fact that, in contrast to the research and extended study approach, the SES is less time consuming. At any rate, it lends itself to speed, since the user does not need to go outside himself for the material and even hypotheses from which to reason. In many cases, but a few minutes may be required to answer its self-directed questions. The truth is that the SES can be used within almost any appreciable interval of time, because almost any period is adequate for the decision maker *somehow* to answer each query. Whether or not increased speed in making the SES enhances its superficiality is an open question. Perhaps it does, but sight should not be lost of the fact that temporal pressure for decision can itself motivate the maker to more intense mental effort.

Many of the more complex approaches to decision making, such as intensive personal investigation, the use of professional consultants and experts, the running of surveys, and the resort to pilot or tentative decisions are costly to the whole resource combination which includes, in addition to time, such factors as energy, inventory, and finances. The Superficial Estimate of the Situation has the advantage of cheapness. It will normally require little beyond the personal time and energy of the decision maker and, because it is usually not an action in great breadth or depth, probably not much of this. This third argument for the SES can be a most potent one for the administrator who is working on an inadequate budget and/or whose effectiveness is judged in appreciable measure on the basis of his economy of operation.

A final argument for this self-estimate of what should constitute the essence of the decision can be based on the character of the questions included in it. The queries here propounded, as the directives of th SES, are designed to draw forth some organized thought—and even analytical judgment—on all aspects of the correct substance of a decision. If any pertinent fundamental item is omitted from their ranks, it is the concluding question: "How does the decision I contemplate fit into the political frame of reference in which the decision must be sold?" This interrogative prod has been intentionally left out, because its inclusion might detract from the primary purpose of concentrating on the substance of the decision and because its many ramifications mark it for special treatment elsewhere.

A special merit of the battery of questions chosen, even excluding the political query, is that they are basic to any study of the proper intrinsic character of a given decision. Therefore, they do not constitute a mere expedient device by which some consideration can be given the necessary decision substance. One may venture, in this connection, a prosaic expression; the questions used can be the "jumping off" points for broader and deeper analysis. The decision maker who employs the SES is not, therefore, necessarily engaging in an isolated or one-step activity. He may be taking the first step in his total investigation and analysis of what he should decide.

The Personal Probe

A number of circumstances may lead the decision maker to undertake a further analysis of what should be the substantive nature of the decision. Often they are nothing more than facilitating conditions, such as available time, sufficient resources, natural curiosity, and an acquiescent or friendly superior. When one or more of these factors encourages further study, the decision maker may embark upon it. Or the circumstances may be more direct motivational factors that virtually force him on. Here one may note a high degree of complexity in the situation, the vital significance of the right decision, or downright ignorance of the facts and nuances of the case. To be certain, they may be—as they frequently are—some combination of conditions that tend to press the decision maker forward.

The personal probe, as the phraseology suggests, is an effort by the decision maker himself. It connotes essentially his individual effort without any appreciable transfer of the burden to a second party, such as, another individual, organizational entity, or professional research agency. In this respect, it is similar to the SES, from which it often is but an extension. Yet it is distinguishable from the SES by the fact of its greater breadth and/or depth. The personal probe, a step beyond the mere recalling, summing up, and concluding from what is already known, attempts to bring into sharper focus that which is not clearly realized and to uncover that which lies hidden.

This is not to imply that the personal probe is necessarily some sort of high level research exercise rarely attempted and best left to those of good academic bent and background. Actually, all decision makers from time to time make use of it. They want or need to know more about the issues or problems confronting them; and so, as thinking beings with a purpose, they proceed to investigate. One might well assume that the formally trained mind would do best in this further study, but he should not forget that the less academically sophisticated individual may have the advantage of a more primitive and realistic viewpoint which can save him from too much balancing of relative advantages and disadvantages as he gropes for the right thing in decision.

No doubt the personal probe can be conducted in various ways. The decision maker may launch into some sort of historical search; he may attempt to look into pertinent policies; he may survey comparable situations; or he may adopt the library approach. As is quite likely, he may do his probing in more than one—if not all—of these frames of reference. Each of these forms of the personal probe has its own peculiarities, merits, and pitfalls. Certainly the strategic decision maker, the individual or entity that seeks to reach that decision right for the particular occasion, will find it profitable to understand their proper usage.

The Historical Search

The historical search may be defined as an investigation of the past by the decision maker to enhance his capacity to decide correctly in the present or future.[4] It is often a most inviting path, for the decision maker commonly is influenced by one or more attraction forces to turn to the decisions and actions of the past taken in the department, company, or some other aspect of his social milieu. Four of these forces can be of such strength that they almost call attention to themselves. Primary among them is memory and the associations it brings to the mind of the decision maker as he gropes toward the "right conclusion." His fear of deciding by himself can be another strong reason for him to turn backward in his study. Of course, his reason for examining that which has gone before may be simply the stark need for guidance in what to decide. Last but not least, it may be politically wise for the decision maker to honor or appear to honor precedent and to emulate predecessors.

The historical search is quite defensible as a preparatory

step to decision making. The psychological comfort to be obtained by relying upon the past, the value of the data and lessons which such study may reveal, and the positional strength to be gained by showing respect for that which has gone before can be potent arguments for the decision maker to look backward.

The head of the developmental engineering office in a large corporation faces the necessity of fixing upon the general course of action to recommend in view of the fact that the next twelve months appear rather bleak as far as the company's business is concerned. He is in a quandary as to what to decide. Shall he plan for retrenchment and economy, for the maintenance of about the same level of activity and expenditure, or for extra effort and outlay? His company has faced similar lean years in 1931, 1937, 1947, and 1960. He determines to look into what it did then, and so he looks up the minutes of the finance committee meetings, the budgets of those years, and the financial statements. The determination to do this and the actual perusal of these documents gives the head of the development engineering office a feeling of closer association with his own frame of reference. He may gain courage from the realization as to what others in his organization have undergone and done. But this is not the only gain from his attempt to analyze the past. He learns that, in each of the previous four bad years, the company has poured more money into sales efforts but not into research and development. He notes also that in each following year net income rose and his department was granted more funds. Clearly, he has obtained knowledge of a successful decision pattern, and so he may take guidance therefrom and move with sounder judgment toward a decision as to what he shall plan. Finally, it should be noted that the minutes of the finance committee reveal its membership, who still happen to be the controlling figures in the company, to have been unanimously in favor of holding to the status quo in research and engineering. And so the head of the engineering development office comes, by his search of company history, into possession of the valuable political fact that his superiors probably may be inclined again to "hold the line." Truly, as this hypothetical illustration attempts to show in bold relief, the decision maker can gain from looking into the past.

But there are dangers involved in the historical research. First, the mere fact of its attraction may seduce the decision maker into looking backward for answers which are simply not there. Second, and worse yet, is the hypnotic result which can eventuate from repetitive dependence upon history. The decision maker who generally relies upon the past to indicate what he should decide may become a sort of a "precedent drunk"—an individual who will not normally think for himself beyond the limits necessary to ferret out what his predecessors decided or did. This hypnosis can proceed from the relative ease of staying in the groove already cut, independent thinking not being necessary. It also can come from the relative safety of not venturing new decisions, which might well startle people because of their strangeness, disturb them because of the unsettling impact, and in general call attention to the maker as somewhat of a radical, if not dangerous, individual.

These dangers are in essence psychological. Guarding against them, therefore, presents a peculiarly difficult subject to discuss. Psychological reaction is a rather individualistic thing; it varies pronouncedly with the individual both in specific nature and intensity. Perhaps the best that can here be done is to prescribe, as it were, a few generalizations which, if observed, can help the decision maker resist the soporific appeal of the historical search.

The decision maker who is tempted to "thumb the pages of history" should remember that history does not always repeat itself. That which is known, possible, and needed seems to vary with time. This is particularly true in the business world, an environment in which the forces of competition, market fluctuations, and secular change are so important.

He should appreciate the fact that he, and every other administrator, probably possesses some unique decision making ability. It is safe to assume that no two human beings—personalities may be a better philosophical term—ever have been or are exactly the same. Most likely physical, mental, emotional, moral, and social attributes are never quite combined in the same way to make a human personality. Yet all of these attributes have a bearing on decision making. The implication here is that each decision maker, because he is different from every other one, may be able to reach a better decision than his predecessors.

The historically minded decision maker would do well also to heed the warning of the scientific historian that not everything which is written or remembered is true. He who would depend heavily on the past may place a measure of further self-restraint on himself by considering the unpleasant truth that what passes for "records of the past" are not infrequently fallacious in toto or degree. This is as true of company records as it is of the more ancient or general documents of man's political, social, and economic life. The profit and loss statement of many American companies, for example, rarely has shown the whole income truth, simply because it has omitted the item of cash flow. Sometimes, as in this case, the reason for the unreliability of the historical record may be recording neglect, and at still other times a deliberate effort at strategy.

Finally, the decision maker intent upon resisting the fascination of the past ought to recognize the brutal truth that the administrator who depends greatly on history may not thereby be maintaining or enhancing his authoritative image. Many people, including particularly a certain type of so-called practical businessman, seem to have relatively little respect for history and for those who look to it for answers. Their attitude is forward looking and, in their dynamism, they tend to deprecate the individual who always insists upon looking backward before he will look forward. Therefore, the decision maker should consider well the possible loss of respect and popularity he can suffer through becoming hypnotized by earlier decisions and acts.

Nowhere in this brief treatment of the historical search has any mention been made of its relation to the conservatism which is an important ingredient in sensible decision making. In a free-wheeling society such as that of the United States, the term "conservatism" is likely to bear a rather negative connotation as meaning reluctance to progress. This, of course, is a perverted meaning of the concept. Conservatism signifies insistence upon sound judgment with respect to change; it counsels caution and moderation, lest change be made simply for the sake of change. The decision maker needs sound judgment; he needs, in other words, to be conservative in the sense that he first considers well the value of the old before he decides on the new. And an evaluation of established goals, principles, policies, and practices demands a knowledge of their nature, their reason for being, and their results. This can be had only by the study of history if it is not so well implanted in the consciousness of the decision maker that he can recall it via the Superficial Estimate of the Situation. It may be said truthfully that, whatever the specific gains and dangers of the historical search, as a form of the personal probe the device at least can be most valuable in supplying the factual basis for the conservatism necessary to decision making.

The Policy Review

In the social frame of reference of every individual or organization there are settled courses of action familiarly known as policies.[5] The decision maker, in some degree, is usually affected by or expected to be influenced in his decision function by some policy or policies. It behooves him, therefore, to make himself cognizant of their nature, for ignorance of them may lead him to non-strategic determination. The superintendent, who is unaware of the company policy that people of non-Christian religious affiliations are to be given time off to celebrate the prime holydays in their faith, refuses a request by a certain obscure sect to be absent on a given Wednesday. Embarrassment to him and the company ensues when the group protests to the general manager, who must reverse the superintendent; and perhaps the effect upon morale is bad.

Now it may be contended that the decision maker would have to be rather dull not to be aware of the policies pertinent to his impending decision. However, this is not necessarily true, for many policies remain or become obscure and intelligent individuals, alert and dynamic, retain or develop a degree of ignorance regarding them. The reasons are varied. Perhaps the policy, enunciated long ago, rarely has been applied and so has become forgotten. It may be what is known as a "shadow" policy, a course commitment made in concession to some pressure but not really desired by the organization and, therefore, not honored by close adherence. It may be, in fact, policy which somehow has never been fully or properly communicated to the decision maker.

Ignorance of policy is sometimes much more than not knowing what the policy formally states, inasmuch as there is much more which can be known about the policy. A policy is a dynamic social reality, and so it has many facets. Why was it formulated? When was it instituted? Who is responsible for it? How much support does it now enjoy? In what manner has it been interpreted? To what degree is it applicable to the problem or issue to be decided? The answers to these, and perhaps several other questions relative to a given policy, can be of as much or even more import to the decision maker than the bare knowledge of the policy statement. They will place the policy in its proper perspective. It is these answers which will make it possible for the decision maker to adhere more closely to the spirit of the policy. It is also these answers that may show him the wisdom and way of escaping from the binding and predestined commitment to mechanical decision that simple knowledge of policy can impose.

Policy study, then, involves both an investigation as to the formal statement of the policy and an interpretation of the policy in terms of its dynamics. Sometimes the same probing techniques will suffice for each task. Perhaps there is available for perusal some running account of its institution and application. This may be, for example, department reports on the implementation of an absentee policy. A superintendent, somewhat more alert than the individual just cited, decides to scan the copies of these reports to the general manager which are filed in the division office. Here he finds the basic policy statement as the manager's office received it on October 11, 1962, as well as the annual summations of time off permitted by his predecessors to employes of the division he heads. Or the running account may exist in a less convenient form as, for example, in the memory of some subordinate, colleague or superior, who will have to be consulted about the policy. The wiser superintendent proceeds to talk with him or to ask him for a written response about the policy, and again he comes off with knowledge as to both the formal and actual character of the policy.

Often—and probably much more frequently—the policy study is not made this easily, for the simple reason that the knowledge sought is insufficiently concentrated. The decision maker, therefore, might well assume a rather far ranging pattern when he undertakes to probe for pertinent policy information. This pattern should be implemented by at least two actions on his part. At the risk of undue repetition, it is here emphasized that he should take whatever steps are necessary to assure himself that he really knows the policy in its formally stated terms. This knowledge is essential as the point of reference toward which he must move if he wishes to conform to policy in his decision making or from which he may gauge the safety of his degree of departure if he desires to violate policy.

As a sort of progression, the decision maker should also take whatever action is necessary to find out what commitment the present pertinent leader or leaders in his environment, be it department, company, or other association, actually have to the policy. Not infrequently successive leaders have quite different views on a given policy and proceed to apply it with more or less vigor than their predecessors used. The decision maker who owes a leader allegiance and compliance, as many decision makers do, can be guilty of an unwise decision if he fails to realize this fundamental fact, for he may then make his determination in terms of a past, but no longer existent, frame of reference.

An example is to be found in the case of the transportation department head in a public utility company who, strongly impressed with the dynamic public relations policy of his recently retired president, proceeds to pledge his trucks to a Memorial Day parade, not realizing that the new president is very economy minded. In fact, a rather subtle lesson is contained in this particular illustration, and it underlines the extreme necessity for a comprehensive study by the decision maker in his policy probe. It is to the effect that sometimes a decision maker, particularly if he is an administrator subject to a higher command echelon, will remain so impressed by and retain either such loyalty or disloyalty to a former superior that he will almost automatically continue to interpret policy under a new superior as he did under the old. His study of policy has not gone far enough to cause him to disassociate himself from a past policy interpretation. This personality hypnosis can be really binding and have a serious and dangerous effect as even Chairman Krushchev must have realized when he divested his regime of such Stalin oriented characters as Secretary Molotov.

In addition, then, to the ranging action just advocated, the decision maker should adapt a rather skeptical attitude toward much of the policy information he does obtain. Unfortunately for the policy studying decision maker, those from whom he can obtain information regarding the present status of a given policy are not always disposed to communicate it wholly or truthfully to him. Even the new leader, uncertain as to what stand he should take on a given policy or unwilling to make a sharp break from the stand of his predecessor, may at least for a time be unwilling to declare himself clearly on it. The new president of the public utility company might not have been willing to broadcast his restrictive interpretation of the company's public relation policy or even to convey such an interpretation to the head of the transportation department. Perhaps he was new in the community or young in experience, and wisely or unwisely was waiting for events to show him what to do. Still, it is not only superiors who may be reluctant to reveal where they stand with respect to a course of action. The decision maker's other associates may hold back. His colleagues—for example, the other department heads—may not respond wholeheartedly to him because of their own ignorance of the situation, jealousy of him, fear of informing him wrongly, or even desire to embarrass the new leader. And, to be certain, his subordinates may respond poorly to his queries for similar reasons as well as for the wish to please him by telling him what they think he wants to hear—a flattery technique used on them probably more commonly than many decision makers of administrative or other higher rank may realize.

The decision maker who would probe beyond the SES can find profit in a review of policies extant in his environment. After all, policies are ground rules, and he who would play well in any game, even if he wishes to violate the rules, can do so more intelligently—with greater chance of success and less risk of penalty—if he knows what they truly are and mean.

It would be remiss not to mention, somewhere in this treatment of the policy search, that about the same comment is applicable to well established procedures. These standardized patterns of action have been omitted intentionally because they are but a "reflection of policy." [6]

The Survey of Comparable Situations

Although no decision demanding situations, as previously emphasized, are identical, it is also probably true that each such situation contains certain similarities to one or more other problems or issues. Moreover, there is always the possibility that a study of comparable situations will reveal something valuable to the decision maker with respect to these similar elements. The other decision makers may be advanced in their study, or in fact already may have reached a decision which time has shown to be right or wrong. They may have greater capacity to decide properly because of their superior intelligence, better training and more experience, or the resources available to them. It is an old platitude that "We can learn from others"; certainly this is as true of the decision maker as of anyone else.

At times, however, the decision maker fails to avail himself of what others and other complexes can teach him. He may be too involved within his own immediate frame of reference, as is all too often the case of the dynamic administrator, to look outside it, time and energy simply being lacking. Perhaps he is a proud person who in the sensitivity or conceit borne of his pride turns his back on what other decision makers could by their behavior give him. Even if he is willing and anxious to study comparable situations, he may not know in what direction to look for one or more such. It may well be that his ignorance of which way to turn for comparison and contrast is the most common barrier to the study of what others are determining or have decided.

To make matters still more difficult, circumstances sometimes add still another obstruction to such barriers to the use of similar situations and decisions. The decision maker may be in a position, or consider himself to be in one, which for political reasons will not permit him to risk showing his hand by inquiring into comparable situations. Mayhap such inquiry would give someone else information of strategic value—usable against the decision maker or his organization. This could be the inherent revelation to superiors that the decision maker does not "know his business" and is, therefore, not to be fully depended upon or that the decision maker's organization is contemplating some competitive move which, now signalled, can be blocked by a countermove.

No precise plan for the correct study of comparable situations can be drawn up; the task varies too much with circumstance. However, it does seem possible to isolate certain principles which, if followed, can help guarantee adequate and politic situation canvassing. In the first place, the decision maker should observe the *Principle of Social Geography*, which holds that lessons to be learned in the field of human behavior, decision as well as action, may be within, near, or far from the investigator's frame of reference and this distance may be in terms of time, nature of organization, or physical distance. The implication is clear—the decision maker should be catholic in his approach to the situation canvass and should not be bound in his search to any traditional or other favored sector.

In deciding upon a legal problem arising out of hazardous

working conditions, the president of a copper mining company may find guidance in the decisions and actions of a marine dredging corporation. The dean of men in a large university may find an investigation of trade union democracy profitable in trying to determine how to supervise student government. The churchman burdened with congregational debt may find helpful hints for its solution in the review of fund raising decisions made and implemented by a charitable organization. Truly, guideposts for the determination of the "correct stuff" to put into a decision may be found here or there, near or far.

In the second place, the decision should respect what may be termed the *Principle of Negative Value*. This tenet states the fact that it can be important for the decision maker to know what not to decide and that, although the first consideration must always be what to decide, negative knowledge is a way of approaching the prime object. Regard for the principle should take the form of a certain intellectual broadmindedness in the sense that the canvassing decision maker should be willing to look into situations which have not been or obviously are not being decided correctly as to substance. There may be great educative value in the mistakes of others. Not only may they demonstrate pitfalls and entrapments to be avoided but, if the person or entity who made or is making the mistaken determination is in some way a competitor of the decision maker or his organization, this knowledge of the error could facilitate truly effective strategy against the erroneous decision maker.

A general sales manager of a paper container factory faces the problem of declining sales under the pressure of developments in the plastics industry. He looks into the experience of two of his principal paper cup competitors. In each case, he discovers that a basic decision was made by the board of directors to ignore the upsurge of the plastic industry and that, subsequently, their sales began to fall. Now he sees that the snob decision was wrong, and he is thus warned not to take it. Moreover, he is in possession of knowledge that he can use against his paper cup competitors—that they are conservatively led and are suffering. He does not yet know what decision to make about his own case, but he certainly knows one not to take. Such negative knowledge may be the most common gain from a situational survey if it is true that decisions are more often wrong than right.

The *Principle of Balance* is another tenet which justifiably demands obeisance by the decision maker who wishes to extend his personal probe into somehow comparable situations. Its gist is that the decision maker, who often is feverishly looking for answers, should neither rush to study and emulate all apparently related decisions nor ignore them as distractions. This is the most nebulous of the guiding principles of situational study by the decision maker, because it demands good judgment in an area where the criteria are neither clear nor definite. "What is a pertinent comparable situation? How many should be tapped by the individual or group contemplating the substance of a determination? How important are the data and lessons to be learned?" These are the questions to be faced in the proper observance of the Principle of Balance. If the probing decision maker will keep them constantly in mind, he will find that they exercise a positive influence for good judgment.

Closely related to the concept of balance is a final guiding rule that can be given the nice title of *Principle of Political Speed*. Time is very commonly an element in the decision situation, and generally a factor somewhat in short supply. The decision maker should always remember that his associates, the organization he represents, or another "public" concerned with the decision may become impatient and make some determination rather than wait for the greatest assurance that the decision made is the best one in substance. He also should bear in mind that his competitors, friendly or unfriendly, may make or commit him to a decision while he is delving into other situations for assistance in making up his mind. These possible dangers suggest that he not commit himself to the situational canvass so deeply that a decision march is stolen on him. He can protect himself from these dangers in one or both of two ways by making up his mind that he will cut off his study when the pressure gets to the determining stage; and by getting the possible other deciders or forcers of decision so involved in the canvass, investigation, or any other type of distracting commitments that they do not see the opportunity to beat him to the "decision" punch or do not have the chance to do so.

A hypothetical case will serve to illustrate both the political danger of too much "canvassing" and the fact that there are ways of nullifying its effect. The personnel manager of a packing plant is pondering whether or not to recommend a self-rating scheme for salaried employees. Since he feels this device would be a rather daring innovation in his company, he undertakes a thorough study of the experiences of ten other concerns who have tried it. The executive vice president is known to be opposed to any such unique device but not yet to the extent that he will issue an order against instituting it. However, the company pot is boiling. The union, even though it has no jurisdiction over salaried personnel, is pressing the executive vice president to head off any positive recommendation by the personnel manager, as it is afraid the idea may eventually be applied to the non-salaried people. Obviously, there is a good chance that a high level stand will be taken against the self-rating device while the personnel manager is considering comparable situations. Fortunately, he is not helpless. The probing personnel manager can guard against an unfavorable decision from the executive vice president during the long canvass period by determining to send his recommendation to the superior official at anytime he feels this individual is near to making up his mind against the rating system and/or he can continue to submit recommendations on other things to the vice president so that he can tie him down with their consideration.

Fortunately, the decision maker concerned over the time factor in his study of comparable problems and decisions can take comfort from the truth that it really is not necessary for him to locate and study all or nearly all of them. "Accurate coverage of reality does not necessarily mean total coverage." [7]

The Library Approach

At this point, it should be realized that the various forms of personal probing so far discussed—the historical search, the policy review and the comparable situation survey—are not mutually exclusive. Each extends into the other, and this is especially evident in the dichotomy of the historical search versus the other two forms. One cannot, for example, review policy without reference to policies made and followed in the past, and this is clearly a form of the historical search; nor can he, by way of further illustration, indulge in an historical search without running into policy and without, at least upon occasion, getting out of the immediate milieu into another situation.

The intertwining character of these various forms of the personal probe is made even more complex by the introduction of a fourth and final variation. This is the library approach. In a sense, it is the most comprehensive of the lot and might properly have been set first, except for the danger of its breadth so overshadowing the others as to make their distinction even more difficult. The library approach simply refers to an effort on the part of the decision maker to read what has been written on the subject of the decisional situation. It can be given a personality apart from that of mere reading—which, of course, may be involved in all the other forms—by holding it to be the purview of more or less public publications on the subject as distinguished from personal and organizational records.

Some decision makers in the United States, especially those who are under the tremendous pressure of administering some dynamic organization or part thereof, probably tend to disdain resort to published literature. This may be due to the fact that the ranks of American decision makers still contain a goodly number with little formal education in management, that American schools and colleges do not really inculcate in students sufficient respect for books and other reading material, or that pertinent literature on the situation at hand is either not known to the decision maker or unavailable to him.

What can the decision maker do to insure adequate usage of the literature on the decisional subject that faces him? Perhaps the answer must be rather negative if the situation demands quick action, for reading takes time; should the situation be such that the decision can be deferred, then of course much can be done by the determined administrator, since the constant improvement in the dissemination of facts and findings is making it progressively easier to acquire most types of information. In general, however, the decision maker who wishes to assure himself that he knows the pertinent literature profitably can engage in the regular reading of published material which is pertinent to his job. This will not only provide him with specific bits and portions of information which he may marshall in his SES and deeper personal probes, but it should also help give him a consciousness of what has been written on many of the matters for decision which may arise in the future to plague him.

It should be realized by all makers of significant decisions that a vast body of literature exists on each of an almost innumerable list of subjects, among which it is most likely his problem or issue will appear precisely or in some related form. And of almost equal importance, decision makers should be aware of the excellent libraries and library services generally available in the United States. The decision maker who ignores that which has been published in his field and/or upon the immediate subject of his concern may be inviting error of decision quite unnecessarily. A surprisingly large portion of the experiences of the human race are easily accessible to him.

The decision maker, hard pressed by his other duties and commitments, can discharge his "obligation" to read in at least two ways which will greatly decrease the burden of library research. He can attempt to build up his personal, his office, or the company library. This does not necessarily envisage great numbers of books, periodicals, brochures, pamphlets, and other publications. Selectivity is as possible in literature as elsewhere; and often a well chosen library, even if small, is better than a large one that, by its size, may overwhelm the decision maker and either confuse or discourage him in his reading. In place of or as a de facto extension of his personal or organizational library, he can establish a bridgehead with the local and other library personnel. The businessman, the politician, the military officer, and even the churchman and educator, who are not library oriented, will find to their surprise that the American library is today generally staffed at least in part by professional librarians who quickly can and cheerfully will obtain from the shelves of their own libraries or on loan from elsewhere most that is published on the almost infinite variety of subjects which have come under the pen.

Reliance On Others

Not infrequently the decision maker may turn to others for assistance in getting at the proper substance of the decision.

This is a prudent course under one or more of the following circumstances: the decision maker knows he does not know what to decide and cannot alone arrive at a sound judgment; he is fairly certain of what the decision should be but wants his intended determination to be corroborated; or he feels political considerations dictate his calling upon others for aid.

For Basic Aid

The first of these circumstances may be seen in the case of an individual inexperienced in decision making or in making decisions of a given type. The young man promoted to office manager from the position of head bookkeeper quite legitimately might ask the head of the mail department, who has held his position for years, what to decide in a flagrant case of tardiness; and, under the same pressure of ignorance, the head of the mail department, never before having supervised women, might consult with the head of the print shop, which employs several women, about the length of coffee breaks he should allow. The thing to be remembered in this connection is that no one individual or entity can be expected to know everything and that therefore, *ceteris paribus*, it is no disgrace to seek guidance. Of course, one caution is in order. The wisdom of seeking aid should, except in cases of dire emergency, be weighed against anything which the request may reveal or any undesirable impression it may make. Requests, and especially frequent requests, for recommendations from subordinates may help create in their minds an image of the decision maker as incompetent and/ or weak spined; and such requests may have similar, if not even more serious, repercussions when made to colleagues and superiors who, because of their rank in the organization or group, are in a stronger position than subordinates to harm the decision maker.

For Corroboration

Wise strategy in seeking aid to confirm conclusions in "deciding what to decide" demands careful selection of the corroborator. There is a temptation, common to many decision makers, to seek support for a decision about to be promulgated by asking rather indiscriminately people with whom they have contact for their opinion on it. Several things may be perilous in this procedure. The people whose opinion is sought may be, as many associates are, individuals who cannot or will not give an objective and significant response. Perhaps they are subordinates, specialists or even generalists who lack the knowledge, insight, and judgmental capacity to give a sound opinion on the decision at hand. Or perhaps they are hangers-on, friends or even "politicians" who out of fear, desire for favor, or affection refuse to give their real evaluation. As a dangerous corollary to indiscriminate seeking of corroboration one should note the possibility of offending wiser and even more influential individuals by neglecting to approach them for help, which may happen if the decision maker feels satisfied with the support he has obtained indiscriminately.

No note of warning about careless selection of parties from whom to seek corroboration would be complete without reference to the old, but infinitely wise, adage that an individual is known by the company he keeps. And so it is with the decision maker—only the implication may bear to him more than the usual import.

The decision maker is commonly a leader, and hence he is often carefully watched by many, and his behavior patterns are duly noted by his followers, colleagues, superiors and enemies alike. Should he turn to the incompetent or the sycophant to test the wisdom of his intended decision, or even already announced conclusion, he may quickly lose a measure of the respect and trust of those who would otherwise support him and the fear of those unfriendly to him.

Not all decisions made or to be made need confirmation. The decision maker may already have reached his final conclusion with every reason to feel that he is right. Furthermore, there may be no political reasons for going to someone else for his stamp of approval. Seeking corroboration may have little purpose but "moral support"—and many decision makers seek this regularly. The suspicion is that they are what may be facetiously and unscientifically described as "support psychopaths." They appear to be so sensitive to the possibility of being wrong that they require stated concurrence from some one or more persons or that they love the flattery of agreement. Decision makers who fall into this category are in effect cripples who cannot stand alone. The best remedy is rigid self-discipline and, if the decision maker cannot impose this on himself, then his friends and superiors can do him a favor by refusing to discuss or confirm his findings and determinations.

For Political Reasons

The decision maker may be quite capable of reaching a proper determination without the aid of others, and he may know it. He may even not need or desire the psychological agreement. But in either or both instances he may still proceed to elicit the help of someone or party because of certain political advantages to be derived therefrom—gains which have little, if anything, to do with the substance of the decision. Among these gains are enlistment of aid in selling the decision, which aid may eventuate from the flattery that a request for agreement commonly carries; cementing of general relations with another or others via the flattery of asking for support; identifying self as the decision maker—and so as a leader; and denying any other individual or group the various advantages of being the initial announcer of a decision reached. There is nothing intrinsically unethical with an attempt to get corroboration for any of these purposes. Yet, the decision maker is on questionable moral grounds when he deliberately plans and/or proceeds to get someone's agreement to his decision by falsehood, bribery, or plain coercion. Moreover, the party whose confirmation is thus illegitimately gained subsequently may prove to be a source of real embarrassment to the tricky decision maker. He may seek revenge, especially if he is somehow harmed by his agreement, or he may at some future time deny that he meant to concur.

But What Others?

Complete silence has been maintained up to this point on the quite relevant question of whose aid the decision maker should seek. A comprehensive reply to this query should include a discourse upon the relative merits and demerits of obtaining aid from individuals and groups inside and outside the decision maker's organization, and from non-professional and professional sources. Since this is a topic which deserves at least a volume in itself, such are its dimensions, the subject will not be treated at any length here. It would be neglectful, however, to fail to set forth at least the essence of what appears to be a rational attitude toward the source of assistance. The decision maker should ask for aid only when he needs it and from those who can and will give it if he really wants it or from those who are unable or unwilling to render it if he does not wish it; and, often of equal importance, he should endeavor to approach for aid or non-aid those whose contact will yield him the greatest political advantage or do him the least political disservice. This is such a simple rule that it seems all too frequently to be violated. The emotion attendant upon approaching, making, or announcing a decision seems especially provocative. It tends to generate a desire to get closer to anyone who can give sympathy, express an opinion, or contribute a fact, lesson, or warning. Perhaps this is all a reflection of the fact that decision making is intrinsically a lonely and fearful job, since it carries with it a measure of obligation to make the "right" determination.

A word of caution seems in order at this point. No matter what or how many experts the decision maker calls upon, he should try not to rely upon their aid completely. The responsibility for the eventual choice of alternatives is his. Moreover, even experts are not infallible. These two factors suggest the wisdom of his learning as much as he can about the decision situation. This is quite possible—at least to the degree that he can learn some of the right questions to ask the consultants.[8]

Conclusion

The "right" decision—the decision most proper to the situation—is not always the conclusion the maker reaches. He may fail by far to make this decision because his talents or resources are seriously lacking. Commonly, he may only render a "good" decision, failing to come to the optimum conclusion because of a variety of circumstances. Or—and this is perhaps relatively rare—he may choose the very best alternative, aided by all that is necessary to do so or even out of sheer fortuitous random choice. But whichever target he hits in his decision making, he generally will have had some time, if only at least a moment—in which to think about its nature. If he is possessed of any appreciable measure of good commonsense, he will make use of this time by contemplating the substance of the decision—and so he will be seen making a superficial estimate of the situation, conducting a personal probe or going to others for help, if of no more important variety than confirmation of a decision he already has reached.

However, the act of contemplating the essence of the decision to be taken is not to be considered as a sort of automatic action pattern into which an administrator some-what naturally moves when confronted with a situation demanding decision. Nor is it to be seen as a necessarily safe pre-decision procedure simply because it is a rational step. The would-be decision maker must be motivated to make the best use of the period of arousal, and he must be his truly strategic self to avoid both the mental and political errors possible in considering what should be the decision. The motivation should come from the decision maker's good judgment and the political wisdom from his strategic astute-ness. Each of these "sources of safety" dictates that the administrator—he who makes decisions in and for the or-ganization—may well devote a portion of his time to the study of the act of decision making as the apex of leadership.

BUSINESS SITUATIONS FOR ROLE PLAYING

SITUATION XVIII

Contemplating the Substance of the Decision

THE TENTH CORPS OF ENGINEERS

A. Scene.   An army unit of construction engineers. The Office of the District Engineer, in which a heated discussion is taking place over the amount of research necessary to reach a proper decision as to the location of a new dam on a medium size southern river. The recommendation on situs must be submitted through channels and ap-proved by the Chief of Engineers in the national capitol.

B. Players.   1. Commanding Officer: Colonel Deshart W. White, an old time professional soldier-engineer who has made so many decisions about dam construction that he feels a high degree of con-fidence in his own, more or less intuitive, conclusions.

2. Principal Engineer: Edward E. Edwards, a graduate of Massachusetts Institute of Technology, and, although still below forty, a recognized national authority on fluvial construction.

3. Consulting Engineer: Constantine Cabott, an employee of almost forty-five years' service who "has seen it all." He feels that it really does not matter what the engineering offices recommend, since the place of the dam really will be determined in the capitol by influential politicians.

C. Situation.   1. The Commanding Officer wants to "hit" his superiors at the nation's capitol early in the budget period with a reasonable decision supported by a tidy presentation of data and drawings.

2. In contrast, the Principal Engineer insists upon researching every foot of the river and basing the ultimate decision on what he calls the real facts. He has no particular sensitivity to the political implications of timing the presentation in the capitol. To a degree, he loves research for its own sake.

3. The Consulting Engineer is willing to agree to almost any sensible recommendation, simply to get the project underway and the decision off the district's hands.

D. Assignment.   1. Allow the class to choose the individual to act as Commanding Officer, directing it to select an individual with political capacity.

2. Ask for volunteers from the class to assume the other two roles.

3. Have this trio discuss the proper amount of study needed to reach the right decision in locating the dam.

4. Invite the class, at the end of the demonstration, to criticize the reasoning of each participant.

NOTES

1. LEON FESTINGER, *Conflict, Decision and Dissonance* (Stanford: Stanford University Press, 1964), p. 3.
2. Brim et al., states, "It is possible to conceptualize three states of nature: competitive, cooperative, and neutral. These serve to summarize the conditions or states under which decision making generally is carried out." They proceed to describe the competitive condition as one in which there is interest conflict as in a labor-management situation; the cooperative condition as a cooperative game exemplified in a friendly situation in which both partners are willing to communicate and form coalitions to their mutual advantage; and the neutral state as one in which the given decision maker is not faced by a "malevolent opponent or by a friendly, co-operative decision maker." ORVILLE G. BRIM, JR. et al., *Personality and Decision Processes* (Stanford: Stanford University Press, 1962), pp. 15-16.
3. For a discussion of the intuitive value system used in decision making, consult IRWIN D. J. BROSS, *Design for Decision* (New York: The Macmillan Company, 1953), p. 86.
4. "Man's search for knowledge is governed by the times in which he lives but the true value of his findings is not." George B. Strother, "Problems in the Development of a Social Science of Organization" in HAROLD J. LEAVITT, ed., *The Social Science of Organizations* (Englewood Cliffs, N.J.: Prentice-Hall, Inc., 1963), p. 17.
5. Mc Farland describes policies as ". . . guides to the actions or decisions of people in an organization. They are the planned expressions of the company's official attitudes toward the range of behavior within which it will permit or desire its employees to act." DALTON E. MC FARLAND, *Management: Principles and Practices* (Second ed.; New York: The Macmillan Company, 1964), p. 122.
6. *Ibid.*, 123.
7. CHRIS ARGYRIS, *Understanding Organizational Behavior* (Homewood, Illinois: The Dorsey Press, Inc., 1960), p. 5.
8. The thought here expressed was suggested by ERNEST DALE, *Management: Theory and Practice* (New York: McGraw-Hill Book Company, 1965), p. 577.

CHAPTER **19**

Administrative Control
as a Function of Leadership

> "Control is a major function of the business adminis-
> trator. It is part and parcel of his leadership role.
> In bold relief, it is the means or act of assuring that
> his subordinates, singly and collectively, keep their
> eyes on the organizational goals as the target, and
> direct their efforts with a maximum of efficiency to-
> ward it. The action components of control are re-
> straint, push, and overseership. The discharge of the
> control function is one of the most difficult of the
> tasks that fall to the lot of the administrator."

CONTROL is one of the most discussed aspects of business
administration.[1] Yet there is considerable disagreement as to
its meaning. The concept is not, however, impossible or even
difficult to define if the broad view is taken. In this sense, it
signifies the means or action by which an administrator sees
to it that his group or any portion thereof, even an individual,
is working with the desired degree of efficiency toward the
goals of the organization. Should he be the top official of
the organization, his group is the entire company as a functioning organism. Should he be lower in the echelon of
command, his group will be a correspondingly smaller, but
not necessarily less lively, group.

Control: A Multi-Splendored Thing

Restraint

The task of control has several facets. Certainly, it does signify restraint. There is a tendency for individuals and groups, as members of an organization, to do things not sufficiently pertinent to the established objectives. In an ideal company or department all time, energy, and motion would be directed at these goals. But the ideal organization rarely, if ever, exists. Individuals, departments, and informal groups unfortunately stray from the narrow path. In Western range vernacular, the administrator must "ride herd" on his people to keep them moving in the right direction.

Forward Motion

It would be quite incorrect, however, to portray administrative control as merely a negative function. It has a definite positive aspect, also. The members of the group not only must be kept in line, but they must also be kept in forward motion. So the administrator should concern himself with facilitation and motivation as an aspect of managerial control. He should see to it that the people and units under him push ahead at the rate which his company or department expects. If the executive fails to grasp that this job is a part of his control behavior, he is likely to end up with an organization on the right path but making little progress down it.

Overseership

And so one sees control in administration as both restraint and push. It has a third aspect which, while inextricably interwoven with these two, deserves to be identified and considered separately because of its great significance. This facet may be called observation and evaluation. (Coordination is omitted here, and in the general delimitation of control, since it is a function of restraining, stimulating and overseeing, that is, since it will result from the fact of effective control.) The administrator must know what is happening or threatening in his area of responsibility as well as the relative importance of these events. It may, in fact, be well to abandon the terms "observation and evaluation" in favor of the awkward but meaningful word "overseership." But whatever semantics are employed, the fact remains the same. Control is in part superintendency. If this component is missing, the executive generally will not know and understand the functioning of his own organization and will not, therefore, be in a position either to correct the direction of movement or change its pace.

Why Control?

Why does the administrator have to restrain, push, and oversee? This action may seem unnecessary or of little import if he formulates and clarifies the organizational goals to all concerned, if he selects only people of wisdom, ability, and goodwill as his employees, if he provides them with the best of facilities, and if he protects them well from distractions. Yet even under these sanguine circumstances, and certainly in the reality of ordinary business life, there are strong interruptive influences at work on his people. It is these forces that necessitate administrative control. In all organizations and organizational situations, a degree of ignorance and laziness will exist; someone or more individuals or units will not know the score or want to perform. Then too, the counter-attraction of non-organizational goals will always be present; some individual or group will be so attracted by or pledged to objectives other than the aims of the organization that they need to be curbed or motivated. Such mavericks particularly contribute to the need for control when lacking in the virtue of loyalty, for without this moral fiber they are likely to go further astray in their pursuit of private objectives. To these relatively simple interruptive forces there must be added a whole category of far more complicated factors. It is the personal characteristics of certain individuals or groups within the organization that make it difficult or impossible for others to work with them. Here one must note the realities of individual differences, the absence of social skills such as the ability to communicate and compromise, and the lack of moral character. But these are all internal interruptive forces. Disturbing pressures from without the company also make themselves felt. Domestic and social demands, government regulations, distracting symbols, and the lure of better opportunities are examples of these external phenomena.

Man—the Object of Control

This discussion is intentionally oriented toward the human factor. The reason is not complex. In organizational life, fundamentally only people require control. Money and things cannot go astray, except insofar as a human decision and/or action allows them to be used wrongly in view of existing standards and goals. Immediately, there comes to mind many phases of and subjects related to control which suggest that it is, at least in part, concerned with the mechanical in contrast to the human.[2] One thinks of procedures and systems, budgets and budgetary control, material and inventory control, production and quality control, and operations research. A canvass of the literature of management tempts him to believe that such mechanical means are sometimes mistaken for the essence of control. But they are in reality only the creations and tools of human minds and hands. It is man, his traits and idiosyncrasies, which must be given the center of attention in a rational analysis of administrative control. More particularly, administrative control strategies involve human beings, and so this chapter on control omits a discussion of all the usual, but interesting, techniques and tools of control which range from records and reports through audits and inspections to substitute administration.

The Place of Standards

The fact that standards of performance and product are basic to effective administrative control does not deny the substance of the above mentioned contention that such control must be people oriented. Of course, these standards are essential, for they are the norms against which behavior is measured and found acceptable or wanting and, therefore, requiring control. Yet, they are no more than this; they have no value in themselves nor are they sacred. This truth is all too often overlooked in the complexities of developing, instituting, and enforcing standards. It is unnecessary to look further for a reflection of such disregard than the almost interminable argument between management and labor over what constitutes an hour's or day's work.

What Does Control Involve?

The task of control is fourfold for the administrator. As just mentioned, he must establish standards against which to measure performance; this is, in fact, an initial step. The second step is to gather and report data on work progress. Next, the results of the measurement are compared with the standards. Finally, corrective action is taken on the basis of the analysis made. One might, however, raise a question as to whether or not correction is a legitimate part of control, or a separate and distinct activity.[3]

The Web of Leadership

Administrative control is a function of leadership.[4] The idea is consonant with the concept of leadership as the capacity to keep followers, to make it possible for them to live together, and to direct them toward the organizational goals, for all three of these aspects are necessary to the assurance of the group behavior that is the essence of the controlled situation. Administrative control has been called group control.[5] The idea is also in harmony with the definition of leadership as an exercise of power. To maintain control, obedience (or more politely, compliance) must be obtained from the members of the company or department.

The Sub-Leader Complex

Leadership in most sizeable business organizations is a task beyond the capacity of one individual to discharge in detail. Hence, the organization finds it necessary to create a hierarchy of leaders, with the chief executive having ultimate responsibility and concomitant power but with the subordinate officials sharing his duties and power. The administrative control "system" must be built upon the organizational structure of leadership diffused. And this signifies that the relations of the chief administrator, the leader at the center of the web, must have proper relations with the subleaders who surround him in concentric circles of descending duty and power, e.g., vice presidents, general manager, department heads, office supervisors, and shop foremen. The figure of speech here used, the web, may cause some difficulty in the light of the fact that the principal administrator may have but one sub-leader in each class. Note the singular of general manager in the above listing of examples of subleaders. Any such difficulty can be dissipated if one takes the view that a single sub-leader standing between the chief executive and tertiary or lower sub-leaders has a multiple personality and, on a schematic presentation, would appear as a circle of separate, but identical, symbols around the chief leader. This idea is introduced in preference to the traditional pyramidal ladder chartings of administration, because the web suggests the focal position of the chief in the control process as well as the circular flow of control through the concentric levels of sub-leaders surrounding him, an almost impossible phenomenon to portray with simplicity in the traditional vertical arrangement.

A degression into this somewhat obtuse laterally circular or circularly lateral control may be profitable. In effect, the concept states that one administrator may exert a degree of control on another administrator of his level, and, in fact, may be the main agent in controlling him. An example is in order. In a medium size soap manufacturing company, the manager of the budget section and the manager of the public relations department are on the same administrative level. The president permits the latter to have great freedom of operation, but depends upon the former to exercise control via the approval and allocation of funds. If the president for some reason, perhaps fear, does not wish "to touch" the manager of public relations, he may depend almost exclusively upon the budget director to hold him down when necessary. The president may even hide behind this financial officer to control others among his colleagues, so that the effect is truly circular on the same plane.

Principles for Handling Sub-Leaders Strategically

The chief executive of the company, if a true strategist, will realize that sub-leaders are best considered a unique class unto themselves in each organization. He will, therefore, study them carefully and, after making an estimate of the situation, work out a more or less definite *modus operandi* for handling them in the interest of control. As is so often true in analyzing administrative strategy, it is here impossible to outline any specific formula to fit all situations. The best that can be done is to think in terms of general tenets for the chief administrator to follow. Although it would no doubt be possible to formulate literally dozens of such rules, one may identify some nine basic principles.[6]

1. *The chief leader should recognize that he must control his sub-leaders.* In general, the president of the company can assure the type of control he desires down to the most lowly employee only by operating through subordinate administrators. He simply will not have the energy, time, and opportunity personally to reach far down into the company family. The necessity for controlling the sub-leader arises from the fact that a subordinate executive may be just as unruly, wrongly oriented, and unreasonable as any non-administrative employee. Unless he can be brought to see and do as the president desires, he very probably will not effect an extension of this desired pattern to his inferiors.[7]

2. *The chief leader should be aware of the fact that the sub-leaders know power.* Their positions will carry a degree of authority, and they may obtain more power from one or more of power's many other sources. Furthermore, they will have exercised it, and so will not only be familiar with its application but will also have developed a measure of independence. These two conditions have both negative and positive implications for organizational control. In respect to the former implication, they may influence the subordinate to resist the chief leader. With regard to the latter, they may help shape the sub-leader into an effective applier of power, so that he becomes a good controller of that portion of the company or company activities under his command.

3. *The chief leader should act as the type of leader he wants his subordinate administrators to be.* Subordinates are no different in their emulative instincts than any other people. Therefore, they will as a class be prone to imitate those with whom they associate, and especially the central figure among them. This emulation is often close, so the lower leader acts very much like his superior. The chief administrator, then, must be careful as to the "figure he cuts." The point is that the principal executive must be a proper "leader's leader," or he will find his shortcomings duplicated in the character or behavior of his lieutenants who have become an extension of him.

4. *The chief leader should realize that his sub-leaders may have, in psychological terms, split personalities.* They may act one way to those below themselves and in quite a different manner to him. He is not to assume, therefore, that

their agreement, promises, pledges, and behavior in his presence will be duplicated in their efforts to control people under them. He should, from time to time, look into their respective administrations. It may be his bad fortune to have lieutenants who color or report affairs falsely to please him and who comport themselves as he wants them to act when he can observe their actions. Sometimes, his subordinates may be simply dishonorable men intent on feathering their nests. More often probably, they are reacting to a strong stimulus to appear successful, which may be coming from such factors as a poor employment market or unusual competition from colleagues for further recognition in the organization. The chief leader himself may be the cause of, or at least a contributor to, this duplicity. His insistence upon very high accomplishment or the impossible may drive sub-leaders to play a game of make-believe with him.

5. Lieutenants can be trained, so the *chief leader should endeavor to educate them in his views of control.* This may not be an easy task, because the sub-leaders may be experienced and/or professional administrators with their own strong ideas and pride. Nevertheless, he can "work on them." There are innumerable ways of educating people. In this case, however, indoctrination through association seems to offer much. It can be a constant persuasion device if the chief leader has frequent and close-contact with his assistant leaders. In addition, it can be a subtle means of indoctrination since the hints and suggestions dropped, and the examples set, can be gauged in dimension and vapidity by the chief. All this is not to overlook the educative potentials of such more formal devices as conferences and formal courses; nor is it to discount the occasional salutary educative benefit to be derived from allowing subordinates to stub their toes by making significant errors in control.

6. Assistant leaders certainly are not always to be regarded as unreliable or completely dependent upon the chief leader in their exercise of the control function. In the main, they have some capacity above the ordinary or they would not be in positions of command and supervision. Therefore, they may appreciate the chief leader's trust in them, they may function better when left on their own, they may be proud of their unaided accomplishment. *And so, the*

chief leader may find it beneficial to morale and accomplishment to allow them to operate with a good degree of freedom. Of course, this may be a risky experiment, for the sub-leaders turned loose can commit serious mistakes which may appear to be the result of the chief leader's lack of control. He also should weigh carefully the possibility of losing more or less permanently through this freedom a measure of control. Sub-leaders accustomed to freedom may be impossible to bring back under control, or may in their moments of independence have done things which make their recapture unfeasible.

7. *The chief leader should not neglect democratic practices in effecting control.* He can, in certain circumstances, use such devices to tie his assistants closely to him. The essence of these democratic techniques, which may range from frequent consultation to formal committee action, is to bring the sub-leaders more into decision making. Normally, it may be expected that they will be more willing to carry out decisions which they have helped make. The chief, of course, runs a risk in the use of democracy as a control device. Those who are allowed to participate in the decision may force or make one contrary to his wishes and needs.

8. *From time to time, the chief leader should dip into the operation of his organization for information purposes.* This is neither to suggest a practice of going over the heads of his assistant leaders or even a habit of mistrusting them. It is rather to recommend the value of first hand knowledge of what is transpiring. Then too, there may be a strategic advantage in letting subordinates know that he knows his own operation. The unfortunate truth is that clever and ambitious sub-leaders can and do isolate the president or other top leaders from the administrative realities of the business. The chief leader cannot allow himself to be an organizational captive in an air-conditioned office, no matter how pleasant the reports read.

9. In the interest of forward action, the *chief leader should be guided by the truth that often he will be unable to control his assistant leaders exactly as he wishes.* He will, therefore, find it wise to accept something less—an optimum compromise. The deciding factors in how far he should go to effect his ideal of control is the net balance of writing off the cost

of doing so against that of not doing so. The theory of games would suggest that the strategic administrator will not always try to maximize his gains.[8]

Bureaucracy[9]

It is impossible to discuss administrative control without treating bureaucracy. To many American businessmen this is a fighting term; it suggests red tape, delay, and even confusion. They reflect the feelings of free men who honor enterprise and are inclined to associate bureaucracy with government and to abhor it as an organizational and behavior pattern of the public agency. Their disapprobation of bureaucracy spills over into the public consciousness where it joins a sort of independent revulsion to things bureaucratic proceeding from individual experience with extreme system in administration.

But bureaucracy is not necessarily a "term of opprobrium."[10] In a proper semantic sense, it is ". . . simply a hierarchical arrangement of unit organizations."[11] As such, it is the typical pattern of large companies and departments thereof just as it is of all big organizations.

The Fact of Inequality

There are a number of features of bureaucracy which must be appreciated by the administrator who would perform strategically the control function. First, there is the element of inequality; units organized on a hierarchical basis will constitute a grouping or society of unequals.[12] From a control viewpoint the implication is, of course, a series of what repeatedly has been termed in this book domination and submission relations. "Each rank is responsible for doing a specific job and is accountable to someone who wants it done."[13]

This fact of inequality which pervades bureaucracy has

two definite strategy implications for the administrator. On the one hand, it enables him to crack the whip with a certain degree of immunity. There is always some one or more individuals or groups below him in an institutionalized status of inferiority from which they cannot and/or will not generally react against supervision and supervisory imposition with full vigor. On the other hand, the hierarchical organization may provide hiding places for non-cooperative subordinates who use their immediate supervisor, and the intermediate superiors above him, as walls to conceal their inaction or independent actions. Perhaps one sees here in this possibility of shelter from the authority of the higher administrator a fundamental reason why so many businessmen detest what they believe to be bureaucracy. There is a necessity for insistence on a good report system so that the location of such pockets of resistance can be ascertained and proper corrective action taken.

Duties Divided and Inherent in the Office

A second feature of bureaucracy is the fact that it involves a "clear cut division of integrated activities which are regarded as duties inherent in the office."[14] This is commonly a source of both joy and pain to the administrator seeking to control his organization, whether it be the whole company or a part of it big enough to have its own sub-units. As an asset, it lends itself to the development and perfection of managerial and operational skills simply because the work to be performed by each unit is repetitive. And also as an asset, it favors on the part of his people the growth of a sense of identification and pseudo-ownership of a segment of the organization, which may reflect itself in their pride of performance. But there are, unhappily, certain negative implications which in a measure may offset the good. The very fact that bureaucracy so decisively categorizes and assigns activities may increase the difficulty of the control problem. By extreme division of duties, it may create so many offices and other units to be controlled that effective control bogs down in organizational complexity. In addition, the very feeling of identification and possession that definite categorization fosters may produce also within each unit a provincial attitude which disdains both intra-company co-operation and positive response to the wishes, instructions, orders, and supervision of higher authority. The unit comes to think of itself as independent, and to act accordingly.

But what can the administrator do to take full control advantage of the division of activities? He can use it to impose a heavier hand upon each subdivision, for this unit, having its work clearly defined and perhaps jealous of it, has less chance, therefore, to get out from under its particular responsibility. Then too, he can change sub-leaders with less fear of disruption, for each unit, being established in place, power and duties within the organization, will be able to function somehow even under the negative effect of management turnover. This possibility of heedless functioning may be enhanced by the fact that the department will probably be organized on a formal basis after the pattern of the total company, for bureaucracy breeds bureaucracy among its members. Its formal structure may enable it to continue to function with less leadership than might be supposed. Finally, the administrator in his effort to control can exploit the fact of division of duties to divide and rule. Since the basic reality of division is already present, the task, now easier, is one largely of accentuating differences among departments or of blocking communications among them, so that each, standing more alone, will be less able to resist his restraint, motivation, and overseership.

The Importance of General Rules

As a third feature of bureaucracy, one must take note of the great significance which general and abstract, but clearly set forth, rules play in its control.[15] Within the bureacratic organization, it is not so necessary to issue specific instructions for each problem and necessary action. Duties are lodged fixedly with study and action agencies and, consequently, often all that is necessary is a careful categorization of problems to be solved and things to be done, so that each will fall into the waiting department. Quite obviously, this places a strategic device of considerable power in the hands of the highly placed administrator. He can through the technique of changing the criteria for categorization redirect the flow of work. The sub-unit can also play games with the category pawn. It can exert a disruptive influence in particular cases by insisting that specific tasks given it do not fall within its legitimate purview, and it may be able to do this even more effectively if it is in a position to point out that the assigning executive is violating the organizational pattern. After all, the members of the organization find both safety and comfort in the knowledge that "this goes here, and that belongs there." A subordinate unit, if led by an astute assistant leader, can give the chief leader real annoyance by showing him to be ignoring the established policy of division of activities. At times, he can almost make it appear that the president of the company, or other high official, is committing a very wrongful act—such is the popular regard in which the members of the organizational family occasionally come to regard the division of work.

Bureaucratic Officialdom

A fourth feature of the bureaucratic organization has to do with the method by which officials get office. It has been said that the pure type of bureaucratic administrator is appointed, either by superior authority or through impersonal competition such as that of competitive examinations. The bureaucratic official is distinguished, however, by more than his appointive status. He commonly holds the position for an appreciable period, his compensation is generally fixed as a salary, and he can usually look forward to a career with the organization.[16] The facts that he is not elected and enjoys tenure have deep control significance. They mean a higher degree of vocational security than would otherwise, *ceteris paribus*, be the case. This, in turn, generally makes the sub-official less fearful of higher authority and, hence, more likely to resist control from above. The higher official, with the responsibility for effectively keeping the organization moving toward its goal, can do at least two things to offset the resisting power of secure assistant leaders. Above all else, he can cement relations with that portion of the higher functionaries who are elected, and this means in the main the board of directors. With their understanding, sympathy and backing, he will be better armed to cope with the true bureaucratic officials ensconced in the continuity of their appointments. But he should not overlook a more mechanical device for handling them, and this is a thorough knowledge of the policies, rules, and regulations by which the company or department lives and operates. Such mastery will help protect him against the legalistic arguments and other resistance of subordinate officials. It may even reveal chinks in their armor, a fact which can be of special importance since the bureaucratic organization lives by the rules and tolerates well discipline for their infraction.

Discipline—an Essential Feature of Bureaucracy

A final feature of bureaucracy which requires mention with respect to administrative control is that of discipline. Bureaucratic organizations stress obedience.[17] Bureaucracy is basically a matter of social relations undertaken for a purpose. In business, this purpose is multifold, but the prevailing objective, that of profits, is in itself sufficient to generate an insistence upon obedience, for disobedience is seen as unfriendly to net income. However, regardless of what the purpose or how strongly it may be pursued, the mere fact that the members of the bureaucratic organization live together in hierarchical arrangement demands compliance. Lacking this, it would degenerate into the anarchy of disorganization and eventually cease to exist, since it could not function. The strategic business administrator will be aware of the fact that rarely, if ever, do all people and groups within a company or department obey every wish, instruction, and order from above. He will be required to discipline at times, but he can do so from the strength of necessity. The members of the organization will stand very considerable discipline in their ranks because the lack of it will create situations unpleasant, unsafe, and unrewarding to them. In fact, it has been pointed out that "bureaucracy is the 'most rational offspring' of discipline."[18]

A Reasonable Administrative Attitude toward Bureaucracy

The strategic administrator should recognize the fact that bureaucracy is something much more than the slavish and sluggish adherence to roles by continuing officials, which unpleasant behavior pattern may, however, accompany it. Bureaucracy, he should see, is the pyramiding of units of organization, and the careful spelling out of unit activities and authority. Seeing it as such, he will realize it to be something with which he must live and through which he must administer in most large companies and even divisions of concerns. This will prove a significant step in realism for many an executive. It was observed, even decades ago, that big and modern companies are fine examples of true bureaucratic organization.[19]

With this reasonable attitude, the administrator will be better able to evaluate bureaucracy in an objective manner and to determine how far he is justified in abandoning non-bureaucratic values in order to avail himself of its advantage. The principal merit of bureaucracy is technical efficiency.

Eliminating much of love, hate, emotions, and other personalized relations and irrational factors, it places heavy emphasis on those considerations, including expert controls, which make for this efficiency.[20] In fact, the more dehumanized bureaucracy becomes, the nearer it approaches its pure type. It can truly be said, "Bureaucracy is the ordering of institutional management to secure the advantages of system."[21] And so bureaucratic administration is described as even superior to other forms of administration—the collegiate, honorific and avocational forms—because it is stable, reliable, predictable of results, and permissive of large scale operations.[22]

Unfortunately, bureaucracy also has certain deep inherent qualities which tend to weigh against its basic virtue of technical efficiency. One of these is its very passion for orderliness, which tends to mesmerize its members into good administrative housekeeping for its own sake. And another is its dehumanization, with prime emphasis upon objectivity, rather than personal considerations, an orientation distinctly unfriendly to initiative and dynamic leadership. Such defects commonly add up to a lack of vitality in administration, which is energy and endurance and capacity to compete and survive. Unless balanced by enterprise, with its expectation of innovation and continued progress, bureaucracy will likely result in considerable lethargy.[23]

Closely related to any evaluation of bureaucracy must be a consideration of the effect of span of control[24] philosophy on the case for bureaucratic organization. It may be defined as the thinking on the number of people whose work one person can supervise and direct. The prevailing thought tends toward conservatism. There seems to be more concern about placing too many rather than too few under one individual. The bureaucratic implications are clear. The smaller the span of control, the more units and, hence, more bureaucracy there will be. The strategic administrator should remember, therefore, that when he argues for fewer people to supervise and direct he is lending his influence to the growth of bureaucracy.

The necessity for a semantic reorientation seems to arise at this point. *Throughout the book, the terms leader, administrator, executive, and official have been used as synonyms of each other.* Such usage is justified if one confines it to the frame of reference of the formal organization and if he takes care to realize that there can be within the informal orbit all kinds of leaders, weak, strong and indifferent, who by their status of informality cannot be administrators, executives, or officials. But the current worry arises from the fact that bureaucracy with its emphasis on continuing and professional officials may make it a bit more difficult for the critical student to accept the quadruple identity. It is suggested, therefore, that when he is really bothered by this sematic marriage he remind himself it is valid only when referring to formal leaders.

Communication as a Control Device

Communication is the very life-blood of administration, and its channels are the organism's circulatory system. An effort has already been made to substantiate this view.[25] However, it is proper to consider communication in a more specific sense—as a device of each of the other activities of administration, for it is an indispensable universal tool. And to no administrative function is it more significant than to control. An enumeration of the contributions it can make to control will provide foci for discussing communication stratagems in control.

To Eliminate or Alleviate Hostility

Communication can be used to eliminate or alleviate hostility on the part of those to be controlled. The prevalence of hostility, as a feeling of antipathy toward others, varies in breadth and depth with specific administrative situations. In a particular company at a given time, it may be almost non-existent, spotty and superficial, spotty and deep, general and shallow, or general and intense. But whatever its degree, the function of hostility is to arouse fighting energy and to contribute emotional motivating force for resistance or attack.[26]

The administrator who faces the necessity for exercising a degree of control, that is, a measure of restraint, stimulation, or overseership with respect to a given individual or group under his management may, therefore, run into hostility toward himself, some other person or persons in the organization, or the organization as a whole. The extent to which its existence will complicate and block his effective control can depend on many factors. But regardless of its seriousness, there are at least three communication stratagems by which he can attempt to eliminate or negate its influence. Among them the most potent is the use of the communication approach best designed to remove or deaden hostile feelings. There are various types of hostility: primary which is a simple, instinctive animal tendency; social, which is associated with highly personal ideas; and ethical, which is also associated with highly personal ideas but which involves reference to standards of justice and sanctions of conscience.[27]

If the administrator analyzes the hostile situation as one of primary or animal anger, he knows that he faces the necessity for removing an immediate obnoxious provocation to the senses.[28] He can, after seeing to it that the provocation is dulled or liquidated, communicate the fact to the hostile party or parties. The office manager can rescind his recent prohibition of the off-premise coffee break and circulate memorandum to this effect among all secretaries and clerks. Of course, even though the communication aspect of the assault on animal hostility is commonly not difficult, the attack itself may not be easy, since the administrator may find it hard to identify the cause of the anger and/or do anything about it when he does discover it. Sometimes, either out of desperation, a desire to stall, or even the more ignoble motive of deceit, an administrator will announce that he plans to correct or rid the organization of the cause of hostility. This superficial action at times does help allay the feeling of antagonism, but it is a dangerous expedient in that the administrator, having announced his intent, may come to think that indeed he has solved the problem or in that, if he goes no further, he runs the risk of being considered dishonest.

Should the administrator consider the hostility to be of the social type, his use of the communication weapon will require much more subtlety. The persons or group which are socially hostile feel that another or others harbor ideas injurious to them.[29] Therefore, the strategic executive will try to communicate assurance of the contrary to the hostiles. This may involve the direct approach in which the administrator in a straight forward manner tells, writes, or otherwise informs them that the suspected party does not harbor ideas inimical to them. In this approach, one sees the president of the company, for example, writing a plant manager a letter telling him that the general manager does not wish to suspend operations in his division. Of course, his success in this employment of communication to help the control function depends upon his prestige with the hostiles and the intensity of their unfriendly feeling. But the necessary assurance may also be communicated by the indirect approach. The administrator may advise, order, or otherwise let it be known to those against whom the hostility is directed that he wants them to take steps to communicate their friendliness to the hostiles. In the indirect approach, the president lets the general manager know he wants the doubts and fears in the plant manager's mind allayed, and he may even suggest or specify how he wants the general manager to do this. The indirect is sometimes the more effective employment of communication. It has the merit of "first-handedness" as far as the hostiles are concerned, for they receive the message of assurance, verbal or non-verbal, directly from those whom they suspect. The hostiles may be less likely to suspect deceitful managerial statements of assurance in the interest of smooth administration.

In case the administrator senses the hostility to be ethical, he may use communication stratagems similar to those pertinent in social hostility. However, there is one difference. Ethical hostiles are people who feel that another or others entertain dangerous immoral ideas against them. In communicating assurance to them, it is, therefore, essential that the administrator know and convey with precision and sincerity his appreciation of the moral values involved. Otherwise, his efforts to assure the hostiles may appear to be a mere covering up or rationalizing of a wrong. And such a conviction can generate further an unusual hostility because it suggests that the administrator is one who does not care whether his people are really treated justly or is himself a conspirator to the injustice. The president, who states publicly for the benefit of the angry union members that there is no collusion between their company and distributors for the benefit of a few pivotal executives, had better let them know he does not condone such action and will not tolerate it, otherwise the union members may be further aroused and include him among the objects of their hostility.

Of course, the matter of ethics is important in all administrative communications aimed at hostility, and sincerity is certainly an ethical quality of prime significance. Hostiles are by virtue of their hostility already oversensitized to what they consider "the wrong." So any deliberate misstatement of fact, false promise, or other seduction will assume enhanced proportions in their minds and constitute grounds for added negative feeling and resistance to control.

To Maintain Contact with the Administered

Communication, in its broad meaning, is the only way that liaison can be maintained by the administrator with those under him. It must thus be seen as a control device *sine qua non*, for control demands the exchange of ideas. The administrator must know the mind of his people to be able to judge what, if any, control they require. He must be able to convey his persuasions, orders, and instructions to them in order to exercise the necessary control over them. There is nothing new in this line of thought. In one sense or another, it has been belabored in most works on administration, and this book is no exception.

But there is one rule of communication which needs repetition and underscoring with respect to all areas of administration. *It is that no administrator can afford to leave communication to chance.* The process is too susceptible to inertia, delay and perversion, and the message itself too prone to error, misconstruction and falsification. Then too, the stakes are high, and this is eminently a fact in the realm of administrative control. There can be no effective control without proper communication.

The supreme significance of communication to control may lead the thinking administrator to include a communication system as a part of his organizational structure. Undoubtedly, many business administrators have sensed the desirability of such action, for numerous companies and their larger divisions do have what may be correctly called communication systems. They have established policies, channels, rules, and regulations to govern the three way movement of messages. Certain aspects of these systems at times obtain exaggerated attention. Advertising gets huge appropriations; democratic practices, popular announcement and notable adulation; and routine intra-company communication, professional study. No doubt the attention which he and his associates give communication convinces many an administrator that *his* communications are satisfactory.

Here is the danger of communication hypnosis. An elaborate communication system with generous financial support can lead administrators, especially the top executives, to believe that right messages are getting to the right places in the right way at the right time. What they may not see is that a communication system may be nothing more than a sham, that is, simply institutionalized motion which moves lots of more or less irrelevant words and paper at times and to parties which have little, if any, need for them. More importantly, what they may not realize is that the very system upon which they depend to furnish them with information and to carry their wishes is actually being perverted to give them misinformation and their subordinates misdirection. The causes for the failure of a communication system are probably not much different from the causes for the failure of any administrative system, or in fact of the whole administration process itself. They no doubt include ignorance, ill will, and neglect on the part of those who manage them, as well as built-in defects. The point of all this is that the communication system, no matter what its appearance, cannot be trusted completely. It is fallible, being a product and tool of human endeavor. And so here is the real pertinent meaning of the basic communication rule. The admonition not to leave communication to chance means that the administrator should view it, as practiced in his organization and as practiced by him, with a most critical eye. His action, especially with respect to control should be one of continual probing of the reliability of message sending and receiving in the organization, accompanied with stern and thorough correction of defects discovered.

It should be remembered that there is a strategy by which

the administrator can somewhat reduce the risk from a deficient or mal-functioning communication system. It is to incorporate the control system into the routines and expectations of the people to be affected by it. This can reduce the need for communication, and thus help to eliminate communication error. It has been asserted that the effectiveness of a control system is determined in no small degree by this inclusion.[30]

To Establish Leadership Ascendancy

More than one-half century ago, a pioneer in sociology observed that there is no algebraic formula for leadership.[31] Nor has all the scientific study in psychology, sociology, and administration yet proved him wrong.[32] In a sense, the nearest one can come to expressing leadership precisely is to state that it involves the personal ascendancy of one person over one or more other people, because leadership connotes followership for the leader and compliance with his wishes. But a prime condition to this personal ascendancy is that those over whom it is to be exercised must possess undirected energy or energy which can be re-channelled.[33]

What has all this to do with communication as an aid to administrative control? Very much, it is believed. The presence of undirected or redirectable energy must be located and measured, and this is the function of information. The possessor may need motivation to free it to the leader and direction to release it properly. And this entails communication as persuasion, order, and instruction.

The strategic pattern of communication which the administrator can follow with most benefit to his control function will vary with the type of leader he happens to be. Leaders can be described as autocratic, democratic, or laissez faire.[34] The autocrat, to be true to his nature, should be quite unilateral in his communication. He should announce policies to his group without consulting it, give firm orders, tell the group only the immediate steps to take but not discuss future plans, praise or blame on his own initiative, and in general remain aloof from the group. The democratic leader, faithful to his species, should see that policies are worked out in group discussion, issue orders only after consultation with the group, sketch out plans when asking his people to do something, publicly insist that praise and blame is a duty of the group, and in general participate in the group. The strategy of the laissez faire leader is properly negative. He does not lead, and leaves the group to itself. So he has little need for communication and its stratagems.[35]

Every administrator, regardless of the type of leader he may represent, should be aware of a trilogy of general facts whose appreciation will at least save him a degree of frustration, if it does not point the way to opportunity for better communication and control. The closer the communicator is to the decision making process, the better he normally will be able to communicate the decision. His understanding of the background of, support for, and antagonism to the conclusion reached should enable him to convey it as information, order, or instruction with better tone and knowledge. A second fact is that real control possibilities lie in communication interaction. Successive replies or feedbacks give the administrator an opportunity to explain, elaborate, retreat from, slow up, or press forward the control objective of the involved message.

A third, and it is feared commonly overlooked, fact of general import is the stark reality that a communicator or recipient of a message, being human, does not respond to all people in the same way.[36] A message sent to a particular personality will usually reflect the clash or agreement coefficient of the communicator with the recipient, and a message received will often provoke a reaction colored by the same factor. For example, an order dispatched to a friend may be warm and incomplete, because the communicator has affection for and trust in him and because he may be fearful of offending him by including too precise an explanation or instruction. A message received from a friend may elicit favorable response without much analysis on his part because of the affection, confidence, and loyalty factor. The point of all this is that the administrator must be careful of weakening his control of his people by neglecting the proper preparation and reception of communications. Above all else in communication, he must view objectively those with whom he communicates. Perhaps the best way for the leader to do this, at least with respect to his assistant leaders, is regularly to appraise their performance.[37]

Motivation: Furnishing the Push

Motivation is the subject for voluminous dissertation. This is probably the result of a rather natural curiosity of man regarding himself. What can be more interesting to him than the reasons why he does things? This subject, of course, is also of prime significance to the business organization. The attainment of its goals demands human action, which may or may not be forthcoming and which may or may not be directed toward these objectives as efficiently as desired.

Motivation—What Is It?

The concept of motivation can be defined in two ways. The administrator generally will hold it to be the stimulation of a person to work toward a goal. He will find expression of this somewhat simplified definition common in the literature of administration, personnel management, and human relations. At times an author in one of these areas will elaborate it slightly. One such elaboration adds the ingredient of complexity and states, "Motivation may be defined as the complex of forces starting and helping a person at work in an organization."[38] Another introduces the element of efficiency, and British literature sometimes gives specific attention to the topic of stimulating efficiency.[39]

The psychologist, who above all others, is most concerned scientifically with the consideration of motivation goes further than defining it simply in terms of behavior with respect to a goal. He not infrequently describes motivation in terms of the pressures or tensions residing in the person and producing the results observed. "Motivation . . . may be defined as awareness on the part of the individual of tension within him which stirs him to action aimed at relieving that tension."[40] This definition from the world of psychology makes it possible to associate with motivation such intriguing synonyms as drives, needs, and desires. These forces, singly or in combination, build up pressure within the individual that upset his equilibrium and, therefore, demand action to restore it.[41] The disturbed individual sees a goal which he thinks will relieve his tension, so he sets his course in that direction. It is clear that he is motivated by two forces: the pressure of his own tension and the pull of the goal. No doubt the relative influence of each will vary with the individual and situation, although it is said that the goal, which is properly termed the *incentive*, furnishes the direction for the action.[42]

Motivation—A Complex Subject

Truly motivation is complex. As a subject of scientific inquiry, it presents real difficulties. Systematic research within a sound theoretical frame of reference is necessary to identify and measure the power of motivating forces in business or any other field of activity.[43] It is believed that much of this investigation still remains to be done. But the business administrator is also confronted with this complexity, although it strikes him in concrete manifestations.

He is constantly discovering paradoxical facts, such as: the same motives produce different behavior in the same people at different times; the same motives sometimes cause different people to act differently; and different motives sometimes bring the same behavior in the same or different people.[44]

Strategic Assumption 1: Common Elements in Human Behavior

The business administrator cannot excuse himself from concern with motivation simply because it is a complicated matter. There are, however, certain fundamental assumptions which appear to have a good foundation in reality and which he can make to guide himself in motivating his people. The most basic of these assumptions is that all human behavior has at least three common elements:[45] it is caused, it is motivated, and it is goal directed. This generalization should clearly indicate to the thinking administrator a fundamental pattern of strategy, namely, that he can direct and redirect his people, and slow down or speed up their efforts toward an organizational goal. Such may seem a very obvious conclusion. However, there do seem to be executives who look upon their employees as more or less human automatons that will move in the same way no matter what is done.

Strategic Assumption 2: Common Motives

A second assumption which will aid the administrator in motivation is that there are motives to which all people will respond somewhat similarly. This assumption will permit him to approach his people with certain general or standard motives. Immediately, there comes to mind the economic reward. In days well past, it was generally thought that people work primarily for money. Considerable investigation of the financial and general economic incentive has been undertaken. In the main, research has cast a doubt on its primacy.

It was observed more than a decade ago by attitude surveys that American workers rate salary and wages not higher than fifth or sixth in their choices of what they want from their job. Ahead of the financial reward generally were placed steady work, comfortable working conditions, a good boss, and opportunity for advancement.[46]

The administrator, however, should not be too quick to abandon the economic incentive as the prime common motivating device. The mere fact that attitude surveys show other things to rate higher in the scale of employee desires does not prove that the economic motive is not central in the motivation conjuncture to which employees respond. It may well be that a number of circumstances are at work to give an untrue picture. In the United States, times have been rather prosperous for a generation and, in the main, for almost one-half century. Good pay for work is probably assumed by most American employees, who may, therefore, not be prone to rate it high. There has been much discussion in recent decades of the overemphasis on materialism. Motives other than the financial have been given more respect. American employees are literate, and may often report their preferences in terms of what convention considers good motives rather than in terms of what they really feel. Finally, money itself is perhaps more desired for its symbolic value than for itself.[47] As a result, employees may not rate it as highly as they really feel about it, since they are thinking of it principally in terms of the things, prestige, status, and power it will bring them.

There is, of course, a warning to the administrator in all this furor about the economic incentive. It is that, while the basic assumption of the possibility of some common motivation is sound, the common motive may be other than money or there may be common motives in addition to money. This enhancement of the range of common motives may well include, for example, the desire for recognition or ego satisfaction. Prominent authority holds this desire to be thought important: "one internal need in common"[48] and "central to other incentives in motivating people."[49] Of course, the category of common motives, whatever their rank, may include among others, status, security, attractive work, opportunity for development, worthwhile activity, personal power and influence, treatment by the boss, freedom and independence, and good supervision.[50]

Strategic Assumption 3: No One Ideal Incentive

A third motivation assumption which the business administrator can make with profit to his performance is that no one ideal incentive exists.[51] An ideal incentive would be one which would cause all members of a company or department to work at the height of capacity, quantitatively and qualitatively with uninterrupted continuity toward the organizational goal. Such an ideal would require enthusiasm of a spontaneous and enduring nature to permeate each member of the group.[52] This does not signify that the administrator should neglect his efforts to improve the motivation in his organization. It is rather a warning that he will be wasting his time and energy if he looks for a panacea factor.

What, then, is the practical *modus operandi* for the administrator with respect to motivation? His attack of the problem clearly must be on a multiple front. Since there is no ideal incentive and since people respond to many incentives and to particular incentives in different ways, it will be well for him to develop and use a *system of incentives*. The system should do two things: provide the particular package of incentives best designed to motivate each person or group, and to accomplish this at lowest cost to the organization. This latter point may require underscoring for some administrators who become enamored at the psychological niceties and theoretical possibilities of refined or experimental motivation proposals. After all, business administration cannot be taken out of the realm of economic considerations.

Whatever packages of incentives an administrator may concoct, he should always remember the "doctrine of the optimum." An incentive system is not, therefore, necessarily to be seen as containing all the finest incentives to an intensive degree. In the first place, such a collection might not produce the best motivation, since the different incentives might clash or negate each other's influence. For example, very high wages for workmen might dull the influence of opportunities for advancement to the position of supervisor. And, in the second place, the package of crystalline incentives might be too expensive. In the light of all this, it is clear that the strategic administrator must come up with a *balanced combination of incentives.*

Strategic Assumption 4: Politic Action Possible in Motivation

A fourth and final guiding assumption for the administrator interested in motivation is the hypothesis that motivation, like almost all functions of administration, can be handled in a more or less politic manner. In other words, it can be done with greater or lesser friction within and without the organization. A few of the more politic considerations will demonstrate the importance of this assumption. Of prime significance is reliance upon self-motivation whenever it appears to the administrator that such is a reasonable expectation. Self-motivation, as here used, is the result of something within the person or his experience that propels him toward the organizational goal with the degree of efficiency desired by the organization. Obviously, it is the ideal personal motivation, because it assures the organization of the greatest individual contribution with little, if any, strain to it. Enthusiasts for self-motivation sometimes praise it as being "always operative" and "self-perpetuating."[53] Truly, they may be a little too optimistic. Free will alone argues that self-motivation may be spotty rather than continual.

The good politics of motivation also argue for what may be called sensitive action. This means that the administrator should endeavor to anticipate when further motivation is needed by his people and to provide it graciously. The term "graciously" may seem out of place in administration. But it opens the door to one of the most egregious errors in management—waiting until employees demand something angrily or actually begin to fight for some additional incentive. If the administrator senses that he will eventually have to provide it—say, health insurance—he may gain much by granting it early or at least with a tone of willingness. Such action, the strategist knows, is simply making a virtue out of necessity.

A leader is no stronger than his friends in the organization. This proposition is clearly supportable if friendship is interpreted to mean loyalty. The friends, then, are seen as the sub-leaders, and employees who generally anticipate the administrator's wants, who regularly do his bidding, and who by and large support him and his actions. However, these close followers also need motivation, and, when the administrator forgets to provide them adequate incentives, he may be embarrassed to find that their responses, upon which he has counted so heavily, may no longer be as strong or even forthcoming. Here is another political consideration in motivation demanding the respect of the administrator. If he does not take care of his own team, he may eventually find that they will not take care of him.

Still another politic dictum for the motivating executive to regard is the necessity for respecting conventions. These are usual ways of thinking and doing things which people honor above other ways. To the extent that a leader can accomplish his purposes without doing violence to convention, he may be wise to do so. Such conservative action will at times avoid for him the disapprobation of popular criticism and the danger of popular punitive measures as well as gain for him real public approval. This is as true of the discharge of the motivation function as it is of any other phase of management. The administrator's publics, especially his own organizational family, expect certain rewards and punishments in particular situations and given in particular ways. For example, his employees may expect overtime with its fine opportunity for premium pay when the company is pressed beyond its normal productive capacity. Overtime and extra compensation are usual in such circumstances. If the administrator fails to give it and hires additional people, even though he may improve the recreation program for all employees, he will be flying in the face of convention and group expectations. And so trouble may be forthcoming. The sane approach would seem to be conventional motivation when feasible.

This appeal for conservatism should not bring one to overlook a final, and completely antithetic, politic consideration —that of innovation. Upon occasion, the administrator may find it strategic to depart from old patterns of motivation. This may involve giving new incentives, extra measures of old incentives, or old incentives in a new manner. The element of the unusual can provide new stimulus to forward action. If it is applied with a degree of surprise, the motivating effect may even be greater. An administrator of a very staidly managed factory, observing that the employees are showing little initiative, suddenly introduces a schedule of paid winter vacations as an addition to the regular summer vacations. The incentive itself, being new, and the shock of its surprise introduction may stir up initiative. The administrator should realize, of course, that innovations, especially if they are well received, may become expected, and the winter vacation pinned on the company as a commitment.

Supervision and the Supervisor

Meaning of Supervision

Control ultimately eventuates in the specific acts of a member of management with respect to some one or more people immediately under his jurisdiction. This individual, whose prime purpose described in brutally direct terms is to see that the work gets done, may be high or low in the organization. His position in the administrative hierarchy is not a factor. The pivotal consideration determining whether he is an administrator, an administrator and a supervisor, or supervisor is whether or not he is immediately in charge of people. If he is, then the official is a supervisor no matter how else he is classifiable. Seen in this light, the supervisor may be the president of the company or the most junior and lowly foreman. (The issue of whether or not the supervisor can also be considered an executive or administrator is perhaps here only of academic interest, although the authors are inclined to believe he should be so identified.)

A goodly measure of precision is possible in describing the supervisor. Detailed definition is provided in federal legislation. The National Labor Relations Act defined a supervisor as "any individual having authority, in the interest of the employer, to hire, transfer, suspend, lay off, recall, promote, discharge, assign, reward, or discipline other employees, or responsibly to direct them, or to adjust their grievances, or effectively to recommend such action, if in connection with the foregoing the exercise of such authority is not of a merely routine or clerical nature, but requires the use of independent judgment."[54] In common with most legal definitions, this statement attempts to cover everything and it has, therefore, required interpretation. Of significance to this discussion is one such interpretative viewpoint by the National Labor Relations Board to the effect that a person might be a supervisor even though he did not do everything set forth in the definition but did responsibly direct other employees.[55] Apparently, the law considers supervisors to belong to the category of management, for it excludes them from the protection of the Act.

In a less legalistic frame of reference, the supervisor may be defined in terms of his duties. It seems reasonable to consider as a supervisor any person whose main duties with respect to his immediate subordinates are (1) the scheduling and assigning of work to them, (2) the coordinating and overseeing of their performance, (3) and the assuring that the work is done well, on time, and economically.[56] Various authorities in the field of supervision are more rigorous and enlarge this definition by adding more functions as, for example, the custodianship of materials and services to the workers.[57] No doubt these are legitimate duties of the supervisor. However, they do seem to be of secondary significance, since they are only indirectly related to the main responsibility of the supervisor, which is *to get the work out.* It has been very aptly said that ". . . the emphasis in his job is largely on the human factor."[58]

The Supervisor—A Leader

Whatever the particular definition one may accept, the effective supervisor must be considered a leader. His is a clear task of managing and directing personnel toward goals with efficiency and concern for both their rights and the rights of the organization (one might go far out, and add "the rights of the public," also). And so the supervisor has many roles: those of planner, organizer, delegator, scheduler, budgeter, observer, coordinator, expediter, disciplinarian, arbiter, counselor, teacher and trainer, communicator and communication center, liaison officer, insulator, public relations man, technician, recorder and reporter, and above all else that of task master and controller.[59] The whole spectrum of leadership stratagems is probably open to him. Of course, he may not be able to practice them in very large dimensions since his domain of supervision is necessarily limited. Strategist he can be, even though he may be a janitor with two assistants—merely a leader in minuscule.

Beguiling as the temptation to discuss supervision broadly may be, it is necessary to bring this discussion back to supervision as an element in control. There would be little purpose served by attempting to identify and analyze all the stratagems the supervisor can use with advantage. To do this would be most repetitious of the previous analysis in this book, since it is devoted to leadership action and the supervisor is a leader. The task at hand, then, is to localize the supervisor in the whole milieu of administrative strategy.

The Supervisor—A Leader at Action Ends

The supervisor is the leader at the action ends of management. He, therefore, has less chance than others of evading managerial responsibility, except to fall back on his immediate superior if he has one. In specific cases this reliance may be quite proper, for example, when the superior has ordered such recourse, when only the superior has the organizational authority to decide, when the higher technical knowledge of the superior is needed, and in extremely unique problems. In general, the supervisor who resorts to the strategy of relying on his superior is running the risk of being typed as a weak or poor supervisor. Officialdom as a rule expects the supervisor to be particularly resourceful because it generally does not wish to be bothered with a multiplicity of operating specifics and details. Workers look to the supervisor for their answers; if he frequently says in effect, "Wait, while I ask my boss," they may lose confidence in him and react accordingly in a negative fashion to his demands on them.

The Supervisor—A Dual Personality

Not only is the supervisor at the focal point of action but he also must from this critical point face in two directions— upward toward management and downward toward his employees. (The lateral frontiers are here purposefully neglected.) To be a good strategist, the supervisor must develop a dual personality—that of manager and that of worker. His problem is understanding each group, keeping them apart, and yet making it possible for them to work together. His danger is that of becoming an organizational psychopath who suffers with administrative schizophrenia. The pressure on him to move in both directions sometimes simultaneously and against almost impossible odds can so bewilder him that he loses contact with the realities of his job and suffers what amounts to a consequent disintegration of his personality as a supervisor. The schizophrenic supervisor engages in irrational conduct such as running futilely in all directions, contradicting his own orders, communicating wildly, becoming angry at small things, and working at a frenzy. If there is any place in the organization where irrational conduct can be costly, it is the supervisory level, because here it is that production is to be assured. The appropriate stance for the supervisor is one of balance. He must be something, but not everything, to all people.

The Supervisor—Both Autocrat and Democrat

The supervisor's position with respect to strategy is made more difficult by the fact that he must function both as an autocrat and a democrat. Autocratic supervision, which means unilaterally making decisions, commanding rather than consulting workers, and often not compromising on performance, will be necessary at times. No organization can operate continuously without meeting occasions when its will must be imposed on its employees—and, of course, the supervisor is the imposer. On the other hand, democratic supervision, which means just the opposite of autocracy, is probably the pattern of supervisory control most successful in twentieth century America. It connotes, at least partly, what has come to be identified as *general*, in contrast to *close*, supervision. The pattern of general supervision permits subordinates to make some decisions for themselves. Its advantages are numerous. The supervisor is freed in a measure to do things commonly of more significance than standing over the workers, such as, training them to perform more efficiently and in general planning and organizing for better results. The worker is encouraged to develop self-reliance and a sense of job enlargement, since he is somewhat his own boss. The worker is also given the opportunity to develop pride in himself as a man and producer, a feeling necessary to good work but seriously hurt by advanced technology and automation.[60] Research studies made by various agencies—the Survey Research Center of the University of Michigan, the General Electric Company, and the Yale Technology Project—came to the similar conclusion that the effectiveness of general supervision is superior to that of close supervision.[61] These findings lend support to the growing conviction that the quality of supervision has a very positive relation to productivity.

The Supervisor—A Skilled Functionary

Moreover, to be a good strategist, the supervisor must develop and exercise supervisory skills. These are numerous and diverse, and include, for example, skills in observing, communicating, directing, training and developing a work force, building and maintaining morale, interviewing and consulting, mediating and arbitrating, disciplining, dealing with unions, and handling community relations. The supervisor cannot be an effective strategist unless he can pursue efficiently his job on all its many fronts. A prominent authority points out that supervision is always a process of adaptation.[62] And strategy, in one of its essentials, is adaptation.

The Supervisor—A Keeper of the Peace

Inter-personal friction is endymic in organizational life. It is almost a certainty that at any given time there will be in a particular organizational unit at least two people who are not "getting along." If friction is allowed to develop, it can reach proportions dangerous to the efficiency which the supervisor must maintain, so he cannot afford to allow friction to go unnoticed. Whether or not he takes positive action about it should be the result of his analysis of its self-liquidating possibilities or of its low potential in contrast to the cost of doing something about it. Should he decide to enter the picture, he should do so with full knowledge of the facts of the case and with the determination to be objective. This is just plain common sense, for it is necessary both to effective mediation and arbitration and to that impartiality which the supervisor must clearly exhibit in order to keep himself from becoming embroiled in the very conflict he is trying to settle, as sometimes happens to peacemakers. But, when all is said and done, the best peace strategy for the supervisor to follow is that of preventing friction from arising in the first place. This requires that he be a student of human relations and a keen observer of his own people, so that he can foresee places and issues at which friction is likely to arise. Oddly enough, the actual preventive steps are generally not difficult. They often involve little more than separating "potential clashers" by a suitable physical distance at the place of work, reducing the frequency and intensity of their contact, letting them and the other employees know that trouble will not be permitted in the ranks, and taking decisive action to rid the department of the individual or individuals who continually stir up unfriendly feelings and fights and who engender feuds.

The Supervisor—A Giver of Orders and Directions

Although administrators are constantly sending down orders and directions to people not immediately under them, it is the supervisor who does most of the actual ordering and directing. Not only does he pass on and implement those emanating from higher office, but he is more or less constantly on his own instructing his people what and what not to do and how to proceed. This order and direction giving is of utmost importance to supervision and control, since the positive response elicited, in the last analysis, constitutes much of the desired progress toward organizational goals. The administrator should see to it that his supervisors give clear orders and directions, and this means keeping directives as simple as possible. It is generally the essence of good managerial strategy to underestimate the understanding of those being ordered and directed, although upon occasion simplicity can be so exaggerated as to offend the subordinate. In addition to keeping them clear, orders and directions should be given so as to make the most of the emotional factor. This means issuing them with a general tone that will match or carry forth the positive feelings of the subordinates and not arouse or exaggerate their negative emotions. So, for example, the wise foreman couches instructions in the language of the employees and gives them on Mondays when they are less tired, but is careful not to use profanity in repeating directions to fatigued individuals late Friday afternoons.[63]

Living the Realities of Supervision

Finally, the supervisor should appreciate the fact of organizational life that his job is no crystal palace in which everything is light and sweetness.[64] Supervision is another of those dynamic social realities which characterize the practical world of administration. It contains peace and conflict, fulfillment and frustration, advantage and disadvantage, success and failure, and joy and sorrow. The supervisor is not necessarily born to the job; he may or may not have a calling for supervision or for some part of it;[65] he may be trained or untrained; he may be fortunate or unfortunate. In short anything can, and often does, happen to him, whatever his qualifications for this job. The pleasant things need not worry him, but he does have certain unpleasant tasks; and it is against these especially that he should prepare and brace himself.

One of his most irritating jobs is the fitting together of the bits and pieces of resources at his command to attain the goal the organization wants him to reach. They may be totally inadequate for the task, and so he will face the necessity for compromise in his techniques and expediency in his combinations. The pertinent thing for him to remember is that basically the organization will seem cruel and is concerned primarily with his getting the work done. No matter how enlightened and benevolent his superiors may be, their measurement of his supervisory performance will be largely that of his results in terms of what they want. His explanatory excuses and his excusatory explanations may well fall on deaf ears or, if they evoke attention, may get him nothing but expressions of sympathy. Few supervisors make much professional headway by appealing for understanding.

Pulling the superiors' chestnuts out of the fire is also an irritating function that falls to the supervisors. Superiors make errors or initiate personal projects which result in the supervisor having to do unpleasant things to follow through on them, to protect the boss, or to save his face. This may be called "supervisory accommodation." Whether or not it is a legitimate function of supervision is a moot question. The hard, cold truth is that almost every supervisor sooner or later must perform it, or run the risk of alienating an official important to his future.

Not the least of the aggravating aspects of supervision is the task of supervising more people that he can handle with the best results. A good deal of attention has been given the span of supervision, and various estimates have been made as to what should be the maximum number of supervisees.

Although these figures are impressive as the result of research and analysis, their magic may consist to no small degree of the mere fact that they are an effort at quantification. Actually, the optimum or the maximum span of supervision, while subject to some generalizations, will be viewed by the strategic administrator as something which varies with many factors: the simplicity and homogeneous nature of the work, the measure of mechanics usable, the ability of the supervisor, the distribution of the supervised and their work, the philosophy and cultural background of both the supervisors and supervised. Span of supervision takes on full meaning in terms of a given situation.[66]

Correction and Discipline

And, of course, correction and discipline must not be forgotten in considering the irritating jobs of the supervisor. Correction may not necessarily be unpleasant. It may not involve more than putting an employee straight in his efforts or personal conduct by helping in some discreet way. It can, however, be irritating to the supervisor when it involves complicated and intense effort or when it is repetitive, especially with the same person or group. Actually, it can be almost maddening when the supervisor is busy with other matters, when he is unsure as to the correction needed, or uncertain as to how to proceed. Yet discipline is by nature likely to be a more disagreeable task, since it involves finding a person wrong and taking action against him.

The strategy of correction is largely summed up in the statement that the supervisor should first analyze what needs corrective action and then take constructive steps. But discipline, dealing as it does with a violation of the will of the organization or of its representatives by one or more of its members, can demand more complicated stratagems.[67] Before he philosophizes his position with respect to discipline, the supervisor should recognize that it is a prominent task of supervisors in general since trouble with subordinates is universal, that it is a basic responsibility of supervisors, and that its purpose is primarily to protect the group and help the offender. This last point needs emphasizing; the purpose of discipline is not revenge, for such contributes little, if anything, to organizational welfare. Having absorbed these thoughts into his philosophy of discipline, the unit manager or foreman can proceed to assimilate principles and stratagems of discipline. A few of these are: (1) make no more disciplinary rules than necessary and inform all members of the organization of them; (2) be sure that an offense has really been committed which deserves discipline; (3) decide to discipline or not to do so by weighing the values of overlooking the offense against the advantages of disciplinary action; (4) make the punishment fit both the offense and the person; (5) avoid unenforceable penalties; (6) decide in view of the dynamics of each disciplinary situation whether the punishment should be assessed and/or imposed privately or publicly; (7) keep punishments within the bounds of justice and morality; and (8) do not hold a grudge against the offender or otherwise make it impossible for him to overcome the stigma of his defection.

The sensible supervisor, even though he may accept discipline as an inherent function of supervision, should not overlook an antithetic course of action. The supervisor who disciplines should also commend good behavior. The supervisor who consistently does not recognize and praise where commendation is due will not long enjoy the most harmonious relations with and positive response from his people. They will tend to see him only as a task master and a policeman. Commendation is not always an easy accomplishment. Good deeds may go unnoticed. They may be performed by individuals or units whose maladjustment to the organization or whose prior record does not endear them to the supervisor and/or their associates. But even then a sound amount of praise might brighten the supervisor's life and motivate the recipient to bigger and better things.

Supervision and the Development of Human Resources

Supervision is not just a routine function in administration which, when performed at all, is satisfactory. It is an activity that, if of good quality, can yield unique results to the organization. Basically, its quality is determined by how well in terms of quantity, quality, speed, and cost the work is gotten out. Certainly, this output implication is the essence of the control significance of supervision. But actually there is another "substantial good," perhaps only partly of control import, which supervision can accomplish, and this has to do with the human relations factor. The far-seeing supervisor will realize that the human resource is the most valuable thing any organization can have. Therefore, in addition to output, this supervisor will concern himself with the improvement of certain human elements. He will attempt to maintain and develop high morale in the interest of present and future performance. He will try to train his people for better performance, and will seek to find more efficient methods for them to use. And he will, after working out a rapprochement with them in their dependence on him, endeavor to give them adequate opportunity to show their own mettle and grow in success and capacity.[68]

What of Systems and the Systems Department?

This chapter has treated administrative control in generalities. It has been a deliberate attempt to show the basic realities of control, unobscured and uncluttered by the maze of mechanics which have been developed to aid in its discharge. Nothing has been said of systems and systems departments. However, these cannot be neglected. They are an important reality of business administration, and the strategic administrator will find himself concerned with them.

In recent authoritative literature, systems are defined ". . . as the coordinating of activities with respect to time and order of accomplishment to satisfy the requirements for the completion of a project."[69] In other words, systems furnish control prior to action.[70] The systems function has grown into a much fuller stature than it enjoyed a few years ago, when it was concerned with writing and charting formal procedures and methods. In many companies, one now sees a systems organization to which the systems function has been assigned. It may have a wide spectrum of duties ranging from mere preparing procedures for filing to drawing up the scheme for coordinating all managerial activity toward the organizational goal. In fact, systems departments have been set up in various companies. The chief work of these departments is to study, analyze, and attempt to improve the systems used by the company in its operations.[71]

The strategic administrator should recognize that systems can do much for the success of his organization or part thereof. A good systems unit, or even systems man can help save operating time, reduce inventories, cut down on errors in cost and delivery date predictions, eliminate superfluous activities, bring more rapid turnover of working capital and lower working capital requirements, and even the faster implementation of top management decisions.[72] The benefits to the company from effective systems work will come through the fact of better coordination.

But the alert administrator should beware of certain risks inherent in systems. One is, of course, the danger of overcommitment. So wonderful may the results of certain system developments appear, that the hard-pressed administrator may go overboard and, e.g., employ high priced specialists and buy expensive electronic machines when much less would fit his needs. Another risk is that of inflexibility. The development and institution of systems is expensive, and they do, after a period of time, generate the feeling of security which comes from familiarity with a routine—so they may be hard to change. And then, to be certain, there is the very real danger that systems and systems devices are still in a rather primitive state. The alert administrator might well, therefore, sit back and wait to see if the great breakthrough of today is not discarded tomorrow. Finally, there are a series of risks implied in questions that can be answered only in each administrative situation: What will this systems development do to the organizational family by way of negative effect on the development of democracy in administration?; Will it block this growth and result in a restoration of autocracy in management?; Will it seduce the administrator into mistaking mechanical answers for decisions and acts of leadership? These are real issues, for they involve important human values to both individuals and the company.[73]

Conclusion

Control is a major function of the business administrator. It is part and parcel of his leadership role. In bold relief, it is the means or act of assuring that his subordinates, singly and collectively, keep their eyes on the organizational goals as the target, and direct their efforts with a maximum of efficiency toward it. The action components of control are restraint, push, and overseership. Although control is often described in terms of assuring proper output, the concept of output should be understood to include all the results the organization seeks. As has been so eloquently put, ". . . an administrator is effective only when the purposes of a business organization and the essential satisfaction of its individual members are being achieved."[74]

Adequate control procedures, methods, and systems do not spring into being automatically, nor do successful control acts occur spontaneously. The discharge of the control function is one of the most difficult tasks that fall to the lot of the administrator. He must have and use a network of sub-leaders, who will normally have to work through a bureaucracy. He will not be able to operate as a controlling force without good communications. His decision making must be wise, or control efforts will be perverted. Proper motivation of his subordinates will be as significant as their intelligent restraint. All his control will go for naught if the function of supervision, which is located at the action ends of management, is not skilled and faithful.

BUSINESS SITUATIONS FOR ROLE-PLAYING

Situation XIX

Administrative Control as a Function of Leadership

THE YONTAN VEGETABLE OIL COMPANY

A. Scene.

A large vegetable oil extraction and processing firm. A special conference in the President's office a few days after an extremely frustrating Board of Directors' meeting.

B. Players.

1. Chairman of the Board and President of the Corporation: Mr. C. Q. Xenephone, an eminently successful immigrant who trusts his own judgment implicity.

2. Vice President in Charge of Finance: Mr. C. P. Plethora, a C.P.A. and an Attorney especially qualified in taxation.

3. Vice President in Charge of Manufacturing: Mr. T. Tasker Trent, a self-made production expert who is provincial in his outlook.

C. Situation.

1. The two Vice Presidents have diametrically opposed views on the issue of whether or not the refinery should be moved. Invited by the Chairman of the Board to do so, they presented their respective cases directly to the Board at its recent meeting.

2. Each Vice President is an intelligent and dynamic individual aggressive in advancing his

arguments. The Board of Directors was confused by the presentations which appeared to them as almost equally meritorious in thought.

3. After some discussion following the Board appearances of the Vice Presidents, who had then withdrawn from the Board room, one of the more elderly of the Directors, a gentleman rather far removed from the affairs of the company, bluntly asked the Chairman why he, as President, had not come to the Board meeting with a definite recommendation.

4. The President, who realizes that each of the Vice Presidents involved has a strong following among subordinate administrators, faces the necessity of effecting a compromise between these two gentlemen. This is his big problem. How, in short, can he exercise sufficient control over these sub-leaders to cause them to come to a workable and politic agreement?

D. Assignment. 1. Let the group select the three individuals to act out the roles of Chairman and President, Vice President (Finance), and Vice President (Manufacturing). Attention may be called to the fact that these officials represent top administrative positions.

2. Ask the three participants to step out of the room for a moment. Then instruct the group to watch for the techniques of handling sub-leaders and of reaching a compromise decision.

3. Use the last ten or fifteen minutes of the session for eliciting group views on the proper handling of the problem.

NOTES

1. Some writers discuss control and control techniques primarily from the viewpoint that control is a function of top management. This feeling seems to be more or less in line with the idea expressed in the statement, "General management is in an altogether different class from departmental

management." See T. G. ROSE and DONALD E. FARR, *Higher Management Control* (New York: McGraw-Hill Book Company, Inc., 1957), p. 6.

For an exposition of the basic process of control, control policies, and control practices with a high echelon connotation, attention is invited to PAUL E. HOLDEN, LOUNSBURY FISH, and HUBERT L. SMITH, *Top Management Organization and Control* (New York: McGraw-Hill Book Company, Inc., 1951), pp. 77-251.

2. A well known analysis of certain aspects of control mechanics is that of BILLY E. GOETZ, *Management Planning and Control* (New York: McGraw-Hill Book Company, Inc., 1949).

3. LOUIS A. ALLEN, *Management and Organization* (New York: McGraw-Hill Book Company, Inc., 1958), pp. 44-45.

4. "Some control of organized activity is a universal necessity

. . . .

The universal necessity for control in some degree arises from the universal necessity for leadership in the accomplishment of joint objectives." RALPH CURRIER DAVIS, *The Fundamentals of Top Management* (New York: Harper & Brothers, Publishers, 1951), p. 628.

5. *Ibid.*, p. 633.

6. An identification of so-called general laws of leadership are essayed by J. F. BROWN, *Psychology and the Social Order* (New York: McGraw-Hill Book Company, Inc., 1936), p. 342.

7. "The meaning which people give a control system in terms of their own outlook is as critical as the technical design of the system." EDMUND P. LEARNED, DAVID N. ULRICH, and DONALD R. BOOZ, *Executive Action* (Boston: Harvard University Press, 1951), p. 122.

8. Suggested by JOHN McDONALD, *Stategy in Poker, Business and War* (New York: W. W. Norton & Company, Inc., 1950), pp. 50-83.

Attention is invited to MAX WEBER, *Wirtschaft und Gesellschaft* (Tübingen: J. C. B. Mohr, 1922), pp. 650-678.

9. Max Weber has given the world the classical analysis of bureaucracy. ROBERT K. MERTON, *Social Theory and Social Structure* (Rev. ed.; Glencoe, Ill.: The Free Press, 1957), p. 196.

10. MARSHALL E. DIMOCK, *Administrative Vitality: the Conflict with Bureaucracy* (New York: Harper & Brothers, Publishers, 1959), p. 3.

11. DELBERT C. MILLER and WILLIAM H. FORM, *Industrial Sociology* (New York: Harper & Brothers, Publishers, 1951), p. 153.
12. *Ibid.*, p. 153.
13. *Ibid.*, p. 154.
14. MERTON, *op. cit.*, p. 196.
15. *Ibid.*
16. *Ibid.*; and MAX WEBER, "Bureaucracy" in H. H. GERTH and C. WRIGHT MILLS (eds. and trans.), *Essays in Sociology* (New York: Oxford University Press, Inc., 1946), as quoted in EDGAR A. SCHULER et al., *Outside Readings in Sociology* (New York: Thomas Y. Crowell Company, 1952), pp. 406-410.
17. ALVIN W. GOULDNER, *Patterns of Industrial Bureaucracy* (Glencoe, Ill.: The Free Press, 1954), p. 22.
18. GOULDNER, *op. cit.*, p. 22, in analyzing Weber's view of discipline in relation to bureaucracy.
19. MAX WEBER, "Bureaucracy" in H. H. GERTH and C. WRIGHT MILLS (eds. and trans.), *Essays in Sociology* (New York: Oxford University Press, Inc., 1946), as quoted in EDGAR A. SCHULER et al., *Outside Readings in Sociology* (New York: Thomas Y. Crowell Company, 1952), p. 411.
20. MERTON, *op. cit.*, p. 196.
21. DIMOCK, *op. cit.*, p. 4.
22. GOULDNER, *op. cit.*, p. 25, in stating Weber's view on the value of bureaucracy.
23. DIMOCK, *op. cit.*, pp. 4-5.
24. Some succinct comments on span of control are found in JAMES C. WORTHY, *Big Business and Free Men* (New York: Harper & Brothers, Publishers, 1959), pp. 100-118.
25. See Chapter XIV.
26. CHARLES HORTON COOLEY, *Human Nature and the Social Order* (New York: Charles Scribner's Sons, 1902), p. 240.
27. *Ibid.*, p. 239.
28. Cooley defines primary or animal anger in terms of that which is immediately aroused by an obnoxious stimulant. *Ibid.*, p. 233.
29. *Ibid.*, p. 238.
30. LEARNED, ULRICH and BOOZ, *op. cit.*, p. 122.
31. Cooley, *op. cit.*, p. 287.
32. In the vein of Sorokin's thought on quantophrenia, one may contend that it is probably impossible to express leadership in numbers. For his discussion of quantophrenia, see PITIRIM

A. SOROKIN, *Fads and Foibles in Modern Sociology and Related Sciences* (Chicago: Henry Regnery Company, 1956), pp. 102-173.

33. Suggested by Cooley. See *op. cit.*, pp. 285-286.

34. J. A. C. BROWN, *The Social Psychology of Industry* (Harmondsworth, Middlesex: Penguin Books, Ltd., 1954), p. 226.

35. Brown suggests these communication patterns of the different types of leaders. *Ibid.*, pp. 225-226.

36. This fact of different response is noted by MARSHALL EDWARD DIMOCK, *The Executive in Action* (New York: Harper & Brothers, Publishers, 1945), p. 218.

37. Attention is invited to the American Management Association publication on appraising executive performance. CARL HEYEL, *Appraising Executive Performance* (New York: American Management Association, 1958).

38. ROBERT DUBIN, *The World of Work: Industrial Society and Human Relations* (Englewood Cliffs, N.J.: Prentice-Hall, Inc., 1958), p. 213.

39. C. H. NORTHCOTT, *Personnel Management* (3rd ed.; London: Sir Isaac Pitman & Sons, Ltd., 1955), pp. 75-76.

40. LESLIE R. BEACH and ELON L. CLARK, *Psychology in Business* (McGraw-Hill Book Company, Inc., 1959), pp. 106-107.

41. *Ibid.*, p. 107.

42. *Loc. cit.*

43. MORRIS S. VITELES, *Motivation in Morale in Industry* (W. W. Norton & Company, Inc., 1953), p. 66.

44. MILTON L. BLUM, *Industrial Psychology and Its Social Functions* (Rev. ed.; New York: Harper & Brothers, Publishers, 1949), pp. 56-57.

45. This assumption is suggested by HAROLD J. LEAVITT, *Managerial Psychology* (Chicago: University of Chicago Press, 1958), p. 12.

46. These findings are summarized in JOHN M. PFIFFNER, *The Supervision of Personnel* (New York: Prentice-Hall, Inc., 1951), p. 237, who acknowledges the information to NORMAN R. F. MAIER, *Psychology in Industry* (New York: Houghton Mifflin Company, 1946), p. 268.

47. WORTHY, *op. cit.*, p. 123.

For a comprehensive exploration of economic incentives which covers symbols, see WILLIAM FOOTE WHYTE, *Money and Motivation* (New York: Harper & Brothers, Publishers, 1955).

48. ALLEN, *op. cit.*, p. 140.

49. *Loc. cit.*, but in reference to belief of Dr. Rensis Likert,

Director of Institute for Social Research, University of Michigan.

50. This enumeration is partly taken from WILLIAM H. NEWMAN, *Administrative Action* (Englewood Cliffs, N.J.: Prentice-Hall, Inc., 1950), p. 449.

51. BROWN, *op. cit.*, p. 202.

52. LYNDALL F. URWICK, *The Pattern of Management* (Minneapolis: University of Minnesota Press, 1956), p. 50.

53. "Self motivation is the highest and most desirable type of motivation. It is always operative. . . . It is self-perpetuating." PAUL ECKER et al., *Handbook for Supervisors* (Englewood Cliffs, N.J.: Prentice-Hall, Inc., 1959), p. 49.

54. *National Labor Relations Act*, Sec. II, Par. 11.

55. ECKER et al., *op. cit.*, pp. 6-7.

56. Suggested by BEACH and CLARK, *op. cit.*, p. 228.

57. Spriegel and Schulz defined a supervisor as ". . . any person who is responsible (1) for the conduct of others in the achievement of a particular task, (2) for the maintenance of quality standards, (3) for the protection and care of materials, and (4) for services to be rendered to those under his control." WILLIAM R. SPRIEGEL and EDWARD SCHULZ, *Elements of Supervision* (New York: John W. Wiley & Sons, Inc., 1942), p. 1.

58. *Ibid.*

59. For an exhaustive list of the duties of the supervisor, see HENRY E. NILES, MARY CUSHING NILES, and JAMES C. STEPHENS, *The Office Supervisor* (3rd ed.; New York: John Wiley & Sons, Inc., 1959), pp. 1-8.

60. This thought on the nature and merits of general supervision is partly taken from GEORGE STRAUSS and LEONARD R. SAYLES, *Personnel* (Englewood Cliffs, N.J.: Prentice-Hall, Inc., 1960), pp. 124-125.

61. *Ibid.*

62. RENSIS LIKERT, "Effective Supervision: An Adaptive and Related Process," *Personnel Psychology* (Autumn, 1958), p. 227, as quoted in NILES, NILES and STEPHENS, *op. cit.*, p. 287.

63. Newman devotes a chapter to direction. *Op. cit.*, pp. 375-389.

64. One of the more interesting portrayals of a happy administrative situation is found in ALAN HARRINGTON, *Life in the Crystal Palace* (New York: Alfred A. Knopf, 1959).

65. This idea of the *calling* for a job is taken from a discussion of the *Unternehem* (owner-entrepreneur) found in HEINZ HARTMANN, *Authority and Organization in German Man-*

agement (Princeton: Princeton University Press, 1959), pp. 28-34.

66. Partly suggested by FRITZ MORSTEIN MARX (ed.), *Elements of Public Administration* (New York: Prentice-Hall, Inc., 1946), p. 442.

67. For discussions of discipline, attention is invited to STRAUSS and SAYLES, *op. cit.*, pp. 284-302; JOHN M. PFIFFNER, *The Supervision of Personnel* (2nd ed.; Englewood Cliffs, N.J.: Prentice-Hall, Inc., 1958), pp. 362-380; and "The Importance of Maintaining Discipline" in *Leadership on the Job.* Edited by the Staff of *Supervisory Management* (New York: American Management Association, 1957), pp. 197-205.

68. This paragraph is inspired in part by EDWARD C. SCHLEH, *Executive Management of Personnel* (Englewood Cliffs, N.J.: Prentice-Hall, Inc., 1958), pp. 95-107.

69. M. S. SHANE, "Fitting Systems and Procedures into the Business Enterprise" in *Organizing for Efficient Systems Planning and Control.* Special Report No. 12 (New York: American Management Association, n.d.), pp. 38-39.

70. *Loc. cit.*
   "It is important to distinguish between 'systems' and 'processes.' In brief, a system facilitates a process; it is the means by which the process occurs." ROBERT N. ANTHONY, *Planning and Control Systems: A Framework for Analysis* (Boston: Division of Research, Graduate School of Business Administration, Harvard University, 1965), p. 5.

71. ROBERT M. GLEASON, "Introduction" in *ibid.*, p. 7.

72. Taken from SHANE, *op. cit.*, p. 41.

73. The risks discussed in this paragraph are largely the thought of MELVIN L. HURNI, "Modern Systems Design," in *Organizing for Effective Systems Planning and Control.* Special Report No. 12 (New York: American Management Association, n.d.), pp. 19-22.

74. DONALD K. DAVID, "Introduction to the Theme" in EDWARD C. BURSK (ed.), *How to Increase Executive Effectiveness* (Cambridge, Mass.: Harvard University Press, 1954), p. 4.
   The danger of too many controls is pointed out by HENRY G. HODGES and RAYMOND J. ZIEGLER, *Managing the Industrial Concern* (Boston: Houghton-Mifflin Company, 1963), p. 142.

A SELECTED BIBLIOGRAPHY

This bibliography consists for the most part of the materials consulted in writing *Administrative Strategy and Decision Making*. Resort was had primarily to "classics" of book dimension in various pertinent fields. The publications listed, representing a highly selected enumeration, comprise a sound reading list, if but a fraction of the literature on administration in general and business administration in particular extant in the United States and the other nations of the Free World.

ALLEN, LOUIS A. *Management and Organization*. New York: McGraw-Hill Book Company, Inc., 1958.

ALLEN, LOUIS A. *The Management Profession*. New York. McGraw-Hill Book Company, Inc., 1964.

ANSHEN, MELGIN and BACH, G.L. *Management and Corporations 1985*. New York: McGraw-Hill Book Company, Inc., 1960.

ANSOFF, H. IGOR. *Corporate Strategy*. New York: McGraw-Hill Book Company, Inc., 1965.

ANTHONY, ROBERT N. *Planning and Control Systems*. Boston: Division of Research, Graduate School of Business Administration, Harvard University, 1965.

APPELY, LAWRENCE A. *Management in Action*. New York: American Management Association, 1956.

ARGYRIS, CHRIS. *Executive Leadership*. New York: Harper & Brothers, Publishers, 1953.

ARGYRIS, CHRIS. *Integrating the Individual and the Organization*. New York: John Wiley & Sons, Inc., 1964.

ARGYRIS, CHRIS. *Interpersonal Competence and Organizational Effectiveness*. New York: Harper & Brothers, 1961.

ARGYRIS, CHRIS. *Organization and Innovation*. Homewood, Illinois: Richard D. Irwin, Inc., 1965.

ARGYRIS, CHRIS. *Personality and Organization*. New York: Harper & Brothers, Publishers, 1957.

BAKER, ROBERT L. (ed.). *Business Leadership in a Changing World*. New York: McGraw-Hill Book Company, Inc., 1962.

BAKKE, E. WIGHT. *Bonds of Organization*. New York: Harper & Brothers, Publishers, 1950.

BARNARD, CHESTER I. *The Functions of the Executive*. Cambridge, Mass.: Harvard University Press, 1956.

618

BARNARD, CHESTER I. *Organization and Management.* Cambridge, Mass.: Harvard University Press, 1952.

BASS, BERNARD M. *Organizational Psychology.* Boston: Allyn and Bacon, Inc., 1965.

BEACH, LESLIE R. and CLARK, ELON L. *Psychology in Business.* New York: McGraw-Hill Book Company, Inc., 1959.

BEISHLINE, JOHN ROBERT. *Military Management for National Defense.* New York: Prentice-Hall, Inc., 1950.

BELLOWS, ROGER. *Creative Leadership.* Englewood Cliffs, N.J.: Prentice-Hall, Inc., 1959.

BENDIX, REINHARD. *Work and Authority in Industry.* New York: John Wiley & Sons, Inc., 1956.

BENDIX, REINHARD and LIPSET, SEYMOUR M. (eds.). *Class Status and Power.* Glencoe, Ill.: The Free Press, 1953.

BERELSON, BERNARD and STEINER, GARY A. *Human Behavior: An Inventory of Scientific Findings.* New York: Harcourt Brace & World, 1964.

BERNAYS, EDWARD L. (ed.). *The Engineering of Consent.* Norman: University of Oklahoma Press, 1955.

BLACK, JAMES MENZIES. *Developing Competent Subordinates.* New York: American Management Association, 1961.

BLAU, PETER. *Bureaucracy in Modern Society.* New York: Random House, 1956.

BLUM, MILTON L. *Industrial Psychology and its Social Foundations.* Rev. ed. New York: Harper & Brothers, Publishers, 1956.

BOND, FLOYD A. et al. *Preparation for Business Leadership: Views of Top Executives.* Ann Arbor: Bureau of Business Research, University of Michigan, 1964.

BRECH, E. F. L. *Management; Its Nature and Significance.* 3rd ed. London: Sir Isaac Pitman & Sons, Ltd., 1953.

BRECHT, ARNOLD and GLASER, COMSTOCK. *The Art and Technique of Administration in German Ministries.* Cambridge, Mass.: Harvard University Press, 1940.

BRIM, ORVILLE et al. *Personality and Decision Making.* Stanford: Stanford University Press, 1962.

BROMAGE, ARTHUR W. *Introduction to Municipal Government and Administration.* 2nd ed. New York: Appleton-Century-Crofts, Inc., 1950.

BROWN, ALVIN. *Organization: A Formulation of Principles.* New York: Hibbert Printing Company, 1945.

BROWN, J. A. C. *The Social Psychology of Industry.* Harmondsworth, Middlesex: Penguin Books, Ltd., 1954.

BROWN, J. F. *Psychology and the Social Order.* New York: McGraw-Hill Book Company, Inc., 1936.

BROWN, WILFRED. *Exploration in Management.* London: William Heinemann, Ltd., 1960.

BURGER, CHESTER. *Survival in the Executive Jungle.* New York: Macmillan Company, 1964.

BURNS, TOM and STALKER, G. M. *The Management of Innovation.* London: Tavistock Publications, 1961.

BURSK, EDWARD C. *How to Increase Executive Efficiency.* Cambridge, Mass.: Harvard University Press, 1954.

BURSK, EDWARD C. (ed.). *The Management Team.* Cambridge, Mass.: Harvard University Press, 1954.

BURSK, EDWARD C. and CHAPMAN, JOHN F. (eds.). *New Decision Making Tools for Managers.* Cambridge, Mass.: Harvard University Press, 1963.

BURSK, EDWARD C. and FENN, DAN H., JR. (eds.). *Planning the Future Strategy of Your Business.* New York: McGraw-Hill Book Company, Inc., 1956.

CADY, EDWIN LAIRD. *Creative Communication.* New York: Reinhold Publishing Corporation, 1956.

CALDWELL, LYNTON K. *The Administrative Theories of Hamilton and Jefferson.* Chicago: University of Chicago Press, 1944.

CARLSON, SUNE. *Executive Behavior.* Stockholm: Strombergs, 1951.

CHAPPLE, ELLIOT D. and SAYLES, LEONARD R. *The Measure of Management.* New York: Macmillan Company, 1960.

CHISHOLM, CECIL (ed.). *Communications in Industry.* London: Business Publications, Ltd. in association with B. T. Botsford, Ltd., 1955.

CHURCHMAN, C. WEST. *Prediction and Optimal Decision: Philosophical Issues of a Science of Values.* Englewood Cliffs, N.J.: Prentice-Hall, Inc., 1961.

CLEETON, GLEN U. and MASON, CHARLES W. *Executive Ability: Its Discovery and Development.* Rev. ed. Yellow Springs, Ohio: Antioch Press, 1946.

COLLINS, BARRY E. and GUETZKOW, HAROLD. *A Social Psychology of Group Processes for Decision-Making.* New York: John Wiley & Sons, Inc., 1964.

CONANT, W. H. *Business Administration.* New York: Gregg Publishing Company, 1945.

COOLEY, CHARLES HORTON. *Human Nature and the Social Order.* New York: Charles Scribner's Sons, 1902.

COPELAND, MELVIN T. *The Executive at Work.* Cambridge, Mass.: Harvard University Press, 1952.

CORDINER, RALPH J. *New Frontiers for Professional Managers.* New York: McGraw-Hill Book Company, Inc., 1956.

CORSINI, RAYMOND J. et al. *Role Playing in Business and Industry.* New York: The Free Press of Glencoe, Illinois, 1961.

COSTELLO, TIMOTHY W. and ZALKIND, SHELDON S. *Psychology in Administration.* Englewood Cliffs, N.J.: Prentice-Hall, Inc., 1963.

CRAWFORD, ROBERT C. *The Techniques of Creative Thinking.* New York: Hawthorn Books, Inc., 1954.

DALE, ERNEST. *The Great Organizers.* New York: McGraw-Hill Book Company, Inc., 1961.

DOLE, ERNEST, *Management: Theory and Practice.* New York: McGraw-Hill Book Company, 1965.

DALE, ERNEST. *Planning and Developing the Company Organization Structure.* Research Report No. 20. New York: American Management Association, 1952.

DALE, ERNEST and URWICK, LYNDALL F. *Staff in Organizations.* New York: McGraw-Hill Book Company, Inc., 1960.

DALTON, MELVILLE. *Men Who Manage.* New York: John Wiley & Sons, Inc., 1959.

DAVIS, KEITH and SCOTT, WILLIAM G. (eds.). *Readings in Human Relations* (2nd ed.). New York: McGraw-Hill Book Company, Inc., 1964.

DAVIS, RALPH CURRIER. *The Fundamentals of Top Management.* New York: Harper & Brothers, Publishers, 1951.

DEARMOND, FRED. *The Executive at Work.* Englewood Cliffs, N.J.: Prentice-Hall, Inc., 1958.

DENNISON, HENRY. *Organization Engineering.* New York: McGraw-Hill Book Company, Inc., 1931.

DILL, WILLIAM R. et al. *The New Managers.* Englewood Cliffs, N.J.: Prentice-Hall, Inc., 1962.

DIMOCK, MARSHALL E. *Administrative Vitality.* New York: Harper & Brothers, Publishers, 1959.

DIMOCK, MARSHALL E. *The Executive in Action.* New York: Harper & Brothers, Publishers, 1945.

DIMOCK, MARSHALL E. *A Philosophy of Administration.* New York: Harper & Brothers, Publishers, 1958.

DRUCKER, PETER F. *The Concept of the Corporation.* New York: John Day Company, 1946.

DRUCKER, PETER F. *Landmarks of Tomorrow.* New York: Harper & Brothers, Publishers, 1959.

DRUCKER, PETER F. *Managing for Results.* New York: Harper & Row, 1964.

DRUCKER, PETER F. *The Practice of Management.* New York: Harper & Brothers, Publishers, 1954.

DUBIN, ROBERT (ed.). *Human Relations in Administration.* New York: Prentice-Hall, Inc., 1951.

DUBIN, ROBERT. *The World of Work: Industrial Society and Human Relations.* Englewood Cliffs, N.J.: Prentice-Hall, Inc., 1958.

ECKER, PAUL et al. *Handbook for Supervisors.* Englewood Cliffs, N.J.: Prentice-Hall, Inc., 1959.

EDITORS OF FORTUNE, *The Executive Life.* Garden City, N.Y.: Doubleday & Company, Inc., 1956.

ELLIOTT, OSBORN. *Men at the Top.* New York: Harper & Brothers, Publishers, 1959.

ELLSWORTH, JOHN S. *Factory Folkways*. New Haven: Yale University Press, 1952.

ETZIONI, AMITAI. *Modern Organizations*. Englewood Cliffs, N.J.: Prentice-Hall, Inc., 1964.

EWING, DAVID W. *Long Range Planning for Management*. New York: Harper & Brothers, Publishers, 1958.

EWING, DAVID W. *The Managerial Mind*. London: Collier-Macmillan, Ltd., 1964.

FARMER, RICHARD N. and RICHMAN, BARRY M. *Comparative Management and Economic Progress*. Homewood, Illinois: Richard D. Irwin, 1965.

FAYOL, HENRI. *General and Industrial Management*. Trans. Constance Storrs. London: Sir Isaac Pitman & Sons, Ltd., 1949.

FEINBERG, SAMUEL. *How Do You Manage?* New York: Fairchild Publications, Inc., 1965.

FESTINGER, LEON. Conflict, Decision and Dissonance. Stanford: Stanford University Press, 1964.

FILIPETTI, GEORGE. *Industrial Management in Transition*. Rev. ed. Homewood, Ill.: Richard D. Irwin, Inc., 1953.

FLORY, CHARLES D. (ed.). *Managers for Tomorrow*. New York: New American Library. 1965.

FOLLETT, M. P. *Creative Experience*. New York: Longmans, Green and Co., Inc., 1930.

FRIEDMANN, GEORGE. *Industrial Society: The Emergence of the Human Problems of Automation*. Glencoe, Illinois: The Free Press, 1958.

GADDIS, PAUL O. *Corporate Accountability*. New York: Harper & Row, 1964.

GARDNER, BURLEIGH B. and MOORE, DAVID G. *Human Relations in Industry*. 3rd ed. Chicago: Richard D. Irwin, Inc., 1955.

GHISELLI, EDWIN and BROWN, CLARENCE. *Personnel and Industrial Psychology*. 2nd ed. New York: McGraw-Hill Book Company, Inc., 1955.

GINZBERG, ELI et al. *Democratic Values and the Rights of Management*. New York: Columbia University Press, 1963.

GINZBERG, ELI (ed.). *What Makes an Executive?* New York: Columbia University Press, 1955.

GIVEN, WILLIAM B. *Bottom-Up Management*. New York: Harper & Brothers, Publishers, 1949.

GLASER, COMSTOCK. *Administrative Procedure*. Washington, D.C.: American Council on Public Affairs, 1941.

GLOVER, JOHN G. *Fundamentals of Management*. Rev. ed. New York: Simmons-Boardman Publishing Corporation, 1958.

GOETZ, BILLY E. *Management Planning and Control*. New York: McGraw-Hill Book Company, Inc., 1949.

GOODMAN, PAUL. *People or Personnel: Decentralizing and the Mixed System.* Toronto: Random House, Inc., 1965.

GOULDNER, ALVIN W. *Patterns of Industrial Bureaucracy.* Glencoe, Ill.: The Free Press, 1954.

GRANICK, DAVID. *The European Business Executive.* Garden City, New York: Doubleday & Company, Inc., 1962.

GRANICK, DAVID. *The Red Executive.* Garden City, N. Y.: Doubleday & Company, Inc., 1961.

GRAUBARD, STEPHEN R. and HOLTON, GERALD (eds.). *Excellence and Leadership in a Democracy.* New York: Columbia University Press, 1962.

GREENWALT, CRAWFORD H. *The Uncommon Man.* New York: McGraw-Hill Book Company, Inc., 1959.

GREENWOOD, WILLIAM T. (ed.). *Issues in Business and Society.* Boston: Houghton Mifflin Company, 1964.

GREENWOOD, WILLIAM T. *Management and Organizational Behavior Theories.* Cincinnati, Ohio: South-Western Publishing Company, 1965.

GROSS, BERTRAM M. *The Managing of Organizations.* New York: The Free Press of Glencoe, Ill., 1965.

GUEST, ROBERT H. *Organizational Change: The Effect of Successful Leadership.* Homewood, Illinois: Richard D. Irwin, Inc., 1962.

GUETZKOW, HAROLD (ed.). *Groups, Leadership and Men.* Pittsburgh: Carnegie Institute of Technology Press, 1951.

GULICK, LUTHER and URWICK, L. (eds.). *Papers on the Science of Administration.* New York: Institute of Public Administration, Columbia University, 1937.

HAIMAN, FRANKLIN S. *Group Leadership and Democratic Action.* Boston: Houghton Mifflin Company, 1951.

HAIMAN, THEODORE. *Professional Management: Theory and Practice.* Boston: Houghton Mifflin Company, 1962.

HAIRE, MASON (ed.). *Modern Organization Theory.* New York: John Wiley & Sons, Inc., 1959.

HAIRE, MASON. *Psychology in Management.* New York: McGraw-Hill Book Company, Inc., 1956.

HANIKA, F. DE P. *New Thinking in Management.* London: Hutchinson & Company, 1965.

HARBISON, FREDERICK and MYERS, CHARLES A. *Management in the Industrial World.* New York: McGraw-Hill Book Company, Inc., 1959.

HARRINGTON, ALAN. *Life in the Crystal Palace.* New York: Alfred A. Knopf, 1959.

HARTLEY, EUGENE L. and HARTLEY, RUTH E. *Fundamentals of Social Psychology.* New York: Alfred A. Knopf, 1959.

HARTMANN, HEINZ. *Authority and Organization in German Management.* Princeton: Princeton University Press, 1959.

HEMPHILL, JOHN K. *Situational Factors in Leadership.* Columbus: Ohio State University, 1949.

HERZBERG, FREDERICK et al. *The Motivation to Work* (2nd ed.). New York: John Wiley & Sons, Inc., 1959.

HESKETT, J. L. et al. *Business Logistics.* New York: The Ronald Press Company, 1964.

HEYEL, CARL. *Appraising Executive Performance.* New York: American Management Association, 1958.

HILL, L. S. *Communications, Semantics, and Information Systems.* Santa Monica: Rand Corporation, 1964.

HODGES, HENRY G. and ZEIGLER, RAYMOND J. Managing the Industrial Concern. Boston: Houghton-Mifflin Co., 1963.

HODGSON, RICHARD C. et al. *The Executive Role Constellation.* Boston: Division of Research, Graduate School of Business Administration, Harvard University, 1965.

HOLDEN, PAUL E. et al. *Top Management Organization and Control.* New York: McGraw-Hill Book Company, Inc., 1951.

HOLLANDER, E. P. *Leaders, Groups and Influence.* Oxford: Oxford University Press, 1964.

HOMANS, GEORGE CASPAR. *The Human Group.* New York: Harcourt, Brace and Company, Inc., 1950.

HOSLETT, SCHUYLER DEAN (ed.). *Human Factors in Management.* Rev. ed. New York: Harper & Brothers, Publishers, 1951.

INDUSTRIAL RELATIONS RESEARCH ASSOCIATION. *Research in Industrial Relations.* Publication No. 17. New York: Harper & Brothers, Publishers, 1957.

JAMISON, CHARLES L. *Business Policy.* Englewood Cliffs, N.J.: Prentice-Hall, Inc., 1953.

JENNINGS, EUGENE E. *An Anatomy of Leadership.* New York: Harper & Brothers, Publishers, 1960.

JENNINGS, EUGENE E. *The Executive—Autocrat, Bureaucrat and Democrat.* New York: Harper and Row Publishers, 1962.

JOHNSON, ROSSALL J. *Executive Decisions.* Cincinnati: South-Western Publishing Company, 1963.

JONES, MANLEY HOWE. *Executive Decision Making.* Homewood, Ill.: Richard D. Irwin, Inc., 1957.

JUCIUS, MICHAEL J. *Personnel Management.* 4th ed. Homewood, Ill.: Richard D. Irwin, Inc., 1959.

JURAM, J. M. *Managerial Breakthrough.* New York: McGraw-Hill Book Company, 1964.

KAHN, ROBERT L. et al. *Organizational Stress.* New York: John Wiley & Sons, Inc., 1964.

KATZ, DANIEL. *The Social Psychology of Organizations.* New York: John Wiley & Sons, Inc., 1965.

KEPNER, CHARLES H. and TREGOE, BENJAMIN B. *The Rational Manager.* New York: McGraw-Hill Book Company, Inc., 1965.

KINGSLEY, JOHN DONALD. *Representative Bureaucracy: An Interpretation of the British Civil Service.* Yellow Springs, Ohio: Antioch Press, 1944.

KNOWLES, WILLIAM H. *Personnel Management.* New York: American Book Company, 1955.

KOONTZ, HAROLD and O'DONNELL, CYRIL. *Principles of Management.* New York: McGraw-Hill Book Company, Inc., 1955.

KOONTZ, HAROLD and O'DONNELL, CYRIL (eds.). *Readings in Management.* New York: McGraw-Hill Book Company, Inc., 1959.

KORNHAUSER, ARTHUR. *Mental Health of the Industrial Worker.* New York: John Wiley & Sons, Inc., 1965.

KRUPP, SHERMAN. *Patterns in Organizational Analysis.* New York: Holt, Rinehart & Winston, Inc., 1964.

LAIRD, DONALD A. *Practical Business Psychology.* 2nd ed. New York: McGraw-Hill Book Company, Inc., 1956.

LAIRD, DONALD A. and LAIRD, ELEANOR C. *The Techniques of Delegating.* New York: McGraw-Hill Book Company, Inc., 1957.

LANDSBERGER, HENRY A. *Hawthorne Revisited.* Cornell Studies in Industrial and Labor Relations, V. 9. Ithaca, N.Y.: New York State School of Industrial and Labor Relations, 1958.

LAWRENCE, PAUL R. et al. *Organizational Behavior and Administration.* Homewood, Illinois: The Dorsey Press, Inc. and Richard D. Irwin, Inc., 1961.

LEADERSHIP ON THE JOB. Edited by the Staff of *Supervisory Management.* New York: American Management Association, 1957.

LEARNED, EDMUND P., ULRICH, DAVID N. and BOOZ, DONALD R. *Executive Action.* Boston: Harvard University, 1951.

LEARNED, EDMUND P. et al. *European Problems in General Management.* Homewood, Illinois: Richard D. Irwin, 1965.

LEAVITT, HAROLD. *Managerial Psychology.* Chicago: The University of Chicago Press, 1958.

LEAVITT, HAROLD J. (ed.). *The Social Science of Organizations.* Englewood Cliffs, N.J.: Prentice-Hall, Inc., 1963.

LEBRETON, PRESTON P. *General Administration: Planning and Implementation.* New York: Holt, Rinehart & Winston, Inc., 1965.

LEEDS, RUTH and SMITH, THOMASINA (eds.). *Using Social Science Knowledge in Business and Industry.* Homewood, Illinois: Richard D. Irwin, Inc., 1963.

LEMKE, B. C. and EDWARDS, JAMES DON (ed.). *Administrative Control and Executive Action.* Columbus: Charles & Merrill Books, Inc., 1961.

LEPAWSKY, ALBERT. *Administration.* New York: Alfred A. Knopf, 1949.

LICKERT, RENSIS. *New Patterns of Management.* New York: McGraw-Hill Book Company, Inc., 1961.

LIPSET, SEYMOUR M. and BENDIX, REINHARD. *Social Mobility in Industrial Society.* Berkeley: University of California Press, 1959.

LITTERER, JOSEPH A. *The Analysis of Organizations.* New York: John Wiley & Sons, Inc., 1965.

LOTHROP, WARREN C. *Management Use of Research and Development.* New York: Harper & Row, 1964.

McCAY, JAMES T. *The Management of Time.* Englewood Cliffs, N.J.: Prentice-Hall, Inc., 1959.

McDONALD, JOHN. *Strategy in Poker, Business and War.* New York: W. W. Norton & Company, Inc., 1950.

McFARLAND, DALTON E. *Management Principles and Practices.* New York: Macmillan Company, 1958.

McGUIRE, JOSEPH W. *Theories of Business Behavior.* Englewood Cliffs, N.J.: Prentice-Hall, Inc., 1964.

McLARNEY, WILLIAM J. *Management Training.* Chicago: Richard D. Irwin, Inc., 1952.

MAIER, NORMAN R. F. *Principles of Human Relations.* New York: John Wiley & Sons, Inc., 1952.

MAIER, NORMAN R. P. *Problem Solving Discussions and Conferences: Leadership Methods and Skills.* New York: McGraw-Hill Book Company, Inc., 1963.

MAIER, NORMAN R. F. *Psychology in Industry.* 2nd ed. Boston: Houghton Mifflin Company, 1955.

Manual of Excellent Managements. New York: American Institute of Management, 1965.

MARCH, JAMES G. and SIMON, HERBERT A. *Organizations.* New York: John Wiley & Sons, Inc., 1958.

MARTINDELL, JACKSON. *The Scientific Appraisal of Management.* New York: Harper & Brothers, Publishers, 1950.

MARX, FRITZ MORSTEIN. *Elements of Public Administration.* New York: Prentice-Hall, Inc., 1946.

MASON, JOSEPH G. *How To Be a More Creative Executive.* New York: McGraw-Hill Book Company, Inc., 1960.

MAYO, ELTON. *Human Problems of an Industrial Civilization.* Cambridge, Mass.: Harvard University Press, 1946.

MEE, JOHN F. *Management Thought in a Dynamic Society.* New York: New York University Press, 1963.

MERRIHUE, WILLARD V. *Managing by Communication.* New York: McGraw-Hill Book Company, Inc., 1960.

MERRILL, HARWOOD F. (ed.). *Classics in Management.* New York: American Management Association, 1960.

MERTON, ROBERT K. *Social Theory and Social Structure.* Rev. ed. Glencoe, Ill.: The Free Press, 1957.

MERTON, ROBERT K. et al. (eds.). *Sociology Today.* New York: Basic Books, 1959.

METCALF, HENRY C. and URWICK, L. (eds.). *Dynamic Administration; The Collected Papers of Mary Parker Follett.* New York: Harper & Brothers, Publishers, 1940.

MILLER, DELBERT C. and FORM, WILLIAM H. *Industrial Sociology.* New York: Harper & Brothers, Publishers, 1951.

MILLETT, JOHN D. *Management in the Public Service.* New York: McGraw-Hill Book Company, Inc., 1954.

MILLS, C. WRIGHT. *The Power Elite.* New York: Oxford University Press, 1956.

MILLS, C. WRIGHT. *White Collar.* New York: Oxford University Press, 1951.

MOONEY, JAMES D. and REILEY, ALAN C. *Onward Industry,* New York: Harper & Brothers, Publishers, 1931.

MOONEY, JAMES D. and REILEY, ALAN C. *The Principles of Organization.* New York: Harper & Brothers, Publishers, 1939.

MOORE, WILBERT E. *The Conduct of the Corporation.* New York: Random House, 1962.

MORGAN, JOHN S. *Getting Across to Employees.* New York: McGraw-Hill Book Company, Inc., 1964.

MORRELL, R. W. *Managerial Decision-Making.* Milwaukee: The Bruce Publishing Company, 1960.

MORRIS, WILLIAM. *Management Science in Action.* Homewood, Ill.: Richard D. Irwin, Inc. 1963.

MORROW, ALFRED J. *Behind the Executive Mask.* New York: American Management Association, 1966.

NEWCOMER, MABEL. *The Big Business Executive.* New York: Columbia University Press, 1955.

NEWMAN, WILLIAM H. *Administrative Action.* Englewood Cliffs, N.J.: Prentice-Hall, Inc., 1951.

NEWMAN, WILLIAM H. and LOGAN, JAMES P. *Management of Expanding Industries.* New York: Columbia University Press, 1955.

NEWMAN, WILLIAM H. and SUMMER, CHARLES E. *The Process of Management.* Englewood Cliffs, N.J.: Prentice-Hall, Inc., 1961.

NILES, MARY CUSHING. *Essence of Management.* New York: Harper & Brothers, Publishers, 1958.

NILES, MARY CUSHING. *Middle Management.* Rev. ed. New York: Harper & Brothers, Publishers, 1949.

NILES, HENRY E. et al. 3rd ed. *The Office Supervisor.* New York: John Wiley & Sons, Inc., 1959.

NORTHCOTT, C. H. *Personnel Management.* 3rd ed. London: Sir Isaac Pitman & Sons, Ltd., 1955.

ODIORNE, GEORGE S. *Personnel Policy: Issues and Practices.* Columbus, Ohio: Charles E. Merrill Books, Inc., 1963.

ODIORNE, GEORGE S. *How Managers Make Things Happen.* Englewood Cliffs, N. J.: Prentice-Hall, Inc., 1961.

Organizing for Effective Systems Planning and Control. New York: American Management Association, n.d.

OSBORN, ALEX F. *Applied Imagination.* New York: Charles Scribner's Sons, 1953.

628 / **Administrative Strategy**

PARKINSON, C. NORTHCOTE. *Parkinson's Law.* Boston: Houghton Mifflin Company, 1961.

PARSONS, TALCOTT. *Essays in Sociological Theory.* Rev. ed. Glencoe, Ill.: The Free Press, 1954.

PARSONS, TALCOTT. *The Social System.* Glencoe, Ill.: The Free Press, 1951.

PARSONS, TALCOTT. *Structure and Process in Modern Society.* Glencoe, Ill.: The Free Press, 1959.

PARSONS, TALCOTT. *The Structure of Social Action.* 2nd ed. Glencoe, Ill.: The Free Press, 1958.

PARSONS, TALCOTT and SHILS, EDWARD A. *Toward a General Theory of Action.* Cambridge, Mass.: Harvard University Press, 1954.

PARSONS, TALCOTT, BALES, ROBERT F. and SHILS, EDWARD A. *Working Papers in the Theory of Action.* Glencoe, Ill.: The Free Press, 1953.

PATTON, ARCH. *Men, Money and Motivation.* New York: McGraw-Hill Book Company, Inc., 1961.

PAYNE, BRUCE. *Planning for Company Growth.* New York: McGraw-Hill Book Company, Inc., 1963.

PETERS, RAYMOND W. *Communications within Industry.* Harper & Brothers, Publishers, 1950.

PETERSEN, ELMORE and PLOWMAN, E. GROSVENOR. *Business Organization and Management.* Rev. ed. Chicago: Richard D. Irwin, Inc., 1948.

PFIFFNER, JOHN M. *The Supervision of Personnel.* Englewood Cliffs, N.J.: Prentice-Hall, Inc., 1951; and 2nd ed., 1958.

PFIFFNER, JOHN M. and SHERWOOD, FRANK P. *Administrative Organization.* Englewood Cliffs, N.J.: Prentice-Hall, Inc., 1960.

PIGORS, PAUL and MYERS, CHARLES A. *Personnel Administration.* New York: McGraw-Hill Book Company, Inc., 1951.

PUTNAM, ARNOLD O. et al. *Unified Operations Management: a Practical Approach to the Total Systems Concept.* New York: McGraw-Hill Book Company, Inc., 1963.

RANDALL, CLARENCE B. *The Folklore of Management.* Boston: Little, Brown & Company, 1961.

REDDING, W. CHARLES and SANBORN, GEORGE A. *Business and Industrial Communication: a Source Book.* New York: Harper & Row, 1964.

REDFIELD, CHARLES E. *Communication in Management.* Rev. ed. Chicago: University of Chicago Press, 1958.

RICE, A. K. *The Enterprise and Its Environment.* London: Tavistock Publications, Ltd., 1963.

RICHARDS, MAX D. and NIELANDER, WILLIAM A. *Readings in Management.* Cincinnati: South-Western Publishing Co., 1958.

RIGBY, PAUL H. *Theory and Economic Analysis of Business Management.* Columbia: Research Center, School of Business and Public Administration, University of Missouri, 1965.

ROETHLISBERGER, F. J. *Management and Morale*. Cambridge, Mass.: Harvard University Press, 1946.

ROETHLISBERGER, F. J. and DICKSON, WILLIAM J. with the assistance and collaboration of HAROLD A. WRIGHT. *Management and the Worker*. Cambridge, Mass.: Harvard University Press, 1946.

ROGERS, KENN. *Managers: Personality and Performance*. London: Tavistock Publications, Ltd., 1963.

ROSE, T. G. and FARR, DONALD E. *Higher Management Control*. New York: McGraw-Hill Book Company, Inc., 1957.

ROWBOTTOM, RALPH W. and GREENWALD, HOWARD A. *Understanding Management*. Manchester, England: Whitworth Press, Ltd., 1962.

ROY, ROBERT H. *The Administrative Process*. Baltimore: Johns Hopkins Press, 1958.

RUBENSTEIN, ALBERT H. and HABERSTROH, CHADWICK J. *Some Theories of Organization*. Homewood, Illinois: Richard D. Irwin, Inc., 1960.

RYAN, T. A. *Principles of Industrial Psychology*. New York: Ronald Press Company, 1954.

ST. THOMAS, CHARLES E. *Practical Business Planning*. New York: American Management Association, 1965.

SAMPSON, ROBERT C. *The Staff Role in Management*. New York: Harper & Brothers, Publishers, 1955.

SAYLES, LEONARD R. *Behavior of Industrial Work Groups*. New York: John Wiley & Sons, Inc., 1958.

SAYLES, LEONARD R. *Individualism and Big Business*. New York: McGraw-Hill Book Company, Inc., 1963.

SAYLES, LEONARD R. *Managerial Behavior*. New York: McGraw-Hill Book Company, Inc., 1964.

SCHEIN, EDGAR H. and WARREN, BENNIS G. *Personal and Organizational Change through Group Methods*. New York: John Wiley & Sons, Inc., 1965.

SCHELL, ERWIN HASKELL. *Administrative Proficiency in Business*. New York: McGraw-Hill Book Company, Inc., 1936.

SCHELL, ERWIN HASKELL. *Technique of Executive Control*. 8th ed. New York: McGraw-Hill Book Company, Inc., 1957.

SCHLEH, EDWARD C. *Executive Management of Personnel*. Englewood Cliffs, N.J.: Prentice-Hall, Inc., 1958.

SCHLEH, EDWARD C. *Management by Results*. New York: McGraw-Hill Book Company, Inc., 1960.

SCHLEH, E. C. *Successful Executive Action*. New York: Prentice-Hall, Inc., 1956.

SCHLENDER, WILLIAM E. et al. *Management in Perspective: Selected Readings*. Boston: Houghton Mifflin Company, 1965.

SCHULER, EDGAR A. et al. *Outside Readings in Sociology*. New York: Thomas Y. Crowell Company, 1952.

SCOTT, WILLIAM G. *The Management of Conflict*. Homewood, Illinois: Richard D. Irwin, Inc., 1965.

SELEKMAN, B. M. *Moral Philosophy for Management.* New York: McGraw-Hill Book Company, Inc., 1959.

SELEKMAN, SYLVIA KOPALD and SELEKMAN, BENJAMIN M. *Power and Morality in a Business Society.* New York: McGraw-Hill Book Company, Inc., 1956.

SELZNICK, PHILIP. *Leadership in Administration.* Evanston, Illinois: Row, Peterson & Company, 1957

SHARP, WALTER RICE. *French Civil Service Bureaucracy in Transition.* New York: Macmillan Company, 1931.

SHARTLE, CARROLL L. *Executive Performance and Leadership.* Englewoods Cliffs, N.J.: Prentice-Hall, Inc., 1956.

SHAY, PHILIP W. *How to Get the Best Results from Management Consultants.* New York: Association of Consulting Management Engineers, 1965.

SHELDON, OLIVER. *The Philosophy of Management.* New York: Prentice-Hall, Inc., 1923.

SHULL, FREMONT, JR. *Selected Readings in Management.* Homewood, Ill.: Richard D. Irwin, Inc., 1958.

SIMON, HERBERT A. *Administrative Behavior.* 2nd ed. New York: Macmillan Company, 1958.

SIMON, HERBERT A. *The Shape of Automation.* New York: Harper & Row, 1965.

SLICHTER, SUMNER. *Challenge of Industrial Relations.* Ithaca, N.Y.: Cornell University Press, 1947.

SLOAN, ALFRED P. JR. *My Years with General Motors.* Garden City, N. Y.: Doubleday & Company, Inc., 1964.

SMITH, GEORGE ALBERT. *Business, Society and the Individual.* Homewood, Illinois: Richard D. Irwin, Inc., 1962.

SORD, BURNARD HAND and WELSCH, GLENN A. *Managerial Planning and Control as Viewed by Lower Levels of Supervision.* Austin: Bureau of Business Research, University of Texas, 1964.

SOROKIN, PITIRIM A. *Fads and Foibles in Modern Sociology.* Chicago: Henry Regenery Company, 1956.

SPENCER, MILTON H. and SIEGELMAN, LOUIS. *Managerial Economics: Decision Making and Forward Planning.* Rev. ed. Homewood, Illinois: Richard D. Irwin, Inc., 1964.

SPRIEGEL, WILLIAM R. and SCHULZ, EDWARD. *Elements of Supervision.* New York: John W. Wiley & Sons, Inc., 1942.

SPRIEGEL, WILLIAM R. et al. *Elements of Supervision.* 2nd ed. New York: John Wiley & Sons, Inc., 1957.

STAGNER, ROSS. *Psychology of Industrial Conflict.* New York: John Wiley & Sons, Inc., 1956.

STECKLE, LYNDE C. *The Man in Management.* New York: Harper & Brothers, Publishers, 1958.

STEIN, MORRIS I. and HEINZE, SHIRLEY J. *Creativity and the Individual.* Glencoe, Illinois: The Free Press of Glencoe, 1960.

STOGDILL, RALPH M. and COONS, ALVIN E. (eds.). *Leader Behavior: Its Description and Measurement.* Research Monograph Number

88. Columbus: Bureau of Business Research. Ohio State University, 1957.

STOGDILL, RALPH M. (ed.). *Leadership and Structures of Personal Interaction.* Research Monograph Number 84. Columbus: Ohio State University Press, 1957.

STRATHER, GEORGE B. (ed.). *Social Science Approaches to Business Behavior.* Homewood, Illinois: Richard D. Irwin, Inc., 1962.

STRAUSS, GEORGE and SAYLES, LEONARD R. *Personnel.* Englewood Cliffs, N.J.: Prentice-Hall, Inc., 1960.

SUMMER, CHARLES E., JR. *Factors in Effective Administration.* New York: Graduate School of Business, Columbia University, 1956.

SUTTON, FRANCIS X., HARRIS, SEYMOUR E. et al. *The American Business Creed.* Cambridge, Mass.: Harvard University Press, 1956.

TANNENBAUM, ROBERT et al. *Leadership and Organization.* New York: McGraw-Hill Book Company, Inc., 1961.

TAYLOR, CALVIN W. *Creativtiy: Progress and Potential.* New York: McGraw-Hill Book Company, Inc., 1964.

TAYLOR, FREDERICK WINSLOW. *Principles of Scientific Management.* New York: Harper & Brothers, Publishers, 1947.

TEAD, ORDWAY. *Administration: Its Purpose and Performance.* New York: Harper & Brothers, Publishers, 1959.

TEAD, ORDWAY. *The Art of Administration.* New York: McGraw-Hill Book Company, Inc., 1951.

TEAD, ORDWAY. *The Art of Leadership.* New York: McGraw-Hill Book Company, Inc., 1935.

TEAD, ORDWAY. *Democratic Administration.* New York: Association Press, 1945.

THAYER, LEE O. *Administrative Communication.* Homewood, Illinois: Richard D. Irwin, Inc., 1961.

THOLE, HENRY C. and GIBBONS, CHARLES C. (eds.). *Business Action in a Changing World.* Chicago: Public Administration Service, 1956.

THOMPSON, C. BERTRAND. *The Theory and Practice of Scientific Management.* Boston: Houghton Mifflin Company, 1917.

THOMPSON, JAMES D. et al. (eds.). *Comparative Studies in Administration.* Pittsburgh: University of Pittsburgh Press, 1959.

TORRANCE, E. PAUL. *Guiding Creative Talent.* Englewood Cliffs, N.J.: Prentice-Hall, Inc., 1962.

TOWLE, JOSEPH W. (ed.). *Ethics and Standards in American Business.* Boston: Houghton Mifflin Company, 1964.

TRECKER, AUDREY R. and TRECKER, HARLEIGH B. *Committee Common Sense.* New York: Whiteside, Inc. and William Morrow & Company, 1954.

URWICK, L. *Committees in Organization.* Reprinted from *British Management* Review. London: Management Journals, n.d.

URWICK, L. *The Elements of Administration.* New York: Harper & Brothers, Publishers, n.d.

632 / **Administrative Strategy**

URWICK, LYNDALL F. *The Pattern of Management.* Minneapolis: University of Minnesota Press, 1956.

VESPER, HOWARD G. *Motivation and Development of Management.* Pasadena: Industrial Relations Center, California Institute of Technology, 1964.

VINCENT, MELVIN J. and MAYERS, JACKSON. *New Foundations for an Industrial Sociology.* Princeton, N.J.: D. Van Nostrand Company, Inc., 1959.

VITELES, MORRIS S. *Motivation and Morale in Industry.* New York: W. W. Norton & Company, Inc., 1953.

VON NEUMANN, JOHN and MORGENSTERN, OSKAR. *Theory of Games and Economic Behavior.* 3rd ed. Princeton: Princeton University Press, 1953.

WARNER, W. LLOYD and MARTIN, NORMAN H. (eds.). *Industrial Man.* New York: Harper & Brothers, Publishers, 1959.

WATSON, THOMAS J. JR. *A Business and Its Beliefs.* New York: McGraw-Hill Book Company, Inc., 1963.

WEBER, MAX. *Gesammelte Aufsatze zur Soziologie and Sozialpolitik.* Tübingen: J. C. B. Mohr, 1924.

WEBER, MAX. *Wirtschaft und Gesellschaft.* Tübingen: J. C. B. Mohr, 1922.

WHITE, LEONARD D. *Introduction to the Study of Public Administration.* Rev. ed. New York: Macmillan Company, 1939.

WHYTE, WILLIAM FOOTE and HAMILTON, EDITH LENTY. *Action Research for Management.* Homewood, Illinois: Richard D. Irwin, Inc., 1965.

WHYTE, WILLIAM FOOTE. *Man and Organization.* Homewood, Ill.: Richard D. Irwin, Inc., 1959.

WHYTE, WILLIAM FOOTE. *Money and Motivation.* New York: Harper & Brothers, Publishers, 1955.

WHYTE, WILLIAM H., JR., and the EDITORS OF FORTUNE. *Is Anybody Listening?* New York: Simon and Schuster, Inc., 1952.

WHYTE, WILLIAM H., JR. *Organization Man.* New York: Simon and Schuster, Inc., 1956.

WILLIAMSON, C. DON. *An Execuitve Operations Technique.* Englewood Cliffs, N.J.: Prentice-Hall, 1963.

WIRTENBERGER, HENRY J., S.J. *Morality and Business.* Chicago: Loyola University Press, 1962.

WORTHY, JAMES C. *Big Business and Free Men.* New York: Harper & Brothers, Publishers, 1959.

YODER, DALE. *Personnel Principles and Policies.* New York: Prentice-Hall, Inc., 1952.

ZALEZNIK, ABRAHAM and MOMENT, DAVID. *Casebook on Interpersonal Behavior in Organizations.* New York: John Wiley & Sons, Inc., 1964.

ZALEZNIK, ABRAHAM and MOMENT, DAVID. *The Dynamics of Interpersonal Behavior.* New York: John Wiley & Sons, Inc., 1964.

INDEX

Action
  contradictory action inherent in strategy, 12-13
  diverse action patterns of strategist, 12-14
  limits to strategic action (See Strategic action: limitations to.)
Adaptability, 29-30
Administration
  ancient subject, 9
  and management, 4
  as gamesmanship, 3, 188
  background of modern in
    administration itself, 9
    business practices, 4-5
    Church, 9-10
    economics, 5
    ethics, 9
    history, 9
    industrial engineering, 6-7
    mathematics, 9
    Military, 9-10
    philosophy, 9
    political science, 9
    psychology, 7
    public administration, 7
    sociology, 8
  concept of, 4
  multi-dimensional nature of business administration, 10, 22
  principles in pairs, 253
Administration by crises
  administrative crises (See Crises.)
  crises as source of opportunity, 121-122
  some questions about, 122
  surprise and crises, 278-279
Administrative objectives
  agreement on (See Reconciliation of administrative objectives.)
  consciousness of, 66-67
  necessity for definite, 88
  provincialism in, 67-69
  variation with individual and time, 66
Administrative strategy
  assuring followership, 49-57
  characteristics of
    contradiction, 12-13
    forward looking, 14-15
    relativity, 12
    right combination of factors, 11
  freedom from binding commitment, 262-266
  hints for exploiting opportunity, 129-130
  limitations of, 15-16
  misleading connotations, 10-11
  relation to Machiavellian conduct, 11
  rules of
    avoiding pitfalls in reorganization to procure and retain personnel, 239
    conditioning individuals, 54-55
    conditioning sub-groups, 55-56
    surprise, 280-281
  situs, 36-38

Administrative strategy (*cont.*)
  some stratagems for
    avoiding overemphasis on human relations, 290-295
    conditioning followers, 50-52
    coping with resources factor in planning, 196-201
    dealing with committees, 351-357
    handling opposition, 99-101, 224-231, 275-277
    influencing reaction to communication, 417-421
    living and working with over-conformist, 299-305
    overcoming precedent, 203-206
    reception of communications, 422-430
    reconciling administrative objectives, 69-82
    stalling, 13-14, 211-212, 268-270, 349
    timing, 266-281
    treating internal conflict, 143-151
Administrator
  description of (See Leader and also Leadership.)
  identified as leader, 454
Alertness
  and two leadership fronts, 27-28
  vital to leadership, 27-28
Authority
  defined as institutionalized power, 95-96
  sharing of, 329-331
Autocracy in administration, 326-327, 588-589

Barrage in communication, 419-420
Behavior pattern of strategist, 12-14
Bureaucracy
  evaluation of, 580-582
  features
    bureaucratic officialdom, 578-581
    discipline, 579-580
    duties divided and inherent, 576-577
    importance of general rules, 577-578
    inequality, 575-576
  reasonable administrative attitude toward, 580-581
  strategy possibilities in features of, 575-576
  true meaning, 575
  typical of big organizations, 575
Business practices, 4-5

Centralization
  and possibilities for reorganization, 244-246
  extreme limit of, 245
Chain of command
  and opportunities for reorganization, 242-244
  nature of, 242
Channels of communication, 409
Church, 9-10
Cliques and gangs
  real power under two conditions, 93
  source of power, 93

633